BRIDGE OF SOULS

ANCIENT PROPHECY. ULTIMATE EVIL.

K.R.M. Morgan

MADBAGUS BOOKS

ISBN: 978-1-5272-2595-4

Cover design by MadBagus

Enochian font by Nu Isis Working Group

Disclaimer

This story provides some of the most detailed and meticulously researched presentations of esoteric practices within contemporary literature. Readers are warned that attempting to replicate such practices may result in serious psychological and physical harm.

Acknowledgements

The author wishes to acknowledge the help and support from his wife, Maddy, without whom this book simply would not have been possible.

The author also wishes to acknowledge the substantial contribution from two individuals, one a former senior Secret Intelligence Officer and the other an advanced initiate within several esoteric orders. Both individuals provided expertise that substantially improved the technical accuracy of many scenes within the book. Any errors or omissions are mine alone.

If you enjoy reading this book please leave a review on social media so others can also discover the adventures of Tavish Stewart.

FOLIO 1 – FROM BENEATH THE SANDS OF TIME

CHAPTER 1 – TAVISH

"The True Beginning of our End." - Act V. Scene 1. Shakespeare's A Midsummer Night's Dream

Stewart Lodge, North of Loch Chon, Stirling, Scotland.
22:00HRS, July 24th, Present Day.

The tree lined driveway, which led away from a pair of tall, black, cast iron entrance gates, was the only break in the four-mile-long dry-stone wall that ran along the Western edge of the B829 Glasgow road, and marked the boundary of the Stewart family estate. The narrow gravel drive ran in a long straight line, away from the main road, for nearly a mile before reaching a deceptively sharp right-hand turn, concealed behind some large glacial erratic rocks and tall heathers. The start of this savage bend was marked by a massive oak tree, that was currently highlighted in the full beams from the distinctive double headlights of a classic, black 1967 Mercedes-Benz 250SE convertible coupe. The fading light of the Scottish summer's day, combined with the dual beams of the car, created long shadows from every tree, making the rough grass and rocks on either side of the thin gravel drive fade out of sharp detail.

Tavish Stewart changed down on the four-speed manual transmission, as he began to push the legendary seven-bearing six-cylinder 2,496cc engine hard. The fifty-year-old car produced a glorious roar, as Stewart accelerated along the straight and caused the long needle pointer to gently creep past 100 Mph on the "VDO" branded speedometer, embedded to the right of the exquisite wooden dashboard. The large white wall tyres made the occasional roadside stone fly wildly from behind the car, as it sped towards the ancient oak tree that marked the well-practiced tight ninety-degree bend, which Stewart had been confronting at speed in various cars since his teens. Tavish, or Sir Stewart as his staff called him to his face, was returning home after what had proved a very long week but, as he became more engrossed in the challenges of pushing the classic sports car to its limits, his mind started to let go of the frustrations of business.

Although he had retired as Colonel of his beloved Royal Scots

Regiment, shortly after the ill-conceived defence review had forced a merger with the Kings Own Scottish Borderers, Stewart still kept a tough schedule as CEO of a successful antiquarian business, that he ran from prestigious showrooms in London, Rome and Istanbul.

Stewart was a large and physically powerful man. Six feet two inches tall and weighing just over two hundred pounds, he carefully maintained his body with a strict exercise regime. Although his dark hair was now flecked with grey he kept it cropped short, which gave him a clean and rugged appearance. A well-trimmed beard covered his defined jaw line and, even though his face clearly showed its age, as he raced the powerful open topped car through his estate, his expression showed that he clearly still relished the joys of life, and this was reflected in his sharp and intelligent grey eyes.

Changing down hard, he took the corner at speed, and rapidly handled a series of less severe bends with an almost perfect trajectory, finally entering a 400 yard straight leading towards a large house, which had clearly been extended over many generations from a once modest sixteenth century farm building. The contrast between the later red brick structures and the earlier natural stone was highlighted dramatically in the dying rays of the setting summer sun, that shone from behind the classic Mercedes as it advanced towards his family home.

As Stewart approached the main entrance to the circular drive, he slowed and extinguished his headlights, as he noticed that, unexpectedly, all the house lights were on. The front doors had been torn off from their hinges and were now propped against a side wall. A large silver Toyota Land Cruiser Invincible was parked directly outside the main entrance. All five doors were open, and the SUV's interior lights spilled over the dark gravel drive, clearly highlighting the figure of a short man, dressed in a paramilitary uniform, sitting in the rear hatch opening of the big SUV. Near to the man, an unidentified dark shape lay on the ground, blocking the illumination of the interior lights and casting a long shadow over the driveway.

Slowing the black Mercedes further, as he started to approach the house, Stewart noticed with growing dismay that the dark shape on the ground was his devoted dog, "Bella", an ancient Irish Wolfhound, now clearly lying motionless in a growing pool of her own blood. A trail of dark liquid showed that the dog had been trying to defend her home against the intruders.

The sound of the approaching sports car had already attracted the attention of the lone figure, sitting on watch in the rear of the Land Cruiser, and in the light from the interior of the large SUV he could now be clearly seen. He was a small man in his mid-thirties, with a military crew cut which made his dark hair look like a shadow on his skull. His deeply pock marked face was gaunt and his mouth showed teeth with heavy tobacco stains. With a cruel gleam in his dark eyes, he drew a wicked looking black polymer 9mm pistol and assumed an arrogant single-handed shooting position, pointing his gun sights towards the approaching vehicle, and squinting as he was forced to guess the exact location of his target due to the blinding rays of the setting sun. He started squeezing off round after round from the NATO stock magazine attached to the fifth generation German Glock 17 pistol.

Inside the Mercedes, the flashes from the muzzle of the gun were closely followed by the sound of hammer like blows on the bonnet, right hand side windshield and exterior of the ancient car. Sitting behind the left-hand drive steering wheel, Stewart was spared any direct hits but he grimaced as he imagined the damage to the pristine fifty-year-old bodywork and his anger was intensified as the full metal jacket rounds started ripping through the wooden dashboard, embedding shards of walnut into the red leather upholstery and tearing the fabric of his Ede and Ravenscroft jacket. As if that was not enough, the cabin space of the sports car began to fill with the highly distinctive smells of the numerous fluids, which were evidently now leaking from unseen damage inside the engine bay.

The Scotsman carefully took in the scene of his dead dog, his home being ransacked, the damage to his car and, finally, the unknown gunman in front of him, who continued to fire 9mm rounds.

Stewart narrowed his grey eyes, turned on the remaining headlights, that had not already been shattered in the hail of bullets, and floored the accelerator on the ancient 250SE. The dazzling beams of light and the unexpected ferocity of acceleration took the gunman completely by surprise, making his remaining shots miss the oncoming car by a wide margin, as fear rapidly replaced arrogance. The figure of the would-be assassin became silhouetted in the dual headlights, as Stewart expertly calculated the remaining distance, before executing a dramatic 180-

degree handbrake turn, resulting in a violent impact as the rear end of the ancient Mercedes spun rapidly around, striking the gunman sideways on as he was running away from what had appeared to be a planned direct forward assault.

Inside the coupe, the collision made the chassis crack ominously and caused the side door windows to shatter, as the car shook violently. When the impact subsided, Stewart casually brushed the broken window glass from his already torn suit and looked, first towards the pulverised remains of the gunman, and then to the dead body of his faithful dog, Bella, before remarking.

"That is for you, old girl."

Noticing movement in the illuminated windows of his home and assuming that there were more heavily armed assailants about to emerge from the front door, he decided his best tactic would be to try and draw these people after him and improvise how to deal with them en route.

Stewart planted his right foot firmly on the accelerator of the car, which now faced away from his ancestral home, and the distinctive black coupe raced away, leaving an ominous trail of engine fluids behind it on the gravel road surface, which slowly intermingled with the copious blood.

Alerted by all the noise, a tall muscular man ran smoothly from inside the house. His deep set brown eyes and long crooked nose made his features look cruel and penetrating, like a bird of prey. His intelligent eyes took in the sight of the escaping Mercedes, and he barked a series of commands in a thick Middle Eastern tongue. From the various areas of the large house four men rapidly appeared, each dressed in identical paramilitary fatigues. Within a matter of seconds, they had exited the building with a remarkable precision, and were seated in the big Land Cruiser making pursuit.

In the distance, Stewart noted, through the rear-view mirror, the huge SUV starting after him some 500 yards behind, and he allowed himself a small smile. However, the pleasure was short lived, as he noticed the vehicle had left the narrow gravel track and was taking a direct route over the fields and rough ground, clearly heading for the single entrance way that marked the edge of the property.

In the pursuing Land Cruiser, the cruel faced leader was speaking into an encrypted Motorola Iridium Satellite Phone. Its bulk and weight seemed old fashioned in an age of tiny handsets, but its size was more than compensated for by its ability to make calls in any environment, even the Scottish hills, where cellular phones were notoriously unreliable due to the uneven landscape. The hawk faced leader was clearly intimidated by the person on the other end of the line, as his face creased with anxiety when he detected displeasure from the other speaker. A rapid dialogue ensued, during which he shamefully revealed that not only had his men failed to obtain their prize, but they had now also alerted their adversary.

Inside the Mercedes, the gauges for engine temperature, oil pressure and fuel were all telling Stewart that his beloved car was dying. Ignoring them, the Scotsman patted the steering wheel fondly.

"Come on, come on, don't quit on me now."

Stewart did not waste time trying to use his phone, he already knew from experience that the nearby hills made normal cell reception impossible down here in the glen. Instead, he focused on his driving, at the same time reaching down into the side storage well of the driver's door to locate a golf ball he had accidently left in the car after his last round.

Back in the chasing SUV, the hawk faced man, known to intelligence services around the world as Issac bin Abdul Issuin, continued his dialogue, but it was apparent that his failure had brought him considerable ill favour with the person on the other end of the large phone. His exasperation was becoming clearer and clearer as his explanations were being ignored and, in the end, it was obvious that the conversation had been abruptly terminated. The other men in the SUV exchanged glances, and pretended not to notice the loss of face encountered by their leader, as they continued the high-speed chase over the rough ground, the large Toyota swinging wildly from side to side.

Meanwhile, as Stewart's Mercedes neared the deserted unlit stone gatehouse, he braked dramatically, losing vital seconds and, in a single deliberate movement, he launched a small white Dunlop DDH Tour Gold golf ball through the glass window of the small stone building. A shrill alarm instantly filled the air and flood lights suddenly illuminated the entire Western perimeter of the estate.

Not stopping for an instant, Stewart changed down and buried his right foot on the accelerator, noting as he did that an ominous burning smell was beginning to fill the cabin, and the once glorious roar of the engine had been replaced by a deep shuddering vibration. Stewart continued to talk to his car, as if it was a close friend, and in some mysterious way it seemed to respond, as the coupe overcame its momentary loss of power and launched itself through the open wrought iron gates, taking a violent right hand turn on to the B829, that wound its way besides the two linked Lochs of Chon and Ard, towards Glasgow.

Stewart took a moment to glance at the luminous dial of his well-worn, Omega watch and pushed the upper start button on the hand wound mechanical chronograph, so he would know how long it would be before the gatehouse alarm brought the police towards him along the narrow road running beside the peaceful loch waters.

Seconds later, the big Land Cruiser followed, mounting the gravel road close to the low stone gate house, from which a piercing 140db siren was now sounding, and was brightly illuminated by the massive spot lights from the tall lighting posts spread around the estate.

Under normal conditions the top speeds of both vehicles would have been closely matched, but Stewart's classic Mercedes was so badly damaged that it was a miracle that it continued to move, let alone exceed 100 mph. Slowly, the pursuing SUV got closer and closer in Stewart's rear view mirror. It's roof mounted spotlights suddenly came on, highlighting the Scotsman so clearly that Abdul Issuin encouraged his men to open their side windows and take pot shots with their Glocks.

"Today just keeps getting better." Remarked Stewart to himself, as 9mm rounds buzzed inches past his head. Realizing he had to make some kind of response or risk a bullet in his back, the Scotsman reached behind him for the button poppers holding down the convertible roof and released and unfolded the fabric, sending a spinning wall of canvas, backwards towards the Toyota, which was now only yards behind.

The unexpected dark shape, that rose into the air and threated to obscure the entire windshield, panicked the driver in the Land Cruiser, almost making the huge SUV veer clean off the narrow road. He only avoided plunging into the icy loch waters by performing an expertly executed emergency stop, but coming to a complete standstill allowed Stewart to gain valuable distance.

The numerous dials and warning lights on the smashed walnut

dashboard of the ancient Mercedes told a sad story. By every measure of engineering the old car should be dead but, by some miracle, it continued hurtling along the loch-side road, carrying its owner on one last run, which was proving to be the ride of its very long life. Finally, reality caught up with it and the faithful old engine cut out, leaving the elegant fifty-year-old sports car to coast gradually to a standstill. As Stewart looked over the rear of the convertible he could see the Land Cruiser, with its numerous roof mounted spotlights, thundering down the narrow B829 road behind him, clearly intent on finishing this evenings confrontation, once and for all.

A Land Rover Discovery, with Central Scotland Police blue and yellow chequered side decorations and flashing siren lights, suddenly appeared in the full beam headlights of Stewart's stationary vehicle, pulling up alongside. With a smile of relief, Stewart jumped from his car, running over to the driver's side window and addressing the two police officers inside. After a very brief exchange, the more senior of the two, a dark-haired female officer, that Stewart recognised as Sergeant Ann Wells, urgently contacted a radio controller in Stirling.

Three minutes later, Keith Smith, Chief Constable of Police Scotland, was disturbed by an unexpected phone call, during an informal dinner party, on his restricted Blackberry phone. Four minutes later, two specially modified BMW Armed Response Vehicles (ARVs) emerged at high speed, with sirens shattering the silence of the night, from Stirling Area Subcommand HQ, racing to cover the fifteen miles to Loch Chon. Each ARV carried normal Police Scotland markings, with an additional distinctive large star on the roof and round markers in the front and rear windows, denoting to aerial surveillance and other police vehicles the specialised nature of each car and that they were carrying Authorised Firearms Officers (AFOs).

Inside the two speeding white BMWs, three highly trained AFOs conversed with each other through a private radio communication system, that was separate from the normal police channels. The main topic of discussion related to the urgent need for more information regarding the threat they were about to face. Their briefing had indicated one person in paramilitary fatigues, using a large capacity hand gun on a member of the public, with deadly intent, and an unknown number of additional armed assailants in pursuit of a civilian vehicle. Ten minutes into their journey, the Bronze commander inside the lead BMW had authorised the use of hollow point ammunition, thus minimising the risk of bullets passing right through the target and injuring innocent bystanders, and the AFOs were now busy loading new magazines into their weapons.

In the pursing silver Toyota Land Cruiser, Issac bin Abdul Issuin continued to bully the driver to get more performance from the large SUV. As they hurtled around a bend in the narrow loch road the flashing police lights of a Land Rover Discovery came into view. The big Toyota burnt rubber from its massive tyres and came to a sudden halt, ending up at a ninety-degree angle, its nose pointing towards the end of Loch Ard.

The police Discovery had moved to occupy a sideways position, blocking the narrow road, and Stewart's black Mercedes remained where it had stopped, facing away from the scene. A short figure, that was clearly a woman police officer, was standing in front of these vehicles, gesturing for the suspects to come out with their hands in the air. The summer night was almost completely silent, as Abdul Issuin commanded his men to get out from their car. As the terrorist leader stepped down from the Land Cruiser, with a single fluid movement he drew his Glock 17 in his left hand, and fired six rapid shots at Sergeant Ann Wells. The 9mm rounds slammed heavily into the officer's Kevlar vest and she fell to her knees, coughing blood onto the dark asphalt road.

Abdul Issuin smiled at the result of his act, and gestured for one of his men to finish the murder of the British policewoman. Dominic Gervac was a thirty something Serbian with little hair on his head, but compensated for that lack with a thick long beard. He marched rapidly, covering the thirty feet between the Land Cruiser and the wounded woman, his boots making a metallic clicking noise as he walked. Finally, he stood before the wounded police officer, and kicked Anne Wells savagely with his right foot. The woman rolled over fully on to her back and emitted a sob. A smile crept over Gervac's face and he started to reach for his gun.

At that moment, Wells moved rapidly, drawing an odd yellow shaped object into both her hands and pulled the trigger. A thin filament leapt from the weapon and a bright spark illuminated the stunned man, as the Police Issue Taser X26 discharged 50,000 volts into the Serbian's groin area. Gervac's body jerked uncontrollably but remained standing, frozen on the spot. Hidden behind the upright figure of the gunman, Wells eased the Glock 17 from his hands and threw it under the police Land Rover. She then pulled the paralyzed assailant to his knees, making sure he still blocked the line of sight from his colleagues, who would assume he was adding some final indignity to her end.

Wells pulled Gervac closer, rapidly guiding his hands behind his back and, in a well-practiced movement, locked both his hands into her police handcuffs. Then she reached to his shoulders and started to drag him slowly towards the police SUV.

A loud shout came from Abdul Issuin, as he realised that something had happened to compromise Gervac. As Wells manhandled the Serbian she called frantically to her partner, Constable Jimms, who was hiding behind the police Land Rover.

"I hope you've got that bloody gun ready, because I am going to need some covering fire?"

The only response was the sound of the young man throwing up, clearly unable to handle the stress of the situation. Wells started to sound more anxious.

"Sir Stewart, I hope you still know how to handle a weapon? I could really do with some help round here!"

Moments later, the air around Wells started to buzz from the volleys of 9mm rounds fired by the terrorists, which exploded around her, as small divots of tarmac flew into the air. She continued to try and drag Gervac, but she could feel the large man's body shudder as numerous rounds hit him. Clearly his team members considered him totally expendable, and were now standing as a group, side by side, firing their Glock pistols, as their targets backed away along the tarmac towards the police SUV.

The answer to Ann Well's question to Stewart came in the form of a series of rapid shots from over the bonnet of the police Land Rover. One of the terrorist gunmen, standing the furthest away from the

Toyota Land Cruiser, doubled over as a 9mm round passed through his right arm, spraying blood and matter out from the back of his sleeve, making him drop his handgun to the tarmac.

A second member of the three-man team groaned and collapsed, holding his left leg, trying to limit the blood that now pulsed rhythmically in a fountain of life from his inner thigh.

Assessing the skilful marksmanship of his opponent, Abdul Issuin moved rapidly back towards the Toyota Land Cruiser but, before he could reach the vehicle, he felt two massive blows to his mid-section that knocked him to the floor and on to his knees, as two rounds fired from behind the police Land Rover smashed into his Kevlar vest.

Winded from the shots, Abdul Issuin dragged himself into the Toyota, and grabbed a composite AKMS 47 machine gun from the back seat. He clicked the folding stock down, so it took the more familiar shape of the AK47, and set the machine gun into fully automatic mode. Slotting a special Russian made 100 round drum magazine into the weapon he stepped back into the line of fire, placing the unfolded stock to his shoulder and aiming at where he had seen the last muzzle flashes, he pulled the trigger and sprayed fully automatic fire over the police SUV.

Back behind the police vehicle, the noise of high velocity rounds penetrating through the steel body of the SUV was deafening. Both police officers were clearly in shock, although the older Sergeant was handling it better than her younger colleague, who was lying very still on the floor and sobbing. In contrast, Stewart seemed remarkably unaffected, apart from the odd graze on his face and his badly torn suit, he looked perfectly composed.

Using an old horn handled double edged dagger, that he had drawn from a black leather ankle sheath, Stewart cut the level three body armour from the dead Serbian and fitted it on Sergeant Wells, while also passing her the Glock 17.

"There are 12 rounds left in the magazine. If that bastard comes around the Land Rover, forget about issuing a warning or using reasonable force, just empty the magazine into his face. I am going down into the loch to swim round and come up behind him."

Just as he was about to descend into the cold grey waters, the barrage of gunfire stopped and the silence of the summer's night returned, only this time broken by the sounds of distant police sirens, rapidly approaching.

Suddenly, two modified BMW ARVs pulled up thirty feet behind the parked police Discovery and three AFOs, dressed in black military fatigues, emerged and quickly moved to the rear of their large vehicles. They grabbed two Heckler & Koch MP5 machine guns and a single Remington 700 Mountain LSS model rifle, with a modified elongated stainless-steel barrel and laser sighting technology, loaded with the 5.7mm 5.8g Full Metal Jacket rounds, capable of penetrating highly specialised Kevlar body armour.

Back at the Land Cruiser, Abdul Issuin noted the arrival of the new police reinforcements with fury at being deprived of his chance to finish what he had started. He sharply called his injured men back into their vehicle and, within seconds, the Land Cruiser's tyres were screaming in protest as the large SUV fled from the scene. In a final act, the rear window exploded dramatically in a shower of safety glass, revealing Abdul Issuin's crazed face, as he unleashed a volley of AK47 rounds, sprayed indiscriminately at anyone who would dare to come after him.

CHAPTER 2 - THE TARTAN KREMLIN

"During interrogation, you must watch for those opportunities that occur in moments when your captor distracts himself, by his own threats or his own acts of violence." - Resisting Interrogation. T. Stewart, NATO Handbook Series

Interview Room C, Stirling Police Area Subcommand,
Stirling, Scotland.
02:00 HRS, July 25th, Present Day.

Stewart looked around the small windowless room where he had been held for the last two and a half hours. Years of training had made it second nature for him to constantly monitor his environment for opportunities or objects that might prove useful should circumstance demand them. So it was, that his expert eye appraised a roughly ten-foot square space, decorated with light blue sound proof wall panels on its upper sections and, below waist height, with white plasterboard and a contrasting dark navy-blue skirting board. A small one-and-a-half-inch wide wooden cabling conduit ran around the mid-level of the room, providing a single electrical socket for the sound recording system. The room's blue theme was continued with some badly worn carpet tiles on a false raised floor that had clearly been conceived as a way to conceal ugly power cables, but such intentions of tidiness had been forgotten tonight, as black cables for a Samsung video camera snaked their way into the room, forcing the sound proof door to be left ajar.

On the left-hand side of the room, as viewed from the partially open door, was a wooden table with metal legs that were bolted to the floor. On the table stood a storage unit filled with stacks of new cellophane sealed audio CDs, some Sharpie marker pens and a grey metal NEAL triple deck CD recorder, with a makeshift microphone fitted crudely into a drilled hole in the centre of the wooden table surface. Set around the table were four armless black plastic chairs, of which one was unoccupied.

Seated opposite Stewart were two smartly dressed men in dark business suits, who had introduced themselves as Detective

Superintendent Alistair McBride of the Serious Organized Crime (SOC) unit, Forth Valley Division and Mr Andrew Cludden, who was a Counter Terrorism Security Advisor (CTSA) with the National Counter Terrorism Security Office (NaCTSO) in London. D/Supt. McBride was a tall thin, dark haired middle-aged officer who, based on the questions he had initiated before the arrival of his NaCTSO colleague, was more sympathetic towards Stewart. In fact, throughout the long session McBride had been noticeably trying to guide the interview to a conclusion since midnight, noting on several occasions for the record that he thought it highly unlikely that a well-respected local resident would destroy his own family's ancestral estate.

In contrast, CTSA Cludden had, from the outset, clearly viewed Stewart as the prime suspect for orchestrating the entire evening's violence. The short blonde thirty-year-old terror advisor consistently exhibited lines of questioning that would, if left unchallenged, keep the interview going as long as possible and end with Stewart being charged with orchestrating the ransacking of his own home, the car chase alongside Loch Chon and the fully automatic gunfight that had totalled his Mercedes and the Police Scotland Land Rover.

The interview had started to go badly when Cludden directly contradicted the opening statement made by D/Supt. McBride, that the meeting was purely a formality to gather information, and stated that he was redirecting the interview in light of undisclosed information he had received from London and insisted Stewart be handcuffed.

From that point, Cludden's questioning became increasingly aggressive, prompting Stewart to request that his legal representative be present, a request which Cludden took great pleasure in refusing. When Stewart responded by declining to be interviewed in the absence of his lawyer, as was his right under Scottish Law, Cludden took further delight in stating this right had been waived as Stewart was being detained under the Terrorism Act and would therefore be held without charge or any legal representation.

Without so much as a pause to give Stewart a chance for thought, Cludden had launched into the Police Scotland advisory, clearly taking McBride by surprise, since by law such a caution should have been issued by him and not the London based terror advisor.

"Tavish Stewart, you are going to be asked questions about the disturbance at Stewart Lodge and several general firearms offences committed on the B829 beside Loch Ard this evening that resulted in the loss of human life. You are not bound to answer, but if you do your answers will be tape recorded, may be noted and may be used in evidence."

Cludden then placed a German composite Glock 17 with an ejected nineteen round NATO stock magazine, both of which were inside a thick plastic Police Scotland Tamper Evident Evidence Bag, on the table in front of Stewart, demanding,

"I am now placing item 56a on the desk in front of the suspect. Sir, I must ask do you recognize this gun?"

Stewart calmly looked into the eyes of the confrontational CTSA, trying to assess the intent of the man, and indicated that he could not be sure but the gun looked similar to those used by the armed assailants who had attacked him earlier that evening.

Cludden glared at Stewart looking for a reaction, and not seeing one he placed two A4 sized papers on the desk, one with computer finger print analysis results and the other which showed a series of numbers and a spectrogram, both sheets held together with a single steel paperclip.

"Would you be surprised if I told you that your finger prints are all over this gun?"

Stewart shook his head and before he could answer the CTSA agent continued,

"…and that your hands have tested positive for Gun Shot Residue (GSR)?"

Stewart could see where this line of questioning was heading and tried to pre-empt it.

"Mr Cludden, as you well know from my formal statement, I arrived home this evening around 22:00 HRS to find my house being ransacked by a team of armed men, who proceeded to pursue my vehicle alongside the loch and who directed semiautomatic and fully automatic rounds at the unarmed police who had responded to the break in. During the firefight, one of your officers requested I provide covering fire using a side arm she had taken while arresting one of the armed men…"

Cludden angrily interrupted Stewart before he could continue.

"Unfortunately, Sgt. Wells and Cons. Jimms are under sedation and cannot verify your story, so you will understand if I view your claims of innocence with some considerable suspicion."

CTSA Cludden then pushed a black and white photograph towards Stewart. The picture was of a youngish man with a long thick beard. Based on the closed eyes and steel surface visible behind the head, Stewart assumed the picture had been taken at the police morgue.

"Killed from multiple gunshot wounds fired from a 9mm handgun, just like this one, that you admit to having fired."

Cludden emphasized his statement by pushing the evidence bag containing the Glock 17 towards Stewart, who responded, still icy calm in spite of the clear attempt to frame him.

"If you care to compare the ballistics reports on the bullets inside this man you will find this gun..." Stewart pointed to the Glock on the table in front of him, "...did not shoot him. I was asked by Sgt. Wells to provide covering fire to protect this man when he was in police custody."

"Bullshit." Snarled Cludden, in a whisper so his words could be heard by the two other men in the room but not picked up by the microphone.

"Sorry? I missed that, could you repeat it for the recording?" Asked Stewart in such an innocent manner that D/Supt. McBride could not help but smile.

CTSA Cludden did not appreciate the joke at his expense and his voice became filled with a clear anger.

"Here is what I think happened. This character..."

he pointed one of his thick fingers at the mug shot of the dead man that rested on the table,

"…had Bosnian currency in his wallet along with an Aeroflot ticket stub from Sarajevo International Airport. You are well known in that country are you not, Stewart? In fact, you are mentioned on several Neo-Nazi web sites as being on a death list for your involvement in hunting down fascist war criminals and bringing them to trial."

Stewart raised his eyebrow sceptically, as if questioning the relevance of events that took place five years ago. The terror advisor continued.

"I think what happened tonight was some kind of payback for your meddling in the affairs of these far-right organisations. Things got out of hand, you called the police and now you are hiding behind the boys in blue to try and avoid the consequences of a situation that you orchestrated yourself, or with persons unknown."

Cludden nodded to McBride, "Detective Superintendent, I would like some time with the suspect alone. I have some restricted material that I believe will cause Mr Stewart to revise his statement and close this case."

McBride looked uncomfortable. "It is highly irregular, but…" the police officer looked at his watch noting the late hour and, hoping for a chance to at least get some sleep that night, acquiesced.

"I will give you ten minutes."

Rising from his chair he noted, "02.15 HRS, Detective Superintendent McBride leaving the room." to the recorder and exited, closing the door as much as he could in spite of the thick video camera cables.

Cludden waited for a moment and then reached over and turned off the NEAL CD unit, before standing and unplugging the Samsung video recorder.

Stewart pretended not to notice and, as though pulling the paperwork towards him to re-examine the mug shot of the dead man, he waited for the moment the terror advisor was focused on the video recorder before he palmed the paperclip and a Sharpie pen from the table into his right hand.

Meanwhile Cludden had turned back towards Stewart. Tearing the Glock from the plastic evidence bag, he inserted the magazine into the stock and loaded a 9mm round into the guns chamber. Now feeling in complete control, he gloated, finally revealing his true purpose.

"You must have really pissed off someone to have such a short notice contract placed on you, and for it to have to happen in a police station. Still I cannot complain. This is a very lucrative gig for me."

He smiled wickedly at the tired and dishevelled man who appeared harmless, seated on the chair before him locked in a pair of steel police issue handcuffs.

"Accidents happen with loaded guns every day. Even in police stations. When some guilty suspect grabs a gun, officers have no choice but to pull the trigger."

Looking at his highly distinctive Luminox watch he pronounced.

"Now let's get this farce over… I have half a million euros waiting to be collected."

The assassin stood and walked closer, placing the loaded Glock 17 in his victim's face so the shot would be point blank. Stewart remained icy calm as he reached out towards the gun with his handcuffed hands, looking as though he was going to plead for his life. Instead he used his left hand to grab and forcibly push the muzzle of the pistol back, exposing the barrel and causing the gun's feed mechanism to jam.

As the assassin found the Glock's trigger stuck fast, his momentary look of puzzlement was replaced by a contorted expression of agony as, from his seated position, Stewart's left foot launched into a snapping kick up into Cludden's groin, while simultaneously ramming the blunt point of the Sharpie marker pen up under the assassin's sternum, causing the already stunned man to collapse to the floor, his lungs and breathing temporarily paralyzed. In a fluid motion, Stewart then took the pistol and, while covering the incapacitated assassin with the gun, manipulated the paper clip as an improvised lock pick to free his handcuffs and use them to secure the paralyzed assassin to the fixed table leg.

He then folded the mug shot of the dead Serbian into his jacket pocket before pressing the concealed panic button on the interviewer's side of the desk, which he had seen when he tied his shoe laces at the beginning of the interview. Only then did he address the semi-conscious man on the floor before him, as he removed the unfired round from the chamber and the magazine from the gun's stock, placing the disarmed weapon on the table.

"Never did like the Glock 17. That reciprocating slide mechanism is a bloody liability."

Seconds later custody officer Clark stormed into the room. Seeing the semi-conscious terror advisor handcuffed to the table leg and Stewart calmly seated, he demanded.

"What the hell happened here?"

Without missing a beat, Stewart replied.

"An assassination attempt, thankfully it went off half-cocked…"

Hearing the commotion and the continuing shrill panic alarm, two other figures entered the small room. The first was a tall middle-aged man dressed in a dark grey suit. He would have looked elegant, apart from the obvious stress and tiredness that marked his features.

Stewart nodded at the newcomer.

"Good to see you, Keith."

Chief Constable Keith Smith, who had obviously been watching the interrogation via the Samsung video feed before it had been disconnected, was standing beside a tall, elegant, middle aged woman with shoulder length brown hair, who was dressed in a dark Salvatore Ferragamo business suit and carrying a Montblanc light tan leather briefcase. She extended her hand to the custody officer while clearly reading his name badge.

"Sergeant Clark? Helen Curren, I am Sir Stewart's legal representative."

She efficiently passed the bemused Sergeant three completed A4 forms along with a Council of the Bar and Law Societies in Europe (CCBE) Lawyer's Professional Identity Card and calmly requested.

"Please confirm you have received Forms 51-7 through 51-9 and have seen my CCBE identity card, for the record."

The clearly shocked and apologetic Chief Constable responded, "That will not be necessary. Given this unforgivable breach of our security, I am terminating this interview."

Tavish Stewart made an attempt to defuse the situation.

"Keith, if I am correct this incident is linked with the earlier attack on my home and, based on what this low life…" Stewart nodded to the assassin who was glaring at him from the floor, "…told me we are dealing with professional mercenaries, for whom killing and breaching the very best security is an everyday business. In that light, I will not be making any fuss about what happened." Stewart looked at Curren who nodded her understanding that no legal redress would be sought for the events of the evening. "But, I would appreciate some freedom to find whoever hired these men and why."

Keith Smith nodded. "Given your history you are undoubtedly well suited for such work, but understand I cannot formally endorse you taking the law into your own hands."

Smith then pulled up one of the battered metal chairs and sat opposite Stewart.

"This is a bloody bad business, Tavish. Armed terrorists making the glens look like Afghanistan and assassins posing as Counter Terror Advisors! The forensic boys say those hoodlums did a really thorough job of going through every room in your home, destroying pretty much everything, and left almost no DNA. Apart that is, from the dead man lying next to your dog on your drive, killed instantly by an unknown massive blunt force trauma. I don't suppose you know anything about that? Hmm?"

"No comment." Said Curren quickly, intervening before Stewart could say a word.

Keith Smith smiled, looking at the experienced lawyer.

"Quite. If you think of anything further that might help us with our enquiries, then…"

Curren completed the sentence, "We will inform you."

Smith smiled again.

"Indeed. Unfortunately, the remains of your Mercedes will have to stay with us for forensic analysis. There are well over sixty rounds embedded in it, so it may take a while. We will also keep that antique dagger of yours, at least until we finish our investigations. In the meantime, we would welcome the chance to begin the interrogation with Mr Cludden, or whatever his real name is, here."

Stewart nodded and exited the small room with Helen Curren close behind.

"Poor bastards." Said the Chief Constable quietly.

Sgt Clark tried to reassure his boss. "I am sure they will soon get over tonight, Sir."

Keith Smith regarded the custody officer, "I didn't mean them, Sergeant. I meant the terrorists."

Outside the three storey brick police station, in the heart of Stirling city centre, the summer night was glorious, with the stars spread out above them like a jewelled ceiling. Curren led the way through the almost deserted police station car park. Stewart walked a few steps behind, clearly enjoying the fresh air, after long hours in the interrogation room.

He was the first to break the silence.

"Are you up for a quick drive into Edinburgh? I'd like a chat with a very old friend, and then we can book into the Balmoral and have one of their famous Scottish breakfasts."

"Who will want to have a chat with you at 3 AM?" Asked the lawyer as she looked at the time on the luminous markers that glowed on Stewart's watch.

Stewart smiled, "You'd be surprised."

Curren raised one eyebrow, and walked towards a striking red Maserati GranTurismo coupe, deactivating the car's alarm as she approached. Stewart made a very short call on his Samsung phone before entering the passenger side door, and then the five litre V8 Ferrari engine growled delightfully, as the Maserati sped out of the car park and towards the M9.

Fifty minutes later, the red Italian coupe came to a stop outside a dark granite building, just off the Princes Street gardens in central Edinburgh. An enormous neon sign above the entrance proclaimed "The Tartan Kremlin". Two large men in black suits stood by the door, preventing anyone from entering the nightclub which was closing in thirty minutes time. A strong breeze blew plastic bags and an empty McEwan's beer can along the curb, making some of the male customers, who were leaving the establishment, put their jackets over the shoulders of their sparsely dressed female companions, to keep out the chill.

As Stewart and Curren walked briskly to the entrance, the two large door men clearly viewed Stewart with increasing suspicion, as they noted the stained and torn suit he was wearing. Thankfully, as if by some unseen signal, the nightclub owner, Lev Bachrach, an imposing grey-haired man with a distinctive broken nose emerged from the doorway, while consulting an old Fortis Cosmonaut watch that was resting under the left sleeve of his dark grey Hugo Boss business suit, and gestured for the doormen to stand aside. He smiled warmly.

"Tavish! My old friend, please come in, and enjoy some Russian hospitality."

Stewart turned and gestured to Curren to join him, and moments later the three of them entered the loud interior of the nightclub. Bachrach briskly led the way through a large auditorium, that had been decorated to look as though the dance floor and tables were located in Red Square. Striking blonde waitresses, with high Slavic cheekbones and heavy makeup, walked past, dressed in Russian Military uniforms with black thigh length boots, whilst carrying drinks on trays. Curren gazed around in wonder, as a laser light show cleverly produced the illusion of crowds walking past and around Red Square. She paused and Stewart gestured to her to follow Bachrach, who was already heading for a reconstruction of Lenin's Tomb. Walking down into the entrance of the mausoleum, the decoration returned to a more normal business format, and Lev Bachrach nodded to a group of large men dressed in dark double-breasted suits, seated behind black granite desks watching video security screens, before he continued on through an adjoining metal door. Stewart and Curren followed rapidly behind, and the nightclub noise was instantly lost as the massive windowless door was shut behind them, and they found themselves inside a thick metal walled room that closely resembled a bank vault.

Hanging in the centre of each wall was an extremely thin, fifty-two-inch SONY display, showing the activity throughout the night club. Bachrach noticed Curren's careful observation and remarked.

"Three inches of steel and four feet of reinforced concrete provides good sound insulation."

Curren glanced at Stewart, who was already seating himself in a stylish metal chair at a long glass and metal table, and commented.

"Impressive security, for a night club."

Bachrach looked at Stewart and asked, "Who is your inquisitive friend with a taste for Maseratis and Salvatore Ferragamo?"

Stewart gestured towards Curren.

"Lev, meet Helen Curren, QC, my long-suffering lawyer."

"Helen, meet Colonel Lev Averbuch Bachrach, formerly of the State Security Agency of the Republic of Belarus, and a good friend of mine from my days in Berlin during the 1980s."

Bachrach nodded and, after shaking hands with Curren, walked to the shining glass topped table, picking up three shot glasses and an unmarked bottle. He unscrewed the top of the bottle and poured three very full glasses. Unlike the stereotypical movie scenes of Russians consuming vodka in a single swift motion, Curren noticed that both men smelt the spirit like wine, and sampled small amounts in their mouths, before swallowing slowly.

Stewart licked his lips and said in appreciation.

"Not bad for a Polish vodka – Belvedere Silver, if I am not mistaken."

Bachrach gave a deep and genuine belly laugh. "Not bad for a decadent Capitalist, I will make a Russian out of you yet. But you did not come here just to taste vodka, did you?"

Stewart stood and picked the crumpled police morgue photo from his jacket pocket, passing it to the Russian.

"Do you think we can find out something about this character, he was one of the group raiding my estate earlier this evening?"

Bachrach took the police mug shot from Stewart noting, as he ran the photograph through a Samsung flatbed scanner on his desk, that based on the numerous bullet holes at least the bastard had died badly.

Consulting a small note book, which he took from a locked desk drawer, the Russian began typing a series of IP addresses into his Lenovo desktop system. Moments later, one of the wall mounted Sony screens transformed from displaying CCTV footage into a modified Skype video conference call, that was answered by a digitally animated picture of a large black wolf which talked in an electronically masked Russian voice. The disguised speech was almost drowned out by a combination of heavy metal music, video gaming noises and numerous other conversations taking place in the background.

Curren whispered, "Are these the infamous Black Wolf Hackers?"

Stewart nodded, "Yes, probably a unit within Spetssvyaz, the modern-day successors to the old 16th Directorate of the KGB."

Bachrach talked to the disembodied electronic voice, clearly describing the task of identifying the attacker of a British friend. There was some back and forth and Curren recognized Stewart's name being mentioned.

Lev Bachrach clearly had considerable influence as the loud heavy rock music and numerous conversations that had been taking place in the background abruptly stopped. In the resulting silence, the Black Wolf avatar was replaced by an image of a dimly lit Moscow internet café, filled with around twenty individuals, almost all with thick glasses, greasy hair and bad cases of acne, who were crammed next to the web cam, eagerly awaiting their instructions.

Lev Bachrach smiled and turned to Curren and Stewart.

"There, now we have the undivided attention of the best computer scientists in the world, let us find out what can be discovered about this man."

Bachrach pressed a series of keys to transfer the photo to the internet cafe. The moment the digital mug shot was displayed the hackers in the darkened room scrambled back to a bewildering range of ancient computers and gaming consoles which were without exception, surrounded by numerous Red Bull cans, chocolate wrappers, Mac Donald's Big Mac cartons and posters of Heavy Metal artists. The sounds of furious typing that filled the air for the next few minutes was interspersed with the odd shout from one of the young hackers, as some clue emerged.

Then a series of photographs and biographical information began to appear on the video screen. The man was a thirty-four-year-old Serbian called Dominic Gervac. He had served with the 11th Infantry Battalion of the 1st Land Force Brigade, garrisoned in Novi Sad, before being dishonourably discharged in 2015. He then joined the ranks of the many mercenary operatives who offer their services within the former Yugoslavia. The hackers found records showing that Gervac had worked for various US and Saudi corporations who needed close protection to support their projects in Libya, Iraq and Yemen.

The most recent activity showed Gervac being hired by an American military and intelligence contractor, who was almost certainly acting as a broker for deniable black ops. Although the financial transactions supporting this latest contract hiring had been conducted through "shell" companies and offshore banks in the Caribbean, a trace on the IP address that initiated the original commission showed that it came from an encrypted Motorola satellite phone, that was currently located in Edinburgh.

With the search completed, Stewart gave his thanks to the teenagers, who were obviously delighted to have a more challenging task than the usual requests to hack email accounts. After Lev Bachrach ended the video chat he handed Stewart a set of A4 sheets that summarized all the information that they had just obtained.

As Tavish Stewart studied the papers his old friend had clearly already anticipated the Scotsman's next request. With a knowing smile, the Russian headed to his desk, a gleaming metal construction that matched their surroundings. Pressing a series of black buttons on a wall mounted key pad behind it, the steel panels forming one of the side walls parted with an audible hiss, revealing an armoury filled with hand guns, automatic rifles, machine guns, knives and on assorted hangers, clothing.

Gesturing to Stewart, Lev Bachrach remarked.

"Please my friend, if you are alone in the world against an unknown opponent, you should at least be allowed to defend yourself."

Curren walked behind Stewart towards the concealed room where she noticed an old photograph mounted on the wall, showing a much younger Tavish Stewart and Lev Bachrach standing next to Mikhail Sergeyevich Gorbachev, the last President of the Soviet Union. All three men were shaking hands next to a flattened section of the infamous wall.

"What exactly did you two do in Berlin in the late 1980's?"

Lev Bachrach laughed, "That is a story for another time."

Once inside the entrance of the hidden room, it was clear that it was as large as the office they had just left and constructed with the same thick steel walls and ceiling. The entire space was filled with three tall racks of equipment, all labelled carefully describing each piece in detail, the number in stock and the ammunition options.

Stewart walked carefully through the racks, evaluating what was available, and having completed his review whistled in appreciation.

"Quite an armoury Lev, I am impressed."

The Russian stood back watching Stewart, and drinking the remains of his vodka.

"One does what one can."

Clearly in his element, Stewart started humming as he studied the various handguns and, after a moment's hesitation, he pulled out a box labelled Sig Sauer P229 MIL-Spec .357 SIG (12 RND MAG). He then bent over and removed a set of five smaller boxes, labelled ".357 SIG Mil-Spec Armour Penetrator", and a carton labelled "S.O.B holster black", which showed a picture of a pistol holster that concealed the weapon in the small of the back attached to a belt.

Lev smiled appreciatively, "The 229 is a nice sidearm."

Stewart nodded, "I'd prefer a revolver, but I need the .357 SIG Mil-Spec Penetrator round."

Bachrach's eyes widened.

"Body armour?"

"Yes. Those scumbags who were raiding my property last night were all wearing NIJ level 3 Kevlar vests."

Stewart began loading one of the empty pistol magazines with the armour piercing bullets, "Next time these bastards try to kill me, I mean to return the favour."

CHAPTER 3 – EDEN

"Know then, that you are more than meat, blood, and bone. The mind has wings, and can pass between the realms of matter and the voids beyond, from whence Self (Cognos), and Substance (Cosmos), both originate as two sides of one essence. The forces (Anunnaki) that formed our world exist still, and can, through the force of will combined with sacred rite, fold realities on each other, and allow the minds from one to spill unto the other. Thus, taught the Utukku when they lay with the fair daughters of men before their fall from heaven." - Stanza 36 - The Anunnaki Eli, 1098 BC

75 Miles South of Nasiriyah, Dhi Qar Governorate, Iraq
17.00HRS, 30th Jan, Seven Months before Current date

The small Cessna plane was cramped and cold. Strapped in his seat directly behind the pilot, Father Thomas O'Neill, of the Pontificia Accademia Romana di Archeologia (Pontifical Academy of Archaeology), stared to his right out of the plexiglass window at the desolate sands 12,000 feet below. O'Neill's dark hair, short beard and pale skin were dusted with a fine layer of sand that got everywhere and made O'Neill look older than his forty-two years. The ancient plane was dirty, bearing the evidence of the hundreds of flights carrying human cargo across the desert. Odd stains covered the seats, and the rubber mats on the floors had deep cuts and missing sections where heavy objects had been dragged in and out of the plane. The smell of vomit and sweat had now subsided as the temperature dropped with their increased elevation, but everything vibrated with the constant hum of the single propeller.

The twenty-seven-year-old US Marine Master Sergeant sitting in the next seat stared at him with a barely concealed hostility. His close blonde crew cut revealed the skin of his scalp, and his face muscles moved continuously as his jaws chewed gum at a rapid rate. The blue eyes were partially hidden behind tinted combat glasses, but showed a lifetime of sights that young men should be spared. The Marine was annoyed to be stuck playing nursemaid to some civilian, who wanted to visit some god forsaken town miles from anywhere, in a region where foreigners were unwelcome and had nowhere to hide from that hostility.

O'Neill avoided the stare and gazed again out of the window. The plane lurched in a pocket of turbulence and the Archaeologist's stomach reminded him of the poor food hygiene of his most recent meal. A couple of Imodiums and some frequent bathroom visits seemed to have stopped the problem, but O'Neill knew the next meal would likely start the cycle again. He shivered. It was much colder than he imagined. He buttoned up the collar on his once white linen shirt and gazed again at the sand dunes beneath him, which resembled an unmoving ocean with wave after wave of sand appearing to wash around stark outcrops of rock, worn down by eons of time. O'Neill reminded himself it was this timeless nature that indirectly was bringing him here. Here was the birthplace of writing that underpinned much of modern civilization and here also was the source of the myths that formed the basis of many modern religions. It was hard to imagine that beneath him was the location of the original Eden, where God supposedly breathed life into Adam and walked with him in that first paradise, where once stood the Tree of Knowledge and the lesser known Tree of Life.

Twenty minutes later as the sun began to fall, the small plane had landed and O'Neill was once again on the ground, sitting next to the Master Sergeant in the back of a battered white 1985 Toyota Hilux pickup, being covered in yet more dust, as the makeshift airport taxi sped along the dirt road towards the small settlement nearby. The Marine continued to chew, but now had switched his attention from O'Neill to the surroundings, his blue eyes continuously scanning all around and keeping his right hand on, or near, the Beretta M9 handgun in the holster at his side. The dirt road had formed endless ripples of hardened mud with the passing of numerous tyres and these caused the old Hilux to shudder violently whenever the pick-up slowed below twenty miles per hour. After what seemed an eternity of spine jarring travel, the lights of a small town approached in the distance. Having passing through some lightly populated areas, the pickup slowed and came to a stop outside a square three storey concrete building which had a single sign, showing in first Farsi and then in English "Nasiriyah Hospital, Dhi Qar Governorate". O'Neill jumped stiffly down from the back of the pickup onto the concrete road and offered a hand to the young Marine, who hesitated before accepting the assistance with the two-large military kit bags the men had brought with them.

Walking towards them was the figure of a slim young woman in her twenties, dressed in a white lab coat, her head and shoulders covered by a stylish grey abeya which obscured her face. By her side strode an officious middle-aged man with a large pot belly, wearing a grey uniform and peaked cap smothered in gold braid, who was either police or military, if there was any real difference in the confusion of post war Iraq.

The young woman was about to introduce herself to O'Neill but was brusquely interrupted by the man who, it rapidly became clear, was the senior government official in the small town, and considered it his duty to make everyone's life considerably more challenging.

"Papers!" He officiously demanded to O'Neill and the young Marine, with a repeated click of his fingers towards both of them. O'Neill started reaching into his back pocket when his companion stepped forward and pointed to the label on his left breast, which read "US Marines" and had a golden parachute with wings above it. For the first time in the forty-eight hours since they had met, O'Neill heard the young American speak in a smooth southern drawl.

"You need any more papers than that, and we will be having some serious problems."

Obviously intimidated, the Iraqi official suddenly looked at his fake gold Rolex Cosmograph watch and, muttering some excuse, scurried off to a dilapidated white Nissan saloon car which he drove off at some speed, leaving the three of them alone in the darkness.

The young doctor watched the Nissan disappear in a cloud of dust and then introduced herself, speaking in an American accent.

"Hello. I am Dr Kaliffia, you must be Father O'Neill?"

O'Neill smiled and extended his hand.

"Yes, and this is Master Sergeant Jackson."

The Marine nodded and picked up the two huge kit bags as if they were empty.

The woman gestured for them both to follow her into the hospital. Inside the building was considerably warmer, and O'Neill unbuttoned the top of his shirt in a futile gesture to reduce the heat. The doctor led them along a narrow corridor, paved with what were once white plastic floor tiles that had since split and become stained. The narrow passage was littered here and there with stretcher beds and cheap plastic chairs that would have looked better suited for a barbecue than a hospital. The walls, that had presumably once matched the colour of the floor, were now covered with hand prints and a mixture of brown and red stains, that showed the poor sanitary conditions that existed for patients in the institution.

They finally turned right into a small office which was crammed with two desks, four mismatched off-white plastic garden chairs, and one ancient Compaq desktop computer proudly displaying a screen saver advertising Windows 3.1. The desks were buried in papers, printouts, blue coloured plastic bags and assorted plastic ball pens. Partly visible beneath the debris was an old Epson dot matrix printer.

Dr Kaliffia hurriedly removed the newspapers, lever-arch files and large fake Fossil handbag that were on the vacant chairs and then gestured for the two men to sit. O'Neill gladly accepted, while Jackson took some steps back and instead stood outside looking down the corridor, clearly more interested in keeping watch than on talking with the doctor.

"I am sincerely sorry for the deaths of your colleagues." Stated Kaliffia.

O'Neill looked shocked.

"The fax said there was one survivor."

She nodded, "Dr Finster. He died at three AM this morning." She made the statement while avoiding eye contact.

O'Neill picked up on her evident discomfort.

"The fax was vague about the details of what exactly happened."

"Yes. That is because no one knows for sure. They were found by the driver bringing the weekly supplies to the site."

"Six people die and no one knows what happened?"

"It is a very remote area. Certainly no one goes there by choice because it has had a bad reputation for a long time."

"What was the cause of death?" Asked O'Neill.

"We are not sure. I was told that the bodies were badly decomposed when they were found and had to be burnt almost immediately."

"What about Finster? You said he died this morning. What was the cause of his death?"

"He was severely dehydrated and had lost a considerable amount of blood. He was lapsing in and out of consciousness. We did what we could but..."

She gestured to her surroundings,

"…this is not John Hopkins."

O'Neill nodded gravely.

"Can I see the body? I knew him and, if possible, I would like to bury him."

She looked startled. Uncomfortable. She looked away again.

"I am sorry, his body was burnt this morning."

O'Neill stared at her in disbelief.

"We faxed you and said I would arrive today. If he died from dehydration and blood loss I do not see why he had to be burnt before I arrived, when you knew I would be here in hours."

Before she could answer, a male voice cut into the conversation.

"Your colleague had other… afflictions, which meant he and the others had to be cleansed immediately."

O'Neill looked up to see Master Sergeant Jackson escorting a short old man with white hair, dressed in a crisp white Thawb, simple leather sandals and carrying a well-used book, that O'Neill saw was an ancient Koran, and with it a log book, that O'Neill recognised as being standard issue to expeditions of the Pontifical Academy of Archaeology.

The old man sat next to O'Neill and made the traditional greeting to the Dr and the Western visitor. "Assalamu alaikum."

O'Neill placed his right hand over his heart and responded.

" Wa alaikum assalam wa rahmatu Allah."

The old man smiled warmly, "Your Arabic is excellent."

O'Neill bowed slightly, "As is your English."

Jackson raised his eyebrows, looked at his green G-Shock Mudman watch, and went back to the corridor to keep his eye on the two kit bags and the entrance.

The old man introduced himself as Ali Alheim, the Sheik for the Dhi Qar region, and wanted to know about O'Neill, The Pontifical Academy of Archaeology, and the reason for his visit, but more importantly for the reason the six westerners were visiting such a dangerous site.

"Mr O'Neill, our two religions have very similar accounts of creation and the other creatures that shared in our creation. Both our religions state very clearly that some of these entities were created before humanity and would exist for all eternity."

O'Neill nodded, "Angels."

"Not just Angels, Mr O'Neill. There were also beings so proud that they dared even to defy God himself."

"The Devil?"

"Devils, plural, Mr O'Neill. Most certainly plural as they are clearly said in both our Holy scriptures to be Legion. Both our religions agree about the existence of fallen immortal beings who, through pride, became cursed to share this physical world alongside us, but they are certainly not with us or for us."

"You believe this?"

"One either accepts the scripture as the word of God or you do not. One cannot simply select which articles of faith you accept and which you reject based on convenience or prejudice."

"So, you are saying that my colleagues were attacked and killed by Demons?"

The old man stared for a moment into the Westerner's opal eyes. Instead of answering he passed the archaeological note book to O'Neill.

"Read it. And then go back home and forget this place. As it should be forgotten until the Yawm al-Qiyāmah."

He rose and, bowing to Dr Kaliffia, went out past Jackson, who observed the old man as he turned left and walked down the long corridor and out into the darkness.

O'Neill turned back to Kaliffia.

"Is there somewhere I can go and clean up, eat and then read through this?" He indicated the log book.

Kaliffia nodded, "Well, there is no Hilton in Nasiriyah, but you are welcome to use the duty doctor's shower and bed, although the cafeteria is closed until the morning."

She stood and pulled back a grey curtain behind her desk, which revealed an iron double bunk bed and to one side, offset from the room, a set of old lockers with cheap Chinese padlocks, and a corridor leading to the chipped glass door of a shower room. Looking at a small steel Pulsar medical fob watch hanging from her breast pocket, she added,

"In fact, I have my rounds, so you and your colleague can have the place to yourselves until morning." She rose and walked out, passed Jackson standing outside, and taking a turn to the right headed towards the wards.

After she had gone, O'Neill called Jackson into the tiny office and showed him the simple accommodation that had been made available to them. The Marine brought in both kit bags and opening a side vent pulled out two rubber door wedges, which he placed under the now closed office door. He looked at O'Neill's questioning face and smiled.

"Marine Corps Universal lock. I sleep better knowing I have at least one closed door between me and whatever..." He rummaged further into his bag exposing the protective plastic cap on the short barrel of a M4 carbine, and pulled out two silver foil ration bags. He threw one casually to O'Neill.

"Get some food into you, and you can have first call at the showers. We can take turns at getting some sleep. You get the top bunk, in case I have to deal with any… visitors."

O'Neill nodded agreement and both men set to eating the contents of the rations, with grey plastic sporks that were inside the "Ready to Eat" military food bags.

Between short periods of sleep, O'Neill starting reading the battered leather log book, whilst sitting at the doctor's untidy desk under the light of a single sixty-watt lamp. Finster's account of the expedition started ordinarily enough. They had arrived in what sounded like the same old Cessna plane that O'Neill had just used, and had rented a series of pickups to transport the six-person team to the dig site in the middle of the desert, some thirty-seven miles South West of the small town of Nasiriyah. Their goal was to re-excavate a site known as E23F, which had originally been surveyed in the winter of 1949 by a British team who identified the Ziggurat as being dedicated to the Sumerian god of Earth called "Enki". The original excavation had not found much beyond a small partly exposed subterranean chamber and the remains of an altar. All other items had long been looted by unknown tomb robbers over the last 4,000 years. Then, in 2008, a team at Harvard had discovered some inscriptions on the inside of a Sumerian clay pot, accidentally smashed during an exhibition at the Smithsonian. The previously unknown inscriptions described an ancient oracle beneath the subterranean temple of Enki, which belonged to the most ancient of the Sumerian time lines. After years of fund raising and waiting for the situation in Iraq to stabilize, the Finster expedition had been sent to determine the reality of an ancient oracle chamber.

The first three weeks of the log book entries continued as would be expected. Ultrasound scans showed what could be a large chamber beneath the existing temple, but there was no clear indication of where the entrance tunnel existed.

A painstaking grid wise examination of the floor of the underground temple commenced in the fourth week of the expedition, with Finster noting in his journal that the expedition members disliked the shifts down below. Poor ventilation and the heat from the electric arc lights made the work extremely hard. In addition, his colleagues reported to Finster that they felt they were being watched and, more curiously, that trowels and other small items left in the excavation area overnight had gone missing, only to be found in other areas of the dig grid.

In the fifth week, the team found the top step of a stairway descending down into the rock floor, that had been completely filled in with sand and small rocks. The painstaking process of clearing the stairway began and, after three days of work, they uncovered the steps and found a sealed entrance which miraculously was intact after nearly 4,000 years. The team had emailed the associated news media about their find and planned a formal press event the following week but, in a terrible tragedy, the entire six-person team had then been found dead or dying the following day. The journal gave no indication of any disease or other cause which could have indicated why they all should mysteriously die.

O'Neill looked up as Jackson entered the small office space in the early morning. The Marine nodded at the log book, "Any goblins or bogeymen?"

O'Neill smiled, "Not one. But someone did not want them to open a sealed chamber they had just found."

"Sounds a lot more likely than the hokum that Sheik was trying to sell you yesterday."

"Agreed. I think we need to see this dig site for ourselves if we are ever going to find out what happened here. Do you think we could get a truck and travel through 40 miles of a restricted Iraqi zone without being detected?"

Jackson smiled, "I thought you would never ask."

CHAPTER 4 - THE REAPER

"Men fear Death, as children fear to go in the dark; and as that natural fear in children is increased with tales, so is the other." - Francis Bacon, Essays

Nasiriyah Hospital, Dhi Qar Governorate, Iraq
04.17HRS, 31st Jan, 7 Months before Current date

Sitting together in Dr Kaliffia's cramped hospital office, the two men spent the early morning hours perching on the uncomfortable plastic chairs under a discoloured single sixty-watt bulb, comparing the sketch map and coordinates listed in Finster's charred log book with the high-resolution satellite map stored on Jackson's DOD GPS enabled Samsung Tablet. Since such technology is not permitted to integrate with the US DOD communication infrastructure, and Nasiriyah was outside the effective secure range of the field radio, then USMC standard operating procedure dictated that Jackson had to resort to more mundane communication technologies to update Command and Control (CAC) on his status, the mysterious deaths of the archaeological team and the urgent need to visit the excavation site.

So, at fifteen-minute intervals throughout the early morning, Jackson's G Shock reminded him to try his luck again with the unreliable Iraqi phone network, using a battered red wall phone which was surrounded by hand scribbled Arabic and dirty stains on the plaster from years of previous use.

At around 04:00HRS the seventh attempt proved successful, and Jackson rapidly went through a complex identification procedure, that culminated in him hanging up and getting a return call from a proficient sounding female Command and Control Officer (CCO), called Lieutenant Weevey, aboard the USS Harry S. Truman (CVN 75) in the Arabian Gulf.

Weevey was quickly briefed on the situation by Jackson and, based on her cool responses and follow-up questions, the mysterious deaths of a Vatican archaeology team and an unplanned expedition, by a single Marine babysitting an unarmed Priest into a potentially hostile foreign desert, left her completely unphased. With a few deft key strokes, she woke a General Atomics MQ-9 Reaper drone, that was slumbering in the Arabian night sky nearly twelve miles above them, bringing its sophisticated surveillance systems to bear on the area surrounding the Nasiriyah Hospital.

Within twelve seconds, it's array of multi-gigapixel Carl Zeiss digital lenses had determined that there was a suitable vehicle nearby, that could take two personnel to the target location with sixty four percent probability of remaining undetected for one hour and twenty minutes. More specifically, Lt Weevey advised Jackson, in a voice that could have been confirming a grocery order, that there was a white, 1989 Toyota HiAce van with an open left side door, parked twelve feet from the rear exit of the hospital, its heat signature showing it had recently been used and therefore could be assumed to be in working order. Further, the angle of its rear suspension gave an eighty-three percent probability that it was close to being fully fuelled.

Continuing in her efficient tone, Weevey informed Jackson that she was now directing the Reaper to use its classified "Gorgon Stare" system to check the proposed thirty-seven-mile route from Nasiriyah to the target GPS coordinates of the archaeological site, from its vantage point in the stratosphere, in both visible and invisible optical ranges. Unbreakable quantum encryption communication systems on the Reaper then transmitted its data, via a dedicated geostationary satellite, to an Advanced Artificial Intelligence System located on the Harry S. Truman, which was capable of instantly comparing detected objects against a comprehensive database, categorising everything from a pregnant camel to a T-99 "Armata" Tank, highlighting any potential threat to a single US Marine travelling with a civilian in a Toyota HiAce van.

Moments later, Weevey's voice resumed, confirming that, apart from the Imam Ali Airbase ten clicks to the West, home to three squadrons of Russian made Mil Mi-17 helicopters, there were no indications of any ground based tactical military assets on the projected route, but that there were three operational ground military assets: an FV103 Spartan armoured personnel carrier (APC), a much older M113 APC and a US supplied IAV Stryker light armoured fighting vehicle. Of these three, the Stryker was regarded as posing a seventy-two percent probable threat to the success of the operation, since it was deployed on one of the stretches of Highway 8 that they proposed to pass. With the first indication of any kind of limitation to their plans, Lt Weevey informed Jackson that, as the Iraqi army was formally an ally of the United States, they could not intervene against "friendly" forces if they decided to intercept them on route. As Jackson put it so succinctly after hanging up the phone, "If the proverbial hits the fan, then we are on our own."

O'Neill considered the situation and, looking at Jackson, offered to go on alone, to which the Master Sgt responded by lifting the two kit bags and, offering one to O'Neill, smiled.

"What? And let you see the bogeyman all alone? No way. Besides, some of those murdered people were American citizens and they deserve payback."

Removing the rubber wedges, Jackson opened the door to Kaliffia's office and headed into the corridor, O'Neill following behind. If the aerial surveillance from the Reaper was correct, then their transportation was 100 feet away, accessible through the corridor and the main hospital reception area. There was no point in trying to disguise themselves, as they both stood out in so many ways. Fortunately, as they started walking down the long hallway, they heard the distinctive Fajr call to prayer, and when they found the corridor opening into a larger space they discovered that all the active staff were on the floor, facing away from them. The double doors to the outside streets were half closed and partially blocked by a delivery of blue plastic water cooler bottles. Quickly sizing up the situation, Jackson picked up one of the full water bottles, pushed open the door and had both of them outside on the street in seconds. The sun had risen, and was shining through a gap between the buildings in front of them, so momentarily it was impossible to see anything more than the immediate ground around them and the sharply defined edges of buildings. The tarmac of the road was obscured in places by small accumulations of sand that had been blown over the town from the surrounding desert.

There was an odd mix of temperatures as the cool air of the night was rapidly being exchanged for the heat of the rising sun. The front of O'Neill's face and arms felt warmth, but his back and unexposed skin continued to register the icy cold of the desert night. While O'Neill was occupied absorbing his surroundings, Jackson had already pulled on his USMC Ray-Ban RB3030 Outdoorsman Sunglasses, and guided the arm of the blinded priest to pick up the water bottle and walk towards the ancient HiAce van, that sat in the middle of the empty street before them. Its left-side door was open, so Jackson quickly moved into the driver's seat, leaving the door ajar so he could still get in and out rapidly, and anyone looking at the vehicle would not sense anything amiss.

Meanwhile, O'Neil had walked around to the back of the van and tested the double doors. One was jammed shut but the other opened with some reluctance. Inside, the rear of the van was filled with a mix of empty and full water bottles, and it was clear that the large container that Jackson had taken from the hospital reception was superfluous. In fact, it was so tightly packed, that without removing four empty bottles the two kit bags, which O'Neill had to drag around to the back, would never have fitted.

In the front, Jackson busied himself working on the electrical wires connecting to the ignition with his brushed steel Leatherman Skeletool and, within a few moments, the ancient diesel engine chugged to life, for what would be its final journey, after nearly half a million miles of service in numerous roles, since its creation in a factory in Aichi, Japan in 1989.

After several unsuccessful attempts to prize open a badly damaged right-side passenger door, O'Neill finally managed to slide in on to a split and stained beige plastic three-person seat and positioned himself alongside Jackson in the front of the old van. The middle seat space between the two men was fully occupied by an assortment of papers in Arabic, Jackson's notes from his conversation with Lt Weevey, the Samsung Tablet, Finster's log book, and an extremely well-worn AK47 assault rifle that had been stashed in a deep split in the seat. Large strips of duct tape adorned the AK47 around the curved magazine, either as a decoration or a repair, it was not clear which. As Jackson struggled with the stick shift gearbox, O'Neill looked around the cab. The first thing which drew his gaze were the large CDs hanging from the rear-view mirror, inscribed in Arabic with text that was from the Koran. The rest of the dashboard area was covered in a piece of faded red Arabic carpet with elaborate tassels, that presumably helped prevent the plastic from melting in the extreme heat, but also gave the atmosphere of a scene out of the Arabian Nights.

Jackson reversed the old Toyota back out of the loading bay at the rear of the hospital, and was gradually coming to terms with the ancient manual gear changes, with fewer and fewer lurches, but he was still producing a sickening metallic grating noise with each use of the clutch. O'Neill looked nervously into the partially smashed left-wing mirror, that shared the same duct tape repairs as the AK47. Surely someone would notice the theft of the van and be coming after them at any moment? The Marine Mstr Sgt must have shared the same concern, as he increased speed at the road junction and turned rapidly to the left, into the main street that ran behind the hospital. Fortunately, there were no other vehicles on the road at this early hour. The dreary two and three-storey shops were mostly closed, and the owners of those that were open seemed preoccupied with the morning prayers. The town was laid out in a grid of blocks, with a mix of grey concrete houses and similarly constructed shops in a well-ordered pattern. Some of the wealthier families had upgraded their homes to have white frontages but, for the most part, the buildings were a depressing mixture of concrete and breezeblocks, with cheap air conditioning units poking from the bedroom windows dripping condensation onto the pavements and streets below.

According to Jackson's hand scribbled notes from the phone conversation with Weevey, the town of Nasiriyah had a simple layout, where every road south eventually fed onto the main North/South Highway 8, at one of two large intersections which marked the beginning and end of the town. It was at the Southernmost intersection where they encountered their first significant group of people. On the far side of the crossing there were around sixteen men standing, talking and drinking coffee, next to a blue Datsun 720 pickup truck, all dressed similarly in cream coloured Thawbs with their heads covered in red coloured Keffiyehs. They had clearly just finished their prayers and a few of them were occupied rolling up sheets and rugs from the ground, which had all been aligned roughly in the direction Jackson intended to turn the vehicle.

O'Neill started to panic, pulling up the old AK47 from its place in the seat and, as he did so, two of the long-curved AK magazines came away from the rifle frame, showing the intended purpose of the duct tape. Jackson reached over and pushed the assault rifle back into its slot deep in the seat, adding. "For fucks sake stay calm. These are road work teams, so just chill and smile before you get us both killed."

Slowing the vehicle, the Marine waved in a friendly manner to the men who, pausing from their discussions, stared at the van curiously and waved back.

Jackson turned right, and the old HiAce headed roughly South, along the two-lane Highway 8 towards a small turning, fourteen miles away, where they would leave the highway for another twenty-five miles of rough track, before they reached the archaeological site E23F mentioned in Finster's log book.

The Master Sgt pressed the old van hard along the modern tarmac highway, framed on either side with rough scrub, rock and sand. Highway 8 had separate lanes for North and South traffic and, apart from some small huts beside a series of lakes on the left-hand side of the road, within the first few miles after leaving Nasiriyah there were no signs of human habitation, just mile after mile of harsh desert.

O'Neill turned to Jackson. "Shouldn't we try and disguise ourselves or something in case we are stopped?"

The Marine glanced at his GShock, which was in chronograph mode and showed that twenty-four minutes and thirty-four seconds had elapsed since they stole the HiAce, and responded.

"My estimate is that they should discover the theft any minute, and then we will be reported to that officious ass we met when we landed yesterday. With luck, he will decide to give chase himself. Worst case scenario is that the ass reports the incident to the central authorities. Since they know who we are and where we are going, I would expect they will not treat the incident as a priority. That should at least give us enough time to get to the excavation site and see if there is any evidence of foul play. It is certain that the authorities will turn up and catch us, but borrowing a water delivery van and visiting an archaeological site where a tragedy occurred is not a capital offence, even in Iraq. I think we may get you some valuable hours at the site."

Jackson smiled adding, "Sometimes it's better to ask for forgiveness than for permission."

As the two men sped along the desert tarmac on Highway 8, back in Nasiriyah, the officious Police Chief had indeed been informed about the theft of the water delivery van and was at this moment sweating profusely as he sat in a white steel chair in front of Sheik Ali Alheim, who in turn was seated in a white and gold high backed seat with deep red velvet finishing. The older man was speaking into an ivory and gold telephone, that would not have looked out of place in the 1920's. Both men were sitting in the Sheik's exquisite courtyard area, which was sumptuously finished in fine carved white marble decorated with texts from the Koran. Water trickled gently from spouts that had been shaped into lion's heads and embedded into the walls and also from an ornate fountain in the centre of the large room, that was carved from bronze into the shape of a large palm tree. The entire effect was both calming and cooling. However, as the Sheik turned on the speaker attached to the classic ivory phone, neither man felt calm or cool.

The voice on the other end of the line was camouflaged by a digital filter, but even that technology could not disguise its chilling menace.

"Excellent. You will permit them to reach the location. I will deal with them once they arrive. Your remaining task is to remove all record of them. And I mean *all* record. Understood?"

The Sheik nodded and gasped agreement into the phone, and then noted he was speaking to the dial tone as the other end had terminated the connection. Hanging up the receiver, the Sheik gestured for the Chief of Police to go. Grateful to be released from the meeting, the fat policeman scurried from the courtyard, still wiping his brow from the cold nervous sweat that was always associated with any dealings with this unknown person, who covertly controlled their lives.

Dr Kaliffia's white Nissan Micra pulled over at the improvised police check point, with the large American police car blocking the road. Two young policemen were sitting in the front of the squad car looking very bored. The young doctor had not seen a road block here on her regular route to the hospital before but, like all Iraqi's, she was used to the routine of having these police checkpoints suddenly appear along the roads. One of the young uniformed men got out of the police car and walked casually to the smaller Nissan. Kaliffia's long black hair flowed over her face from out of her grey abeya headdress, as she leant over her right front passenger seat searching for her papers within her fake Fossil handbag. The last sensation the young doctor felt was a violent impact against her head, as a 9mm round slammed into her left temple and her blood splattered over the inside of the small car. The police man emptied three more rounds into her body, turned and walked back to the squad car, where his companion had already started the engine, then rapidly drove away leaving another roadside killing that would never be solved.

A few hundred yards from the callous murder of Dr Kaliffia, the squad car turned off from the main road into a yard, hidden behind ten-feet-high concrete walls. Moments later, the air rang out with an enormous explosion, followed by a large fireball which consumed the squad car and instantly incinerated everything within a sixteen-foot radius.

Back in the Toyota HiAce, O'Neill was gazing absently out of his window at the clear blue sky as they sped along the highway. He noticed the silhouette of a small single engine passenger plane, repeating the same route that he and Jackson had taken into Nasiriyah yesterday. As O' Neill watched the Cessna start its approach, a thin tendril of smoke leapt from the ground into the air heading inexorably towards the tiny white aircraft. When the rocket trail met the Cessna, the plane transformed into a grey smoke cloud and, moments later, there followed a sound similar to a firework exploding. At first O'Neill could not comprehend what he had just seen. Then, as the smoke cloud remained hanging in the air where the aircraft had been moments before, the full horror hit him. He pulled Jackson's right arm and pointed to the cloud muttering.

"I... I... think someone just shot down the Cessna we travelled in yesterday!"

Jackson slowed, looking carefully at the narrow smoke trail and the larger grey smoke cloud that still hung in the sky.

"Dude, that's not cool. Not fucking cool at all."

He pulled the van off the highway on to the hard shoulder, quickly got out and walked around to the back, opening the double doors. Moments later he had the two-large kit bags out and was standing on the rear of the van with a pair of binoculars, looking at the smoke trail and cloud that were now starting to disperse.

"Shit, shit, shit..." Jackson exclaimed and clambered back down to the open kit bags.

O'Neill had joined him around the rear of the van and queried.

"Did you know someone on the plane?"

"Yeah, our hopes of getting out of here alive." Retorted Jackson.

"What do you mean?" Said the puzzled O'Neill.

Jackson patted O'Neill's shoulder.

"Someone is cleaning up, CIA style, and I have a feeling we are part of the mess."

As he spoke, he started pulling thick body armour from the kit bags, followed by small packages that contained ceramic plates. With a rapid practiced hand, he inserted the plates into the front and back of the body armour and started to repeat the process with a second set, clearly intended for O'Neill. Then came two heavy ceramic helmets covered in a thick camouflage pattern.

The priest looked on horrified.

"You expecting trouble?"

Jackson looked at O'Neill and smiled,

"No shit."

Next out of the bag was a wicked looking USMC issue OKC-3S bayonet in a black plastic holder, which Jackson duct taped upside down (blade uppermost) on the chest section of his body armour, so he could grasp the handle quickly. This was followed by six small spherical green objects marked "M67 fragmentation", that fitted on clips attached to the left side of Jackson's chest. Finally, the Marine pulled an M4 Carbine from the bag and, rapidly removing the protective cap, started checking the mechanism. Once he was satisfied that it was working smoothly, he took six spare magazines for the M4, taping them together into pairs with the magazine openings in opposing directions in each matched pair. These were then fitted to his waist band. Finally, he broke open a box marked M433 High-Explosive Dual-Purpose Rounds and stored them into fittings on his body armour.

His preparation complete, Jackson turned and looked at O'Neill, who was still struggling to get his front and rear body armour panels to attach together. After some assistance, the Archaeologist was kitted up, but looked very awkward as they walked back to the front of the van. The Marine got into the cab and pulled up the old battered AK47. He carefully checked the two spare magazines and the one currently in the rifle. All three were full of the heavy Full Metal Jacket (FMJ) 7.62mm rounds. Jackson grunted appreciatively

"Well, that's ninety more rounds than we should have and, say what you like about the AK47, it always brings something to the party."

He turned to O'Neill and handed him the machine gun, while his own M4 now rested in the space it once occupied.

"Ok, O'Neill. If I am correct, the rules of the game just changed and I don't think we are in Kansas anymore, so now our plan is we get to your site as quickly as possible, take pictures of what happened, and then try and get away before whoever is cleaning up comes to deal with us."

Before starting the engine again, Jackson walked once more to the back of the van and pulled out the heavy bottle stand and all but one of the full water bottles. He then got back in the driver's seat and accelerated back onto the highway. The old diesel engine started to smoke out of the exhaust as Jackson pushed the accelerator to the floor.

Back in Nasiriyah, the exquisite courtyard of Ali Alheim was again the meeting place for the Police Chief and the Sheik. The two men sat in their respective places. Around them the sounds of fountains filled the air, interspersed now and again with the buzzing of the numerous flies that gathered over their rapidly decaying bodies.

CHAPTER 5 - BENEATH THE SANDS OF TIME

"There is a Magical operation of maximum importance: The Initiation of a New Aeon. When it becomes necessary to utter a Word, the whole Planet must be bathed in blood." - Aleister Crowley "Magick in Theory and Practice"

Highway 8 Southbound, Dhi Qar Governorate, Iraq
07.12HRS, 1st Feb - 7 Months before Current date

With very little other traffic on the highway they soon reached the right hand turning, taking them onto the twenty-four miles of desert track, that led to the coordinates in Finster's log book. The going was rough, and with Jackson now pushing the old van to its limits, it was a violent ride. The tough Marine's face was set in strong determination as he ignored the oil and temperature gauges. Inside the cabin, the continuous movement made everything rattle noisily, and O'Neill had to hang on to Finster's log book, the Samsung and spare AK47 magazines to stop them flying all over the place. The CDs hanging from the rear-view mirror swung wildly. As they surged forward down the narrow track, that was probably a dried-up river bed since it was lower than the surrounding ground, and snaked left and right in long meandering arcs, thick dust clouds rose behind them combined with an increasing pall of black smoke from the engine. As the minutes ticked by, the volume of the thick smoke increased and soon completely obscured the vehicle's trailing dust cloud, marking the death of the faithful old van. As O'Neill looked at the choking fumes that were visible in the rear-view mirror, it was clear that the Toyota HiAce would not last much longer. But, just as he thought the engine would finally fail, the Samsung tablet started flashing and vibrating. They had arrived at Finster's dig, the location known as E23F. The area resembled a Martian landscape. Sand and rock were the only things visible for as far as the eye could see in every direction.

Jackson brought the van off the dirt track and stopped in a sixteen-foot-wide area, that had clearly seen a large amount of recent traffic, since the sand was etched with numerous tyre tracks and marks. As the Marine Mstr Sgt exited the vehicle he knelt and examined some of them, before looking at O'Neill, who was walking around the van holding Finster's log book, the Samsung tablet and the AK47. The two spare magazines protruded awkwardly from his cargo pants pockets. Dragging the kit bags from the HiAce, Jackson extracted what looked like two house bricks from one of the bags, each labelled M18A1 "Front toward enemy". He strapped one brick in the front of the vehicle, linked to the two front doors, and the second in the rear, directly behind the two rear doors and linked to their opening.

O'Neill watched and said, "Is that really necessary?"

Jackson replied, "If it comes to it, then yeah, every time."

They shared the load of the two kitbags and walked up a small pathway, that had clearly seen considerable use in the recent days. As they reached the top of what was obviously an ancient manmade structure, they could see several blue nylon tents that had been flattened completely. The smell of rotting meat hit them moments later. The remains of the tents were surrounded with flies which swarmed around the entrance flaps. Thomas O'Neill gagged and doubled over as he involuntarily threw up. Jackson was, in contrast, unmoved and opened the nearest tent and entered it. Moments later he emerged, walked over to the vomiting Archaeologist, and took a well-used Canon EOS 1D Mark III camera from around O'Neill's neck. The Marine then returned to the first tent, and the sound of the camera started to compete with the noise of buzzing flies. Moving on to the next tent and then the next, he repeated the procedure, carefully recording the horrific scenes inside.

Jackson returned to O'Neill and squatted down next to the Priest, handing him back the Canon. "All five people are accounted for and all have been killed with multiple 7.62mm automatic rounds."

Jackson held up a couple of the ugly big bullet cartridges.

Rubbing the tears from his eyes, O'Neill asked.

"But why? What possible reason would anyone have to kill all these people? And why did the doctor lie about having burnt the remains."

Jackson squeezed the Archaeologist's arm.

"Obviously we were never expected to come here and find out for ourselves. Let's have a look at this new level they had just discovered, before they were murdered."

As the two men rose, Jackson rummaged again in one of the kit bags, and pulled out three olive coloured canisters with red tops. He ripped the ring pulls off canister after canister, and dropped them on the ground as they walked. Pretty soon the entire area was pouring forth thick red smoke, which rose high into the air highlighting their position for miles all around.

O'Neill looked in horror and tried to pick up the nearest belching smoke canister.

"Are you insane? Everyone will know we are here!"

Jackson momentarily removed his dark sunglasses, looked right up into the sky above them and answered.

"I sure hope so."

Milliseconds after Jackson had pulled the first smoke grenade, twelve and a half miles above them, where the blue sky becomes the icy cold of outer space, the General Atomics MQ-9 Reaper had noted the red smoke. Its memory systems checked the GPS coordinates and noted they were the same as the location that had been entered as a target some hours earlier. This fact alone prompted it to conduct a further analysis. Within seconds, it had initiated a spectrometer analysis of the smoke at the forensic supercomputer array in Langley, Virginia. The result back from Langley showed there was a ninety-three percent probability the smoke was from a USMC issue AN-M18 distress grenade, although scans of the area showed no potential threats in the immediate vicinity. Activity logs on the command and control consoles on the USS Harry S. Truman in the Arabian Gulf and in Langley began to flash an amber watch.

O'Neill and Jackson walked up a well-trodden path to a small mound, some 100 feet higher than where the tents were pitched and the multitude of flies feasted. Once at the top, they found a series of massive cut stone blocks, originally supporting walls for a stone roof, which had partially collapsed down into whatever had lain beneath. As the two men looked down from the ledge, it was clear that they were standing on top of a large manmade structure, some 330 feet long and 100 feet wide, that must have had an entrance now buried under many feet of debris.

The large rock blocks that had comprised the roof now lay, as a new floor, some thirty feet beneath them. As only one third of the roof had collapsed, the rest of the interior space was hidden in stark darkness under the remaining portion. The ill-fated expedition had placed a scaffold and walkway against the nearest exposed wall, and the two men descended down the makeshift wooden stairs, still carrying the two kit bags, which Jackson insisted they take with them. When they reached the bottom, the Marine checked that both men had their oppressively heavy body armour correctly fitted and that the protesting O'Neill wore his ceramic helmet. Before leaving the scaffold, Jackson placed another of the M18A1 bricks, with its invisible wires attached to the steps.

As the two men walked towards the darkness under the remaining roof, there was a sudden movement to their left, and a large white object moved into the light. In an extraordinarily rapid motion Jackson dropped his kit bag, went down on one knee, and drew his Beretta M9 handgun, pinpointing the weapon expertly on the target, which revealed itself as nothing more than a tarpaulin blowing in the breeze.

The Marine slowly returned his M9 to its holster and stood looking at the tall walls surrounding them on all sides and the single way out, saying.

"Let's finish ASAP. This is a great place for a last stand, but a real lousy location to get caught if you intend to have a future."

O'Neill and Jackson paused only briefly, to attach powerful battery powered lamps to their helmets, and then walked under the overhanging roof. They found some more scaffolding from the excavation team, which provided a makeshift set of twelve wooden steps down from the fallen roof sections that they had been standing on, and gradually they descended into the darkness of the ancient temple. The first thing that struck O'Neill was that every surface had a carved image on it, each richer and more detailed than the last. In some places, vivid red and blue colours remained, although obviously faded. Huge winged beings appeared everywhere in the images, together with human forms shown either in adoration or at work inscribing cuneiform onto clay tablets, while the winged beings pointed to their words that were being transcribed. Other images showed the Sun, Moon and Stars being wrenched from the skies by hideous claws, and cities lying destroyed under bird like talons. Elsewhere, rivers flowed with bright crimson and the river banks were full of dead or dying human forms.

Jackson turned to O'Neill and gestured at a carving of a massive winged being, that was literally plucking the heart out of a King while he sat on his throne.

"Not exactly peace and goodwill to all mankind."

O'Neill smiled at the sarcasm of his friend and replied.

"Christians, Jews and Muslims know them as The Watchers. They were angelic beings who were tasked with watching over the creation of the Earth, but who fell under a Qliphothic thrall of matter and found the daughters of men so pleasing that they procreated with them and produced monstrous creatures, called the Nephilim. After breeding with the daughters of men, the Watchers taught human beings agriculture, building, writing, art, war, religion and magic. Either for breeding with us or for giving us this knowledge or both, they were cast out of heaven. They are the origin of all our myths related to supernatural evil."

Jackson looked puzzled.

"You lost me man, klop this and nephew that?"

O'Neill nodded.

"Sorry, they are ancient metaphysical terms. In the Middle Eastern and Semitic languages, the ancient word Nephilim means "fallen ones". Some scholars suggest that since the Watchers were nonphysical beings they could not couple with human females, but rather corrupted them so they could incarnate through them. In contrast to the Nephilim, the Qliphoth are the nonphysical potential for evil in our Cosmos, the literal shadow or husk of evil, and in the most ancient texts the Qliphoth are said to be the left-over forces or entities from previous creations. Gods from a past before our God, who seek nothing more than to destroy everything so their older Universe can be made to return."

Jackson looked at O'Neill.

"You are starting to scare me man, you sound like you believe this shit."

O'Neill looked embarrassed.

"These are some of our most ancient myths, Jackson. A way for humanity to try and explain who we are, where we came from, and how suddenly, around six to ten thousand years ago, we went overnight from bashing rocks together to acquiring expertise in agriculture, building, medicine, art and writing."

Jackson looked at another massive carving on one of the stone columns, this time showing a huge claw crushing the sun, fluid pouring from it and being drunk by a gaping mouth with dozens of long tongues, which were barbed and ripping chunks from the dying star.

"Ok, so this is bogeyman HQ?"

O'Neill smiled and pointed to cuneiform engravings next to some of the less gruesome tableaus.

"This is the temple of "received wisdom". It is supposed to be where the Watchers instructed mankind. It is also supposed to be the location of the Garden of Eden."

Jackson looked at the large carving that filled the furthest wall, which showed another of the long tongues emanating from a cruel looking mouth, but this time entwined around a tree and then probing the mouth of a naked woman.

"And the proverbial snake in the apple tree?" Jackson asked.

O'Neill had not yet noticed the furthest carving, as he was totally engrossed in a pictogram that was engraved into the side of the stone passageway which led down into the chamber, that had been excavated by the archaeological expedition immediately before their brutal murder. The exposed carving showed a winged creature pointing to a carefully prepared table, that had numerous multi-coloured squares etched into it, each containing a curious symbol that was unknown to O'Neill, while human scribes watched via a mirror like object that was suspended above the table.

O'Neill took several pictures of the engraving and replied to Jackson in a distracted tone.

"Yes, Eden is the site of the Tree of Knowledge and Eve's seduction by the Serpent."

"Doesn't look much like a seduction." Responded Jackson.

O'Neill looked up and towards the carved scene on the furthest wall.

"Oh. Yes. Well seduction was often a way of describing being spiritually corrupted or possessed. We have softened many of the myths related to these beings over the millennia."

Jackson walked over to O'Neill, and both men looked down the gaping stone stairway into the darkness.

"What exactly is supposed to be down there, O'Neill?" Asked Jackson.

"The Oracle Room, where the Watchers instructed man on everything from agriculture to religion." Responded the Vatican Archaeologist.

As the two men started descending down the rock stairway in single file, with Jackson leading, they came to another engraving. A priestess was pointing to letters on the same table but this time one of the awful tongues was attached to the back of her head. Scribes were shown sitting around the priestess restraining her from what looked like violent body spasms. In the far corner of the scene, the bodies of other priestesses were shown, stacked on top of one another, three bodies deep.

The sound of the old Canon camera filled the confined space of the passageway, as O'Neill went to work recording the scene.

Jackson turned to him.

"Doesn't look like any kind of instruction I would want."

O'Neill responded.

"The tongue must be their way of showing a body falling under the influence of one of the entities."

The Marine replied. "Judging by the number of dead bodies, it doesn't look like something one should try any time soon."

O'Neill chuckled.

As the two men continued down the steep steps of the passageway, the engravings abruptly stopped. The walls had been recently cut by powerful drills which had left thick rock dust everywhere. The drilling and clearing of the engravings continued down the remaining seven steps to the bottom of the passageway. As O'Neill looked around the subterranean chamber, it became clear that everything had been removed with a near surgical precision. All that remained was thick dust on the floors and bare rock on the walls and ceilings. The two men were in a completely bare stone chamber.

"Someone sure wanted this stuff and not just some antiquities collector."

Jackson knelt and, picking up a highly specialized titanium drill bit from the floor, he continued. "It would take considerable logistics to remove all this material so completely."

"Agreed…" said O'Neill, as he fired off the Canon to record the state of the chamber.

"It certainly provides a motive for the murder of the excavation team."

At that moment, there was a slight shake of the entire chamber around them, followed by the sound of two dull thuds in rapid succession.

"Times up, O'Neill. That was the two claymores in the HiAce. Let's get out of here if we can."

The two men exited rapidly back up the stone steps, their boots covered in the white rock dust. As they emerged from the passageway there was another violent explosion much closer to them. At the far end of the temple the scaffolding collapsed, broken like matchsticks, and a large cloud of dust and a smell of cordite filled the entire temple chamber.

Jackson pulled O'Neill to a position behind one of the large columns, as an American voice called out. "Sgt Jackson, exactly how many claymores did you sign out of the stores?"

The Marine looked carefully at where the voice originated, and saw six men in USMC uniforms standing at the top of the wall and, for the first time since they arrived at the site, O'Neill saw the Marine Mstr Sgt smile.

Two hours later they were all on an enormous Sikorsky CH-53E Super Stallion Helicopter, high above the sand and rock of the desert below, heading back to the USS Harry S. Truman for debriefing.

Five black body bags were fastened to stretchers that were in turn clamped on to the metal floor of the cabin, while O'Neill and the Marines were strapped into fold down bucket seats at the rear and front. After two days and nights without sleep, the Archaeologist was soon slumped in his seat snoring, while the seven marines exchanged friendly banter.

O'Neill's dreams blended seamlessly into the noise and movement of the helicopter. They were flying over the same desert landscape but it appeared very different. The river below them was running crimson red and the river banks were stacked high with small shapes. O'Neill did not need to look closer to see what they were, vividly recalling the temple engravings. A sudden air pocket made the helicopter lurch to one side, and one of the black plastic body bags fell open revealing an arm. It twitched and then, in a sudden movement, grabbed O'Neill's leg in a grip that felt like it would crush his calf bone.

Another air pocket, and the head of one of the Archaeologists suddenly emerged from its plastic covering, its dead eyes moving to look straight at O'Neill. Its slack jaw twitched abnormally left to right and then a low grating inhuman voice spoke, clearly in ancient Aramaic.

"Priest of Rome. We are back..."

O'Neill woke screaming. One of the USMC medics came over to him and said,

"It's ok, Father. The nightmare is all over."

O'Neill looked deeply into the medic's eyes and replied.

"No, I fear it is just beginning."

CHAPTER 6 - SCONE AND CROMBIE

"We sleep safe in our beds because rough men stand ready in the night to visit violence on those who would do us harm." - George Orwell

Prince's Street, Edinburgh, Scotland.
05.54HRS, July 25th, Present Day.

By the time that Curren and Stewart emerged from Lev's offices in the basement of the "Tartan Kremlin", the glamour of the nightclub had faded, along with the laser projected images of Red Square. The stunning Slavic waitresses had been replaced by middle aged women cleaners in blue overalls, and the loud music had been exchanged for the buzzing and vibration of floor cleaning equipment. As Lev instructed some of the remaining security staff to open the large black double oak doors to the outside world, Curren and Stewart voiced their thanks to the Russian and walked out into the morning light onto the grey cobble stoned pavements of Edinburgh's city centre. There was another fine summer's day in prospect, but right now it felt decidedly chilly.

Curren's beautiful red sports car sat parked where she had left it, under the watchful eye of the night club's security staff. The only difference was that the discarded beer cans, empty crisp packets and other mishaps that were scattered over the pavements last night had been cleared away, as if by magic, by the efficient street cleaners. The drive to the Balmoral Hotel took just a couple of minutes, with only the odd taxi to be seen in the city centre. The parking valets on duty at the Balmoral dealt efficiently with the arrival of the Maserati, with its rather shabby looking gentleman passenger and contrastingly elegant woman driver. On entering reception, Stewart was instantly recognised by the Duty Manager, Ian Hiscock, who booked them into the Scone and Crombie suite and rang through their breakfast order to the kitchens. Scrambled eggs on lightly toasted wheat bread, orange juice, a large pot of French Roast coffee and semi-skimmed milk for Stewart, while Curren opted for whole-wheat toast and Seville Orange Marmalade with a pot of Vienna Roast coffee, taken black.

Stewart explained to Hiscock that, while Curren had an overnight bag with her, he had been deprived of his belongings due to an unfortunate series of events. The Duty Manager looked sympathetically at Stewart's ripped suit and indicated that this was no problem, discretely providing the Scotsman with a small red leather Dunhill toiletry bag from under the dark oak reception desk. Stewart nodded his appreciation, while the Duty Manager waved away the bell boys, took Curren's bags and led the two guests to the Scone and Crombie suite himself. Inside the sumptuous apartment, the high panelled walls were painted in a muted magnolia which matched perfectly with the luxurious cream coloured deep pile carpets. The eye was immediately drawn to the fireplace, where a tall mirror hung above it with antique prints showing Scottish flora on either side and two inviting high-backed chairs were positioned nearby. The bed itself had a luxurious dark blue velvet cover with embroidered gold patterns which complemented the polished black granite bedside tables.

"Very nice." said Curren.

The Duty Manager acknowledged her thanks with some pride.

"If either of you need anything, then please just let us know. Your breakfasts will be with you shortly." With that he left, closing the high double doors behind him.

Curren, upon discovering the doors to the ensuite, gave a grateful sigh and remarked to Stewart.

"I am going to freshen up before breakfast." She then walked into the white marble themed bathroom, which was decorated with 1960s prints of Sean Connery from movie stills of that period, and started eagerly opening the complementary toiletry bottles.

The hawk-faced Issac bin Abdul Issuin was again talking in an agitated manner into his encrypted Motorola Iridium Satellite Phone. He was in the front passenger seat of the badly damaged Land Cruiser, which was now parked in a deserted backstreet called Distillery Lane, near Haymarket railway station in Edinburgh. Standing on the pavement, with the left rear side door open, the driver was doing what emergency first aid that he could on the two men who had been on the receiving end of Stewart's shooting earlier that evening. Thankfully, the worst of the bleeding had been stopped but it was clear that both men needed to have urgent medical attention in a hospital.

Abdul Issuin finished his call, opened his door and stepped down to the pavement. He then carefully removed his body armour and combat fatigues, dumping them in the front seat and, in a swift motion, drew his Glock hand gun and rapidly discharged two rounds each into the driver and the two injured men. Abdul Issuin had timed his shots perfectly as a long goods train passed through the adjacent Haymarket station, but still the six loud volleys reverberated around the tall stone buildings. After checking that all three men were dead, he placed an explosive device on the rear seat near the bodies, and started walking calmly away towards the railway station, where he rapidly blended into the crowds of commuters all heading into the main Edinburgh terminus.

Nine minutes after his train pulled away from the platform, heading to Edinburgh Airport, uniformed police arrived at the scene of the abandoned Land Cruiser and started setting up a cordon around the perimeter. As two male officers approached the pavement, coming alongside the SUV, there was an enormous explosion which scattered fragments of the vehicle against the nearby buildings, followed seconds later by numerous small shards of razor sharp glass from the shattered tenement windows, which rained down on the tarmac of Distillery Lane. Three police officers were killed instantly and four others were seriously injured. In the warlike carnage that had unfolded beside Haymarket station there was now silence and an ominous black smoke cloud rose into the clear blue morning sky.

Forty minutes later, Abdul Issuin was dressed in a dark blue Hugo Boss business suit, collected from a prearranged locker at the airport, and was sitting in the executive departures lounge having purchased a Lufthansa business class single to Frankfurt travelling under his false Canadian passport. As he sat drinking a Costa Coffee Grande latte, listening to Mozart on his iPhone, he watched the arrival of six athletic looking men, who all shared the same dress sense and who had just arrived on the Aer Lingus flight from Dublin. Their identical black Samsonite bags were marked with the discreet "Maelstrom" logo of a black whirlpool, marking them out to anyone who recognised the symbol, as employees of an American company known to hire elite ex-special forces operatives in order to provide a wide range of clandestine services to select organizations, that included the Central Intelligence Agency.

The six Maelstrom operatives were met in the arrivals lounge by three men in dark business suits and matching Ray Ban sunglasses, who were from the US Consulate at Regent Terrace in Edinburgh. The consulate had received an encrypted instruction, called an "Operational Flash", directly from the Office of the US Secretary of State earlier that morning, which had provided very specific details of the support to be provided to six arrivals coming in on the 08.30 Dublin flight.

The consular staff obviously had a very good idea how extraordinarily dangerous these six men could be and were clearly in a hurry to pass them two sets of car keys. The leader of the Maelstrom group enjoyed their discomfort and made a point of taking his time, introducing himself as "David" and shaking the hands of all three of the consular staff, before accepting the two Volkswagen key fobs being rather frantically offered to him. Their task completed, the three US consular staff rapidly departed, to the continued amusement of the Maelstrom team, who then walked out to two, brand new, jet black Volkswagen Caravelle Business vans. In what was obviously a well-practiced drill, they rapidly swept the two vans for any form of electronic tagging or surveillance devices, and then distributed the black canvas holdalls and tactical grab bags, that were contained in the rear storage areas of the two vans, among the six team members.

The grab bag for each man, contained latex gloves, a new black Heckler and Koch Mk 23 Mod .45 Pistol fitted with a Knight Armament suppressor, two twelve round magazines and one box of fifty 144 Winchester Ranger T-Series .45 jacketed hollow point rounds.

The larger holdalls contained two Heckler and Koch MP5 N 9mm submachine guns with stainless steel silencers, and ten boxes of fifty 9mm Winchester Ranger T-Series jacketed hollow point rounds. There were also packs of sealed medical syringes, a selection of various 200ml medication bottles with latex sealed tops, and twenty plastic wrist ties.

As the two black Volkswagens pulled away from the airport car park, Abdul Issuin was already two miles above Scotland, seated in his luxurious business class seat, reading an editorial in the Scotsman Newspaper about last night's armed raid on the stately home of Sir Tavish Stewart.

In a side bar, the paper provided a brief biographical summary of

Sir Stewart, proclaiming him as one of Scotland's unsung modern military heroes. The young Stewart went to England to read for a degree, gaining a double first in Archaeology and Anthropology at Hertford College, Oxford. At Sandhurst, Stewart had excelled, graduating with the Queens Medal in recognition of the college's highest recorded scores in military, practical and academic studies. In his family's regiment, he served with distinction in Cyprus, Northern Ireland, Germany, the Middle East and finally Bosnia, where he was awarded the Victoria Cross for single-handedly defending a refugee camp against attempted genocide by a vastly superior rebel force. Before being promoted to full Colonel and regimental commanding officer, he brought General Kolon Zeferski and Surgeon Major Seff Razsof to face trial at the International Criminal Tribunal for the former Yugoslavia at The Hague, for grave breaches of the Geneva Conventions, violations of the laws or customs of war, genocide, and crimes against humanity. Thanks to evidence collected by Stewart, both men were found guilty of their role in the systematic killing of over 7,000 civilians and the horrific torture of over 200 women and children. He was knighted by Queen Elizabeth II for services to the UK armed forces in 2005.

However, he resigned his commission when the British Government announced the merger of his beloved regiment "The Royals" with the "Kings Own Scottish Borderers". Disillusioned by what he felt was a betrayal by the British Government of a two-hundred-year old tradition, he then threw himself into establishing "Stewart's Antiquarians" as Scotland's leading art and antiques dealership, trading in rare and high value items, with offices in London, Rome, Istanbul and a warehouse near the railway terminus in Edinburgh. Abdul Issuin finished reading the biography, folded the newspaper and settled back to sleep in his seat.

Curren woke in the sumptuous bed, with the midday sunshine pouring through the windows of the Scone and Crombie suite. She sleepily fumbled on the top of the bedside cabinet and pulled her stainless-steel Jaeger le Coultre Reverso to her face, so she could check the time. It was seventeen minutes past one in the afternoon. With some shock she realised that, after her delicious breakfast, she had fallen asleep and had been out of it for five hours.

Stewart was sitting at the desk by the window, already shaved and looking immaculate in a light grey Ede and Ravenscroft suit, that had been couriered to him from his tailors. From the bed, Curren could smell the light scent of Hermès Concentré d'Orange Verte, Stewart's signature scent.

He was talking with four different people via a conference call on a new black Samsung phone, using its speaker phone function, so he could simultaneously write with his right hand and leaf through some documents with his left. He evidently had sensed that Curren was awake, since he waved briefly, an elegant Mont Blanc ballpoint still grasped between his fingers. The other participants on the call were the heads of operations in Stewart's offices in London, Rome, Istanbul and Edinburgh. Curren had met them at various board meetings, and visualised each of them as they spoke.

Mohammed Sek ran the Istanbul office, and was an enormous bull of a man, whose smooth accent and flattering words hid an absolutely ruthless nature. By the tone of his voice, he was clearly very upset to learn about the events of last night. Jeffery Sonnet, from the London office, sounded like a 1960s BBC News announcer, but again his elegant voice hid a hard man who had proved himself useful in numerous tight situations. Mario Donne, from the Rome office, was the oldest of the group and was blessed with some unusually close contacts with the Italian underworld that made him better informed than many national intelligence agencies. Finally, the gruff sounding Hamish McSwan, ran the company warehouse in Edinburgh.

Right now, Hamish was providing the group with details about the shipment of a collection of sixteenth century books and papers, that had been purchased by Stewart at an auction in Prague the previous week. Since many of the items needed to be authenticated, they were meant to be transported directly to Stewart's family estate rather than the company warehouse in Edinburgh, but the consignment had been delayed at UK customs, and it was eventually delivered to the warehouse instead. Unaware of this last-minute change, Stewart had been heading to his family estate to do the cataloguing, and had arranged to have the house to himself for the weekend so he could work undisturbed.

The group agreed that someone had obtained detailed knowledge of these plans, and had considered it an ideal opportunity to acquire an item within the Prague consignment. Stewart's description, of the ransacking of his house and the subsequent assassination attempt in the police station, became the focus of discussion, everyone trying to speculate on who could be behind such a bold operation and, more importantly, what such a person or organisation would do next. Sonnet was just saying he was sure that there would be another attempt to seize the Prague consignment when Hamish interrupted, reporting that two black vans had just parked outside the warehouse and four men were entering the premises, with two others remaining outside. There was the sound of muffled voices, one of which belonged to Hamish, and then what sounded like three rapid hammer blows, followed by the sickening thud of something heavy falling onto a hard floor.

Stewart instantly picked up his phone and called into the handset.

"Hamish? Hamish?"

The only response was the sound of the phone being hung up and then the dial tone. Without terminating the conference call on his mobile, Stewart picked up the hotel phone and called reception, demanding in a forceful voice.

"This is Tavish Stewart in the Scone and Crombie suite, please can you have our car brought to the front of the hotel immediately, it is extremely urgent!"

Stewart hung up the hotel phone and, speaking into the mobile, instructed Jeffery Sonnet in London to call the Edinburgh police, and inform them that there was a suspected armed robbery in progress at their Cranston Street warehouse. Stewart then terminated the mobile call and turned to Curren.

"Right, let's see how fast that car of yours really was…"

Curren responded by throwing Stewart the black key fob, with its distinctive silver trident symbol, saying.

"You mean IS!"

Stewart walked rapidly through the double doors of the suite, with Curren following close behind. As the Scotsman started taking the stairs down to reception two at a time, he replied.

"Sadly, under the circumstances, the past tense is probably going to be more accurate."

Thinking of Stewart's wrecked Mercedes from last night, Curren sighed with resignation, as the pair rapidly descended the stairs to the lobby of the hotel.

CHAPTER 7 - THE SILVER LEAF FOLIO

"There is, however, a tradition in the Roman Church that the manifestation of this mystery is reserved till the last times." - Éliphas Lévi, Transcendental Magic: Its Doctrine and Ritual, 1896

1 Prince's Street, Edinburgh, Scotland. EH2 2EQ
12.54HRS, July 25th, Present Day.

When Curren and Stewart reached the elegant revolving door of the Balmoral's Princes Street exit, Curren's red Maserati was waiting for them, standing out conspicuously amongst a string of black taxis in the small layby outside the hotel. It had been parked in the natural direction of traffic towards the Waverley Bridge, so once Stewart had entered the driver's side he cut around in a 180-degree turn. It was the middle of Friday lunch hour, so the traffic along Princes Street had come to a virtual standstill, stuck at the North Bridge traffic lights. Assessing the congestion at the traffic junction ahead of them, Stewart steered the Maserati back towards the parking bay of the hotel but, instead of stopping, he accelerated between two street sign posts, briefly mounted the pavement and drove over the pedestrian crossing, turning right onto the North Street Bridge. Stewart immediately floored the five litre Ferrari V8 and took the sports saloon along the empty bus lane, emitting a glorious roar from the twin exhausts and causing the drivers trapped in the congested lanes to beep their horns in envious frustration.

Curren kept her left hand over her eyes as the car's acceleration pushed her back into the leather bucket seat. Although she was deliberately trying not to look at the road, she could see on the dashboard that they had accelerated to well over 100 mph and had gone through at least one red traffic light. Stewart's feet danced over the three metal pedals on the floor as his right hand gracefully held the steering wheel, his left occupied with the frequent gear changes. He worked hard at keeping the engine revs high and swerved with an amazing skill to avoid the busy city traffic and numerous pedestrians. They had now reached the junction with the High Street and Stewart made a vicious left-hand turn, that had the left rear tyre burning rubber smoke. They passed John Knox House, red lining the 470-horse power engine at nearly 8,000 RPM and flew through another red traffic light, just missing a white Transit van and silver Ford Mondeo. Crossing the junction with Jeffery Street and making another violent left turn, that had Curren hanging on to the roof straps, they finally pulled up on the left-hand side of Cranston Street. On their right was a large warehouse, hidden behind two high stone walls. To one side of the open wooden double gates was a brushed metal sign that read "Stewart's Antiquarians".

Curren sighed with relief, patting the dashboard.

"Well, what do you know Tavish, not so much as a scratch or a bullet hole."

The sound of a police siren began to get closer and, from behind, appeared a large BMW R1200RT Police motorcycle, slowing as it came to a halt on the steeply sloping cobbled street. The siren stopped as the rider pulled up, removed his helmet and dismounted.

Curren continued.

"But, I don't think your license is going to be so lucky," she watched from her side mirror as the rider started walking towards them but, just as he was about to reach the back of the car, another figure, dressed in black combat fatigues and body armour, emerged from the open double gates of the warehouse and called to the policeman.

The road traffic officer stopped in his tracks and addressed the new arrival who, with a false air of camaraderie, wrapped his arm around the policeman's shoulders as if to share some confidence. Instead, he suddenly stuck a hypodermic needle into the officer's neck and within seconds, the police motorcyclist crumpled, only being kept upright by being physically supported by his assailant.

Stewart, who was also watching the events behind the car, turned to Curren, saying.

"Take off your shoes, get out of the car and run as quickly as you can down the street, NOW!"

Curren looked at Stewart and saw the deadly seriousness in his face, as he gestured for her to go with his left hand.

"Get going. There is going to be a complete shit storm here. Run as fast as you can, and don't look back."

Curren removed her shoes, opened her side door and emerged onto the pavement in a full run down the steep curved street. Thanks to the high walls on her left side and the bend in the descending road, she was obscured from a clear line of fire almost immediately.

Stewart timed his exit from the car simultaneously with Curren and, opening the side door, he faced the two men behind the Maserati. Immediately that Stewart came into view, the attacker dropped the unconscious police officer to the ground like a sack and rapidly went to draw a long-barrelled gun, which had been concealed in the small of his back.

Stewart was faster, much faster, and made use of the time taken for the falling police officer's body to block the line of sight between him and his adversary to cover the ground between the two men.

He caught his opponent's rising gun arm before it completed its draw and simultaneously, as he caught the gun hand, delivered a devastating elbow blow into his assailant's trachea with the full forward momentum of his body. Stewart followed through the natural motion of his attack with a vicious twisting action on the gun arm, rotating it against the joints of the wrist, elbow, shoulder, and neck in turn. The technique was executed so quickly and with such force that, rather than throwing his opponent, it shattered the joints. Each made a hideous cracking noise as they burst out of their sockets, the final twist producing a loud click from the broken neck vertebra of the gunman.

The killer's gun rattled to the cobblestones, he buckled to his knees, gasping and twitching wildly, as he fell prone to the ground. The entire exchange took less than five seconds. However, Stewart had no time to celebrate his survival, as another figure had already emerged from the warehouse gates.

This tall and athletic newcomer was also dressed in the same black combat fatigues, complete with body armour. His intelligent grey eyes rapidly and professionally locked onto the smartly dressed older man standing over the body of his colleague on the cobbled street. He instantly drew up a wicked looking Heckler and Koch MP5 N 9mm submachine gun, that he had been carrying across his chest. As the weapon was unslung from its classic carrying position, the black colouring of the stock of the gun contrasted starkly with the shining stainless-steel silencer that protruded oddly at the end of the short barrel.

The moment that Stewart recognised the classic drawing action of his opponent across Cranston Street, his body flowed into Onegai

Shimasu, a rapid Jujitsu forward roll that swept Stewart's body past the suppressed hand gun lying on the cobble stones. Grabbing the weapon, he continued the roll to the far side of Curren's Maserati, leaving him squatting behind the huge rear tyre.

Deadly three round bursts of 9mm Winchester Ranger T-Series hollow point rounds started pounding into the red body work of the Maserati, passing clean through the car and hitting the stone wall behind it. Shards of granite spat into the air around Stewart, nicking his hands and face.

Ignoring the injuries, the Scotsman checked the safety on the HK handgun he had just acquired and removed the long suppressor, rolling it down the pavement to divert the attention of the shooter. As the automatic fire followed the movement of the rolling barrel, Stewart dropped down under the car, drew the sights of the HK on his opponent, exhaled and shot two rounds in rapid succession. Across the road the Maelstrom operative screamed and collapsed to the floor, each of his kneecaps smashed by a single .45 hollow point round. The screams were short lived, as Stewart fired another deadly accurate single head shot, the instant his opponent was on the floor.

Emerging from behind the remains of Curren's car, Stewart looked briefly up at the CCTV camera located on the lamppost above him, as he walked calmly across the street towards his warehouse. He paused, as he passed the dead man's remains, to examine the contents of the tactical grab bag strapped to the body's waist band. As he knelt, he remained facing the warehouse entrance with his weapon pointing towards the closed double doors, using his peripheral vision to watch for any movement. Stewart unclipped the black waist bag and poured the contents on to the road. The sets of syringes, medical bottles, and cable ties were noted with a grunt, along with the whirlpool logo on many of the items. Stewart completed his examination of the bag's contents by retrieving an extra magazine of .45 ammunition and one of the apple sized grenades, marked M67 Fragmentation Composition B, from the belt of the dead man.

Framing his Heckler and Koch pistol in his bent left elbow, stabilising the extremely powerful handgun and making it impossible for anyone to wrestle the pistol from him, he entered the warehouse courtyard.

Meanwhile, approximately one mile south from the gunfight, in the central control room of Police A Division located in Saint Leonard's Lane, Chief Constable Keith Smith watched the CCTV feed from Cranston Street on a large TV screen. He was surrounded by several senior police officers and pressure was mounting on him to send in the Firearms and Public Order (FPO) specialists, that he had kept on standby now for over five minutes. Smith raised his hand and spoke to the senior staff around him.

"Send in paramedics now to that Road Traffic Officer and get the FPO to contain the area, but they are not to intervene and only to fire if fired upon. I do not want any more dead police officers."

The Divisional A Commander, Collin McBreay, replied,

"But what about that armed civilian?" Pointing to Stewart, who was coldly firing the modified .45 rounds deliberately into the engines of the two Volkswagen vans, rendering them into useless lumps of metal.

Keith Smith smiled grimly.

"Hmm... well it looks to me like he is making a good job of ensuring the suspects do not get away. Apart from some reckless driving, as far as I have seen, Sir Stewart has acted purely in self-defence against lethal unprovoked attacks, and he is about to engage a group of armed terrorists who are using lethal force and have broken into his privately-owned premises. Under Scottish law, I would say he can pretty much do whatever he wants."

McBreay interrupted.

"But based on what we have seen so far, he will probably kill them all!"

Chief Constable Smith shook his head.

"Knowing Stewart, I doubt he will kill them all. He will want to know who sent them."

Stewart walked slowly to a small corrugated iron outhouse, attached to the right-hand side of the warehouse, and shot the padlock off in a smooth single-handed motion. He pulled open the wooden door and stooped his six feet two inch frame, so that he could enter the small building. Moments later he emerged, holding a large first aid kit.

As he walked back towards the main warehouse he approached

sideways, with his back to the thick stone wall. Reaching the right side of the entrance, he casually removed his jacket, which he then deliberately threw past the opaque glass of the warehouse doors, in a slow arc. As the jacket's shadow flew past, the doors and metal wall surrounds shredded under furious 9mm automatic gunfire.

Stewart calmly picked up the M67 grenade, without removing the arming pin, and threw it through the nearest right-hand side glass window, shouting loudly "grenade!" as he did so. The response was rapid. Another man, this time shorter and heavier set, ran at full speed through the doors, smashing them apart. Stewart's reaction was smooth and immediate. His body sweeping to follow the projected path of the man, Stewart's HK barked twice in rapid succession and the newcomer fell to the ground dead, just short of the nearest of the two black Volkswagen vans. Stewart then turned to face the open door and walked slowly inside, pausing only to retrieve his jacket and the first aid kit.

Inside the entrance area, the figure of an older man, with thick grey hair, lay face down in the direction of the entrance doors, in a pool of blood that was already starting to congeal on the red tile floor of the reception area.

Stewart knelt and felt for the pulse of the prone figure at the carotid artery in the neck.

"Sorry Hamish, I could not get here in time." He said, as he slowly placed his jacket over the head of his old friend and put down the first aid kit.

Six feet and five inches from Hamish's body, to the left of the entrance area, was another set of double doors which led to the main warehouse, where the consignments were stored before being catalogued. Right at the back of the entrance area, behind a battered old oak table that served as a reception desk and work area, was a large grey metal cabinet labelled "Sentinel Warehouse C02 Fire Suppression System". Stewart walked silently around the desk and opened the metal doors to the fire system. Inside the tall metal frame was a control panel that was comprised of two dials side by side, one marked "PSI" and the other marked "oxygen %". Under these two dials there was a blue stop cock valve and red button marked "Alarm Free Operation". Stewart unscrewed the safety stop cock to fully open and pressed the red button. The system shook slightly as it started to work and the pressure dial jumped steadily to three Bar. Stewart raised his left wrist and started the chronograph on his Omega, as the oxygen % dial began to creep down from twenty percent.

Walking out of the warehouse, he picked up Hamish's thick wood walking stick from beside the desk and stuck it through the twin door handles, jamming them closed. Back out in the courtyard, he walked to the discarded contents of the Maelstrom grab bag, collected a handful of the plastic wrist ties, calmly checked his chronograph, retrieved his Samsung phone from his front left trouser pocket, and made a call.

Stewart spoke briskly.

"Frank? It's Tavish Stewart, yes, it has been a long time. Kosovo, yes, a bloody bad business. Listen, I am working to a bit of a tight schedule, so I will get right to the point. A half dozen of your men have raided my Edinburgh warehouse. Yes. Six of your men raided my warehouse. Unfortunately, half of them have failed to survive, and right now,"

He consulted his Speedmaster again,

"The survival of the remaining three is in the balance."

There was a pause as the other person spoke in an agitated manner.

"Can I assist them? Well, here is how it is Frank. They are trying to take something of mine and I want to know who paid Maelstrom to come and get it."

Another pause.

"Yes, I know, Maelstrom never divulges its clients. But you will admit these are unusual circumstances and I would like to avoid the need to come and see you to obtain the information by more… direct means."

Another pause with increasing agitation from the other speaker.

"Thank you, Frank. I appreciate your assistance. My fax number, ah good, yes, given the circumstances the London office would be best."

Stewart closed the call, consulted his Speedmaster chronograph again and, looking up to the CCTV, beckoned to the viewer at the other end of the camera to come. He then turned and walked back into the warehouse carrying the wrist ties.

Fifteen minutes later, Chief Constable Keith Smith was standing beside Stewart with a large number of Firearms and Public Order (FPO) officers, gathered in front of the warehouse. Three semi-conscious Maelstrom operatives were lying face down on the floor outside the building, trussed up like proverbial turkeys, with their hands, feet and neck tied expertly together behind them with Ty-Rap Polyamide grey nylon cable ties. Their assorted weapons were assembled on a brown blanket provided by the forensic officers. Hamish's body was being extensively photographed, as were the bodies of the three dead Maelstrom operatives.

Curren stood barefoot beside Stewart, as he surrendered the HK Mk 23 .45 to an FPO officer, who placed it in a plastic evidence bag. Unnoticed by everyone, she had acquired a dark brown leather Etrivière II Hermes document holder, that had been passed to her by Stewart, during the commotion when the police arrived.

"And you still have no idea why your premises have been targeted twice in twenty-four hours?" Asked Keith Smith.

Stewart shook his head.

"But I can tell you these are a completely different group of men. Different weapons, and different approach."

Smith responded,

"We have found the bodies of the men we suspect were your assailants from last night."

"Can I see them?" Asked Stewart eagerly.

Smith shook his head.

"All burnt to a crisp in a car bomb explosion next to the Haymarket Station earlier this morning. Someone took great care to cover their tracks."

"And then hired these professionals." Added Stewart, as he nodded to the three tied up men.

Curren interrupted by coughing and looking pointedly at her bare feet. Both men followed her gaze. Smith nodded.

"Yes, of course. We will want to ask you both some further questions so please make sure we have a contact address and," he looked at the police team examining the remains of Curren's red Maserati.

"I will get a car to take you back to your hotel. The Caledonian?"

"The Balmoral." Responded Stewart.

"Of course," smiled Smith, "and thank you."

Stewart raised a questioning eyebrow as he and Curren started walking to a waiting Police Land Rover Discovery.

"For not killing them all." Concluded Smith.

Back in the Scone and Crombie suite, Stewart and Curren were gathered around the large oak desk near the window, looking at the contents of the Hermes document holder that Curren had carried unnoticed from the Cranston Street incident. Stewart used his Samsung phone camera to provide his colleagues in London, Rome and Istanbul with a clear view of the item he had taken from the unconscious Maelstrom operatives at the warehouse.

The auctioneer's note from Prague was still attached to what was clearly an ancient binding for four square shaped stone tablets, roughly the size of a child's hand. The retaining fastenings and silver holding frames for the four tablets were richly engraved in Arabic script, as was the outer protective silver binding cover.

Only the first of the tablets remained inside the silver binding. This emerald coloured stone had been beautifully carved with a script that was not recognized by any of the team. The other three tablets were missing but their silver housings were intact. The note from the Zimbrug Antique House in Prague said.

"Item 34/5/a. 11th Century Arabic Tablet Housing. The script on the one remaining tablet in this 11th century silver binding has a striking similarity to texts in the Ashmolean, dating from the 17th Century that were donated by the British antiquarian Elias Ashmole. At the time of Ashmole's bequest of these materials, he reported that they were recovered from a lot saved from a fire at the Mortlake home of the late English Mathematician, John Dee, on 26th Jan 1679."

Jeffery Sonnet interrupted the silence of the group.

"I will chase my contacts at the Ashmolean and the British Museum to see what they can tell us about this silver tablet holder and the emerald tablet. I will also have the research team here fax you everything we can find about Dee and this unknown language."

The deep voice of Mohammed Sek added, "I have some colleagues in Eastern Europe. I will see what provenance exists for the silver frame."

"Jeff," Stewart asked, "What progress have you made with respect to the payment details of who issued the contract to Maelstrom?"

Sonnet laughed.

"You must have been persuasive as Foster faxed the bank details and a copy of the written instruction they received to undertake the job. I have faxed copies to your hotel and to the Istanbul and Rome offices."

The Italian accent of Mario interjected.

"I have my network tracing who is behind the bank transfer. But it is 7pm here, so it will be tomorrow before we get any answers."

"Excellent, Gentlemen," concluded Stewart, "In that case I think we resume tomorrow and in the meantime Helen and I will take an early dinner at Hadrian's."

Tavish Stewart was in a deep sleep. After saying goodnight to Curren he had retired to an adjoining room, where he had eventually been overcome by fatigue while reading about the Elizabethan Mathematician John Dee. Papers were piled around him on all aspects of Dee's life, that had been faxed from the researchers at the London office. Just before falling asleep, Stewart had focused on the Enochian language that looked so similar to the markings on the one remaining stone tablet. Papers with the strange script were in his right hand and strewn over his chest as he slept.

In Stewart's dream, he was walking through the slippery, cold, grey mud of a refugee camp in the grip of a Northern European winter. He was dressed in his Royal Scots Uniform but with a blue UN Peacekeepers beret. The dark laces on his black Magnum Classic CEN boots were stained with wet grey mud, that had formed into a slippery gunk that penetrated everywhere.

Around him makeshift dwellings, cook houses, and latrines were filled with the smell of thousands of frightened displaced people. But something was wrong, it was too quiet. The camps were always filled with noises of people talking, crying, praying, even screaming. But this was totally silent. Then he saw the first of them. Dead skeletal faces on the ground looking up at him. Dead children clutching at their parent's arms, also dead.

A relentless heavy rain fell from a dark sky, making everything even more miserable. Stewart noticed his clothes were soaked, but oddly he did not feel cold or wet.

The jet-black night sky was suddenly illuminated by the flash of artillery rounds landing close by on either side of the camp, in a thick conifer forest that surrounded the tent city. Each bright flash was accompanied seconds later by a deafening explosion, that shook the ground and scattered stones, along with brick sized clumps of earth, high into the air and filled the nostrils with the thick smell of cordite.

As Stewart walked, he found himself standing before a massive trench that had been dug ten feet deep into the grey mud. The trench was sixteen feet wide and thirty feet long. Sacks of quick lime had been stacked ten bags high beside the left most side of the trench. Blowing in the wind, several empty bags rolled along the ground and were carried into the pit. Stewart knew what was in the lime pit, and although he did not want to see the bodies he knew that he must. His feet stopped at the edge and he felt compelled to look down. Due to the darkness, thankfully all he could see were shapes. He noticed that he was holding the silver folio from the warehouse close to his chest, like one would hold a baby or frightened animal. Then came another barrage of artillery rounds, whistling high in the air. Stewart waited for the flash that would light up everything brighter than day.

The ground shook and then came the brightness. The sunken pit was illuminated and Stewart could see hundreds of bodies huddled together in a random mess of arms and heads and legs. The hideous images of genocide flashed before him, except the victims were all priests. Representatives of all religions, mixed together and united in one thing, death.

FOLIO 2 - THE SANATORIUM OF ST MICHAEL

CHAPTER 8 - THE PRIDE AND THE GLORY

"It was pride that changed angels into devils." - Saint Augustine, 420 AD

10, Downing Street, London, SW1A 2AA
08.32HRS, July 26th, Present Day.

The applause of the enormous crowd filled the Oslo city hall. A multitude of faces were illuminated by the flood lights, showing an auditorium crammed with A-list celebrities, all standing and applauding at a single figure. British Prime Minister, Simon Brinkwater, a smooth-talking career politician in his early forties, beamed with delight, as he clasped the Nobel Peace Prize in his hand and waved it above his head in a victory salute to the world. He approached the lectern, positioned in the centre of the auditorium stage, preparing to give the speech of his life but, as he did so, the Oslo city hall and its spotlights began to fade away, as he felt his shoulder being gently shaken by Amanda King, his blonde, thirty something Personal Assistant, who was on "long term loan" from a global investment bank.

Brinkwater reluctantly pulled his face from the handmade jasmine silk pillow. The air was becoming filled with a wonderful mixture of fresh coffee and the sophisticated tones of Baccarat Les Larmes Sacrees de Thebes perfume. His gaze was drawn from the deep pile nineteenth century Mohatashem Kashan carpet, acquired from Saddam Hussein's private apartments in 2003, that covered the partly exposed floor boards under his Baldacchino Supreme Bed, a souvenir from the palace of Minyar al-Gaddafi in 2011, to the view of King's impossibly smooth long legs. Her electric blue mini stilettos made the Prime Minister reflect that the pleasures of being woken in Downing Street outweighed even his dreams of a Nobel Prize.

Amanda King smiled at the desire in Brinkwater's face and slowly placed a wooden tray on the bedside table, laden with a stylish steel pot of freshly brewed Harrod's Kopi Luwak coffee, a plate of Paul Rhodes wholemeal cut toast fingers, two Jones Bros boiled eggs and a cut crystal bowl full of F. Duerr & Son Seville Orange Marmalade. Besides these items was a sterling silver tea spoon and knife which reflected the ornate ceiling in their highly polished surfaces. Alongside the tray lay the Prime Minister's 18kt gold Tag Heuer Monaco Steve McQueen Leather Automatic Chronograph, it's custom case back engraved with the logo of the same investment bank providing Ms King's services, showing that it was almost eight thirty in the morning.

Amanda King walked slowly over to the full length Georgian window and pulled open the long dark curtains, revealing a bright shining summer morning through a partly open third floor window, that overlooked the well maintained back garden at 10, Downing Street.

"Mmm. Good Morning, Prime Minister!"

She exclaimed, as she felt the warmth of his naked body behind her, and the cold air from the open window on her thighs, as her bamboo silk Coco Chanel skirt was pulled gently up. She smiled, but firmly took hold of his wandering hands and guided him away from the window and back to the breakfast tray.

"But I am not hungry…" Brinkwater exclaimed, and added more quietly, "…at least not for food..."

King smiled again.

"Your wife is next door. Besides you have the Uqari delegation in forty-five minutes."

The Prime Minister groaned with mock disappointment and, returning to the bed, he sat and started pouring himself a dark coffee into a plain white china mug.

Amanda King straightened her blue Chanel business suit, positioned herself on the far edge of the bed and started rapidly running through the main newspaper headlines, with a specific focus on the political sections summarising the various scandals afflicting the other politicians, both at home and abroad. The Prime Minister snickered at various articles, remarking how that rumour had been deliberately passed to the specific journalist concerned. The daily newspaper reading ritual was abruptly interrupted by another young woman, Susan, who could have been King's sister. The Prime Minister clearly liked a very specific type of assistant. As Susan started her daily financial briefing, Brinkwater deliberately and purposefully smashed the top off the first egg, and began systematically dipping his pre-cut toast fingers into the yolk, sucking the rich yellow sticky liquid from the wholemeal bread.

While Susan summarised the financial pages Brinkwater reflected how the strategy of endless low interest rates and enormous quantitative easing had flooded the markets with unlimited credit, creating enormous increases in wealth for the extremely rich, just as the financial advisers had said it would. The main backers for his political party would be grateful, very grateful. He reflected momentarily that he should push for larger bonuses for the honorary board positions he held at the five global investment banks.

Susan concluded her summary of the financial news and left, with a rather secretive smile directed at Simon. As her bright red nails closed the enormous black double doors to the Prime Minister's bedroom, Amanda King reasserted her role as Simon's primary focus by dramatically placing a blue wool Chittleborough & Morgan three-piece suit, with a matching handmade white shirt, on the bed along with a set of new Hermès woven white cotton boxers and Falke black socks that matched a spotless pair of black Sutor Mantellassi Oxford brogue shoes.

Brinkwater nodded approvingly, finished the last spoonful of egg and walked purposefully to the adjacent bathroom, where King now stood in the doorway holding the engraved rams horn handle on a classic Thiers-Issard cut throat razor fitted with the "7/8 Dominator" blade.

Forty minutes later, an immaculate Brinkwater was seated in a leather Chesterfield chair inside the Downing Street first floor reception room, listening sympathetically to HRH Crown Prince Hussein Niezweem, who was seated in the left of the pair of luxurious red leather chairs that were placed strategically by an open fire place.

Dressed in a white and gold dishdasha, HRH was clearly a very unhappy man, a deep frown having formed on his bearded face. His hands moved in an agitated manner, as he held an envelope and his 18kt gold iPhone. His four-person entourage, all dressed in gleaming all white dishdashas, shifted uncomfortably in the surrounding chairs as the Crown Prince growled out short broken English sentences. Brinkwater tried to smile disarmingly. Under normal circumstances, this smile calmed even the most irate listener, but today either it was missing one of its mysterious elements or the Crown Prince was seriously annoyed.

Brinkwater made a mental note that someone should have properly vetted the intentions of HRH for this meeting, as they were supposed to be talking about importing birds of prey for veterinary treatment in the UK, but instead there was an incomprehensible barrage of complaints about the British Government failing to live up to its obligations.

The Crown Prince pressed on with his angry tirade, asserting that there had been a clear understanding that the Western governments would neutralize certain "undesirable nations" within the Middle East region, thus enabling those who followed the "one legitimate form of the true religion" to be united as God intended. The four-person entourage of the Crown Prince nodded in strong support of this final statement. Hundreds of millions of pounds had been paid privately to Western leaders, to properly motivate them in their mission, and they had failed. Not only failed, but now they had gone behind their friends' backs and made a nuclear energy alliance with their enemy! With that final statement, the Crown Prince dropped his hand dramatically on to the arm of his chair and sat back into the luxurious leather. There was an awkward moment of silence. Brinkwater smiled insincerely and began a string of platitudes intended to reassure that no promises had been broken, but he was interrupted by the Crown Prince, who calmly stated that unless Britain stood by its commitments he would reveal all the invoices, the massive fund transfers and the full details of the empty promises made by the Western leaders, to the media, so the people could appreciate fully the true nature of those who led their nations. Brinkwater was about to respond when the Crown Prince rose, along with his entire group, and stormed out of the room leaving the PM looking lost at how the meeting had gone so badly wrong. Rising from his chair he growled.

"Get me Gerald, I will be in the office." As he walked out of the door.

Amanda King reached for her Apple iPhone and, within moments, was talking to the mysterious Gerald Seymour.

Ninety minutes later, Brinkwater was seated in a black leather executive chair in front of a ninety-inch LG 8K TV in the second floor Downing Street office, whose windows had been bricked up during the 1980s as a countermeasure for electronic eavesdropping. A dense iron wire mesh was still clearly visible under the floral wallpaper in several places. The large TV screen was split into two sections, the left side showed a high definition video chat and the other the BBC 24 Hour News. The video chat was streaming live from the Washington, DC offices of the legendary "fixer", Gerald Seymour, CEO of Maelstrom Media. Seymour's status as a "miracle worker" had been assured since his direct interventions during the 2008 financial crisis, that enabled the financial sector to receive unprecedented tax payer financial support. Gerald's guidance to the G7 nations meant that the five main investment banks did not just survive, but went on to establish a mutually supportive relationship with select world governments, based on tax payer assured debts of over 175 trillion USD. Since the beginning of this financial Corporatocracy, enormous wealth redistribution projects had been conducted under the pretence of central bank interventions. Although relatively unknown by the general public, Gerald Seymour was now established as the "go to person" for all financial Corporatocracy interests.

Dressed in his trademark black roll neck top, his close-cropped hair showed his jaw muscles flexing as he smiled at the broadcast that both men were watching. A BBC newsflash described a terrorist network that had just been uncovered, controlled by the Uqari government. At the moment of the newsflash it was unclear exactly how far the network ran, but police sources confirmed that members of the royal house were under arrest at Paddington Green Police Station. Simultaneously police raids were taking place on Uqari Embassies worldwide.

Video footage showed armed police removing an unconscious man in regal Middle Eastern dress, while medical staff administered to other similarly dressed Arab men before they were also helped away by armed police into large black vans. Talking head segments, from the UK Foreign Office and US State Department, showed worried looking civil servants expressing concern about possible "fake news" and misinformation campaigns that could be launched from the now discredited Uqari government. A series of documentaries, describing the terrorist atrocities of the House of Uqar, were being advertised for the coming evenings.

Brinkwater smiled broadly, "Good work, Gerald."

On the screen, Gerald nodded and his disembodied voice issued a command, which brought Amanda King immediately through the office doors, her iPhone held to her head, obviously in direct communication with, and taking instructions from, Seymour. She walked over and dropped the Uqari Crown Prince's personal belongings, including the distinctive Gold iPhone, on the table in front of the Prime Minister.

The TV coverage switched to the international reaction to the breaking news that Uqari government officials had been arrested in Washington, Paris, Berlin and Geneva. The Arab League was making loud protests and coverage showed small gatherings of men, in some unnamed desert, firing AK47 machine guns into the air and burning the US and British flags.

The announcer then switched to the financial news, where the lead story was an announcement from billionaire ecologist Nissa Ad-Dajjal, who had caused disbelief at a media event in the Swiss resort of Grindelwald, by claiming to have solved the world's energy problems, having developing a super-efficient source of electricity.

The banner headline at the bottom of the screen announced.

"Promise of Free Energy from Swiss Billionaire, Dr Nissa Ad-Dajjal."

The footage switched from the heavy set, balding male news announcer, to a sleek black Bell helicopter that landed on a concrete roof helipad. The nearest rear door opened and a tall dark-haired figure emerged and walked purposefully towards the podium. The beautiful forty-year-old woman was dressed in a classic black business suit, with a crisp plain white cotton shirt, and a pair of black Christian Louboutin business pumps. Nissa Ad-Dajjal consulted her Gold Rolex GMT Master II watch and began her speech without any papers or teleprompter.

"Royal Highnesses, Members of the Diplomatic Corps, Distinguished Corporate and NGO Leaders, Members of the Press, Ladies and Gentlemen. It has been thirty-eight months since I last had the pleasure of addressing you, on the occasion of my retiring from the corporate world. Since that time, I have involved myself in establishing the international headquarters for the Unity Movement here in the beautiful and peaceful Swiss Alps. Today I have asked you all to come here for a very special announcement."

Ad-Dajjal turned, and a massive thirty-foot-high holographic image of a complex machine with numerous moving pistons, was projected into the air behind her. The crowd gasped at the detail and vividness of the 3D holographic image.

"Over the past three years, Unity has been working on the development of a new energy system, that generates electricity from a process called GeOthermic Generation or GoG. This system uses the minor temperature differences that occur naturally around us to expand and contract a thermo-sensitive compound, which powers the motion of a simple turbine."

The large 3D holographic display showed how the thermosensitive compound expanded with slightly warmer temperatures, pushing the piston up, and then cooler air caused the compound to contract, pulling the piston down.

Ad-Dajjal smiled, as she could clearly see she had the complete attention of the large audience.

"The GoG system is nothing new, being a modernization of the Sterling Engine first developed in 1815. What is new, is the macro application of such a technology, so that it can serve as a primary energy generation system to replace fossil fuels. This so-called Macro GeOthermal Generation, or MaGoG technology, allows the small GoG generator here at the Unity Headquarters to supply the entire energy needs of this community and the extended community of Grindelwald, without the need for burning fossil fuels, releasing carbon into the atmosphere or requiring any financial contribution from the users."

The crowd started applauding spontaneously. Ad-Dajjal had to hold up her hand to stop the clapping before she could continue.

"Thank you. But this was only the beginning..."

The large 3D hologram now switched to a movie of a massive production facility that was manufacturing large scale MaGoG systems.

"Over the last eighteen months, Unity has invested heavily in the mass production of MaGoG systems and we will be offering these generators to the nations of the world, free of charge. We project that within three months MaGoG will deliver us all from our dependence on fossil fuels, reducing global carbon emissions and therefore averting global warming. Further, it will liberate developing nations, by providing limitless free energy for schools, hospitals and agriculture. Deserts will be made to bloom and the need for oil, one of the primary causes of armed conflict, will have been removed forever."

The massive 3D holographic image shifted to showing the shipment of MaGoG systems throughout the nations of the world. Graphic charts showed exponential reductions in fossil fuel consumption and the resulting dramatic decline in green house carbon emissions. The images then shifted to show applications for limitless free power, with desalination plants irrigating deserts into productive arable land and peoples from developing countries being liberated from trade dependence on fossil fuels, enabling them to focus on education, medical care and quality food production.

As the full implications of these statements began to be absorbed by the listeners, any further speech was made impossible as the assembled crowd rose to their feet, clapping spontaneously, in admiration of the genius and simplicity of the announcement.

Ad-Dajjal smiled and waved to the crowd, then walked purposefully to the stairway leading into an elegant three storey wooden building behind her, leaving her audience standing and still applauding her speech.

As the news story continued to break, Gerald's section of the screen transformed from one of calm and control to panic, as each of the numerous phones on his desk started to ring, and the sound of incoming video chat requests filled the loud speakers like a crazed dawn chorus. As if by some kind of spreading contagion, the numerous phones in Brinkwater's office also began to ring.

CHAPTER 9 – UNCLEAN SPIRITS

"Satan's greatest achievement in these times has been to make us believe that he does not exist, and that all can be fixed on a purely human level." - Pope Francis, 2014.

Greg Café, Pontificia Università Gregoriana, 1 Piazza della Pilotta, Rome 19:00HRS, July 27th, Present Day.

Father Thomas O'Neill sat alone in the sleek modern surroundings of the Greg Café, within the Pontificia Università Gregoriana, or PUG as it was popularly known to the faculty and students. Within it's million book library, some of the rarest and most valuable documents related to Christian belief can be found, making the PUG the highest seat of theological learning in the Roman Catholic Church.

For the past six months, after his extraction from Iraq by the US Marines, O'Neill had been attending a post-doctoral seminar programme titled, "Discarnate Intelligence: Theological and Historical Perspectives." Along with a group of eighteen select clergy, psychiatrists and theologians from around the world, he had come to hear lectures given by some of the most respected experts in the field. His attendance had been strongly recommended, by his superiors at the Pontificia Accademia Romana di Archeologia (Pontifical Academy of Archaeology), as a way for him to deal constructively with the nightmares and panic attacks that had plagued him after his return from Iraq.

The lecture programme had taken O'Neill back into the classroom as a student for the first time in over a decade and the change in routine had, he admitted with retrospect, been good for him. The scenic daily walk to Piazza della Pilotta, the more relaxed schedule and the elegant surroundings of the PUG building, had reduced his stress levels and the terrible nightmares had become less frequent. Within the first few weeks, he had settled into a pleasant routine of rising at 8.30 AM, having a leisurely breakfast in Rome's Scottish themed hostel, the "Nag's head" on the Via IV Novembre, before arriving at the PUG building, where his lectures seldom started before 11 AM.

The scepticism of his fellow students towards any kind of

phenomena that did not fit into the established scientific paradigm meant he had spent the classes seated alone, at the rear of the large C008 lecture theatre. He established a location which he began to regard as "his" and, once seated in the old carved wooden bench on the back row, he focused on listening rather than contributing to discussions that fixated on increasingly obscure or improbable explanations that could dismiss each documented case of discarnate intelligence that was presented. Fortunately, as the classes progressed, the more sceptical students slowly stopped attending and eventually there were only a handful of the more serious scholars remaining, including O'Neill.

Most lectures had been historical or theoretical in nature, covering all aspects related to the academic program. Some presented the background for the complex process required by Canon law to recognise a case of demonic possession before exorcism could be authorised by the local Bishop. Other talks explained the differences between recognised psychiatric disorders and demonic possession, whilst further seminars referred to references contained in the historical records held in the PUG archives, arguing for the existence of non-physical intelligences devoted to good and evil.

Through the months of study, O'Neill learnt that possession was not recognised by the DSM-5 or the ICD-10 formal psychiatric diagnostic processes and this meant that the sceptics had no shortage of recognised disorders which they proposed as explanations for the case studies presented to them. These included complex combinations of Tourette's syndrome, epilepsy, schizophrenia, conversion disorder and dissociative identity disorder. Such combinations of psychiatric symptoms were theoretically possible but they were highly unlikely and certainly not able to explain the radical mental and physical changes that were shown to take place during possession, or the phenomena such as gnosis (access to hidden knowledge), xenoglossy (speaking unknown languages) and macro-psychokinesis (large scale movement of objects or the influence over events), that were required to be formally documented, by multiple independent witnesses, before a case would be regarded by the Roman Catholic Church as being a Demonic Possession.

Over the course of the last two millennia, the Church had developed a clear classification of the types of interactions with non-physical intelligences, the so called "ordinary influence" and the much rarer "extraordinary influence". The so called "ordinary influence" appeared as thoughts, desires or urges to commit some act that would inadvertently increase the global sum of distress or suffering in the world. Such acts were disguised as ways in which an individual thought they could gain a small short-term advantage, without thinking they would cause direct harm to others. Most often, such deeds were done secretly without general knowledge. A person would justify their action as helping themselves but, in reality, the chain reaction of events caused by these small "ordinary influences" increased the global sum of distress and suffering.

Over the past fifty years, the general population had focused increasingly on the importance of their own immediate self-gratification and personal entitlement, and less upon the greater good of the world in which they lived. In a clear sign of "ordinary influence", as people became more focused exclusively on their own desires, they ceased to show an appreciation for good in the world. The Church became marginalized into minor social roles within a society that believed itself beyond concepts of good and evil, and focused only on maximising personal self-interest.

Through a gradual process of desensitization in the media, the importance of moral responsibility had declined dramatically. Individuals felt increasingly comfortable with committing acts that would provide them with minor short-term benefits, at the cost of increasing the distress and suffering of those around them. The paradox was clear. As material standards of living appeared to increase, happiness declined. Such decreases in happiness were, the Church claimed, explained by the "ordinary influence" of evil having become much more widespread than at any other time in the past.

As the strategy of extending "ordinary influence" had proved so successful, the overall numbers of cases involving "extraordinary influence" had significantly declined in the last thirty years, but they still did manifest and, if anything, they had become more theologically extreme. "Extraordinary influence" being defined as when non-physical intelligences make a direct and unequivocal intervention over the life of an individual. Such "extraordinary influences" were classified by the Church into four major forms: Possession, Obsession, Oppression and Infestation.

Possession, the rarest "extraordinary influence", is where a nonphysical intelligence takes full control over a person's mind and body. In most cases, the person concerned willingly seeks such full control as an act of devotion to Evil. The Church terms such willing submission as "Subjugation". There are also much rarer cases, where the person who becomes possessed has no conscious knowledge of the possession, and has not given their consent for the substitution of their consciousness with that of another non-physical intelligence. In such rare, non-consensual possessions, the victim is regarded as morally blameless.

Obsession, involves a non-physical intelligence influencing the thoughts and ideas of an individual and directing them towards destructive goals that often involve suicide or murder or both. Obsessive attacks frequently influence dreams and sleep patterns, to deliberately weaken the mind and body of the victim.

Oppression, is where a non-physical intelligence deliberately intervenes in the daily life of an individual, bringing them a series of misfortunes in every aspect of their life. This is done systematically to bring the individual and their family misery, often as a direct intercession from one person to a power of Evil, to harm another.

Infestation, which can often be an accompaniment to Oppression, is where a non-physical intelligence negatively influences physical spaces, buildings, objects or animals. This can also produce some of the phenomena called preternatural decay, where systems fail well before they should, dwellings fill with foul smells, food rots before its natural time, and once loving animals become hostile and destructive.

The majority of the lecturers had taken note of the prevailing sceptical attitude of their audience, and had presented their materials in a way that minimised any possible paranormal explanations. Except that is, for the sixty-year-old Father Hugo Verchencho, Chief Exorcist for the Vatican. Unlike the other presenters, who talked in vague theoretical or historical perspectives, Fr Verchencho presented real life cases that suddenly transformed the lectures from safe, theoretical perspectives into something much more menacing.

Verchencho showed how the four types of extraordinary influence took place in real world settings, and he brought the victims of these influences of Evil into the lectures. Through interactive presentations with the class, these poor unfortunates presented their own perspectives on their situation, in some cases before and in others after, the release provided by a sanctioned exorcism.

Initially, Verchencho's presentations were received with little respect but, as the nature of the cases being presented became more menacing and obviously genuine, either through disbelief or shock, the student numbers dropped dramatically.

By the final weeks of the Exorcist's lectures, very few of the original class members cared to attend the presentations of those who were currently victims of "extraordinary influence" and in the process of being considered for the sacrament of exorcism. One of the exceptions was O'Neill who, since his own experiences in Iraq, had questions that his own belief demanded be answered. So, as the class numbers shrank, O'Neill moved from his regular seat at the back of the hall closer to the front. It was initially because of this movement that O'Neill came to the attention of Fr Verchencho, but it was clear that something else had noticed as well. It started with what appeared to be an incoherent mumble from one of the case study visitors, awaiting the decision as to whether their symptoms warranted an exorcism.

Mrs Susan Widee, was an attractive Dutch business woman in her late forties, from Leidsche Rijn in central Holland, who had started forgetting small parts of her day, and later found that she had spent hours doing violent or antisocial acts that she would not normally consider. These lost periods of time grew in frequency and duration, until Mrs Widee was referred by her general medical practitioner to psychiatrists at the University Hospital in Utrecht. There it was discovered that Mrs Widee was suffering from a multiple personality disorder, that manifested as lost periods of time for each of the personalities. If that was all, then her case would have been one among many each year, but in routine video analysis of the CCTV in her hospital room, scratches could be seen spontaneously appearing on the walls around her bed while she slept. Further inspections and subsequent research revealed that the random scratches were Nabataean dialect (Aramaic) and similar to curses attributed to "Ulacin", pre-Islamic forms of discarnate entities called Djinn, mentioned in an unpublished Jordanian sub collection of the Dead Sea scrolls.

Although none of the personalities that manifested in Mrs Widee at the Hospital appeared demonic, the curious incident with the scratches flagged her case and attracted interest from the resident University parapsychologist, Dr Ivan Van Ringe. He conducted further observations and, while performing analysis of interview sound recordings, discovered some of the personalities exhibited apparent knowledge of events that had not yet occurred. The statements were inserted into conversations in such a manner that they would never have come to attention, ranging from complaints about specific weather events, such as lightning strikes on churches, to statements about the terrible injuries that had occurred at a motorway multiple collision. The statements in themselves would pass as normal, except that they had not yet occurred at the time of the interview.

Things came to a climax, when Van Ringe attempted to discuss these phenomena with Mrs Widee during a recorded interview using a hidden camera and voice recording. On the video tape, Mrs Widee is seen to listen to Van Ringe comment on the writing on the wall and her precognitive awareness of events, finally asking her if she knew anything about these matters. The facial expression of Mrs Widee was clearly seen to change, becoming more sinister. She tilted her head, so that she looked directly into the hidden camera, and pronounced one single word, "LeLaA", which, in the (Aramaic) Nabataean dialect, means "Fool".

As Verchencho played this chilling video segment to the class, Mrs Widee rose suddenly from her chair, where she had sat silently for the past forty minutes as her case was presented, and walked slowly across the stage like some predatory bird, occasionally cocking her head from side to side, whilst all the time looking directly at O'Neill, and then exclaimed in a perfect Nabataean dialect.

"Priest of Rome, we would talk with thee."

Verchencho watched this strange sequence of events with considerable interest, then he walked quickly and quietly to the woman, who remained motionless gazing intently at O'Neill and, gently massaging her neck, he guided her slowly back to her chair and the two attending nurses. Once she was seated he turned, dismissed the four other members in the class, and indicated with his left hand that O'Neill should come with him.

Verchencho's small office was located in a basement within a non-descript 1960s five storey concrete building, 600 feet inside the walls of Vatican City. The Swiss guards clearly knew the Chief Exorcist well, since they waved him through the three security perimeters and gave O'Neill a curious look. Once inside the small office, Verchencho spoke for the first time in the twenty minutes it had taken them to travel from the PUG lecture theatre.

"So, kindly explain why a first century pre-Islamic Djinn wants to talk with you."

The old Exorcist sat behind his desk in an old high back leather chair, linked his hands and looked at O'Neill keenly.

O'Neill carefully explained about his motivations for attending the course, the details of the doomed Finster expedition and the archaeological evidence for ancient discarnate intelligences.

After listening carefully, and without comment for nearly an hour, Verchencho asked O'Neill to pack an overnight bag and to meet him at the Greg café in the PUG at 7 pm. They were, he explained, going to visit the Sanatorium of St Michael, near San Pietro della Ienca in the Mountains of Abruzzo, where they could, perhaps, find out some answers to O'Neill's questions.

O'Neill's battered grey Crumpler satchel rested incongruously on the stylish transparent green plastic chair next to him, his arms resting on the minimalist wooden table, as he re-read the hand-written journal he had recovered from the ill-fated Finster expedition into the Dhi Qar Governorate of Iraq. O'Neill was at heart a field Archaeologist and never felt truly comfortable in so called civilised surroundings. Within the nineteenth century structure of the PUG, the Greg café added an unexpected clean modern image, interlaced with more traditional touches like the glass etched copy of a sixteenth century Dutch world map on the ceiling. For the seventh time in as many minutes, he consulted his worn steel Nite Mx10 watch and then looked at the International News, that was being shown on a wide screen television above the row of steel coffee makers.

The recent announcement by Nissa Ad-Dajjal of the free distribution, by the Unity foundation, of clean renewable energy generators, had sparked a dispute between the poor and rich nations. The USA and Europe argued that the MaGoG system needed years of careful evaluation by the major energy firms before it could be used with any assurances of safety. The developing nations argued that this was simply a tactic to continue the existing domination of the energy markets by the major Western powers.

An emergency summit of the G7 had authorized a joint military blockade on the European ports of Rotterdam, Hamburg and Antwerp, where the first MaGoG units were being sent to some of the poorest nations in Africa. The cameras showed enormous US and British aircraft carriers blocking civilian container ports. These scenes changed to angry exchanges at the United Nations, where the Secretary General had appealed for calm and called for an emergency meeting of the Security Council, to try and resolve the growing conflict.

In another rare TV appearance, Nissa Ad-Dajjal, looking deeply distressed, appealed to the US President to ease the blockade and allow free energy to save the world from certain destruction by its continued use of fossil fuels.

O'Neill's thoughts about the conflict were brought to an abrupt end by the appearance of Fr Verchencho, who was going to drive them across Italy into the Mountains of Abruzzo, to the Sanatorium of St Michael, devoted to the care of Exorcists who had themselves fallen under the "extraordinary influence" of Evil.

CHAPTER 10 - LONDON CALLING

"This melancholy London – I sometimes imagine that the souls of the lost are compelled to walk through its streets perpetually. One feels them passing like a whiff of air." - William Butler Yeats (Golden Dawn initiate 1890 "Demon est Deus Inversus" the Devil is God Inverted.)

1 Princes St, Edinburgh, Scotland. EH2 2EQ
07.52HRS, July 28th, Present Day.

Tavish Stewart emerged from a traditional British black cab, dressed in a Balmoral Hotel complimentary grey sweat shirt and matching jog bottoms that showed perspiration consistent with a regime of hard physical exercise. As was Stewart's habit when in Edinburgh, he had spent from 6.30 to 7.30 AM at the Edinburgh University boxing club, making intensive use of the heavy bag, kettle weights and speed skipping ropes. His body now had that healthy glow and freedom of movement that only comes from the "noble art of self-defence" associated with the Marquis of Queensbury. Although Stewart was skilled in numerous martial arts, his regular exercise regime focused on boxing techniques because they emphasized stamina, distance and timing skills that naturally carried over to other forms of combat.

Returning to the Scone and Crombie suite, Stewart shaved and showered using the consumables in the Dunhill overnight bag, thoughtfully provided by the duty manager, Ian Hiscock and concluded by setting the shower to an icy cold temperature that, he recalled his Japanese Aikido instructor telling him, strengthened the vital energy of the mind and body. He emerged into the shared living room, smelling of Hermès Orange Verte, dressed in a plain cotton light blue shirt, a pair of light coloured chino trousers and comfortable brown brogue shoes, all provided overnight by Ede and Ravenscroft in Frederick Street.

Curren was in a plain Dior white silk robe, laying the table for breakfast, which had just been delivered to the suite in a set of warmed containers carefully arranged on an elegant steel and chrome trolley. The table was soon filled with plates of yellow scrambled eggs on lightly toasted wheat bread, freshly squeezed orange juice, a large pot of freshly roasted American blend coffee and a rack of whole-wheat toast accompanied by Seville Orange Marmalade.

The sleek LG widescreen television in the living room was muted, but showed news reports on the ongoing UN security council debate about the Unity MaGoG energy devices. Stewart turned up the sound with the remote and sat opposite Curren, gesturing for her to start eating and pouring her a generous coffee, while both watched the UN coverage.

The US Secretary of State, the respected retired General Martin Dore, was presenting recently gathered intelligence that showed the MaGoG systems could be rapidly transformed into weapons of mass destruction, and that they posed a clear threat to the security of peace loving nations. Dore's points were illustrated by highly realistic CGI animations showing MaGoG systems exploding in strategic capital cities, recognisable by their landmark structures, interspersed with stock footage of injured women and children.

His counterpart, Sir Reginald Twiffers, the UK's Foreign Secretary, followed with a presentation that backed up the statements from General Dore with what was claimed to be evidence from within the Unity organization, that support engineers, who would be provided with the MaGoG systems, could, once the generators were in place at strategic locations around the world, convert them into weapons of mass destruction within a matter of forty-five minutes. As a consequence of these revelations, Unity had unilaterally been declared by the US and the UK as a Terrorist organisation, its financial assets had been frozen, and a warrant had been issued for the immediate arrest of Unity leader, Nissa Ad-Dajjal.

The other member states of the Security Council looked seriously shocked by these revelations and, as the TV coverage moved away from the debate to gauge the reactions of the other UN diplomats, it was clear that representatives from the developing nations and ecological groups remained highly sceptical about the claims, either that the free and clean MaGoG generators could be converted to WMDs or that Unity was a terrorist organisation. As the news coverage moved to the apparent suicide of a leading US ecological energy expert, who had disputed that MaGoG could be converted into a WMD, there was a loud knock on the exterior door to the suite and Curren took the remote and turned off the TV, while Stewart went and opened the door to the first of three separate delegations from various police departments that wanted to interview him that morning.

Aside from the numerous bureaucratic details that the different officers demanded for their extensive paperwork, they also reported on the progress of their investigations into the damaged house and warehouse. This was accompanied by more questions for Stewart about his role in the violent deaths at both locations.

The police and Stewart's own staff reported independently that his ancestral home had been systematically burnt with military grade thermite incendiary devices, effectively removing any possibility of a forensic investigation, and causing such extensive damage that, it was estimated by Stewart's estate team, it would take two years of refurbishment before it would be habitable again. Worse still, since the event had been classified as a terrorist attack, insurance would not cover the cost of the extensive rebuilding that would be required.

The surviving CCTV records did show the Land Cruiser chasing Stewart's Mercedes through the estate gates, but all other recordings had been systematically deleted by highly skilled professionals. The police had found who they believed to be those responsible for the attack on Stewart's home, but the bodies had been destroyed by a military grade high explosive device along with the Land Cruiser believed to be used in the raid. Again, all forensic evidence had been effectively removed, making further investigation impossible. The three Maelstrom operatives captured at the warehouse had been released overnight, along with the assassin who had posed as a terror advisor, under the rights of diplomatic protection and privilege accorded to US Consulate staff after high level interventions to the British Prime Minister. At the specific instruction from Downing Street to the CPS, no charges were to be pressed against Maelstrom or its staff.

Stewart took all these revelations stoically, only becoming clearly emotional while giving instructions about Hamish's funeral, which would now take place very quickly as the police had terminated their investigation into both the house and warehouse break-ins at the direct instruction of Downing Street. After spending nearly three hours with the different police representatives, Stewart was at last able to turn his attention to the overdue telephone conference with his key staff in Istanbul, Rome and London.

In London, Jeffrey Sonnet reported having some success with his contacts at the Ashmolean and the British Museum, while in Istanbul, Mohammed Sek had found what looked like a solid paper trail, providing a historical linkage between John Dee and a silver leaf folio.

Based on what the two men had found, the Elizabethan magician Dr John Dee was reputed by several independent sources to have possessed what was supposed to be a magical silver book containing four emerald tablets that, allegedly, could be used to create a bridge between the Human and Angelic worlds, in order to gain esoteric knowledge in return for bringing about the end of days on earth. Prior to Dee's ownership, many individuals had been known to have tried to use the emerald tablets, including Roger Bacon in the thirteenth century and Heinrich Cornelius Agrippa von Nettesheim in the fifteenth century. It is from Agrippa's estate that Dee was thought to have acquired the silver book, as there were recorded ledgers in the Grenoble city archives for the sale of assorted books and diverse jewels from the estate in 1578 to a John Dee.

Dee's use of the silver book commenced in the 1580s and by 1582 he and his assistant, Edward Kelly, explored Angelic communication in such detail that they recorded an entire Angelic language, through which they became increasingly detached from reality. They ended their esoteric adventures at the Court of Rudolf II, the Holy Roman Emperor, trying to convince him of an impending end of days. It was believed that Dee's silver book became one of the prized exhibits, alongside the Voynich manuscript, in Rudolf's "cabinet of curiosities" (Kunstkammer) housed at Prague Castle. Although the "Kunstkammer" was looted by Swedish troops, who sacked Prague Castle on the 26th of July 1648, it is known that the collection still included all four emerald tablets in 1805 because Francis, Holy Roman Emperor, gifted three of the tablets to the Church so they "could be kept safely apart until the appointed end of days". Allegedly, one tablet was to reside with the Pope in St Peters, one with the Eastern Pope in Constantinople and the third was to be buried in the desert along the Silk Route to China. The silver book and the first emerald tablet remained in Prague, where it passed into a private collection in 1806 at the time Napoleon broke up what then remained of the Holy Roman Empire.

"Interesting, it looks like whoever is after the folio is motivated by its purported esoteric properties. Guys, I need to speak with someone who could authenticate and comment on the folio from an esoteric perspective." Commented Stewart, after Jeffery had completed describing all the information he had been given.

"I will arrange it," replied Sonnet, "How soon can you be down here?"

Stewart looked at Curren and then his watch and replied,

"We can take the train and be with you this afternoon. I will text you the ETA, once we have finished here and boarded the train."

"Sounds good, I will meet you at Kings Cross."

Sadly, there had been less success tracing the payment details to find out who had issued the contract to Maelstrom and ordered the raid on Stewart's warehouse. Mario's underworld contacts could only confirm that the silver folio was estimated to be worth less than 2,000 USD on the black market, and therefore no financial motive could be inferred for the effort and cost that had been expended to hire the US based Maelstrom corporation for the raid on Stewart's warehouse in Scotland. Everyone agreed that, whatever was motivating the attempts to steal the folio, it was probably not financial.

Sonnet's trace of the money trail had led him to l'international Bund SA, a small firm of attorneys in Geneva Cité-centre, but inquires to the company led to a dead end as the premises had been destroyed in what was believed to be a gas explosion, yesterday morning. The two survivors who had been recovered from the burnt-out building were currently in intensive care at the HUG (Hôpital Universitie Geneva) at Rue Gabrielle-Perret-Gentil, suffering from such extensive burns that they were thought unlikely to survive.

"These bastards are as thorough as they are ruthless," declared Stewart,

"but let's force their hand to come and get this and when they do we can get them."

He raised the silver folio and, as he did so, Curren gasped involuntarily as an icy breeze came from nowhere, sending the net curtains billowing like a ghost into the room. Stewart smiled, sensing that at least something appeared to agree with his proposal.

The check out from the Balmoral was a far more refined process than their check in had been, two days earlier. Since Stewart had acquired some replacement clothing during his brief stay he had opted for a simple Victorinox CH 25 Tourist Wheeled Backpack, while Curren retained her original Louis Vuitton cases. Lev's "gift" from the Tartan Kremlin was safely stored in the inner zipped compartment of the CH 25, which Stewart insisted on carrying himself. Ian Hiscock had made the train bookings for them on the 1.30 PM fast service and insisted that two of the hotel staff carried Curren's four bags along the pavement to the platform.

Waverly station was uncharacteristically quiet, it's heavy glass ceilings and black iron supporting pillars emphasizing its Victorian splendour that even the grey sky, that had suddenly materialised, could not spoil. The first-class section of the 13.30 HRS "SKYFALL" train was located at the rear of the ten carriages, near the dining car. The 91-class locomotive, 91107, had been named in 2013 after the James Bond film. The 007 livery and etching on the windows were now long gone, but Curren appreciated the irony in the link with the fictional spy, given the strange circumstances that they now found themselves in. As the train pulled away from the station, at the start of its four-hour journey to London, a smartly dressed waiter approached their table and Curren playfully asked for a "Vesper Martini", shaken and not stirred, whilst Stewart predictably declined the cocktail and instead opted for a twelve-year-old single malt Glenfiddich. An hour or so later, while Curren worked on her Lenovo Carbon ThinkPad, catching up on email from her offices in London, Stewart catnapped.

His dreams were a mix of memories that had him walking through deserted streets. After a while, he began to recognise the river on his right side was the Thames and that he was in London. Not in the centre but further South, in the suburbs right in the heart of the commuter belt. He reflected that the subconscious mind was an odd thing, with all that was going on to dream of somewhere that was far removed from his activities. He found himself on a small two-lane road with an old-fashioned zebra crossing, complete with Belisha beacons. To his left, he could see in vivid detail a block of 1960s brick flats, and to his right was a four-storey modern 1970s designed house with large glass windows, its lower ground floor made of red brick and its upper storeys covered with a dark painted wooden planking. The details were so vivid that Stewart could almost reach out and touch the nearest building. A tree lined paved path beside the house led towards the river and Stewart set out down this path noticing, as he progressed, how the building changed from the wooden 1970s style to something much more Victorian in appearance. As he passed a sign that proclaimed the development to be "Tapestry Court", he found himself suddenly descending down a set of steps into an old brick lined underground passageway, that was crumbling away and forming a covering of dust on his well-polished brown brogues.

A thick wooden doorway stood to one side of the subterranean brick passage and, as Stewart entered, he became keenly aware of thick smoke filling his nostrils and making his eyes water. As his vision adjusted he saw that he was in a room that was filled with a mix of broken weaving machines and empty bookcases. Stewart realised that his dream was removing layer upon layer of history from this place, bringing him eventually to what must have been Dr John Dee's magical laboratory.

In the centre of this alchemical study was a wooden table engraved with oddly shaped characters, that were from the same alphabet as those found on the Prague emerald tablet. Upon the table were four indentations that were clearly formed to enable all four tablets to have been assembled on its surface. Lying close beside them was a small red stick, John Dee's wand, that was painted in three sections with the ends coloured black. The ritual instrument had been placed so that a golden finger ring, also inscribed with strange characters, was held at its midpoint.

As Stewart walked closer, he became aware of an odd shadow to one side of the table. It flickered strangely, being there one moment, and then gone in the next. The room became filled with a sound like something scuttling on a wooden surface. Suddenly, the wand broke into two parts, sending Dee's magical golden ring spinning across the floor towards the edge of the shadow, as the source of the strange noise was finally revealed. From the darkness a nightmare shape emerged, a skeletal talon reached out and grasped its ancient bony fingers around the sacred object. Stewart's final image was of John Dee's ring being crushed into a flattened shape, like a coin, that was then left to spin across the floor and fall through the boards into the dark Thames below.

CHAPTER 11 - THE LEGACY OF DEE

"It is by the straight line and the circle that the first and most simple example and representation of all things may be demonstrated, whether such things be either non-existent or merely hidden under Nature's veils." - Dr John Dee, Monas Hieroglyphica, 1564

A5202 Kings Cross Station, Euston Road, London N19 AL
17.55HRS, 28th July, Present Day.

Jeffrey Sonnet, Director of the London office of Stewart's Antiquarians, sat in the luxurious "Solitaire" finished leather driver's seat of the black Overfinch Range Rover, parked outside Kings Cross railway station. From behind a set of mirrored Oakley aviator sunglasses, his eyes scanned the station doors looking for Stewart and Curren. Although in his fifties, Sonnet retained the lean, clean cut look that he had been famous for throughout his commission with the Guards and later in the Foreign and Commonwealth Office (FCO) working for Her Majesty's Secret Intelligence Service (SIS). Sonnet's short light brown hair had started to show the salted grey of middle age, but he kept it in a traditional parting on the left that he felt showed classic good taste. At only five feet eight inches tall, he had learnt from an early age that the only way to gain respect from others was by strength. So, he had devoted himself to excel at sports both when he was at Eton and then at Christ Church, Oxford, where he gained a blue in the varsity boat race, although "the other place" won on that occasion. Now well into middle age he, like his boss, kept himself in top physical condition.

A few years ago, when Government budget cuts forced the FCO to lay off numerous senior staff, he had leapt at the opportunity to work with former colleague Sir Tavish Stewart and the two had come to share a passion for tracking down the rarest and finest examples of antiquities from remote and difficult locations. Thanks to Sonnet's hard work, the New Bond Street premises of Stewart's was renowned, even among the most demanding Middle Eastern clients, as the place to acquire exquisite items that would highlight your excellent taste and deep wallet. Sonnet consulted the dual display of his black cased Breitling

Chronospace Military, just as Stewart and Curren emerged from the modern glass frontage of the station. Seeing the Range Rover 165 feet away at the far edge of the pavement, Stewart steered the trolley containing their combined luggage towards Sonnet.

Midway across the expanse of paving, a thin tall young man wearing a black beanie hat, black cargo pants and a bright red T Shirt, was performing tricks on his customised "Loaded Chubby Unicorn" longboard. A small crowd had gathered to see him complete a range of increasingly complex jumps, 360-degree spins and finally, a high-speed run that allowed him to lean at an extreme angle. This final show of skill was abruptly ended by an unnoticed stone, that caused the longboard to spin from under the rider, and made him fall violently straight into the path of Stewart and Curren. The resulting impact caused the luggage trolley to overturn, as the skateboarder spilt onto the concrete surrounded by Curren's Louis Vuitton bags. As the young man rose, he rubbed a large bloody graze on his forehead and apologised sheepishly, as he helped handle the overturned luggage back onto the trolley. The enraptured crowd moved on, only one or two caring enough to throw a pound coin in the cardboard box for donations. By the time the excitement of the collision was over, Sonnet had opened the fold down tailgate on the Range Rover and taken each bag in turn from Stewart, after a firm shake of hands. Curren exchanged a single cheek kiss with Sonnet, before getting into the sumptuous rear of the long wheelbase Overfinch, the front passenger seat being filled with a long leather case which protruded from the foot well right to the interior ceiling. Once inside, Curren helped herself to one of the chilled Fiji water bottles stashed in the centre console, while Stewart enquired on the progress of locating someone who could comment on the esoteric aspects of the silver leaf folio and its emerald tablet.

As the sleek black Range Rover moved off, a white Ford Mondeo with Metropolitan Police ANPR Interceptor markings, pulled slowly from the curb some sixty feet behind and kept itself one or two cars behind the SUV, as both vehicles joined the busy London traffic.

Inside the police Mondeo, Issac bin Abdul Issuin sat in the driver's seat, carefully watching and following the direction of the Stewart's Antiquarians Range Rover. He was dressed in Metropolitan Police "working dress" of short sleeved white shirt and black trousers. His name badge proclaimed him to be "SGT James Shorting" and the stab vest was a tight fit. For those who took the trouble to look carefully, his hands were covered in white latex gloves and forensic shoe covers obscured his sand coloured Bates USMC DuraShock boots.

Seated beside him, wearing similar latex gloves, was the tall thin skateboarder, who had removed his black beanie hat and pulled off his baggy red T Shirt to reveal a white police short sleeved shirt, and was now struggling in the confined passenger seat to get his stab vest on as the car moved through the traffic.

"Did you place the tracking devices?" Asked Abdul Issuin.

"Yes, exactly as you showed me, one on each of her bags." Replied the young man, who had just noticed the two dead bodies lying in the back seats, partially covered by a red first aid blanket.

"Did they give you any trouble?" Asked the nervous young man, as he nodded at the two bodies. Abdul Issuin shook his head with a wicked smile, as he cut the Mondeo through a red light, to follow the Range Rover down Upper Woburn Place and into Endsleigh Gardens.

Back in the Overfinch, Sonnet had explained that he had located a group in central London with a reputation for seriously practicing ritual magic. The group called themselves "The Temple of Thoth" and their head, Elizabeth Fitz-Glass, had agreed to see the three of them at their offices and temple, located near Gordon Street behind the Wellcome Trust.

The elegant stone facade of the rest of the row of four storey houses was in stark contrast to the red brick of number 14a, which sat slightly back from the other properties that comprised this section of Gordon Street. Stewart, Curren and Sonnet left the Range Rover in one of the vacant parking spaces on the Gordon Square side of the road and walked over to the four white stone steps, that led to the plain black four panel front door with a single round brass handle in the centre. The other noticeable feature was the four separate Yale locks neatly placed one under the other. As the three of them approached the front door, they did not pay any attention to a police car that drove past them down Gordon Street.

Stewart noted the four locks and raised his eyebrow to Sonnet, just as the door opened and they were greeted by a young freckle faced woman with striking blue eyes and long blonde hair, that was tied into a single braided ponytail down the entire length of her back. Her face was fresh, and seemed full of an innocence and purity that was unusual in the modern world. While her clothes were elegant, they were extremely plain being made of a natural undyed white cotton.

"You must be from Stewart's Antiquarians?"

She enquired, as she gestured for them all to come inside into a white marble floored entrance hallway, that was thick with the smell of rose incense from several rows of burning joss sticks placed on a dark metal side stand. The four walls of the entrance hall were a pure white but with the outline of a very large triangle painted in black on each. Two of the triangles were orientated point uppermost and the other two triangles with the point down, one of each pair having a single line bisecting them horizontally. Under each triangle was the name of one of the prime elements, Earth, Water, Fire and Air. The room had a single black iron light fitting which illuminated a ceiling painting of a person in orange robes, seated in a meditation pose in a Himalayan mountain range.

"I am Susan. Ms Fitz-Glass asked me to bring you to her immediately on your arrival."

With that announcement, she led them up a narrow flight of stairs at the rear of the entrance hall. The walls of the staircase were covered in old photographs showing groups of students surrounding the same woman at various points in time, with her becoming older and surrounded by fewer and fewer students the further they progressed up the three flights of stairs.

On the right side of the corridor on the third-floor landing was an open door, which Susan led them through and then closed behind her. Seated at a huge dark wood desk was a woman who looked like the archetypal sweet old lady, with pure white hair and piercing blue eyes that were hidden behind a pair of round glasses. Her desk was covered in papers, with the single decoration of a vase of bright sunflowers. The office was noticeable for its lack of computers or telephones.

The walls of the room were covered in photographs from places and meetings that obviously held some significant memories. Behind the desk was an exquisitely detailed painting of the Egyptian God Thoth in his form as Ankher, with the head of an Ibis, and the lunar disc as a crown. The bare wood floor boards of the room were covered with a thick and clearly ancient hand threaded Turkish carpet, on which were placed three wooden guest chairs. Rising from her desk, Elizabeth Fitz-Glass addressed the group, while gesturing for them to sit. Susan stood quietly by the door.

"I am Elizabeth, you must be the three people who wanted to talk about some talisman you think may be connected with John Dee's Enochian Magick. I hope that you are mistaken."

Meanwhile, outside in Gordon Street, the police Mondeo had stopped beside the Overfinch Range Rover, turned on its flashing roof lights and what appeared to be two police officers emerged from the front of the vehicle, leaving the doors open. Abdul Issuin approached the SUV with a black box the size of a large mobile phone which had numerous dials and switches on it. With a well-practiced sequence, he turned one of the dials and the SUVs lights flashed, indicating it was unlocked. Rapidly releasing the rear tailgate doors, he began systematically going through Curren and Stewart's luggage. While Abdul Issuin was checking the luggage, his colleague stood in the road looking towards 14a, where Stewart, Curren and Sonnet had entered.

Having completed his search of the bags, Abdul Issuin closed the rear tailgate doors, pulled a small gas cylinder from the left pocket of his cargo trousers and walked round to the left front passenger side of the SUV. Opening the door, he pulled the bonnet release, raised the hood and installed the nozzle from the radio-controlled gas cylinder into the ventilation system of the Range Rover. Within moments he had closed the bonnet, reset the remote-control locking, returned to the police car and driven to a vacant parking spot four spaces away from the SUV.

Back in the third-floor office of 14a Gordon Street, Stewart had explained his acquisition of the items from the Zimbrug Antique House in Prague, the subsequent two violent attempts at robbery and their attackers callous disregard for human life. Elizabeth listened intently and enquired if they had brought the object with them. Carefully removing the silver folio from around his neck, where he had been wearing it under his shirt via a length of black nylon paracord threaded carefully through one of the empty holes, Stewart handed it to Elizabeth, who held the object carefully, if somewhat gingerly, through a silk handkerchief that she had produced from her left desk drawer. She first examined the silver case and then opening it, was clearly amazed by the sight of the carved emerald stone held within.

"Interesting," she eventually said, having examined the tablet with great care for around five minutes, during which time Curren, Stewart and Sonnet waited with increasing expectation.

"I never thought it was real," she smiled, remembering she was with company.

"Most occultists are familiar with the Smaragdine or Emerald Tablets of Hermes, the Greek god of magic, that are claimed to hold the secrets of Nature. But few are aware that the translations publicly available are a deliberate forgery, created in the sixth century by an Arab alchemist, Jabir ibn Hayyan, in his text "Kitāb sirr al-ḫalīqa", or the Secret of Creation and the Art of Nature."

"And you believe this is one of the genuine emerald tablets?" Asked Curren.

"I would have to do some more research but, based on what you have told me, someone certainly appears to think so." Replied Elizabeth.

"So, we are looking for someone who is deeply into Greek alchemy. Do you know of anyone who might be prepared to kill for this… Smaragdine?" Asked Stewart.

"The Emerald Tablets are not just a Greek creation."

Elizabeth rose from her chair and walked round her desk, reaching for several thick old books from the bookshelves that covered one of her walls. She opened each of the books at different pages on her desk, showing Chinese Taoist Jade Books that existed before the separation of heaven and earth, Sumerian tablets of lapis lazuli called the "giš-null-gal", written by demonic scribes and said to contain forbidden knowledge, and finally ancient Islamic texts showing the Archangel 'Israf'il as owner of a "jewelled tablet of fate".

"You see," continued Elizabeth "The tablets are mentioned in the pre-history of all cultures as the most powerful keys to all creation and destruction, controlling the final of the forty-nine so called ethers that make up our creation."

"So, the person seeking this tablet believes that it will bring them some secret power?" Asked Curren.

Elizabeth walked back behind her desk and picked up the silver folio with her silk handkerchief, answering the lawyer as she did.

"Not just power, but absolute power over all creation. Based on how they have behaved so far, I believe the person is seeking to gather all four of these tablets to complete a very specific ceremony. The forty ninth call."

"A ceremony to do what exactly?" Asked Stewart.

"They probably believe that they are going to open a bridge between our creation and those creations that preceded ours. Perhaps even create a new one in their own image." Replied Elizabeth.

"And how exactly is this all linked with John Dee?" Asked a sceptical looking Stewart.

Elizabeth looked at him, considered and then reluctantly continued.

"John Dee was the last human being with sufficient intellect to be truly recognised as worthy by the entities involved with these tablets. Dee attempted to complete this ultimate magickal operation in the early 1580s. Using all four tablets he made direct contact with intelligences, that he believed were Archangels, prepared to share their divine knowledge with him. Finally, after years of preparation, during a ceremony in Prague, which has been greatly misinterpreted by historians, Dee discovered the true nature of the entities he was communicating with and broke off his attempts at completing the ceremony. Returning to England, he left the four tablets with the Holy Roman Emperor to be kept safe from human eyes until the end of days. Dee died a broken man, knowing how close he had come to destroying everything. After his death, some fragments of Dee's magical diaries came to light, and these partial notes are the basis of all modern Enochian Magick. Fortunately, intellects on the scale of Dee's are few and far between, so subsequent attempts at using Enochian Magick to communicate with Dee's Angelic intelligences have had very limited success. Still, the dangers of using the methods are such that many traditional Magical schools, such as mine, shun the entire system as too dangerous to use."

"We know the tablets left by Dee in Prague were eventually donated to the Church, when the Holy Roman Empire fell to the French." Said Sonnet.

"Yes, to split them up and send them to the four corners of the world. Prague, Rome, Constantinople, and the Deserts of the Djinn." Confirmed Elizabeth.

"What about the engraving on the tablet, can you read it?" Queried Curren.

"It is better if it is never read." Responded Elizabeth hastily, handing back the silver folio to Stewart.

"You see the ultimate ceremony promises to merge the previous creations with this current one to create a new heaven and earth... but only one creation can exist at any one time. The ultimate power promised is in fact to destroy the creation we live in now. I can tell you this. The person seeking these tablets is of a very rare intelligence. You should take enormous care, as communication with these entities corrupts the mind, so your adversary may be unable to see the final end to which they are working… the destruction of everything."

CHAPTER 12 - THE SANATORIUM OF ST MICHAEL

"Those who consider the Devil to be a partisan of Evil and Angels to be warriors for Good accept the demagogy of the Angels. Things are clearly more complicated." - Milan Kundera

Sanatorium of St Michael
near San Pietro della Ienca in the Mountains of Abruzzo
04.17HRS, July 28th, Present Day.

Father Thomas O'Neill woke amid unfamiliar surroundings and to the persistent deep ringing of a large church bell. As his eyes adjusted to the weak light coming through a small arched stone window, set high in the wall above his simple cot bed, the tritium vials on his Nite Mx10 watch told him it was 04.17AM. He pulled himself upright and with an effort got out of bed. The stone floor was surprisingly cold on his bare feet and the cool temperature in his small monastic cell provided a strong motivation to get rapidly dressed. He opened his thick wooden door with its simple latch and emerged into a long narrow stone corridor. Even at this early hour, the hallway was busy with a line of robed figures all walking silently in the same direction, all the time being joined by yet more priests emerging from their individual rooms set around a classical ecclesiastical quad.

It was too dark for O'Neill to see clearly the sculpture that stood in the centre of this quad although just enough light was cast from the open cell doors to show the outline of a vast serpent being trampled underfoot, a vicious lance piercing its dragon like head.

The figures emerging from the cells were all dressed similarly in full length black robes with white dog collars at their necks, marking them as belonging to the same order as O'Neill, Jesuits. O'Neill's light chinos, black fleece and timberland boots were a stark contrast but he was not conscious of any critical glances as he reached a large double door and entered a small chapel. Once seated on a wooden bench near the entrance, O'Neill expected a standard Matins Mass but the service began with the litany of the saints in Latin, focusing on the prime archangels, followed by Psalm fifty-three and then into a variant of the

Latin Rite of exorcism, with the entire congregation being the subject of the sacrament.

In his walk to the chapel O'Neill had felt the weather was going to be set for one of those fine days in the mountains but, as the priest leading the rite reached the exhortation to

"…crush that roaring lion..."

there was a flash of lightning, followed shortly after by a distant thunder clap. Clearly the sudden mountain storm was raising the humidity, as the air within the chapel began to feel cooler and O'Neill found himself shivering involuntarily, as his breath started to become visible. The weather front came closer as the ceremony continued. By the time they had reached the reading about Jesus Christ confronting Beelzebub, a full storm was raging.

Lightning flashes illuminated the chapel interior through the stained-glass windows, which displayed in vivid colours scenes of the War in Heaven, the thunderclaps now following instantly behind. The winds became so violent that the ancient building was shaking and it felt so cold that O'Neill wondered if, when they emerged, they would find one of those freak summer storms had blanketed the church with a covering of snow and ice.

Just when it seemed conditions could not get worse, the storm evidently found some new thermals to feed from and grew into one of those rare super cells that occurs once every decade. It unleashed enormous hail stones that pounded the slate roof and shook the glass in the windows, so it became impossible to hear the service. The lightning became so bright it burnt its image into O'Neill's retina, so that he could see vivid white lines in the momentary darkness after each flash, and the thunder became so strong that it made the air move in sudden pressure waves inside the Chapel, making papers flutter wildly into the air and fall slowly to the stone floor.

As the priest reached the invocation to God to banish

"Every Satanic power of the enemy, every spectre from hell"

the electrical potential of the monster storm found the lightning conductor of the chapel and there was an enormous discharge, that made the air inside smell of sulphur as the oxygen and nitrogen atoms were transmuted, and the copper lightning conductor glowed red with the heat. The freak electrical charge in the air made the candles flutter wildly, casting odd shapes and shadows in the dark corners of the church. Suddenly, with that massive discharge completed, the storm had expended its power and there was a calm that clearly was unexpected, as the Priest shouted his injunction,

"I adjure you, ancient serpent, by the judge of the living and the dead, by your Creator..."

into a silent and still chapel.

When O'Neill finally emerged at the end of the service, he expected to see evidence of the terrible destructive power of the storm, instead there was just a feeling of a perfect summer's day in the mountains. From the cloister, the large stone statue of St Michael slaying the Great Dragon was now fully revealed in the morning light. The stern magnificence of the archangel, with its enormous wings and right foot placed deliberately on the head of his victim, was in stark contrast to the dejected look of the dragon that was clearly about to be flung into the bottomless pit.

"Never feel pity for him," said a stern voice and O'Neill turned to find Fr Verchencho.

"Breakfast is in thirty minutes. Eat well, as your body needs to be grounded in the material world for your meeting with our star patient this morning!"

With that Verchencho strode away purposefully towards his cell, which was differentiated from the other doors with a large silver Chi Rho painted on it. While the others returned to their rooms, O'Neill decided to take advantage of this free time before breakfast to look around the eleventh century sanctuary. They had arrived in the darkness of the early hours of the morning after a long drive across the width of the Italian peninsula, so he had no clear idea of his surroundings.

Walking to the far South end of the cloister, O'Neill pulled back a large flat iron bolt and opened a smaller door, that was set into the huge main double doors, causing the morning sunlight to stream into the quad. Outside of the sanatorium the true magnificence of their isolated mountain location could be appreciated. As far as the eye could see there were no signs of human habitation, only the distant peaks of other hills. Towards the North was a single dirt roadway which led off to the nearest summit around two miles away. There was no sign of the usual electrical and phone cables that followed the country roads in most of mainland Italy. The sanatorium clearly relished isolation.

Verchencho's ancient square angled Mercedes 450SEL 6.9 saloon could be seen in the parking area, thick dust covering its black bodywork. Its specialised suspension had been raised, giving the forty-year-old car an extra two inches of ground clearance that, combined with the seven-litre engine, had been put to practical use in the expert hands of O'Neill's host on the winding mountain roads last night.

At the edge of the dirt track were a number of unmarked graves, in what was clearly an unconsecrated burial ground. The unkempt nature of these graves was in contrast to a much smaller graveyard, that was located next to the sanatorium, which had more traditional Christian symbolism. As O'Neill walked round the eleventh century structure of the sanatorium, he noted the dozens of lightning conductors protruding from the roof and, set into the exterior stone walls at each of the cardinal points, was a statue of one of the four archangels dressed in the full plate armour of a medieval knight, complete with broadsword and shield.

As he made his way around the outer walls back to the entrance, O'Neill's Timberland boot struck what he thought was a remnant of a rail or tramway but, with some additional scraping, it soon became clear that someone had gone to considerable effort to construct a thick cast iron ring around the entire perimeter. Re-entering through the small door, O'Neill became aware of the delicious smell of cooking and headed towards the small refectory for a hearty breakfast, before his meeting with the mysterious patient who would, supposedly, answer all his lingering questions from Iraq.

CHAPTER 13 – LEGION

"And the great Dragon was cast out, that old serpent, called the Devil, and Satan, that deceiveth the whole world." - Revelation 12:9. King James Bible

Sanatorium of St Michael
near San Pietro della Ienca in the Mountains of Abruzzo
10.00HRS, July 28th, Present Day.

The section of the sanatorium devoted to the care of those suffering from "extraordinary influence" was marked by a double set of large iron gates, cast in a repeated crucifix pattern, before which lay an ancient wooden drawbridge spanning a deep chasm that seemed to go down into the very bowels of the Italian mountain. The outer gates had a sign declaring "No sharp objects" in both English and Italian. In addition to surrendering his keys, O'Neill was efficiently searched from head to toe by one of the four full time attendants who managed the entrance security. As they were both frisked, Fr Verchencho explained that only three of the thirteen cells were currently occupied so they had only need of one full time ordained psychiatrist, along with five sisters from the Augustinians delle Vergini, an eleventh century convent in Venice, who had provided nuns for St Michael's specialist mission since the twelfth century.

Crossing over the drawbridge and between the two iron crucifix gates, O'Neill felt a deep chill pass through his whole body, doubtless caused by the icy waters of the mountain stream beneath him. Shivering, he unconsciously rubbed his hands together and noticed his breath forming thick steam in the icy air. The second set of iron gates had thin strips of badly worn wood set into specifically designed hollow sections in the cast iron, forming an enormous crucifix that towered above the visitor. O'Neill recognised sections made of cedar, cypress, palm and, above where the head would be placed, olive wood, together with inscriptions in ancient languages. The lowest inscription was in Latin and was just legible. "Iesus Nazarenus Rex Iudaeorum." For a second time that morning, O'Neill felt a chill run through him.

The long stone clad corridor on the other side of the second gate felt so icily cold that O'Neill wondered if the area was being deliberately refrigerated. But, as he passed one of the numerous old style thick radiators that were regularly placed along the entire length of the corridor, he was surprised to feel that it was scalding hot. O'Neill reflected that the icy mountain stream, that he had encountered at the bridge, must pass underneath the entire length of this section of the building.

Fr Verchencho stopped directly outside the third cell door and one of the nuns, Sister Teresa, a tall middle-aged woman who had accompanied them from the gates, retrieved a set of keys from her waist belt and unlocked the thick wooden door, with a plain paper label attached to it, which simply stated "Fr Chin Kwon".

O'Neill was not sure what he was expecting when he entered, but certainly not an elegant looking forty something man, dressed in the classic orange robes of a Buddhist monk, with his long dark hair tied into a ponytail behind his head. The man was seated cross legged on the stone floor in a Tibetan Padmasana Vajragya Mudra lotus pose, with his hands resting on his knees. His ring fingers and thumbs were linked in what advanced Yogis would recognise as the Agni Vardhak Mudra, designed to increase bodily temperature. A visible heat shimmer could be seen rising from the seated figure so, although the room felt bitterly cold, clearly Fr Chin Kwon was coping. Maybe one of the hot water radiator feed pipes went under where he was seated, reflected O'Neill. Although the cell was the same size as the one loaned to O'Neill it seemed much darker. The numerous large spot lights that had been fitted must have been exceptionally low wattage, as they failed to penetrate the shadowy darkness in each of the cells four corners.

Large sections of the white plaster walls were painted with a perfect black script in Sanskrit, Aramaic and some form of Sumerian cuneiform, that O'Neill could only partially decipher even with his archaeological expertise. He was unsure of what the other words meant, but the Sanskrit writing was a series of sutras related to necromancy, and the cuneiform was a description of the War in Heaven, but written using an unusual form of personal pronoun.

A cultured voice in a clipped British Oxbridge accent addressed the visitors.

"I have been looking forward to meeting you for quite some time, Dr O'Neill. Please excuse my surroundings, I would offer you a chair but I am not permitted such luxuries."

O'Neill was momentarily taken aback by the personal greeting, but rapidly regained his composure.

"Thank you, Father Kwon. I am so sorry to find you in such a condition."

The cultured voice chuckled, "I fear Father Kwon is…." there was a significant pause

"Not quite himself. But then he was interested in certain of the Tibetan esoteric practices related to the transference of consciousness. So, there is some poetic justice in his situation, and the circumstances required I acquire some more... material means to address the physical world."

With that remark, the body that had been totally immobile in its Yogic pose, with his head bowed and eyes closed, opened his fingers, turned his head directly at O'Neill and opened his eyes. There was a subtle humour that could be read in the face but it was combined with some profound feeling of something being very wrong. It felt like one of those moments experienced just before some terrible disaster, when your mind cannot accept what is happening. The effect was so startling, that O'Neill could not help but take an involuntary step backwards. Verchencho clearly felt it as well, since he reacted by reaching for a large silver cross that hung around his neck. The cultured British accent changed effortlessly into perfect, but rather formal, eighteenth century court Italian, addressing the Exorcist.

"Oh Hugo, I did not intend to startle. There is no need for your Nazarean symbols. You know that I could walk from here in any of," the seated figure gestured with his left hand towards Sister Teresa, who had been standing silently by the door since their entrance. At his gesture, she dropped the keys she had been holding in her right hand, clearly experiencing a momentary loss of coordination, but then straightened and, taking a strange bird like step towards the two startled priests, she regarded them with that same awful gaze that O'Neill had experienced moments before from the seated figure and continued the sentence in that same formal eighteenth-century Italian.

"... the physical vehicles who guard this form. I have submitted to this confinement so we can have this specific meeting and conversation."

Verchencho reacted violently with a roaring stream of words, in a guttural language that was totally unknown to O'Neill, which coincided with an apparent electrical power surge as the small room was suddenly brightly illuminated, and filled with a powerful smell of burning flesh that must have been blown into the cell at that very moment from the nearby refectory.

The electrical power surge caused three or four of the twelve spotlights to blow explosively, sending shards of broken glass scattering in the confined space. Sister Teresa fell in a swoon to the ground, like a puppet whose strings are cut, and the seated figure shook and groaned in what clearly was violent pain. The continued electrical instability meant that the small cell was repeatedly plunged into moments of total darkness, as the lights rapidly cycled from full power to total black. The extremes of light and darkness caused a form of strobe illusion, as the seated figure, who rocked back and fore in agony, seemed for some moments to be transformed by the dark shadows into some hideous impossible creature.

As Verchencho's powerful voice continued his raging invocation, O'Neill found himself experiencing a deep visceral fear beyond anything he had ever imagined, and he could hear his own voice repeating the Lord's Prayer like a small child. The Exorcist eventually became silent. Moments passed, and the lights began to return to their former stable but dimmer setting. O'Neill sensed a crisis had passed, he stopped praying and knelt beside Sister Teresa, who indicated that she was recovered enough to call for a replacement to take over her duties. As she used the intercom by the door, the seated figure remained with his head bowed and he spoke again in the clipped British accent, but this time with a more mocking tone.

"The Tongue of Angels, Hugo? You know you are supposed to have the Holy Father's written consent. There really is no need to go all Old Testament on me, I meant no harm to the virgin, and I certainly did not intend to alarm Dr O'Neill. But it is productive in this circumstance that we have no more… pretence."

Verchencho retorted coldly, "Fine words from (the Exorcist used the Ancient Greek διάβολος diábolos) The Slanderer."

O'Neill interjected.

"What circumstance?"

The seated figure lifted his head and smiled.

"You will not like it any more than I, but circumstances mean that we will have to work together... or perish together."

Verchencho snarled. "What nonsense is this Semjâzâ of the Grigori? You know The Church will oppose you and all you stand for, until the Christ returns to consign you forever into darkness."

The seated figure issued a deep growling snarl, that was so deep that the stones in the cell floor could be felt vibrating through O'Neill's thick soled boots.

"You DARE to name me?"

The electric lighting flickered again and the room suddenly became much colder. O'Neill noticed that not only was his breath forming large clouds of steam, but the roof of the cell was starting to form a layer of heavy frost. O'Neill had stopped searching for natural explanations for the phenomena he was experiencing and instead crossed himself.

The British accent regained some of its former composure.

"You name me from your knowledge of the most ancient story of all, but know that there are always two sides to every story. Your scientists struggle to find an origin for creation, in truth they do so because creation is an instant transformation, from one complete state to another complete state. Each creation is simply a transformation from one former creation into another, with different physics and… different power structures. When one understands that there is one specific process to initiate such change and that whichever intelligence initiates that process becomes the next supreme being, one can aspire to use such a transformation to become the ultimate power."

Verchencho interjected, "Yes, but you failed, didn't you?"

The seated figure gave a sigh, "If you say so. I do not talk in the past tense, Hugo. For there is another who seeks to reunite the four sections of the most ancient book that was cast down from heaven with me."

"So why would you seek to stop them?" Asked the Exorcist.

"Simple," replied the clipped British voice, "Because if I cannot be God, then no one else can be. Let me work with the Church to stop this impostor and we can both return to… our more… traditional roles."

CHAPTER 14 - THE JENNA-EL-MOOTFAH

"Whoever said the pen is mightier than the sword obviously never encountered automatic weapons." — Douglas MacArthur

Gordon Square, Bloomsbury, London, England WC1
19.20HRS, 28th July, Present Day.

Issac bin Abdul Issuin was experiencing a rare moment of satisfaction, in what had been a particularly frustrating assignment, as he listened intently to the report coming from his encrypted Motorola Iridium Satellite Phone. A search and thorough interrogation of the staff at the Balmoral Hotel in Edinburgh, by Maelstrom team two, had revealed that the silver relic had almost certainly been brought to London. Further, his own search of the luggage in the Range Rover, now parked directly ahead of him, had convinced him that one of the three targets carried the item on their person. He had intended to render the small group unconscious and interrogate them at his leisure, having placed the gas canister in their vehicle but, now he knew where the item was, the non-lethal option was no longer necessary.

As he continued to reflect on the setbacks of the past days, he came to the realisation that, as Tavish Stewart had caused him so much personal embarrassment and difficulty, it was fitting that he had arranged that this Scotsman would die here, with his friends, in this quiet London square, that represented so much about the British establishment that Abdul Issuin despised.

As if in answer to his desire to bring a rapid and deadly conclusion to this assignment, two jet black Volkswagen Caravelle Business vans drove in close formation from Endsleigh Gardens down Gordon Street. The last of the two vans stopped in the road next to the police Mondeo, while the leading van continued to the South end of the square and slowed, allowing three heavily armed men to disembark from the side sliding door in a smooth, well-practiced manoeuvre. The men, all dressed in identical black commando suits with black Kevlar helmets, quickly huddled into kneeling positions behind a large old iron sign that declared cycling and ball games to be prohibited in the green space.

Meanwhile, Abdul Issuin and his young Longboard riding assistant removed the stolen police stab vests that they were wearing, deposited them on the bodies of the two dead Police Officers in the back and, exiting the Mondeo, rapidly entered the open side door of the waiting Caravelle.

Abdul Issuin's next act was to speed dial a pre-set number on his Motorola. Inside the boot of the police vehicle, a Nokia 106 mobile started to ring and initiated a one-minute delay to the PETN-based detonating cords connecting to a small green plastic suitcase labelled "US DOD M85: 16 x M112 block demolition charge".

As the two Volkswagen vans sped away in close formation down Byng Place towards Tottenham Court Road, a massive explosive pressure wave erupted from the parked police Mondeo, lifting the rear section of the car up and sending fragments of metal, plastic and road asphalt in a sixty-foot radius, devastating the surrounding buildings and setting off dozens of car alarms around the once tranquil square.

As Stewart, Sonnet and Curren were descending the stairs to leave 14a they felt the pressure wave, followed a second later by an enormous thumping sound that made the foundations of the building jump. The windows shattered and pictures fell from the walls. Susan, who was showing the three guests to the main door, would have fallen headlong down the steep stairs had not Stewart caught her. In amongst the numerous car alarms, Elizabeth Fitz-Glass's voice could be heard calling to her granddaughter to come and help her, as she had suffered some serious glass cuts. Curren offered her assistance and she and Susan hurried back up the stairs, whilst Stewart and Sonnet went to investigate the source of the explosion. As they emerged from the front door of 14a, they saw a black smoke cloud rising at the far end of Gordon Street and heard a sound that both men recognised as automatic gunfire.

Down at the South end of Gordon Square, the three men left from Maelstrom Team five, who had unsuccessfully raided Stewart's

Warehouse in Edinburgh, were led by Col. "Mad" Brad Wilson, a six-foot six-inch mountain of a man in his late thirties, with a shaved and tattooed head. Before joining Maelstrom, he had spent twelve years with the 1st Special Forces Operational Detachment-Delta (1st SFOD-D), better known as Delta force, at Fort Bragg, North Carolina. Second in command was "Rocky" Rocio Rodriguez, a short powerfully built man in his mid-forties, who had served in the Argentinean "Compañía de Comandos 601" based in Campo de Mayo, Buenos Aires, before joining Maelstrom. The final of the three men was William "Willy" White, an Australian with a dark criminal past, who had been recruited to Maelstrom from the French Foreign Legion, based at their headquarters in Aubagne, France.

To say that that the three men had a grudge against Tavish Stewart would be something of an understatement. When they were offered the chance to make amends for their humiliating defeat and the murder of three of their former team members they leapt at the opportunity, even declining the usual fee for such "extreme prejudice" eliminations.

After sheltering from the explosion, behind the "no ball games" sign, the three men rose, removed their sound protection ear plugs, and did a final weapons check.

Brad Wilson inspected the feed on the black unsuppressed Heckler and Koch MP5 N machine gun on his chest, loaded with 9mm Winchester Ranger T-Series jacketed hollow point rounds. His side arm was the standard Maelstrom Heckler and Koch Mk 23 Mod .45 Pistol, loaded with 144 Winchester Ranger T-Series .45 jacketed hollow point rounds. His Interceptor Body Armour carried numerous loaded magazines on specially designed harnesses. Strapped to his right calf was a wicked long Sykes Fairbairn commando knife.

Rodriguez also carried the Mk 23 .45 handgun, but instead of the MP5 N he had opted to carry a Maelstrom special item, the Luigi Franchi SPAS-15 12-gauge shotgun, with an eight-round magazine. His body armour reflected his choice of weapon, holding a variety of lethal and non-lethal rounds.

In contrast to his two team members, White carried his own personal weapons, a Remington Model 870 pump action shotgun and a 9mm Browning GP-35 Mk. III Hi-Power. As White completed checking his shotgun, two Metropolitan Police cycle transport officers, in high visibility jackets riding mountain pedal cycles, entered the South of Gordon Square from Byng Place. Seeing the three heavily armed men in paramilitary dress, they demanded they put down their weapons and lie face down on the pavement.

The big American smiled and exclaimed.

"More faggot unarmed Brits... here, this should bring that Scottish prick running right into our sights." He sprayed the nearest unarmed officer with two short three round bursts from his MP5 N. The six Winchester Ranger T-Series rounds passed through the Police Officer's stab vest like it was tissue paper, and his body jerked before falling to the road. His colleague tried to move his pedal cycle around to escape, but he too suddenly spasmed as another two short bursts of death erupted from the US manufactured machine gun. The loud cracks from its unsuppressed barrel reverberated around Gordon Square, deliberately letting their quarry know that death was coming for them.

The three-man Maelstrom team then split up, with Rodriguez and White going through the central green park space of Gordon Square to emerge at the North end, while Wilson walked calmly down Gordon Street towards Stewart and the parked Range Rover.

At the other end of the small road, Stewart and Sonnet had viewed the callous murder of the two Police Officers. Both men could see the single heavily armed figure walking steadily towards them. Stewart turned to his friend.

"Jeff, can you get the Range Rover over here, while I get Helen?"

Sonnet's response was to set off into a run, down Gordon Street, directly towards the armed figure that walked confidently towards them, only slowing his pace as he carefully made his way through the debris that littered the road surface.

Whilst unlocking the Range Rover with the remote key fob, Sonnet could see that all the armoured glass in the Overfinch had already formed into a characteristic spider web pattern, where it had shattered from the high velocity impacts. Reaching the driver's front door, the massive SUV started swaying, as the approaching Maelstrom gunman started to spray the vehicle with bullets, deforming the bodywork and causing thin shards of metal and paintwork to fly wildly around, cutting Sonnet's left cheek and forehead.

Sonnet managed to pull the driver's side door open, but had to quickly withdraw behind it, still outside the Overfinch, as the large Maelstrom commando appeared on the pavement beside the SUV, grinning as he pointed a menacing machine gun and opened fire again.

Holding the door handle, Sonnet could feel each of the 9mm rounds smash into the International Armoring Corporation (IAC) reinforced steel and Kevlar structure of the SUV's door. Knowing that even the Armormax bullet proofing could not survive such sustained abuse, he reached beneath his leather jacket to his Galco Executive shoulder holster and drew his old FCO service pistol, a well-worn Walther Polizeipistole Kriminalmodell (PPK). Taking aim around the door, Sonnet peered through the now heavily cracked glass, and the ancient .380 barked a total of nine times, sending its rounds slamming into the chest of the figure of his attacker at 1,000 feet per second.

Wilson grinned as his Maelstrom Interceptor Body Armour absorbed the light rounds without harm and he heard the click of an empty magazine from Sonnet's weapon.

"Is that it? Everything British is so fucking underpowered. Give me your best shot!"

Just as the big American prepared to raise his weapon to finish things, a shadow appeared beside Sonnet saying in a Scottish Accent.

"If you insist..."

There was a deafening roar as Stewart's Sig Sauer P229 Special spoke, sending it's 90 grain SIG .357 MIL Penetrator round at nearly 2,000 feet per second, impacting Wilson's chest with nearly 700-foot pounds of energy, sending the big man rocking backwards. Unlike the reaction to Sonnet's rounds there was no hilarity, instead a tiny bullet sized hole appeared at the left edge of the ceramic plate in Wilson's chest armour, and a golf ball sized lump of Kevlar, from the front of the Interceptor vest, burst from his back, flying some sixteen feet away onto the pavement. The huge American looked startled, blood started to pour from his mouth, as he fell to one knee and then slowly backward with his MP5 firing wildly up into the air, until Stewart walked round the open SUV door and fired a second round into the American's skull, pronouncing,

"Remind me to send a case of Vodka to Lev..."

Sonnet came next to Stewart and nodded to the SIG handgun.

"I have to get one of those..."

At that moment, the SUV started rocking wildly again, as two more armed figures became visible from the North end of Gordon Street. Both carried powerful shotguns that blasted alternatively at Sonnet and Stewart from around 165 feet further up the street. The much heavier shotgun rounds impacted the already damaged armoured windshield and it was clear that within moments the glass would fail. Regardless of the impending failure, Stewart assumed a firing position from behind the front door and again the air was filled with the fierce roar of the SIG.

Rodriguez was closest and had assumed a defensive position on the other side of Gordon Street, behind a parked red Fiat Panda. Stewart directed his fire at the side of the Fiat, the specialised SIG .357 Penetrator rounds going clean through the entire car structure and impacting into the stone walls of the house fronts behind the car. Seeing the car was no barrier to Stewart's deadly volley, Rodriguez rapidly retreated from car to car away from the now badly battered Range Rover, while White unleashed a barrage of heavy covering fire from his Remington.

"I hate to say it Jeff, but as good as this SIG is we badly need something with a bit more…"

Stewart never finished the sentence, as he saw Sonnet retrieving the long leather bag that had been resting in the front passenger seat and opening the six sets of leather fastening straps to reveal the contents.

"It cannot be..." exclaimed Stewart, picking up an exquisitely carved steel and wood nineteenth century shotgun with the maker's mark "Holland of Bond Street" and a barrel that looked like it could fire tennis balls.

"Sir Samuel White Baker's "Jenna-El-Mootfah". I thought it was just a legend… and, based on the paperwork, it's just back from a complete restoration… please tell me you have some ammunition?"

Sonnet smiled, as he pulled open another large leather satchel to reveal a dozen 1.3-inch (33.7 mm) diameter solid bronze shells, beautifully engraved with the inscription "Jenna-El-Mootfah - Child of a Cannon - eight ounces - 225 grams."

Stewart began to smile, "Must have a bitch of a recoil,"

clearly doing some rough calculations in his head,

"Roughly 15,000 ft. lbs of energy?"

Sonnet grinned, "Nearer 17,500 ft. lbs."

"Well, we have seen what the modern American and German technology can do... let's see what a little nineteenth century British classic gun smithing can bring to the party."

Stewart broke open the barrel on the huge gun, entered the monstrous bronze shell, closed the breach with a loud click and placed the long barrel between the open door and the body of the SUV, pointing down Gordon Street.

At that moment, Rodriguez rose from behind the far side of a large silver Jaguar XF saloon car, having placed himself in the safest position behind the far rear axle and began discharging round after round from the SPAS-15 12-gauge shotgun. The armoured bodywork of the Overfinch began to disintegrate, large sections of shredded Kevlar were now exposed in the metal chassis, and heavy twelve-gauge military rounds were entering the vehicle, causing seat stuffing to fly around within the cabin.

Just as the situation of the two men sheltering behind the remains of the Range Rover looked dire, there was a bright flash, followed by what sounded for all the world like cannon fire. The SUV became hidden behind thick clouds of black smoke as half a pound of brass accelerated at nearly twice the speed of sound towards the Jaguar.

The 3500-grain round hit the Jaguar saloon car with nearly 25,000 joules of energy, flipping and rotating it into the air like a toy, before it landed on the pavement crushing Rodriguez onto the iron railings. Back at the Overfinch, the recoil of the enormous two bore gun had ripped the door off its hinges, forcing Stewart and Sonnet to advance to the shelter of the white Vauxhall Antara, that was parked in front of the wrecked Overfinch on Gordon Square. Both men searched carefully for the remaining man, Stewart holding the Jenna-El-Mootfah and Sonnet the SIG.

While Rodriguez had been unleashing a barrage of twelve-gauge rounds, White had decided on a subtler approach. Walking away from the battle he had used his Remington Model 870 pump action shotgun to demolish the four Yale locks that protected the 14a Gordon Street front door. Once inside, he had found two women on the ground floor, one of whom was wearing the silver relic around her neck. As he moved to pull this dark-haired woman with him as a hostage, the younger blonde girl had rushed to her defence. Grabbing White's hand, Susan had tried to wrestle Curren free but instead she found herself only with one of the man's black Kevlar gloves. She died moments later, with a look of surprise on her face, as the Australian followed up with a precise stab with his commando dagger into the blonde girl's solar plexus and up under her ribs. Susan's white cotton clothes rapidly turned crimson, as she fell backwards to the marble floor.

White retrieved the now bloody blade and placed it with the point against Curren's throat, dragging his hostage out into the street. Moments later, Stewart and Sonnet saw the former French Foreign Legion Sergeant guiding a blood soaked Curren at knife point towards them. Curren walked on tip toe in front of White, trying to avoid the wicked stiletto blade from cutting deeper than it already had. The blood from her wounds and the splatter from Susan, meant that she looked like she had come from an abattoir. White was in complete control, and called to Stewart and Sonnet to lay down their weapons and to kneel in the centre of the road with their hands on their heads.

Back inside 14a, Elizabeth Fitz-Glass knelt beside her granddaughter's dead form, tears dripping from her eyes and mingling with the thick blood that flowed over the white marble floor, making a macabre ink blot pattern around the body. Tightly clutched in Susan's dead fingers was the tactical Kevlar glove. Stifling her tears and with a determined expression, Elizabeth gently pried the glove free and, reaching to her head, pulled a thick wad of her own hair away in a violent motion. Taking the strands of hair, she began winding them around the Kevlar glove, binding the fingers and thumbs tighter and tighter, until they formed the rough shape of a man. Fitz-Glass then rose and walked calmly out of the broken front door and onto the pavement, only pausing to pick up one of the many fine shreds of glass that now littered the once peaceful street. As she walked calmly towards the figures of the Australian and Curren, she slowly and deliberately ran the sharp glass against her palm, causing her own blood to mingle with her hair and the Kevlar figure. Once within sixty feet of the standoff, she pushed the glass shard deep into the neck of the poppet.

Far above them on one of the roof windows, a sudden gust of wind disturbed some of the explosion debris, causing a twelve-inch razor sharp piece of broken window pane to fly off the window ledge into the strong wind. The aerodynamic shape of the fragment caused it first to hover and then to glide rapidly like a giant paper airplane. Just as suddenly as the wind had come up it subsided, so that the section of glass plunged downwards towards the road.

Stewart and Sonnet knelt defeated before the Australian, awaiting their certain execution, when there was a flash of rapid movement. The long shard of glass buried itself deep into the back of the Australian's neck, severing the third and fourth vertebrae and killing him instantly. As White's body fell forward, revealing the lethal projectile protruding from his neck, Elizabeth Fitz-Glass walked deliberately up beside Curren and threw down a small blood-stained object onto the Australian's dead body. She reached over and gently removed the silver folio from the neck of the stunned Curren, who was still clearly in shock.

"This object brings nothing but destruction… so it must never fall into the wrong hands. All the ancient legends regarding the Emerald Tablets make mention of a Knight from the North who will stand, with a doubting priest of Rome and a Fallen Angel, against the darkness. Having met you Sir Stewart, I have no doubt that you are the intended custodian of this relic,"

She handed Stewart the silver folio.

"You must vanish before the authorities arrive and take the relic from you, making it easier for it to fall into the wrong hands and thus allow the evil that is seeking it to reunite all four parts. With the help of your two friends, we can keep the authorities occupied and will no doubt enjoy their hospitality for some time. But you Sir Stewart have, I would suggest, an urgent quest to find yourself a doubting priest of Rome."

Sonnet and Curren signalled their agreement, and Stewart reluctantly acquiesced. He gestured to Sonnet to give him the SIG, wiping it carefully with the fabric of his jacket to remove his finger prints, then switched it with the Hi-Power in the dead Australian's holster and collected two of the Browning's thirteen round magazines, placing them in his jacket pockets. Shaking hands with Sonnet and giving Curren and Elizabeth a hug, Stewart walked quickly down some steps to a basement passageway that led from Gordon Street to Gower Street.

FOLIO 3 – THE FEMALE OF THE SPECIES

CHAPTER 15 - COBRAS AND OTHER SNAKES

"Maelstrom provides Governments with enormous opportunities in terms of outsourcing security and intelligence operations. Our clients benefit not just from having access to multiple national intelligence data sets, but also from Maelstrom's intimate knowledge of every other nation's security and intelligence services. At the highest level of our business tariff, clients are able to directly influence the actions of target nations, because it is Maelstrom who already controls them." - Frank Foster – President and CEO, Maelstrom

Conference Room A, Cabinet Office, (COBR, often referred to as COBRA)
70 Whitehall, London, SW1A 2AS
21.11HRS, 29th July, Present Day.

The mood was sombre in the blandly decorated first floor conference room, as a low-resolution TV feed projected onto the furthest wall showed the devastation in Gordon Square. The BBC News was devoting an in-depth exclusive on the event, asking the same question to assorted experts,

"Why didn't the intelligence services provide any warning?"

A running banner at the bottom of the screen showed that at least six people were dead and seventy-eight wounded.

Prime Minister Simon Brinkwater muted the sound and turned to the assembled group. Prior to watching this latest update on the television, he had listened to acknowledgements of failures and ignorance from everyone around the long dark wood table. They were all, without exception, thought Brinkwater, relics of a bygone way of approaching security, insular and inefficient.

Clive Basildon, Director General, MI5 and Brigadier Tony Green, Director, United Kingdom Special Forces (UKSF), had rather predictably closed ranks and indicated that any and all failures were from either the Secret Intelligence Service or the Police. Their offices could only respond to threats when they were informed about them.

Dame Cynthia Sinclair, Director General of SIS and Sir Alan Williams, Chief Constable of the Metropolitan Police, were currently in a situation where they were receiving intermittent and incomplete information on their smartphones, as their staff desperately played catch up on an event that had already ended. As was always the case, the journalists were the best informed in the first twenty-four hours after an incident.

Brinkwater gave a dramatic sigh. The stress and late hour meant that the air felt stale. He would rather be back at Chequers, where he had been planning to spend the weekend. The only interesting sight from the dirty windows of this nineteenth century building were the few remains of Henry VIII's tennis courts. Fortunately, Gerald Seymour had come up trumps again. A way to show these incompetent establishment dinosaurs how security and intelligence could be outsourced to corporate resources at reduced cost and dramatically increased efficiency.

"Well, we have heard everything your combined services have available, so let's make way for more modern alternatives. I have invited Mr Frank Foster, CEO of Maelstrom to our meeting today to see what his organisation can do to assist us in this crisis."

If Foster could feel the animosity from the gathered heads of UK security, intelligence and policing, he did not show it. While Brinkwater had been introducing him, one of his staff members had turned off the old Cabinet office video projector they had been using and turned on a state of the art projection system that split into six separate views. At that moment, three of the screens were showing aerial views of Gordon Square from small drones that were flying just above tree height. The feeds were in visible and infrared light. From these images, it was clear that the road and green space were being examined by numerous police officers carrying plastic evidence bags.

Another screen showed central London, focusing on Gordon Square, with a title "routes detected", the fifth screen was a blank list showing "financial transactions" and the final screen showed a facility where smartly dressed operatives were surrounded with an extraordinary range of state of the art equipment.

As Frank Foster walked to the front of the room, his three staff members handed out envelopes containing an information pack, a pen and a small lapel badge with the Maelstrom whirlpool logo. The assembled group exchanged glances that clearly showed a mixture of surprise and discomfort, as they began to contemplate potentially dramatic changes to their respective roles.

"Thank you, Mr Prime Minister, for giving us this opportunity to provide assistance to your colleagues."

Foster smiled a fake greeting at the assembled group and nodded to one of his assistants, at which point three of the screens switched to showing the feeds, from what were clearly combat helmet Point of View (PoV) cameras, of Gordon Street and Gordon Square during the recent terror event. The dark plume of smoke from the car explosion was clearly visible and the sound of automatic gunfire could be heard.

"Jesus Christ!" Exclaimed Cynthia Sinclair, "How did you get this?"

"And under whose authority are Maelstrom conducting armed manhunts on UK soil?" Demanded Alan Williams.

The footage continued to run. It was heavily edited, only showing the perspective from the wearers of the helmet cameras being shot at by two figures huddled around a heavily damaged Range Rover on Gordon Street.

Frank Foster highlighted a series of freeze frame shots, showing a specific individual shooting with extraordinary skill at whoever had been wearing one of the cameras. The figure was enhanced and displayed next to a formal military portrait of Sir Tavish Stewart.

There was a gasp of shock from Brigadier Tony Green.

"Colleagues, our detailed analysis shows that our principal suspect is a Tavish Stewart, working with three associates,"

Pictures of Jeff, Helen and Elizabeth filled separate screens.

"Who, we believe, cause a clear and present danger to the United Kingdom."

There was a moments silence.

"Are you seriously suggesting that a former Colonel and recipient of the Victoria Cross is a terrorist?" Asked Clive Basildon, clearly incredulous.

"And your second suspect Jeffrey Sonnet was the SIS section head for Moscow."

Added Cynthia Sinclair, in a tone that indicated growing contempt.

"I can understand your reluctance to accept the truth, that is why I prepared the evidence summaries in the envelopes that have just been distributed."

As the assembled group opened and read the materials there were more comments of incredulity from the heads of MI5 and SIS.

As one of the Maelstrom staff at the remote intelligence centre described the full extent of the monitoring that was now being brought into play to find their target, Cynthia Sinclair searched in her red Gucci handbag, retrieved and then dropped a well-worn copy of a NATO handbook entitled "Escape and evasion under a surveillance state" by T. Stewart" on the conference table remarking,

"Do you have any idea who you are hunting?"

Just as Frank Foster was about to respond, there was a cry of delight from the Maelstrom control room. Tavish Stewart had made some purchases on his credit card at the Students Union shop at University College near Gordon Square, a batch of numbered travel cards for London Buses and Underground trains, along with some blue London University hoodie sweat tops.

Foster smiled.

"Got him! Begin surveillance on the use of those travel cards and," turning to the Police Commissioner.

"Your uniformed officers can start looking for people wearing blue London University hoodies. Use all available street patrols and your CCTV. Hop to it."

Just as the Commissioner was about to make a protest about the proper COBR platinum gold–silver–bronze command structure, there was another loud triumphant cry from the Maelstrom command centre. Stewart's credit card had just purchased an advance train ticket online for the 23.50 HRS from Euston to Edinburgh, the last train of the evening.

The projected route through the underground to Euston and then onto Edinburgh now appeared in flashing red on the screens, along with the locations where the credit card had been used.

The baby faced Brinkwater began to laugh like a spoilt public-school boy who has just humiliated a rival.

Foster looked pointedly at Dame Sinclair.

"Stewart is not as impressive as you thought, my dear. But your misplaced faith is understandable as all of you,"

He gestured grandly to the whole group.

"Are about to be relegated to the museum. Watch and learn".

Foster instructed his staff at the control room to move three Maelstrom teams to Euston Station in preparation for Tavish's arrival. Just as he turned to his three smartly dressed colleagues, who were assisting him in the COBR conference room, there was a further announcement from the Maelstrom control room. More train tickets were being booked. The screen showed the departure stations, each appearing one after the other, as if on an airport departure board.

Canonbury
Malden Manor
Ealing Broadway
Earlsfield
Tadworth
Tattenham Corner
Hackbridge
Rainham
East Croydon
East Dulwich
Abbey Wood
Malden Manor…

The list grew, as all 366 London stations appeared one by one. The routes began also to appear on a separate screen in red. Gradually the entire London public rail and bus network became highlighted.

Sinclair and Commissioner Alan Williams exchanged a knowing glance at each other as the head of SIS started to gather her things to leave.

At that same moment, the automated ANPR Interceptor systems began to report movement of Stewart's car registration plate. Foster begin to look increasingly stressed as the screen displaying the road network of central London began to light up, showing multiple scanned sightings of the same registration plate moving everywhere within central London.

As if not wanting to be left out, the screen tracking the financial transactions began to load information rapidly, displaying credit card purchases all over central London and then at hundreds of international locations. The high-resolution tracking map was now a solid red showing activity on every bus, rail and road within the central region.

Brinkwater stared at Foster with anger, demanding.

"What the hell is happening?"

Cynthia Sinclair smiled as she exited the room, answering for all of them.

"Tavish Stewart is what is happening..."

CHAPTER 16 - THE HUNTED

"Certainly, there is no hunting like the hunting of man and those who have hunted armed men long enough and liked it, never really care for anything else thereafter." -- Ernest Hemingway, "On the Blue Water" Esquire, April 1936

Gower St, London WC1E 6BT
19.48HRS, 28th July, Present day (one hour before the COBRa meeting)

Stewart took a moment to dust off the assorted debris that had accumulated on his jacket, trousers and shoes, before walking calmly up from the basement passageway that he had followed from Gordon Street. He emerged onto the Gower Street pavement and turned towards the UCL (University College London) Students Union entrance, with an ease that made him look like he did this every day, and calmed the numerous thoughts that were running through his head.

Around him police vehicles, fire engines and ambulances screamed their assorted sirens as they rushed to Gordon Square, paralyzing all other traffic. The summer sky was filled with the sound of police and TV helicopters that fought for the space above him. At the end of Gower Street, opposite Waterstone's book shop, were parked two black Ketterer Continental Motorhomes with Maelstrom whirlpool livery. The rear tail gates were open and a group of five men, all dressed in black combat fatigues, assisted by three uniformed police officers, were removing four small reconnaissance drones from within the two massive vehicles. Stewart noted the location of the Maelstrom mobile command centres with a wicked smile, as a plan started to form in his mind.

Inside the Student's Union building, Stewart went straight to the student shop, which was having a late-night sale for the foreign exchange students and, rapidly scanning the range of clothing, he gathered up around thirty blue London University hoodies. Taking them to the single staff member he asked about travel cards explaining as he purchased the hoodies and thirty numbered travel passes, that he was hosting a group visit. After paying with his credit card, Stewart walked deliberately across the entrance hall, pausing only to remove one of the "Welcome to UCL" signs from a notice board, and then made his way into the student dining room, which was only partly full.

Selecting several empty tables near the exit, he rearranged them and spread out all but one of the travel cards and all the hoodies in an inviting circular pattern, around the "Welcome to UCL" poster he had removed. Most of the hoodies and passes had already been taken by the time Stewart exited the building. He walked at a steady pace along Grafton way to Warren Street underground station, where he took the Victoria line to Oxford Circus using the remaining travel card. On exiting Oxford Circus, he left the travel card conspicuously on one of the ticket dispensers where it was rapidly taken by a tired looking man struggling with bags of shopping, who smiled at his good fortune to get free travel home to Notting Hill, but who unwittingly now spun an electronic false trail that would drain the coming search effort.

Consulting his Speedmaster Chronograph, Stewart noted he had taken twenty-seven minutes to get from Gordon Square to Stewart's Antiquarians New Bond Street premises, including his detour to the UCL student's union. By his estimation, he had thirty minutes more before his world would be enveloped in a thick electronic net.

The shop front was closed, with a thick steel shutter painted with fancy Stewart's Antiquarians signage, but the office space above was accessible through a side door, up two flights of narrow stairs which were covered with a well-worn black and white tile pattern linoleum.

Once inside the first-floor office space, Stewart strode purposefully to the communal washroom and, by accessing a pair of concealed handles located behind the small plastic shower unit, slid it sideways into the corridor. The floor under the movable shower had two sets of rails set into it that ran the length of the tiling, with the exception of a central drainage fixing.

The exposed wall behind the shower space revealed a thick metal Leopold Feuerstein custom safe door, that looked like a cross between the entrance to a bank vault and a nuclear bunker. The door opened with a hydraulic hiss in response to Stewart placing his eye to a small lens that was embedded in the metal. A motion sensing strip light immediately came on, revealing a long narrow room around six and a half feet wide and twenty-three feet long, which ran the entire length of the first-floor office. The walls and floor were made of a single welded structure, marked occasionally with the Leopold Feuerstein logo. Alongside the racks of precious antique items, waiting to either be shipped out to their new owners or catalogued, were stashed a number of canvas storage bags, in a wide range of shapes and sizes, resting on tall black metal shelving.

Stewart identified a big army kit bag which he opened and quickly retrieved a stack of thirty thin self-adhesive car registration plates, all bearing the same number. Taking these plastic plates, he closed the concealed strong room, exited down the stairs and walked towards Oxford Street, where he encountered a line of empty parked taxis whose owners were taking a hurried dinner. Taking care not to attract attention, Stewart rapidly placed ten of the sticky plates on the cabs and then walked on. When he reached the main thoroughfare of Oxford Street, he worked his way beside each passing double decker bus as they pulled into the nearby bus stops, attaching the remaining registration plates before the vehicles set off again along their different routes.

Returning to the Stewart's Antiquarians first floor office, Tavish Stewart sat at the secretary's desk and called Anna, his regular contact at the Omega 24-hour travel agency that operated from offices in Charing Cross. Although she thought it was an unusual request, Anna made the 366 long distance rail bookings in the exact order Stewart requested and charged them to his personal credit card. Hanging up, Stewart then logged into the office Lenovo workstation and went to web sites in Holland, Poland and Russia in order to do some deliberately insecure online transactions. Within moments, his debit card details had been passed to numerous servers which proceeded to rapidly empty one of his smaller petty cash accounts. Stewart smiled as his Samsung smartphone alerted him that his last transaction had been rejected due to lack of funds, knowing a time-consuming series of false electronic trails had been established.

Consulting the accumulated time on his Speedmaster, he gathered together his smartphone and bank cards and put them all into the microwave on high power for five minutes so they could no longer be used to track him. The bright arcing light from the shorting electrical components, combined with the acrid smell of melting plastic, filled the small office space. As this "silicon zapping" took place, Stewart changed into some very old military fatigues, worn black leather boots, and a black woollen beanie hat that he had taken from the old kit bag, and checked the contents of a battered sixty litre camouflage bergen backpack.

Taking a one litre bottle of whisky from an Ikea drinks cabinet in the small office kitchen, he took a swig and then doused a much larger quantity from the bottle over his jacket and trousers, lamenting the waste under his breath. Grabbing fifteen tea bags from the cupboard, he made a quick cold brew in the office tea urn, which he then poured into the now empty whisky bottle.

Remarking to himself that he smelt like a distillery, he turned off the office lights, walked over to the windows, opened them slowly and, assuming a kneeling position, aimed a small black Webley Typhoon .177 break barrel air pistol at the CCTV cameras that covered this area of New Bond Street. The small calibre air pistol made an almost silent report three times, each followed by the sound of breaking glass. Stewart returned the small pistol to a side pocket in his backpack and, after checking that the microwave had done its work on the cards and electronic items, he put the entire molten mess in a bowl of water and exited to the street below.

Down on New Bond Street it was now much quieter, the lull between people going home after work and those going out for a night of fun. Temporarily free from the CCTV observation, Stewart opened one of the first street bins he found, checking carefully in case of sharp objects, and rubbed his face with a used newspaper to give himself an unwashed look. Finally, he took a bit of unfinished pizza and dabbed it carefully on his top and trousers to complete the "homeless veteran" look he was cultivating.

Moving down one of the nearby dark alleyways, he was almost immediately accosted by two men, brandishing a baseball bat and demanding he hand over his backpack. Issuing some platitudes in a strong slurring Scottish accent, he staggered towards them clutching the whisky bottle in his left hand. He bumped into the nearest of the two men, blocking the baseball bat and delivering an upwards sliding atemi strike with the edge of his right hand against the man's carotid artery. The man's legs buckled, as he fell, senseless to the alley floor, filling the enclosed space with the distinct smell of urine. Following the natural path of his advance, Stewart bumped immediately into the second man, catching an attempted right hand straight punch and transforming it into an elbow overextension (a variant of Maki Hiji Nage) which, with an effortless switch of balance, put him behind his opponent, enabling him to deliver a wickedly rapid shime-waza sleeper hold. Within six seconds, the would-be mugger was semiconscious and began to twitch uncontrollably in his deep muscle groups, as if in a macabre kind of dance.

Minutes later, two unsteady figures made their way down Conduit Street, through Regent Street, where Stewart paused to discreetly deposit a small parcel in a public post box, and then headed up to Oxford Circus. They were avoided by passers-by and ignored by the police, appearing to be just two more of London's vast army of homeless people. The pair finally settled down for the night at 9.45pm in the door front of Waterstones book shop, at the junction between Gower Street and Torrington Place, directly in front of the two enormous Maelstrom Ketterer Continentals.

Tavish Stewart expertly surveyed the scene, looking for any security weaknesses that he could exploit, as he needed to get some time inside the control suite to learn what Foster's goons were planning. Maelstrom had set up enormous arc lights around their two mobile command centres, powered from a single Hyundai HY12000LE-3 petrol generator located between the two vehicles. Stewart noted that they had only posted two guards to patrol the perimeter of the area around the vehicles, each armed with the standard Maelstrom Composite H&K MP5 N machine guns that he had seen at the Edinburgh warehouse. Foster only recruited from former special forces personnel for Maelstrom, so Stewart knew that such guard duties would be as unwelcome as they were unfamiliar for these men and, just as he expected, by 10.30 PM the two operatives had started to become bored. By 11.00 PM they had stopped their moving patrols and fixed their positions at separate ends of the mobile units, each under one of the powerful lights.

Stewart took this as his cue, carefully stopping the systematic pressure point sedation of his doorway companion. Within minutes, the would-be mugger started to show signs of increased awareness and finally lurched to his feet, stumbling into a run onto Gower Street up towards the Euston Road. This sudden movement created an irresistible distraction for the two bored Maelstrom guards, who both chased and then tasered their target. As this scene unfolded, Stewart calmly carried his backpack from the Waterstones doorway and silently rolled into the darkness under the nearest Ketterer.

In the confined space, under what was the accommodation unit, he donned Viper heavy military knee and shin pads, that made the lower part of his body look like he was preparing to play a cricket match. As Stewart had planned, dealing with the tasered man and calling in the police had fully occupied the two Maelstrom guards, allowing him the time to unpack a length of Akzo Nobel expanding latex hose from his backpack and connect the exhaust of the noisy Hyundai generator to the air intake for the right hand Ketterer unit, which Stewart had identified as the Maelstrom command and control centre.

By 11.45pm a police van had picked up the mugger and the two guards shared a cigarette together under the single arc light near Gower street, discussing what evidently had been the highpoint of their evening. Stewart maximized the opportunity of having both guards located together in a single location, by reaching into his bergen and silently casting numerous small ball bearings along the far side of the two Ketterers and then, pulling the pin on an airsoft TLSFx Thunderflash M12 flash bang grenade, expertly rolled the M12 down the full length of the two massive vehicles.

Just as it seemed the excitement was over for the night, the two Maelstrom operatives noticed the sound of a small metal object rolling along the tarmac, followed by a brilliant flash of light and a thunderous loud bang resonating from the vehicle furthest away from them. The flash-bang made the two guards instinctively run down the side of the massive Ketterer Continentals to investigate, but their rapid dash was abruptly brought to a halt as both men lost their footing on the numerous tiny metal spheres that were now spread invisibly over the tarmac.

As the two men tumbled to the asphalt, Stewart used his jujitsu knee walking (Shikko Waza) skills, combined with the protection given by the thick knee pads, to slide over the ball bearings, strike both men unconscious and drag them under the accommodation module, where he rapidly bound them with some nylon paracord into a classic jujitsu Nawajutsu rope restraint.

Time was now against Stewart, as he was acutely aware that he could be discovered by a random police patrol or Maelstrom unit at any minute. Taking a deep breath, the Scotsman entered the second Ketterer and, finding the three operatives inside unconscious from the carbon monoxide they had been inhaling for the best part of an hour, he quickly had the three sleeping bodies join the two guards tightly bound under their own mobile accommodation trailer.

Aware of the ever-increasing danger of being discovered with every passing moment, Stewart rapidly disconnected the exhaust tube from the generator and vented the control room to purge any remaining fumes. He then removed the four metal wheel chocks and climbed into the cab of the massive Ketterer Continental, using the key he had found helpfully labelled in a cabinet inside the now empty control room.

The massive Actros fifteen litre Mercedes engine started first time and Stewart allowed himself a small smile as he deliberately made an illegal right hand turn down Malet Street, ignoring the No Entry signs. Steering the vehicle down the A400 past St Martin in the Fields, down the Mall, past Buckingham Palace to the A302, then along the A202, he crossed Vauxhall Bridge, finally parking the Ketterer in an empty car park at 89 Camelford House. Although surrounded by CCTV cameras, even at such a late hour the enormous trailer attracted little attention, as many artists used the area for overnight parking when performing with the London Philharmonic Orchestra.

After Stewart had expanded the Ketterer's double pop out mid-section, he rapidly entered the luxurious white control room and seated himself in the central control seat. He quickly searched through the numerous video feeds stored within the state of the art surveillance system and was able to find the full unedited footage from the three-man Maelstrom team that had attacked Gordon Square.

Viewing the live Maelstrom drone camera feeds, that were being accessed by numerous news networks, Stewart switched the data sources. Soon TV Channels in the US and Asia picked up the recording showing Maelstrom operatives murdering two UK police officers, shooting at Jeff Sonnet, brutally stabbing an unarmed woman and holding a female hostage at knifepoint. The POV cameras clearly showed the savage and merciless aggression of Maelstrom, that contradicted the official UK government statements regarding the Gordon Square incident. As Stewart monitored the major news networks, the real events at Gordon Square gradually became the leading news. The BBC was the last to stream the new footage, using it, almost reluctantly, to replace the previous Government coverage of Sir Stewart being a terror suspect on the run.

However, Stewart ignored all this, as he had become distracted by one of the other recordings on the Maelstrom system. It showed a luxurious bedroom with a familiar male figure seated in an ornate antique wooden chair, wearing only a shirt. His black shoes, expensive suit jacket and trousers lay discarded next to a Chanel silk pencil skirt on the wooden floor, forming a trail to the chair. Standing next to him, with her long naked right leg raised so that her six-inch Louboutin high heel rested on the groin of the seated man, was a stunning blonde. She adopted a totally dominating stance, while British Prime Minister Simon Brinkwater was encouraged by another male voice to inhale more of a white powder from her exposed thigh. As Brinkwater shuddered in ecstasy, the camera angle widened to show corporate spin doctor Gerald Seymour directing the entire scene from a live video feed.

A female voice behind Stewart diverted his attention.

"Never did like that little prick."

Cynthia Sinclair looked elegant but tired. She wore a long black trench coat over a dark blue silk Prada business suit along with classic four-inch black heels. In her hand, she held a small black Colt 380 Government pistol.

"I didn't think the video gave a clear enough view to tell if it was small."

Stewart replied as he rose from his seat, kissing the Chief of the British Secret Intelligence Service in an embrace that spoke of intimacy.

Sinclair closed her eyes, clearly glad that Stewart was safe. Then she pushed him away.

"You smell like a distillery. Bloody taste like one too!"

She gestured to the control room.

"Couldn't you steal anything smaller?"

"It was all they had available." Replied Stewart mischievously.

Sinclair walked back to the open door of the control room, and gestured for someone to come in.

"Brinkwater will resign before dawn. I will see to it personally."

She placed an emphasis on the word personally that left no doubt of her feelings towards the Prime Minister.

"I assumed you might want to talk with Frank Foster,"

continued Sinclair,

"So, I had him followed to a nice little place by the river. Thought you might like to take a boat trip and drop in on Frank for an early breakfast."

A man wearing a neoprene military wetsuit carrying a C8 SFW Carbine (L119A1) entered the control room. He was not wearing any insignia, but introduced himself as Lt. Collins of Z Squadron Special Boat Service (SBS).

Stewart kissed Sinclair and said, "What would I do without you?"

CHAPTER 17 - THE FEMALE OF THE SPECIES

"...it would be the arrogance of men never to consider that the Belial (Babylonian Tiamat, Queen of the abyss, bringer of the end of days) would be fair of form, promoting peace and promising a fairer world. Drawing universal admiration for fearlessly opposing centuries of corrupt self-interest that perpetuated injustice and poverty. She has no desire for anything in this creation and that makes Her the more dangerous for She will use any and all to get what She desires..." - Bahman Yast: Zoroastrian Apocalyptic Prophecies

35°31'42.9"N 25°13'37.0"E
Aboard the 283m "Tiamat" Migaloo M7 Submersible-Yacht,
Sea of Crete, 50 Nautical Miles North of Heraklion, Crete
13.00HRS, 29th July, Present Day.

In the exclusive world of the super-rich, possessions cease to be just a measure of success or return on an investment. Instead, as one's wealth increases, there comes a moment when your power, influence and riches exceed those of the nation in which you live. For most of us, possessions and especially dwellings, provide security from the uncontrollable elements of existence. However, even enormous stone walls, isolation and the best security in the world are little protection once one becomes perceived as a threat, or as more often happens, your success attracts the envy of those who wield the reins of Government. For when Governments wish, property can be seized, assets confiscated and even monarchs have ended their lives imprisoned.

For this reason, although land based mansions can provide a sound investment and a mark of status, for those whose success and power are so great as to provoke such envy, the private yacht provides an incomparable sanctuary where the super-rich and powerful can live free from the potential sanction of any nation or its often-vicious tax regimes. In this world of superyachts, the Austrian bespoke shipbuilder Migaloo is renowned for one-off designs which, for those who have no budget restrictions, can provide ocean going sanctuaries whose only limit is the imagination of the client.

The Tiamat was special even by the extraordinary standards of

Migaloo. Measuring nearly 1000 feet long this sleek grey blue ship was as large as many military battle ships. Like such vessels, it was endowed with a double reinforced armoured hull and multiple watertight bulkheads. Its lines were designed for extended periods in international waters and intercontinental voyages, easily capable of maintaining its cruising speed of thirty knots even through the seventy knot winds and the 165 feet high storm surge of a full hurricane.

The interior provided its owner with the luxury of a seven-star hotel, thanks to its luxurious furnishings and, with a staff of over 100 highly trained individuals, every imaginable whim could be catered for on this incomparable vessel.

It's onboard hydroponic agriculture units, vast stores, wind turbine generators and desalination units meant it could remain at sea for three years between refits. Its roof helicopter landing sections allowed for not just the landing of incoming aircraft, but also enabled the yacht to maintain its own long-range helicopter and four wicked looking armed drones, that could be stored internally within the massive ship's upper bulkheads. The rear of the vessel contained its own small docking station for water craft up to sixty-six feet in length. This small harbour was also capable of being withdrawn within the lower bulkheads, for the Tiamat had one extra feature that was not immediately obvious from looking at its sleek profile. This long vessel was not just a floating fortress, it was also fully submersible to a depth of over 1000 feet, where it could cruise at eight knots for the full duration of its three-year operational ocean-going time, thanks to its small twin nuclear turbine engines.

On board, Frank Foster sat uncomfortably on a small wooden seat that would have been more fitting for a school child. The jacket from his two-thousand-dollar grey silk Armani suit lay neatly folded next to his 18kt Gold Panerai watch, black Gucci shoes, red Prada silk tie and grey cotton Hugo Boss socks, which were all deposited carefully on the wooden floor to his right, beside his small chair. In front of his bare feet lay his gold plated classic colt .45 1911 automatic, it's closeness constantly tempting him. But he knew it was a deliberate psychological ploy to reinforce his feelings of helplessness, trapped in the centre of the ocean, and the gun would almost certainly turn out to be empty, humiliating him and only making his final punishment worse. Sedated and tied with plastic cable ties, on similarly uncomfortably small chairs alongside him, were the semiconscious slumped figures of a man on Foster's right, and two women on his left.

In front of the older of the two sedated women, stood a small brass three-legged table which was covered in ancient Sanskrit writing. Carvings of some hideous stylised demons decorated the upper part of the three table legs, while the foot of each was shaped into a set of three thick bird like talons. Resting on the small table top was a decorative ivory and ebony box that contained three small stylised daggers set into a red velvet cushion, with unusual and exquisitely finished corkscrew twisted blades made of gold, silver and iron. At the end of the leather handle of each dagger was an ornate jewel, that would not have looked out of place in a maharajah's crown. Each knife hilt held a different gemstone, a red ruby for the golden blade, a blue sapphire for the silver and a green emerald for the iron one.

The two unconscious females beside Foster were dressed in one-piece cotton blue Metropolitan police evidence suits, which were standard issue when items of clothing were taken for forensic examination. In contrast, the unconscious man was still dressed in his leather jacket and chinos, having been removed from police custody before being processed.

Foster had organised for the three of them to be relocated from their Paddington Green holding cells to his riverside London base for some "quality time", so that he could get the three of them to reveal everything they knew about Tavish Stewart, and probably a few things they did not know they knew, as the process of interrogation took its full toll.

But Foster's plans for the weekend had been abruptly interrupted when Maelstrom's excessive force in Gordon Square had become public knowledge. Such exposure threatened not only Foster and Maelstrom but also those who coordinated and nurtured his worldwide private Intelligence empire, from the shadows of the Corporatocracy that now controlled Governments worldwide. So, Foster had been snatched unceremoniously, along with his three captives, to face whatever had been decided would maintain the illusion of the democratic rule of law.

He was, he estimated, some twenty feet away from a large metal and glass desk, where an impossibly beautiful woman, dressed in a black Chanel linen trouser suit, sat in a luxurious white leather chair viewing the latest TV news feeds. The office walls were formed from electronic glass that could be made transparent or opaque at the desire of the owner. At that moment, they were acting as high definition screens that soundlessly streamed numerous live TV channels.

The news focused on the growing tension between the countries of the developing world, who were all eager to enjoy the promise of free energy so they could be rid of their dependency on Western oil companies, and the alliance of developed nations, who claimed the revolutionary Unity Magog generators were covert weapons of mass destruction that would destabilize world peace and therefore had to be stopped, at any cost.

The news showed massive rallies in Africa, Asia and South America, with hundreds of thousands of people marching to demand free access to Magog. The ticker tape news headlines ran at the bottom of the large screens that filled the walls:

The UN security council had passed unanimous resolutions demanding that all Magog technology be destroyed by UN appointed teams of weapons inspectors.

UNITY global financial assets had been frozen by the western coalition to counter the threat of terror posed by the distribution of Magog systems.

Dr Nissa Ad-Dajjal had announced she was coming today at noon to make a sworn statement to explain the harmless nature of the Magog systems at the offices of the African Union, at Rue des Pâquis in Geneva. Pictures showed hundreds of press and paparazzi already waiting.

The blockade of all European shipping ports to halt delivery of Magog continued.

Tributes to Dame Cynthia Sinclair were coming in from all parties in the House of Commons, after a fatal car crash had been reported to have killed the highly respected head of British Intelligence, last night outside Chequers. Simon Brinkwater, British Prime Minister was quoted as saying "Her death was a significant loss to the Nation and his thoughts were with her family".

The nationwide manhunt continues for suspected terrorist mastermind Sir Tavish Stewart.

Foster allowed himself a smile at the last two news items. At least that bastard Stewart was suffering and would be sure to lose everything when he was caught. That was only fair, given that he was certain that the Scotsman would have killed him only hours earlier, had he not been air lifted from his London riverside retreat moments before two black inflatables had powered up the Thames.

Foster recalled looking back from the cabin of the sleek Airbus Helicopters X3, as it accelerated to nearly 310 mph away from the mayhem unfolding beneath, while a dozen highly trained commandos poured onto the tree lined lawn where moments before he had been ushered into the copter's passenger compartment by a tall man with a hawk like face. The Maelstrom teams guarding his base certainly had not lived up to their marketing description in the company literature of "being the equal to any of the world's elite special forces", as all twenty-five men had surrendered before the sound of the escaping helicopter had faded.

Looking again at the tall, elegant, raven-haired woman at the desk ahead of him, Foster suddenly felt grubby. He had not slept for two days, he badly needed a wash and a good night's rest. Sadly, he knew he was unlikely to get either as his fate now rested on the mercy of someone who was as cold and ruthless as she was beautiful. And she was extraordinarily beautiful.

Nissa Ad-Dajjal had just concluded a video conversation with Imed Zimba, Head of Delegation for the African Union at the United Nations in Geneva. After some initial reluctance, he had succumbed to the threat of revealing his personal involvement in people smuggling and drug trafficking within North Africa. The intelligence gathered from global internet, phone and banking surveillance provided invaluable leverage to blackmail and control any and every individual on the planet, no matter how powerful or protected, should the need arise. The war on terror had created a convenient pretence to record everyone's weaknesses, and it was inevitable that such power would be gathered and nurtured by the few who were strong enough not to hesitate to use it for their own ends. This office on the Tiamat was the apex of a pyramid of control that had been cultivated for nearly two decades, gradually encouraging government after government to outsource its intelligence operations to the more cost effective private sector. Budget stretched nations had been systematically encouraged to outsource their needs to more "efficient" commercial partners but, by the time the Ministers of State realised the error of giving such total control to a private interest, it was too late, their own personal corruption and depravity made them slaves of their new master or, as it turned out, mistress.

With her complete control over Zimba acknowledged and her detailed instructions noted, the woman turned her attention to the CNN news coverage, which was now reporting the apparent arrival of Nissa Ad-Dajjal's entourage at the African Union's permanent delegation at the United Nations in Geneva, Switzerland.

Two jet-black BRABUS Mercedes-Benz G500 "4x4 squared" SUVs with "UNITY" signage on their doors and rooftops entered the long circular driveway, that was filled with the world's press. The mirrored windows on the two heavily modified SUVs showed hundreds of cameras and eager faces seeking to catch a glimpse of the now legendary woman, who was either a force for equality and freedom or a threat to world peace, depending on your perspective. As well as numerous handheld cameras, the news coverage included aerial views taken from several small drones that occupied the air space above the scene.

The CNN reporter explained that in response to the Western Alliance's freezing of Unity's financial assets, a crowdfunding campaign had been started yesterday and was already in excess of 90 million US dollars.

As the two vehicles reached the entrance of the African Union's permanent delegation, their doors opened, first to reveal the black suited personal protection team, and then the tall figure of a black-haired body double, dressed in Ad-Dajjal's signature white Chanel trouser suit and large dark sunglasses. As the awaiting journalists pressed forward, already shouting their questions, a number of the camera drones dropped their pretence of filming and suddenly opened fire with remote controlled 9mm machine guns. The 600 rounds a minute fired indiscriminately from the four drones into the mass of people caused a sickening chaos, as the survivors ran over the fallen bodies of the wounded and dying.

The quickest thinking of the news crews started replaying the footage, trying to determine if Ad-Dajjal was among the wounded, and speculation was already mounting about who could have undertaken such a callous attack on unarmed civilians.

Within minutes, there was official confirmation from the Right

Honourable Imed Zimba, Head of Delegation for the African Union, via telephone to the CNN offices in London, that Ad-Dajjal was injured but had survived and was now under the formal diplomatic protection of the African Union. Further, she would remain as a diplomatically protected guest at the permanent delegation offices for as long as she required protection from the disgraced Western Alliance.

Meanwhile, cameras outside the African Union building showed the two Unity SUVs taking as many of the wounded away for medical help as they could, followed by a stream of ambulances and armed Swiss police arriving at the scene. A large grey NATO NH90 tactical transport helicopter landed on a nearby green space and deposited around thirty armed troops wearing joint NATO and Maelstrom insignia. These troops made an attempt to enter the permanent delegation but, by now, the entrance was blocked by a group of African female staff, many of whom had heavily blood-stained clothing, linking arms to show the protection they were now giving to Ad-Dajjal. The troops settled for creating a perimeter around the building with, as was noted by several of the news services, their guns all pointing inwards towards the entrance.

The dark-haired woman in front of Foster viciously pinched the flesh between her thumb and forefinger until a tear ran down her cheek, then cleared her throat, as she clicked a remote control on her desk and initiated a ship to shore international call. On identifying herself, she was rapidly put through to the twenty-four-hour live news desk at the BBC. In a performance that could have won her an Academy Award, she sobbed and gushingly told of her concerns for all those who had been so callously murdered and their families. She would, she promised, see that Unity's crowdfunding resources would cover all the expenses for those injured in this unprovoked attack. When asked what she would do next by the interviewer, she requested that everyone take time to reflect on the brutal actions being taken by the rich to protect their own selfish interests. Finally, controlling her emotions, she closed her call repeating that her only desire was to share her Magog system with the world, so everyone could enjoy the benefits of energy taken for granted by the rich without harming the environment.

With a single click of her long red painted nails on the remote control, Dr Nissa Ad-Dajjal made the walls return to transparent glass, revealing a blue ocean as far as the eye could see on all sides. As the screens completed their transformation, they began to retract into the bulkheads and the floor where Foster and the others were seated began to move slowly outwards, finally extending some sixteen feet over the ocean, open on all sides. The sea breeze wafted a strong smell of salt and ozone over him. Foster now sat facing into the centre of the massive yacht with his back only a few inches from the gently swelling water, which occasionally lapped onto the decking and over his bare feet, soaking the expensive clothes piled beside him. The thought of taking his chances in mid ocean ran through his mind, as he heard the sound of high heels on polished wood. He looked up to see that the tall raven-haired woman was walking towards him with a confident stride that he would normally have found highly seductive, but now just filled him with a deep dread of what she would do next.

She was now close enough for him to smell her spicy hand blended perfume made exclusively for her by Merati-Kashani in Dubai. Pausing beside Foster and picking up his gold plated 1911, she weighed it carefully in her right hand as she walked in front of the group. The three sedated bodies were still slumped forwards oblivious of everything around them, including the tepid sea water that flowed occasionally around their feet.

"You know Frank, I was always taught by Horoagi, my Karate Sensei, to eliminate the greatest threat first," She smiled,

"It might surprise you that this old lady,"

She pulled Elizabeth's face up, holding the old woman's cheeks with the red nails of her left hand, and looking at her like a bird of prey might look at a stunned lamb or rabbit,

"Is the greatest threat amongst your small group. Not while her mind is rendered powerless like this of course. But she has... abilities... beyond your simple military techniques, Frank. Abilities that mean that to deal with her thoroughly (she put an emphasis on the word thoroughly) one must destroy what the Yogis term the three sacred seed atoms that bind the Sushumna, or the Silver Cord that runs between lives, like a thread holds a string of pearls."

She smiled and briefly closed her eyes revealing her expertly applied MAC dark eye shadow, as she placed Foster's .45 colt on the small brass table in front of the unconscious figure of Elizabeth. Picking up the golden corkscrew dagger she ran her long red fingernail across the tip, and seemed to be lost in a moment of short lived ecstasy, before moving rapidly and expertly pushing the thin golden corkscrew blade deep into the chest of the unconscious woman in front of her.

Elizabeth's eyes flashed open, suddenly fully aware and, as the blood began to pour slowly from her mouth, she looked defiantly into the eyes of her killer.

"Oh yes, my dear Elizabeth... I am gifting you an exit from the endless cycle..."

Ad-Dajjal sounded like she was talking to a small child who had woken from a nightmare. Never leaving Elizabeth's stony gaze, she smiled as she calmly took the iron corkscrew dagger from the box and expertly thrust it into the old woman's solar plexus. Elizabeth's breathing became erratic, making deep and disturbing rattling noises, which only stopped when Ad-Dajjal thrust the third silver blade expertly into the forehead of Fitz-Glass. As the old woman's body started its journey into death, each of the jewels lost their lustre and fell, in turn, like ripe seeds to the floor. Rolling briefly on the hardwood deck, they were picked up in the flowing seawater and snatched away to the depths of the blue Mediterranean, leaving the blade handles looking somehow empty and unfinished.

Checking that the knives had truly done their work, Ad-Dajjal once more took Elizabeth's head in her hands and stared contemptuously into her face. Suddenly, in what must have been a final death spasm, the old woman coughed and spat a huge deposit of red blood and mucus at her tormentor. For a moment, it seemed that Elizabeth smiled, before the life finally passed from her eyes.

Ad-Dajjal snarled like an angry animal and took several steps backwards, before wiping the blood from her face with her right sleeve, picking up Foster's gun from the table and firing three rounds at the old woman, into her head, heart and her stomach. The total silence after the three deafening gunshots was only interrupted by the sound of the gentle ocean swell. Foster had seen numerous executions in his career, but few done with such emotionless efficiency, and a deep and unfamiliar fear began to form in the pit of his stomach as he realised there were no limits to the cruelty of this beautiful woman.

Having watched the last of the stones roll into the water, Ad-Dajjal raised her right leg so that her steel Gianvito Rossi stiletto heel rested gently on Elizabeth's left shoulder and slowly pushed the chair backwards over into the ocean, where it disappeared swallowed by the waves.

Behaving as if nothing had happened, Ad-Dajjal turned and strode confidently back to her desk still carrying Foster's golden 1911, which she placed casually on the left-hand side of her glass desktop. Sitting back in her white leather chair, she opened a side drawer and withdrew a bespoke makeup kit in a long Louis Vuitton Malletier leather case. She calmly removed the last remains of Elizabeth's blood from her face and expertly reapplied her flawless makeup.

A short instruction into her desk phone, summoned a tall dark-haired female carrying a freshly pressed Chanel linen top identical to the one Ad-Dajjal was wearing. Replacing the blood-stained jacket, Ad-Dajjal dismissed the staff member and began two short international video calls, one to Zimba at the African Union and another to Mohammed Al Pess, Mayor of Hebron in the Palestinian West Bank. Both men were peremptorily issued a set of detailed instructions, without any pretence of respecting social conventions. Clearly, they were both in situations where they had no option but to comply with whatever was demanded of them.

Ad-Dajjal then used the remote to resume watching the global news, which was covering the next development in the ongoing Magog confrontation. The city of Hebron had made a surprise announcement, moments before, that it would defy the western coalition embargo and install a Magog generator, which was going to be transported by road from Switzerland to Palestine. A message from the African Union in Geneva, apparently from the injured Dr Nissa Ad-Dajjal, appealed for people to come from around the world to form a human shield around the Magog, as it was transported from Unity HQ in Grindelwald to Hebron. Already, only minutes after the announcement, there was evidence that people from nations around the world were gathering to escort the free energy device, in a growing international defiance of the western coalition.

While the news continued and the world moved ever closer to its most divisive global confrontation, Foster watched Nissa Ad-Dajjal walk leisurely to one of the walls where an enormous map of the planned route for the Magog system was being displayed. Long red nails traced its predicted progress down through Europe until they reached Istanbul, where her right forefinger finally settled on the 470 bed "Medipol Hospital", that lay directly in its path. A slow sensuous smile played across the perfect face.

CHAPTER 18 - THE DARK GODDESS

"In the beginning, Adam was of both male and female. In time, the female separated from the male, but neither would submit to the other, as they were both of the same dust and divine breath in the image of God. At the demand of Adam, the most perfect woman was turned out of Paradise and, after consorting with Iblīs (Satan), became the mother of devils. She is called "El-Karineh" in Islam, "Lilith" by Judaism. After Lilith had been driven from Paradise, God created Eve out of one of Adam's ribs, making a breed of imperfect mortal beings." - Based on the Islamic Traditions of Lilith

35°31'42.9"N 25°13'37.0"E
Aboard the 283m "Tiamat" Migaloo M7 Submersible-Yacht,
Sea of Crete, 50 Nautical Miles North of Heraklion, Crete
10.00Hrs, 30th July, Present Day.

Frank Foster was escorted down a series of steep steps and into an immensely long passageway in the bowels of the massive ship, by two tall powerfully built women dressed in white jumpsuits. As they marched behind, his escort maintained a disciplined fifteen-foot distance from him, which was standard operating procedure when escorting high risk prisoners. The two women had collected him from his cabin moments earlier and, holding what Foster recognised as a military variation of the multi shot X3 Taser, gestured that he should accompany them. After a poor night's sleep, he was in no mood to experience the electrical shock so he complied with their instructions.

Overnight, Foster had been detained in a small cabin which, although simply and elegantly furnished, was barely disguised as a holding cell. The white walls, ceiling and floors were all made of high impact resin, formed over a steel structure that had been designed to effectively resist any damage. The lights were set behind the white plastic in regular spaces in the walls and the single door was a work of art from a security perspective, with no exposed joints or hinges, and again made of a strengthened white resin skin over a steel base. Even if he had still retained any of his weapons, escape would have been impossible. The bed was a series of metal strands formed into a web and fashioned into a hammock. The sink and toilet were simple one-piece stainless-steel constructions. The water was supplied with a motion sensor, as was the shower. Food had been left for him on a metal table that was welded into the floor, along with a single metal chair. A small loaf of wholemeal sliced bread, some pre-cut cheese and a mixed bowl of fruit had been provided to last for dinner and breakfast, which Foster had picked at intermittently. The area of the small room that contained the sink, toilet and shower also provided a bar of unperfumed coal tar soap, simple toothbrush and a battery powered shaver. On the table, alongside the food, was a simple red cotton two-piece suit but no shoes. Clearly his captors wanted him comfortable, clean and fed, but never to forget he was a prisoner.

The walk from the cell made Foster realise just how enormous the ship was, and its great size was being deliberately used to dramatic effect in this long dim corridor that must have run the whole length of the vessel, and led towards a single golden door some 600 feet away. At equidistant intervals, statues of mythical goddesses lined the passageway, each carefully lit within its own alcove, so that the eye was unavoidably drawn from one figure to the next as one walked along it. The corridor had been deliberately designed to highlight the fact that each goddess was the only light in an otherwise dark existence.

The floor was decorated in a repeating pattern of scale like shapes that turned the entire length of the corridor into a representation of a gigantic serpent, with its head sculpted in a huge relief on the distant golden door. As Foster walked closer he could see that the snake was in the process of consuming a large sphere, overlaid with a mosaic of blue and gold depicting the outlines of the continents and oceans.

The goddesses that lined the corridor were each from different cultures and ages, but they all shared some aspects that made it clear that they were a personification of the same being. All were beautiful but portrayed in their darkest form, seducing the innocent, inciting evil, encouraging vice and corruption, or invoking darkness upon the earth.

Foster was far from an expert on ancient mythology, but he could recognise some of the cultures and periods of the statues, as he was marched slowly towards the head of the Great Serpent. Each was clearly an original that had been very carefully sourced to form this unique procession way. Some were extremely ancient and must have required great skill to move and relocate.

The Sumerian Ishtar was shown seducing a king on a ritual altar, while holding a long sacrificial blade in her left hand, hidden behind her back.

Kali, the Indian goddess of destruction, was portrayed dancing on the corpse of the supreme male god Shiva, while followers of the goddess strangled enraptured sacrificial victims with red silk scarves.

The Aztec goddess Itzpapalotl was depicted kissing each of the night stars, extinguishing them one by one, so there was nothing but cold darkness wherever she had extended her love.

The Greek goddess Ate was immortalised seducing and trapping Zeus, king of the gods into chains, casting the world into disorder, darkness and endless suffering.

Laufeia, the Norse goddess of destruction and evil, was to be seen drugging the mead of Odin and nailing his body to the Yggdrasil Tree, bringing forth Ragnarök, literally the "Twilight of the Gods".

Finally, as Foster approached the great golden door at the end of the corridor, there was a flowing sensuous silver statue of the Islamic and Jewish Lilith, consorting with a giant black serpent made of a highly polished smooth onyx. The snake was crushing a representation of the Tree of Life, carved from dried unpolished cedarwood, in order to create a darkness where souls would be condemned to endless solitary despair. Although this final composition was as suffused with evil as all the others, the form of Lilith had been fashioned with such skill that it evoked a sensuality that was missing from the previous statues.

On approaching the serpent's head doorway, a concealed mechanism made the mouth of the snake close over the representation of the earth, before the whole dropped away into a hidden recess in the floor. Simultaneously, the lighting behind Foster went out along the entire length of the long passageway so that the only illumination came from the path ahead, showing a floor that sloped down and to the left in a sixteen-foot diameter spiral that was aligned with the shape of the ship's hull.

The curved sides of the sloping walkway were made up of large stone sections that had been removed from some ancient site and set in careful order, to make an enormous sixteen-foot-high by twenty-foot-wide frieze. The scenes portrayed on the stone walls had been painted and many of the colours were still vivid, hinting that they had not been exposed to daylight during the passing millennia.

As he walked down the curved slope, Foster could see cuneiform writing which presumably described the series of carvings depicting the progress of a ritual, where priestesses sat, restrained by assistants, before a large stone table top composed of a grid of roughly forty-nine by forty-nine squares, each containing a symbol or letter.

In each of the scenes, the priestess was pointing to specific symbols in the large table grid, while beside them scribes were shown recording everything onto soft clay tablets. The images were even more remarkable because of the long blood red forked tongues, that were shown embedded deep into the back of the priestess's spines and skulls. As the frieze continued, it was clear that the restrained women were being controlled by these "tongues", which connected them to a partially obscured creature, with bird like talons, that towered over the tiny humans. The bodies of these raptor like monsters were hidden behind the depiction of a blinding light but, it was made clear from the frescoes that any interaction with these creatures resulted in death, since stacks of bodies were shown piled up after each ceremony.

When he reached the bottom of the curved walkway, Foster felt he too had been transported back in time to some ancient subterranean temple. It was hard to accurately estimate the size of the room but it must have been nearly sixty feet wide and at least 300 feet long. The walls were a continuation of the stone frieze from the walkway and must have shown every documented interaction with these terrifying red tongued beings.

The main illumination in the chamber came from numerous traditional oil wick lamps set into alcoves around the edges of the walls. These created a dim, inconsistently flickering light that made large areas of the floor space alternate between being visible and suddenly vanishing into impenetrable darkness.

In the centre of the temple, Foster could see what looked like the original stone table that had been shown so clearly in the carvings in the entrance. The space around it was the only area in the dark chamber that was well lit, by four enormous black candles that produced copious amounts of a thick and intoxicating smoke. This incense filled the air throughout the temple with the distinctive heady smell of Hyoscyamus Niger, the so called "black henbane", that was so widely used in ancient ritual incense to induce extreme altered states of consciousness. Four large male figures stood, dressed in white robes, at each corner of the ritual table, facing away from the table itself. Their faces were obscured and covered by a deep cowl hood and each of them carried a large primitive double handed axe that made their presence deeply menacing.

Near to the Oracle Table, but facing away from the temple entrance where Foster was now standing, was the distinctive tall figure of Nissa Ad-Dajjal, dressed in a blue silk creation that closely resembled the robes worn by the high priestess shown on many of the wall carvings. Ad-Dajjal was focused on a female figure directly in front of her. Foster recognised the seated figure as Helen Curren, the lawyer connected with Tavish Stewart. She was sitting on one of four simple stone blocks set into the floor, located between Ad-Dajjal and the Oracle Table.

Although Foster and his two escorts made some noise when they entered the otherwise silent chamber, Curren remained fixated, her pupils abnormally enlarged, looking only at the tall dark-haired woman standing before her. For her part, Ad-Dajjal seemed equally preoccupied staring down at Curren, there clearly being some mesmeric connection between them that excluded all other distractions.

Curren was dressed very simply in an off the shoulder white linen robe that covered the rest of her body right down to her ankles, leaving only her feet exposed on the cool stone floor. Her hair was neatly combed but still wet, where she must have come from the shower and been brought directly to the temple. Although she wore no makeup, her look of total calm and focus gave her an unusual beauty, like a statue frozen in time, completely absorbed, and having lost awareness of everything around her.

Ad-Dajjal was talking to Curren, not in a conversational way but in the tone of how one would talk to an animal that needed reassurance. Curren responded but in a very quiet voice, almost as if she was talking to herself. Even though Foster was now standing within ten feet of the conversation it was impossible to hear clearly what was being said.

After a few minutes, Ad-Dajjal thanked Curren, turned and nodded to the two guards who had escorted Foster to the temple. Although he could only have been in the area for at the most twenty minutes, Foster was finding the thick intoxicating incense overpowering and, when combined with the powerful drugs that had been placed into the food he had consumed in his cell earlier, he was unable to offer any resistance as the two female guards guided him gently to sit on one of the stone blocks next to Curren. He was dimly aware that he could no longer feel his legs and his arms were as heavy as… his internal observations were cut short by a woman's voice that sounded as sweet as honey and felt just as good.

"Hello, Frank..."

Ad-Dajjal smiled as she spoke, and Foster felt like the sun had come out from behind a cloud on a dark winter's day. He had always thought she looked beautiful but now, with a mix of the tropane alkaloids hyoscine (scopolamine), hyoscyamine (L-atropine), and atropine (DL-hyoscyamine) flowing through his blood, she was simply the most perfect thing he had ever seen, the only thing that mattered. Her words took on an importance that transcended anything Foster had ever imagined possible.

Foster's mind began an irresistible descent into the velvet darkness of a deep somnambulistic trance, only to be awoken at the very last moment by a loud sound that, in his drug induced state, felt like an ice pick shattering his brain. A piercing cry of rage sounded through the hall, reminding Foster that he was not in an ancient temple in the presence of a goddess, but was a prisoner on an enormous hybrid vessel that was the headquarters for the clearly psychotic woman standing before him. The startling realisation made him shake his head to try and clear it, and he became aware that Ad-Dajjal was addressing three uniformed men, who were reporting that Jeffrey Sonnet had overpowered his two escorts using a concealed belt knife and stunned them with their own tasers, before taking one of the small motor boats and escaping towards Crete.

While Foster was fighting the powerful tropane alkaloids flowing through his blood, Jeffery Sonnet was soaking wet and standing in a small sixteen foot wide diving chamber, located somewhere in the lowest levels at the rear of the enormous vessel.

Sonnet had woken in a small white room with very elegant but basic furnishings. He resisted the temptation of what was probably drugged food and water and focused instead on determining the optimum angle to hide behind the door when it opened. Once he had the location set in his mind, he began a series of Goju Ryu Karate exercises, to warm his body and eliminate the remaining chemicals that were still flowing through his blood.

He did not have to wait long and, as the door to his cell began to open, Sonnet retrieved his long slender Bowen belt knife, which had remained undiscovered when he was detained at Paddington Green. Fortunately, no one had recognized the Bowen belt buckle was a weapon at the police station or when he was brought onto the ship. That oversight meant that the wicked four-inch blade was available now to be rapidly placed under the throat of the guard, who was unlucky enough to open the cell door. Seconds later, there was a flash and Sonnet felt the lead guard's body convulse uncontrollably, as the second guard misfired his military x3 taser accidently hitting his colleague. Sonnet's SIS training kicked in and he instinctively returned fire from the multi shot Taser still held in the hand of the first guard's rigid body, which acted as Sonnet's shield. With both incapacitated, Sonnet quickly dragged the two men inside his small cell, and struck each of them hard behind the skull, so that he knew they would remain unconscious for long enough for him to escape. He made no attempt to restrain the two men as his plan needed them both to raise the alarm.

Leaving the small room, Sonnet rapidly gained his bearings and headed to the rear of the ship where, having the element of surprise, he dealt with the three men operating the Tiamat's retractable harbour by using one of the cell guard's X3 tasers. Searching the unconscious bodies on the deck, he took a 40mm steel quartz Tag Heuer Aquaracer watch, which he calibrated with its blue aluminium rotating bezel to give him a rough estimate of the time that had elapsed since his escape around four minutes earlier.

Taking four fully compressed diving tanks and an Italian Semer flare gun with three shells, he selected one of the two classic Riva motor launches moored at the retractable harbour and powered the sleek wooden vessel to its maximum speed directly away from the Migaloo. When he judged he was around 800 yards away from the ship, he slowed the launch to a crawl, cut the fuel lines with his Bowen knife, propped up the four pressurized dive tanks into a visible position next to the fuel lines, and rolled elegantly backwards over the side into the ocean. Once he was some distance from the launch, he fired the flare gun towards it. The combined effect of the small boats movement and swell of the ocean made him miss with the first two rounds, but his third shot hit directly and the flare ignited the leaking fuel, causing the pressurized air tanks to explode, ripping the small wooden boat apart and within minutes sending it to the depths below, leaving very little debris.

Sonnet began to swim with a strong practiced stroke back towards the large Migaloo, which was visible in the distance. Thirty minutes later he was close to the ship and, after deliberately hyperventilating, he began a slow and graceful free dive in the crystal-clear waters under the gigantic vessel. At a depth of around sixty feet, his efforts were rewarded when he saw a small 20 foot square diving access port, towards the rear left of the ship and slowly he guided himself up into the pressurized diving chamber. After silently emerging into the small pool, he carefully looked around the interior to make sure it was empty, and thankfully it was deserted. The air in the confined space smelt strongly of an odd mix of salt, iron and rubber as he inhaled deeply after his long dive.

Sonnet found himself floating in what looked like a small swimming pool with high metal sides and, at the far end, a thick metal ladder that led up onto the dimpled black rubber floor of the room. Suspended on metal struts above the water was a bright orange one-person submersible.

In the furthest corner stood a grey metal pressurized door with a large circular screw handle, rather like those on a submarine, and the thick grey metal walls inside the sealed diving chamber were gently sweating moisture due to the cold damp air coming off of the sea water. In another corner, was a stack of diving equipment, gas cylinders, welding torches and, hanging from the rig that held the submersible, a rubber cased remote control unit to lower and raise it to and from the water.

The room had evidently been designed to act as an emergency control centre for recovery operations, because one whole wall of the sixteen-foot square area had a control panel with a series of screens showing CCTV camera feeds from around the entire vessel. By trial and error Sonnet found the feed from the temple complex, showing a tall and strikingly beautiful dark-haired woman talking to three men dressed in identical uniforms to the guards he had encountered earlier. The woman was obviously issuing commands with a clear authority. Other CCTV feeds from around the vessel showed two unmanned drones being prepared on the upper decks. Sonnet assumed they would be sent on a search for the missing launch, hoping there would be insufficient debris from the sunken Riva to be found quickly. While scanning the numerous camera feeds from around the ship, Sonnet's expert eye fixed on a small two-person Robinson R22 marine helicopter, located behind the drones, and a plan started to form in his mind.

The camera feed from the temple now showed the semi-conscious figure of Curren being carried to the exit slope by two guards, leaving behind a man, who Sonnet vaguely recognised from his recent briefings with Tavish Stewart, as being the CEO of Maelstrom. He was seated and looking very disorientated. Sonnet used the control panel in front of him to pull up more CCTV feeds, so he could follow Curren as she was carried along the long passageway and back to the holding cells near the rear of the ship, while he set the other screens to show the temple and wide panoramic views around the vessel.

The two unmanned drones had set off circling the area, and thankfully did not appear to have found any trace of the sunken launch as they continued to extend the area of their search. Meanwhile, the tall woman in the blue Greek styled dress had the drugged Maelstrom CEO carried to an elaborate ceremonial chair, set in front of what Sonnet now recognized as a scrying table that he recalled seeing in one of Elizabeth Fitz-Glass's books. Although Sonnet was primarily interested in following Curren's progress through the ship on the CCTV cameras, he became increasingly fascinated by what was unfolding on the temple feed. Two of the four large axe wielding guards were now holding Frank Foster down into the ceremonial chair, while the tall dark-haired woman looked like she was chanting so forcefully that her face began to show heavy perspiration.

Frank Foster struggled wildly against the men restraining him and the video feed began to cut out intermittently, as blinding flashes of light wiped out the camera's automatic light level adjustment. The flashes seemed to originate around the large table and, as they intensified, they showed Foster screaming with an irrational terror at whatever he could see or sense. The camera continued to struggle with the abnormal light levels and, at the centre of the table, strange shadows and shapes formed that stirred the most primal fears of the human imagination. Just when it looked like Foster would literally scare himself to death, he suddenly became extremely calm, his hands moving slowly, his fingers pointing at specific letters or symbols on the table before him.

Sonnet had to pull himself away from watching the unfolding scene in the temple, as he could see Curren being placed in holding cell B on deck two, some eight floors above him, close to where he himself had been held earlier. Looking in one of the thick manuals that had been left on the top of the control panel, Sonnet began searching for the process involved to override the safety features of the twin diving chamber airlock doors, that prevented the whole ship from becoming flooded. Once he understood the steps he needed to take, he carefully used the remote to lower the orange submersible, so that it sat in the diving bay and blocked the outer hull doors from automatically closing when the airlock became compromised. As soon as Sonnet initiated the emergency override for the doors of the diving chamber, a deafening klaxon sounded throughout the enormous ship. His diversion now fully under way, Sonnet rushed from the pressurized chamber just as the Mediterranean began to flow rapidly through the lower decks.

Outside in the corridor, the noise of the alarm was even louder and was accompanied by a change in the ships lighting, from ambient to a menacing red. The grey metal corridors were ankle deep in cold water as Sonnet made his way up the spiral staircase. As he left the service levels, the stairway changed from a utilitarian metal spiral stairway, with screw down hatchways between each level, to some wide carpeted stairs similar to those found in a luxurious hotel.

As Sonnet rapidly ascended the interior stairs to the level where Curren was being held, several crew members rushed past, so focused on the flooding that they paid no attention to him. Taking full advantage of the unfolding chaos, Sonnet opened the white metal door and helped the disorientated Curren from her cell, guiding her along the corridor back to the central stairway that led to the upper sections of the boat.

After three flights of stairs they reached the highest level of the ship, where Sonnet knew the small flight deck was located. He lost valuable time following a corridor that led to an open-air swimming pool, before backtracking to find the hangar deck. All hands were occupied in the lower levels of the ship and the two drones were still continuing their search, so the bay was empty, apart from the Perspex and the blue grey metal shape of the tiny Robinson R22 marine helicopter with its two-large orange water landing floats. The small flight deck was well organized and Sonnet blessed his luck that the key to the Robinson was clearly labelled on a rack behind the flight controllers desk.

After opening the Perspex doors, he carefully strapped Curren into the passenger seat and then, trying to remember his basic SIS pilot training, turned the ignition on the right hand of the small black metal dashboard and removed the red button guard over the rotor switch on the left of the central console. Nothing. Sonnet began systematically pressing buttons within the tiny cockpit. As he continued to struggle to get the Lycoming O-360 four-cylinder turbines started, he expected to be surrounded by armed guards at any moment but, thankfully, after a few sputtering attempts the engines caught. The tiny helicopter wobbled and lurched over the small take-off area, before Sonnet finally got the hang of the single steering control and pulled up and away from the silver-grey ship beneath them.

Back on board the Tiamat, the life faded from Frank Foster's eyes, blood pouring from every orifice, as he slumped and fell to the stone floor of the temple.

CHAPTER 19 - BY STRENGTH AND GUILE

"All men dream, but not equally. Those who dream by night in the dusty recesses of their minds, wake in the day to find that it was vanity: but the dreamers of the day are dangerous men, for they may act on their dreams with open eyes, to make them possible." - T. E. Lawrence

Willow Manor, Willow Ln,
Wargrave on Thames, RG10 8LJ, UK
03.00 HRS, 29th July, Present Day.

The two Zodiac Futura Commando FC420 Black Rigid Deck inflatables bounced over the grey Thames water in the predawn light, their thirty horsepower Mercury three-cylinder four stroke outboards powering the thirteen-foot-long boats through the water at just over thirty knots. Each boat carried six men dressed in identical unmarked black neoprene wetsuits, their L119A1 machine guns slung across each of their chests, Sig Sauer P226 handguns at their sides and modified Sykes Fairburn daggers strapped to their calves.

At the short briefing, before leaving Vauxhall, Stewart had been introduced to the group during a video replay of the recently aired full footage of the unprovoked Maelstrom team attack on Stewart at Gordon Square. The goal of their mission, to capture Frank Foster, had then been discussed using detailed surveillance photographs, architect's diagrams of the six-bedroom house and a mock-up of the lawn and riverside approaches to Willow Manor. Stewart had given some first-hand intelligence about the likely weapons being used by the Maelstrom operatives, and the SBS men asked brief specific questions about the three civilians, who had been taken from Paddington Green to Frank Foster's residential address for interrogation. Each man had been provided with a recent picture of Curren, Sonnet, Fitz-Glass and Frank Foster, in order to minimize any confusion with respect to identities once the commandos were on site. As a final action, the men synchronized their black PVD cased versions of the British Ministry of Defence (MOD) issue Cabot Watch Company (CWC) diver's watches, and the group embarked onto the two sleek Zodiac boats.

Stewart sat in the middle of the lead boat alongside Lt. Collins, his bergen rucksack stowed in a watertight rubber cover bag at his feet. Before leaving the dockside at Vauxhall bridge, Stewart had been able to change into a snug fitting MOD issue wetsuit that was now covered in the heavy spray generated from the prow of the speeding inflatable. After thirty minutes of motorised progress up the length of the Thames, they reached the so called "Millionaires Row" stretch of the river and the two inflatable boats silenced their engines. The men took out collapsible black plastic oars, that had been stowed on the deck of each, and began to paddle in a smooth well practiced action that made the two craft slide silently through the water.

As they approached their target it became clear that someone had tipped off Frank Foster. Approximately 800 yards before they reached their designated landing area, Collins gestured to Stewart to note the sleek grey Airbus Helicopters X3 rising up from a clearing on the expanse of lawn in front of the house and speeding away, keeping low and maximising its distance over altitude. Several guns became targeted on the fleeing aircraft anticipating a "fire at will" command.

"Hold fire! Hostages may be onboard!"

Collins called into his ARC X24 radio throat microphone, that formed the operational communications for his eleven-man team. His anger could be clearly seen, even under the heavy black camouflage paint that made his face blend so perfectly with his black military wetsuit.

Stewart had been issued the earpiece but not the X24 throat mic, so he could only listen to the short tactical messages that passed between the men to coordinate their movements and responses. Collins manually disengaged his microphone for a second and shared his concerns with Stewart.

"Operational security has been compromised."

Stewart nodded his grim agreement with the assessment and added,

"Is there any way to contact Sinclair? We need to warn her she may be going into a trap!"

Collins nodded and began talking into his microphone, evidently on a separate frequency as Stewart could not hear what was being said back. The message clearly having been sent, Collin's voice came over the operational channel.

"Proceed and engage at will. Repeat. Proceed and engage at will."

At these words, the dozen SBS commandos flowed like a black liquid from the rubber inflatables on to the lawn. Each man had been assigned an area of the grounds to cover with their suppressed C8 SFW Carbines. As soon as they reached the line of tall weeping willows, some five yards from the river's edge, two preselected commandos climbed specific trees providing superior observation and covering fire, if needed.

The remaining men covered the rest of the 100 yards leading to the manor house rapidly, some openly in the centre of the lawn, others at the edges of the garden and some within the neighbours' grounds. The advancing centre group of five commandos were surprised to find twenty-five Maelstrom guards sitting cross legged on the front lawn, hands on their heads and with their weapons already neatly stacked in front of them, clearly happy to surrender without a fight now that the target individuals had already taken flight. However, their smiles were short lived, as they had thick restraints applied to their wrists and ankles, before a ventilated black hood was expertly placed over their heads, rendering them totally helpless, as they sat under the careful watch of two of the SBS commandos, who now guarded them.

Stewart kept a relative distance of three to five yards back from the central group of SBS men, letting them do their job. Unlike in the movies, where they portray a constant two-handed carry, Stewart held his 9mm Browning High Power in his right hand, straight down by his side, ready to be fired in an instant, the relaxed carrying style not taxing his shooting arm. He moved facing sideways towards the house, presenting the smallest possible target, unlike the face-on stance so often popularised in the media.

Within ten minutes after landing, Collins had his team surrounding the manor house. Upon his order three men climbed to the roof using specialised carbon fibre expanding ladders and waited outside the skylights, while two additional three-man groups gathered by the front and rear doors. Stewart looked away and covered his ears, while the multiple sets of flashbang grenades gave the separate teams a momentary tactical advantage on entering the unknown spaces. There were no gunshots and within four minutes the commandos began to radio in confirmation that the manor house and its surrounding grounds were free from further threats.

After the order to secure the premises had been issued, Lt. Collins emerged from the front door, surrounded by the remains of the thick flash bang grenade smoke, and gestured for Stewart to enter.

The house was elegantly furnished, with plain wood floors covered with thick Persian carpets. The walls were undecorated and all painted a uniform magnolia. The kitchen was a mix of black granite and oak, with an enormous Aga wood cooker/boiler combination and a long well-worn oak farmhouse table, with twelve matching wooden chairs. The South facing wall had a series of four double glazed doors that looked out over the lawn they had just crossed. The living room was dominated by a massive real wood fire place, which was surrounded by four classic leather sofas, with a rich Indian rug on the floor.

Everything in the house spoke of luxury and had been chosen to provide a relaxed atmosphere for its guests, who would welcome the break from their financial, commercial or political wheeling and dealing in the city, except for two windowless rooms in the basement that had been clearly set up for less innocent purposes. The walls and floors of these two subterranean spaces were covered in white tiles, and there were ridges in the floor leading to a large steel central drain. Two plastic covered reclining dental chairs were set into the floor of each room and beside them were metal tables covered with a sickening selection of surgical knives, saws, spikes, hammers, knuckle dusters, rubber hoses, multi coloured acid bottles, needles and labelled syringes. The walls on one side of the room had metal cabinets where more items were clearly labelled.

In one of the two rooms, on a metal side table, lay a few personal effects that Stewart recognised as belonging to Curren, Sonnet and Elizabeth Fitz-Glass. Sonnet's Breitling, Curren's engraved JLC Reverso and an amulet of some kind, shaped like a mummified bird, that he had seen around Fitz-Glass's neck. As Collins made an excuse to leave the room, so he could update central command, Stewart continued to look through the assorted items left on the table, pocketing Sonnet's SIS emergency kit and picking up a grey (non-military issue) ARC X24 radio set that he fitted into his ear. The radio channel was pre-set and the voice on the frequency was clearly Lt. Collins. Stewart made a quick check with the SBS issued earpiece he had been wearing and confirmed that this grey civilian head set was set to a different channel from the one that Collins had been using to coordinate their mission. The agreed call signs that had been assigned at Vauxhall were missing, instead there was a detailed set of instructions that "Jackal" should expect the delivery imminently and that he was expected to dispose of all assets and liabilities on site and then return to the agreed extraction point.

Stewart put his issued earpiece back in just as Collin's voice announced, over the SBS operational channel, that they had been stood down with a two-hour window for collection by road transport, but that they were to expect a VIP prisoner imminently who was to be taken to the holding rooms in the basement. In the meantime, six men were to bring the hooded Maelstrom operatives from the lawn into the main living room.

When he emerged up the stairs and through a white metal door into the kitchen, Stewart found Collins in good humour making a "brew" for his men. As the steaming mugs of tea were passed round, the Scotsman made an excuse and, uncharacteristically, fumbled inside the depths of his rucksack, that he had insisted, in spite of numerous sarcastic remarks, on bringing with him from the Zodiac when they landed.

As the men relaxed around the kitchen table, Stewart offered to share the contents of the leather flask that he had eventually retrieved from the depths of his backpack. As the Glenfiddich was passed around he made a joke of not taking any tea since he did not wish to spoil the Single Malt. Collins was also noticeable for avoiding the tea and after he filled a large glass from the flask, Stewart was left with only a rather small measure after his generosity to the twelve men.

The celebrations were interrupted by the sound of a single Zodiac arriving at the river's edge. Through the multiple glazed kitchen doors Stewart could see a group of three heavily armed men, dressed identically to the other SBS operatives, escorting a restrained and hooded figure from the newly arrived craft over the expanse of lawn towards the house.

Even at a distance the prisoner looked familiar to Stewart and, as they passed through the tree line, he could see it was a female wearing a distinctive dark blue Prada silk jacket and pencil skirt with matching four-inch heels. The elegant look was spoilt as the skirt was badly torn, exposing her left thigh, and the left four-inch heel was badly bent. Even under such conditions the woman still held herself with dignity and walked with a gait that Stewart instantly recognized, sending a cold chill right through his body. Stewart could sense the attitudes of the men around him subtly changing, dropping the pretence of cooperation and replacing it with a much colder appraising look that he had seen many times before, always when some form of betrayal was about to unfold.

Making the most of any time remaining to him, he faked rubbing his eyes from tiredness and, stifling a yawn, his hands momentarily covered his mouth, allowing him to conceal a small thin metal strip that he had taken from Sonnet's SIS emergency kit in the interrogation rooms below. Moments later, the figure that had been seen being escorted over the lawn had reached the house, was pushed into the kitchen area and the hood removed.

Cynthia Sinclair's thick dark hair was out of place and her makeup smudged by the head covering she had been forced to wear. Her classic silk Prada suit was stained and creased from being confined and transported on the Zodiac, but she still managed to maintain an elegant, defiant pose as she scanned her captor's faces, seeing the gun muzzles that were directed towards her and towards, she noted, one other figure in the room. Her frown broke into a smile when she saw Stewart.

"Ah... I had wondered who was going to save me."

Stewart smiled,

"Up until a few minutes ago, I was rather hoping the same about you."

And then, ignoring the numerous gun barrels pointed at them both, he walked over and embraced Sinclair with a kiss that initially surprised her but that she rapidly accepted. She returned the embrace by placing her tied hands over Stewart's head, so they could better exchange a long and passionate moment. The tenderness was broken by Collins.

"Enough, you two old lovebirds."

He turned to his men,

"Escort them both downstairs and get them ready for interrogation. Take extra care with him."

With that abrupt command, Stewart was roughly pulled from Sinclair's embrace. His Browning 9mm pistol was taken from his waistband and the pair of them were led at gunpoint by a four-man team down the stairs to the basement, Stewart being instructed to place his hands on his head and walk very slowly. Once they reached the bottom of the narrow stairs, they were both guided into the interrogation room on the right and each placed into one of the two specialised seats.

Stewart and Sinclair were carefully covered by different commandos, each with C8 SFW machine guns, while two other SBS operatives professionally tied their arms and legs to the steel frame of the chairs with strong thick blue plastic cable ties. Once both Stewart and Sinclair were secure, the four commandos left them to go upstairs and enjoy another brew. While his men went off to relax, Collins chose to focus on his two prisoners, regarding them both like a small child who cannot decide which Christmas gift to unwrap first.

After some moments of silent thought, he calmly walked towards Sinclair, looking at Stewart, as he unleashed a cruel backhand strike across her face, with a sickening smack that filled the small room and caused her head to fly violently to the left. Sinclair did not make any sound but as her head turned back, blood flowed copiously from her mouth and down her face, in thick rivulets that stained her silk top crimson red.

Stewart responded.

"Whatever they are paying you we can double it."

Collins turned in response,

"Stupid old fool. By the time we have finished, you will both have given me all your money, that is just before you beg me to put you out of your misery."

Sinclair coughed violently with the blood that was still flowing. Collins grinned, clearly impressed with the damage he had caused with such a simple blow.

"Let's start with you, Stewart. One of my clients badly wants some ancient relic you are carrying. Tell me where it is and you can spare your lover from the worst of it."

"Very well. If you promise to release Cynthia." Bargained the Scotsman.

"Not a chance my friend. She is worth one million euros to my Chinese clients for all the information in that pretty head of hers. But I will promise you a quick death if you tell me where you have that object."

Stewart looked his full years, tired, beaten and utterly defeated. He slowly nodded.

"Let me up and I will show you in my backpack."

Collins laughed,

"Nice try. I will go."

And he strode out of the room, his boots clearly audible as he went up the stairs to the kitchen, where Stewart had left his backpack and where his men were relaxing. For a moment, a brief smile passed over Stewart's tired face, and he wondered how long it would take Collins to discover his little surprise, which he had prepared whilst he was supposedly fumbling for the whisky flask.

The moment Collins left the room, Sinclair began to reach forward in her chair and, producing the sharp blade from her mouth, began working furiously on the cable ties on her left hand, clearly not caring that she was spreading blood everywhere.

Suddenly the house shook as if hit by an enormous earthquake. The violent movement was followed almost instantaneously by a tremendous pressure wave that literally threw everything around the room. Large sections fell from the ceiling and the walls shattered, fragments of tiles flew wildly throughout the enclosed space cutting any exposed skin. After what felt like an age there was a silence that was broken eventually by Sinclair shouting, clearly deafened by the blast.

"You know Tavish, you could have killed us both, but I have to admit that was perfectly done."

Stewart smiled.

"Thanks.... maybe a tad less explosive next time."

As Sinclair released herself rapidly, using the covert blade in her hands, she smiled,

"I sincerely hope there will be no next time!".

CHAPTER 20 - THE VATICAN ARCHIVES

"As there is in Heaven but one God, so is there here one Pope." - Frederick I, Holy Roman Emperor, 1155 AD

Apostolic Palace
00120 Vatican City
10.50HRS, 31st July, Present Day.

The traditional image of the Vatican is of an organisation steeped in ritual and tradition, focused exclusively on its long past. Although it is true that there are parts of the church that rigidly hold to age old customs, the core of the institution is run as a modern multinational corporation. Here, in the upper floors of the ornate stone building that form the Pope's official residence, the main conference room contains state of the art technology, with electronic countermeasures against eavesdropping and sleek LG 8k screens integrated tastefully into the rich nineteenth century oak wood panelling. The long thin smoked Barovier & Toso glass conference table has touch screen information systems integrated into the surface of the table top. The seats are each hand made by Del Giudice, in a rich dark leather that adds a sumptuous feel of luxury for anyone who is fortunate enough to gather at this most exclusive table.

The serious men gathered today were each as qualified and competent in their respective business disciplines as any Silicon Valley executive. For the Vatican is not just the centre of a religion, it is also the heart of one the biggest businesses in the world.

At the head of this distinguished group, the CEO was a charismatic man, who as well as having responsibility for the continued fiscal sustainability of one of the biggest and oldest organisations in the world, is also the religious head for over 1.2 billion human beings.

His Holiness Pope James was a tall, thin, sixty-seven-year-old man, with a thick shock of white hair that had a habit of forming a wild looking display, that had become his signature look so loved by his large following of Catholics and non-believers alike. In his five years in office, this thin man had shown a depth of compassion that transcended secular barriers, and had introduced interfaith humanitarian initiatives that had saved millions from suffering. His popularity had grown to such an extent that he was cited by Forbes as one of the world's top ten influencers.

At the moment, his long slender hands were holding a thin cigarette that he smoked with a clear disregard for the "Non-Fume" signs on the walls. Several others around the table were sharing the habit, not in an act of defiance, but because of the nature of the materials being presented to them by the Head of Vatican Security, Conrad De Ven. A thick set man in his early forties, De Ven had a lightly tanned shaved head that added to his very clean athletic look. His jet-black Armani suit accentuated the powerful frame of his trained body.

De Ven's family had entered into the service of the Holy See before the second Crusade and had established a reputation, generation after generation, for being its most faithful guardians. His security division was separate from the Swiss Guard and reported directly to the Holy Father. It acted to investigate and deal with whatever threats might arise against the Church, its faith and its continuation. Over the centuries and through many crises, his family had faced numerous threats, but what they were addressing today was singularly different in its extent and possible damage to the Holy Church.

Conrad De Ven's strong face betrayed his dismay at the information that was being displayed to everyone on their eighteen-inch table top 8k LG screens, fed from the innocent looking brushed metal verbatim USB stick that had arrived anonymously in the post yesterday. The memory stick had been clinically wiped to remove all means of tracking, and there was a laser etched message on the casing demanding that the board meet at 11am to await a call to the Pope's private unlisted video link.

It was clear from the contents that for the past decade someone had collected vast and detailed information about every senior member around this table, and every cardinal, bishop and officer within the worldwide church. Phone calls, text messages, emails, faxes, and paper letters had all been digitized and then carefully indexed. Every misdeed had been documented, from the selling of confessional information, illicit deals, sexual liaisons of every description, abuses of trust, financial corruption, interference in the political independence of nations and even the sponsorship of terrorism. The information was coded and sorted by individuals, countries and even themes, allowing searches that, in a matter of seconds, could expose and destroy every diocese and individual in the modern Catholic church.

Each man around the table was busy searching their own records and finding their worst fears confirmed. Every one of them was ruined personally and professionally. Some hung their heads, others paced the thick carpeted room. Even the Holy Father was shown to have had several affairs and, since coming to office, to have abused his access to privileged information for personal financial gain. Pope James could see the group was descending into chaos.

"My brothers, stop thinking just of the personal consequences. We must consider our Mother Church and face this challenge with the grace of our Lord, so that His legacy continues."

His fellow clerics begrudgingly acknowledged the reasoning behind his words and resumed their seats, focusing on the Holy Father.

"Let us listen and then do what needs to be done."

He nodded to De Ven.

"Conrad, do the best you can to trace the origin of the call."

The Head of Security nodded, and everyone's attention focused on a large 8k LG screen mounted on the side wall, in between the portraits of the previous Popes, that lined the wooden panelled walls.

932 miles away on an enormous superyacht in the sea of Crete, a set of long delicate red fingernails initiated an encrypted audio call that would be routed through several anonymous dedicated satellite TOR relays. The complexity of the connection process was hidden by the simplicity of the act and, within moments, the beautiful tall dark-haired woman was leaning back into her sumptuous hand finished Bear Emporium white leather chair, carelessly exposing her Eleganti Havana stockings from within a deep split in her black Dior silk robe, her legs made to look impossibly long by a pair of black Jimmy Choo stilettos that extended luxuriously under her glass desk. Based on the smile that ran across her flawless face, she was enjoying every moment of her power over the entire Catholic Church. Her pleasure was also evident in the tone of her voice...

"Your Holiness…" she purred.

"I assume you have had time to review the materials that I sent you yesterday?"

"Yes, we have."

Pope James responded firmly.

"Mmmm… Good... then we understand each other perfectly."

Her voice sounded almost flirtatious.

"You have all been so... delightfully wicked... and in so many... imaginative ways... but I demand no Mea Culpas or Hail Marys."

She laughed,

"Just a recognition of your options... or rather lack of them."

As she talked, her long fingers picked up a delicate silver cross and chain from her dark glass desk and slowly started to wrap the chain around her long fingers. Letting a sensuous smile play across her face, she raised the crucifix close to her red lips and watched her breath form condensation on the small embossed figure of Christ.

"There is only one... small thing I want." She stated.

"Small?"

The Holy Father was clearly anticipating some outrageous demand. The woman's voice on the other end of the audio link sounded like she regarded blackmailing the entire Church of Christ as some kind of school prank.

Her voice came back sounding ever more seductive.

"Yes, James … small... in comparison to your collective... sins… a single tiny item from your enormous collection in the archives. Why, I am sure you will hardly miss it. Especially when I could ask for so much more… couldn't I?"

Pope James hesitated.

"What is it that you want, Miss... what should we call you?"

The voice on the other end of the line laughed in a delightfully teasing tone.

"Oh, James... I am sure you and your brothers will call me all sorts of things. But honestly, I do not care because we will not interact again once you have delivered the item to my representative, the Vatican archive item indexed TG345. You can look it up... A small emerald engraved tablet donated by the last Holy Roman Emperor as his empire fell. As I already said you do not even know it exists so... you will not miss it."

"My representative will call for it tomorrow at 10am your time… he will collect it… from..."

She paused, as she contemplated the options offered by the unique situation. She slowly blinked her expertly made up eyes in pleasure. Her red painted nails gently lowered the silver crucifix into a white-hot crucible, that she had ritually prepared prior to making the call. The silver cross melted violently and rapidly into a glistening mess, hissing dramatically and causing steam to rise high into the air in front of her. Within seconds, the silver crucifix was consumed by the heat and was gone. She sighed in pleasure at the symbolism, and then slowly continued in the same sensuous tone that a lover might use to entice her man.

"The high altar in St Peters."

She sighed once more, this time more deeply than before, filled with delight at her domination of the church and all it represented. Her tone then changed becoming much harsher and demanding.

"If you refuse, James, I will publish everything to the media. If you harm my representative, I will publish everything to the media. If you follow my representative..."

She stopped and her tone softened again. Returning to her seductive resonance.

"You are all clever men so I need not become unpleasant. We will not talk again. Thank you for your..."

She paused and laughed,

"Full cooperation."

Her long red nails clicked the handset and the connection was lost.

There was a deep silence in the conference room. De Ven was the first to speak.

"Nothing on the trace. The signal was routed through a series of anonymous satellites and could have originated anywhere."

A moment later, Dr Antonio Abatescianni, Cardinal Archivist of the Vatican Secret Archives, interjected. A long-haired man wearing wire frame glasses and sporting a thick grey beard, he was dressed in a light herringbone patterned grey cassock and was seated towards the far end of the long conference table.

"She is correct. Article TG345 is a small four inch engraved emerald tablet that was donated to the archive on August 5th 1806 by

Emperor Francis, at the fall of the Holy Roman Empire to Napoleon. It is supposed to be one of a set of four similar items that were split between a private archive in Prague, the Church of Rome, the Eastern Church in Constantinople and one other location along the old Silk Route. Some notes from the time of the donation mention of a deep concern about the four tablets always being kept apart to avoid bringing about the end of days."

Pope James smiled sadly.

"Given this very real threat, a danger to the continued existence of our beloved Mother Church and our own reputations, I do not think we need concern ourselves with some romantic tale. Are we all agreed to comply with this proposed exchange?"

There was no hesitation among the assembled group. As the Holy Father looked around the table he could not just see raised hands, but a group of desperate men who were clinging to their one hope of salvation.

The entrance to the Archivio Segreto Vaticano is located in the Porta di S. Anna via di Porta Angelica. Access is through a pair of tall stone gate columns, decorated on their tops by an ornate pair of carved stone eagles. The steel gate sections are hidden behind enormous thick iron plates welded to the frame, so there is no clear view from the main thoroughfare into the small street beyond. Some way beyond the impressive gates marks the entrance to one of the world's largest repositories of ancient books, letters and significant artefacts that lie stored in over fifty-two miles of shelving. The modern Italian sign hangs next to a much older one written in Latin, its rich Gothic script "Archivum Secretum Apostolicum Vaticanum" partially faded by time. A large wooden door, set into an impressive archway, has a smaller entrance set within it, and this gives access to a security area.

De Ven was well known and respected within the whole of the Vatican, but still had to go through the formal visitor registration process. Once inside the bullet proof glass barriers, with his visitor's badge attached to his left lapel, he was met by Dr Abatescianni who, after shaking his hand, led the way down a set of stone steps underground and into a long wide corridor with single light sockets in the centre of a slightly arched ceiling. The corridor stretched at least 400 yards into the distance and, at regular intervals along the walkway to the left and right sides, were storage rooms with signs indicating the year the items had been deposited. Looking in each room De Ven could see modern concertina sliding storage systems and INERTSAFE300 (IG541) halogen and nitrogen gas feeds protruded from the ceilings in each room, alongside complex sets of automated fire, heat, water and smoke detection equipment. Since De Ven could see the dates on each of the side chambers, he walked on towards the rooms labelled 1806, even when Abatescianni had paused at 1817.

The Cardinal Archivist smiled.

"An understandable assumption Mr De Ven, but although this specific item was donated in 1806 it did not make its way to our care in Rome until 1817, when the French Republic finally allowed the transfer of numerous archive items that had, until that time been stored in France."

The two men entered the 1817 storage room and moving the sliding storage system finally lifted up a small wooden box labelled "TG345". Inside the small box was a rather tiny engraved stone tablet resting on a blue velvet lining.

"So much trouble for such a small item." Said the Cardinal sadly.

De Ven nodded and, pulling a steel parker pen from his inside jacket pocket, quickly signed the paperwork he had been given at the reception desk. Handing the signed papers to Abatescianni, the head of Vatican Security took the small wooden box and walked slowly back to the entrance. As he exited the building, with the item in a plain black holdall, he checked his Swiss Army chronograph, and wondered who would be "the representative" that he would meet in front of the high altar at St Peter's in thirty minutes time.

Issac bin Abdul Issuin walked purposefully across St Peter's square towards the enormous basilica. His watchful eyes were hidden behind a pair of mirrored Ray Ban glasses. A crisp black cassock flowed around his legs, exposing the high shine on his black Frank Wright dress shoes, as he walked up the sets of steps to the massive church. Inside the entrance the enormous ceilings curved high above him, painted in rich golds with images of angels and saints carved exquisitely from the finest marbles. Abdul Issuin ignored the splendour around him and headed with a singular purpose to Gian Lorenzo Bernini's large Baroque sculpted bronze canopy over the high altar, marking the burial place of St Peter.

Checking his black carbon Luminox watch, Abdul Issuin noted with satisfaction that he had arrived at exactly the assigned 10AM. Seeing Conrad De Ven, standing beside one of the columns, he nodded at him and gestured for him to come closer. The two men stood for a moment face to face, the distaste clear in De Ven's frown, while Abdul Issuin simply smiled and took the wooden case that was being held in front of him.

Ignoring the Vatican Head of Security before him, as though he was of no consequence, Abdul Issuin opened the wooden case, removed the emerald tablet and placed it inside a sleek metal and resin radio isolation case attached to a length of cord, which he placed around his neck and under his cassock.

Walking away smoothly, Abdul Issuin noted that he was being followed by four dark suited men but seemed unconcerned. As he descended the marble entrance steps, the Vatican security detail headed towards two waiting black Audi A6 saloon cars, obviously intending to follow their target. Abdul Issuin increased his pace down the final few steps, where he nearly collided with a pretty young woman riding one of the numerous scooters that fill the centre of Rome during rush hour. Instead of being irritated, Abdul Issuin smiled at the driver and promptly mounted the passenger back seat of the bright red Vespa scooter. Within moments, they had merged into a melee of identical red Vespa bikes, each driven by similar looking pretty girls and with a mirrored sunglass wearing priest riding as a passenger. The mass of scooters circled briefly, mixing themselves together deliberately, and then just as quickly disappeared in different directions into the bustling city morning traffic. The two Vatican cars delayed too long deciding which scooter to follow and ended up losing the entire group.

Back in the board room, the worried men received the news of the pickup with clear relief. The Holy Father smiled at the assembled group but his confidence was short lived. Private land lines and assorted mobile phones around him began to ring in a coordinated and insistent manner. As each man around the table checked the incoming messages on their phones the board room doors opened, letting in a string of Personal Secretaries seeking their respective senior managers, each with looks of serious concern. It quickly became clear they were all reacting to the same shared crisis. The world's media was demanding comment on a dossier of misdeeds that had just been released to the press.

The CNN world news feed was quickly directed to the shared conference room screen. The headlines were their combined nightmares.

"Massive scandal breaking - Catholic Church in Ruin."

CHAPTER 21 - ANY PORT IN A STORM

"It is vain for the coward to flee; death follows close behind; it is only by defying it that the brave escape." - Voltaire

Willow Manor, Willow Ln, Wargrave on Thames, RG10 8LJ, UK
04.37HRS, 29th July, Present Day.

After Sinclair had cut Stewart free from the blue plastic restraints on his arms and legs, the pair picked their way through the debris that covered the interrogation room floor and entered the corridor. The entire basement was in darkness as the lights had all shattered from the blast. Thick segments of plaster were scattered across the floor and panels of plasterboard hung from the ceiling. Getting up the stairs involved removing several large blocks of masonry that obstructed the higher steps.

The thick white metal door to the kitchen was badly deformed, having absorbed most of the blast, and fell loudly from its hinges when pushed, revealing charred carnage in what remained of the enclosed eating area. Blood and tissue were spread over every surface. The air was filled with a foul mix of smells from burnt meat and cordite. While some men had been pulped by the blast, others were intact and looked like they were merely sleeping.

Ignoring the stench and mess they checked the bodies for weapons, Sinclair finding a SIG 226 handgun, which she rapidly dismantled to check the movement still moved freely. Stewart discovered a Maelstrom H&K MP5 machine gun, and after he too had checked the mechanism, slung it over his shoulder and put some spare magazines in his pockets. The pair worked in a highly professional and systematic manner going through each room, with one of them offering cover while the other searched every hiding place. Within eight minutes they had visited all of the rooms in the bomb blasted site checking for any survivors. There were none.

Back in what remained of the kitchen, Stewart looked around the remains of the elite force, clearly saddened at the loss. Sinclair gripped his arm.

"It was them or us. Come on."

She led him from the shattered house down to the moored Zodiac. As they walked she looked at him, concern clear in her eyes,

"When was the last time you slept?"

He shrugged and smiled wearily back. In the boat, they consulted an old-fashioned plastic covered Ordnance Survey Map, rather than risk the modern GPS system giving away their trail. Sinclair clearly had a longstanding backup plan for just such a situation, as she gave Stewart precise directions and the pair moved back down river, now in the glare of the morning sunlight.

After twenty minutes, they went past the Royal Botanical Gardens on their right, eventually bringing the small boat ashore at a private waterfront near Waterman's Art Centre, on the left bank. It was still only 5am so the trendy landing area was deserted. Stewart expertly worked on the Zodiac, rapidly deflating the air chambers and opening the drainage points, so the dinghy was soon lost in the depths of the Thames.

The pair then walked quickly through the streets, both acutely aware of how conspicuous Stewart looked in the SBS wet suit. Eventually they reached an unremarkable two-bedroom terraced house, it's upper storey clad in fake white wood, located South of Griffin Park, the Brentford football club ground. The house was only distinguished from all the others around it because, rather than a usual Yale lock, it could only be accessed by using an electronic keypad.

Sinclair rapidly got them inside and they both went into the basic IKEA kitchen to prepare some food. After cooking up some scrambled eggs, bacon, hash browns and Cumberland sausages from the well-stocked tall white Hotpoint fridge, the pair showered in the modern white tiled bathroom. Everything in the house was new and prepared for visitors who used such safe houses in a wide variety of situations, all of which were crises. The one bedroom had an IKEA king sized bed and a set of crisp new sheets and pillows, that had to be unpacked from their cellophane wrappers.

Stewart interrupted the mundane task of unwrapping the bed clothes, by drawing Sinclair's shapely gym honed body closer to him and kissing her tenderly, before the pair made love. They explored each other's body with a wild and passionate abandon and, only later, did their lovemaking show the gentle tenderness of an established couple, where each knows the secret desires of the other, and uses that intimate knowledge to explore the limits of pleasure. Afterwards they lay together, eventually falling into that deep sleep that so often follows the most ardent of lovemaking. They slept for over nine hours, with Sinclair's toned brown arms holding Stewart, while they slumbered.

Tavish Stewart was the first to wake and, leaving Sinclair sleeping, made his way into the living room of the small house, which had been outfitted as a store room with racks and shelving providing clothing in all sizes. The range of equipment on offer in the room was deliberately selected with an emphasis on providing practical high-quality items that would not draw attention to themselves or their owner. Unlike in the movies, real life covert operatives use equipment that allows them to blend into their surroundings.

Stewart chose a black roll top, dark Urbane Cargo pants and a pair of tan Salomon Quest 4D II GTX boots, along with some rapid drying blue oxford style shirts and socks, from a range of Tilley clothing that he knew was hard wearing and dried rapidly. Features that were ideal for the kind of light, rapid travel that lay ahead of him.

To the right-hand side of the wooden clothing alcoves, were three metal tables covered in sets of plain white cardboard boxes, labelled with their respective NATO stock numbers (NSN), indicating their formal selection for government use. The weapons table provided a choice of two guns, a 9mm Walther P5 (NSN 1005-99-978-4952) for personal protection duties and an old two-inch snub-nosed Colt Cobra .38 revolver which, if it ever did have a paper box with an NSN was now long misplaced.

Stewart selected the Cobra for its small size and light weight. He placed it in a small black North Face 28L "vault" daypack along with a black Cordura ankle holster, three "speed loader" plastic revolver reloads and two boxes of Federal Premium 129 grain "Hydra Shock" jacketed hollow point (JHP) rounds. Although Stewart would have preferred something with more stopping power, he had learnt from experience that the timing, accuracy and placement of shots were the major deciding factors in real world gunfights.

To the left of the boxes of ammunition, Stewart had found a small selection of tactical fixed blade and folding knives, all packaged in the same plain white cardboard boxes. After carefully examining them he chose the US designed Scimitar folding tactical knife, supplied by Cold Steel. Its failproof titanium lock made the blade the equal of any fixed blade once deployed, despite its small size, and was able to effortlessly penetrate through body armour, including plate metal. In Stewart's opinion, the best knife was the one you could carry at all times, so size and weight were more critical than blade size or steel type.

Next to the weapons were square cardboard boxes labelled NSN 6645-01-356-5944, containing a solar powered atomic clock synchronised Casio G-Shock 5600, which Stewart took as a backup to his trusty but now battered Speedmaster. In addition to the weapons, Stewart took a handful of British Government "escape and evasion" leather belts, each with fifty gold sovereign coins in the stitching, and some plain paper envelopes containing pound, dollar and euro notes in non-consecutive numbers, each envelope totalling 5,000 pounds. Finally, for a jacket, Stewart had selected a black Web-tex soft shell, which again he knew was utterly reliable against the harshest environments. After outfitting himself as best he could for the escape and evasion that lay ahead, Stewart had eaten a simple meal of cheese slices and whole meal bread, as he watched the News on the BBC 24-hour channel.

The explosion at Foster's retreat formed the main story and was being blamed on a gas leak. In other news, in spite of the footage showing the murderous violence perpetrated by Maelstrom in Gordon Square, the man hunt for Tavish Stewart continued, with Home Office spokespersons making it clear that the full sophistication of the bleeding edge of surveillance technology was now being applied to the search for him.

British PM Brinkwater had made an appeal to the public to support the "Helpful intervention and assistance from the private Maelstrom operatives" but his image as a strong and incisive leader was undermined, as it was becoming clear that his decisions and policies were directed by a small group of advisors from the private sector. All pretence of democratic interest and representation was falling rapidly from his office.

The news concluded with a local London newscaster warning about congestion around the football grounds. Listening carefully, Stewart decided that he would leave the safe house to coincide with the Brentford match that was scheduled that evening. Having synchronised his new Casio watch to its radio controlled atomic source, he wound his scuffed Omega and corrected it's time against the Casio.

He loaded the Colt Cobra with .38 ammunition along with the three revolver speed loaders and, having fitted the Cordura holster around his right ankle, he spent some time practicing drawing the gun with his left and right hand, to check for unexpected snagging or obstructions. He followed a similar practice routine, drawing and opening the Scimitar folding knife single handed from both left and right sides, from its location in his right front trouser pocket, where its folding clasp was the only tell-tale sign of its presence.

Having completed his preparations as best he could, he then made some strong black French Blend coffee for the sleeping Sinclair and took it to the bedroom.

"So soon my love?" She asked sadly as she took in his fully dressed appearance.

He smiled softly, sat on the bed and they kissed.

"The city is alive with people and technology looking for us. Be careful, C."

She smiled, "Don't you worry, honey. Never underestimate a woman who has been wronged!"

After a tender parting, Stewart left the safe house and made his way on foot through the growing crowds, picking up a Brentford supporters scarf and hat from a one man stall a few yards from the safe house. Now blending in perfectly with the hundreds of other middle-aged men, he headed slowly towards a chain of small high-end marinas along Point Wharf lane, where he deposited his football garb in a large wheelie bin. Walking along the range of hobby craft and more serious boats, he eventually found an unlocked gate at mooring B4, that had been left open while an owner was unloading his green Range Rover Sport, walking back and fore to a newish wide beam fibreglass pleasure boat called Emerald with supplies, presumably for a planned trip.

Stewart slipped through the open gate, and hid effortlessly among the shadows on one of the other empty yachts. When the owner of Emerald left and locked up, Stewart boarded the now fully loaded boat. After picking the cabin padlock, he took the small boat down the Thames at a slow five knots, taking every effort not to draw attention to himself. By 3AM he had cleared the Isle of Sheppey and made Ramsgate by 5AM. Entering the small marina as dawn was breaking, he found an empty mooring in the long storage basin, and made a swift exchange of Emerald for a gleaming new fixed keel Jeanneau Sun

Odyssey 30i yacht, with a "For Sale" sign attached, that was moored next to a sailing centre, its windows filled with pictures of expensive boats in a wide range of prices.

Onboard the Jeanneau, the teak finish on the floors, worksurfaces and beds retained their factory waxing, the red leather interior seats were covered in protective plastic and its stern was as yet unnamed. The new Yanmar 3YM20 21 HP, 15.3 Kw engine protested at first but soon fired up and Stewart rapidly transferred food and supplies from the Emerald along with a selection of navigation maps, a radio, compass, torches and waterproof clothing, before filling the fifty-litre fuel tank from the dispenser near the sales booth. The food supplies fitted easily in the storage bins under the sofa seats in the main cabin space, and the Emerald's thirty pound propane calor gas canister was quickly connected to the small two ring cooker in the galley. Stewart put the remaining maps, compass, torches, cups, plates and cooking utensils into the storage cupboards behind and above the sofa seats, and the clothing into the tiny wardrobe in the rear master bedroom, as he took stock of his new home.

Within an hour, he had finished preparing the yacht, now informally named Cynthia, then slowly made his way out of Ramsgate, switching from the slow diesel engine to sail once they were in the channel. Sitting at the helm in the rear of the small boat, Stewart turned on the Anschütz Autopilot Pilot Star D navigation system to track his exact position and set a heading towards the small town of Serooskerke Schouwen on the Dutch coast, around sixty-two miles from Rotterdam. Within a few minutes, his entire journey had been uploaded to the global navigation systems that supported the Anschütz autopilot, and his route was shown as a series of blinking course adjustment points on the digital map on the navigation screen before him.

Stewart reduced the sails down to sixty five feet as Cynthia made for the French coast, making sure that he was seen and his course logged by numerous cargo vessels, as they adjusted course to give sufficient clearance to the smaller vessel and its planned route.

Approaching closer to Calais, he encountered a greater variety of different sized vessels, and made a point of waving to every passing yacht. As the day progressed, he let the autopilot steer the ship, while he grabbed some sleep in the small master bedroom as Cynthia passed the historic World War Two landing areas at Dunkirk and grew closer and closer to the Dutch coast. By nightfall, his position was shown on the illuminated navigation screen as being opposite the Dutch coastal town of Westkapelle. Having consumed a warm meal from one of the tins of Hunger Breaks "All Day Breakfast" in the galley, and having prepared a one litre steel thermos flask of strong Nescafe instant coffee for the night ahead, Stewart turned off his running lights, disconnected the state of the art navigation systems and turned 180 degrees about course.

With the power from a full 460 square feet of sail, a thirty-five-knot wind and the Yanmar 21 HP engines, Cynthia more than tripled her average day time speed, which would have been logged by the computerised navigation systems. Should his acquisition of Cynthia be discovered by Maelstrom, then at least they would start off by searching the Dutch coast.

Under the cover of darkness, Cynthia pushed through the rough channel swells, showing her racing pedigree as she headed past Calais and towards Brest at nearly sixteen knots. Sitting at the large wood and steel helm, Stewart's face showed how much he relished the challenge of pushing the thirty-one-foot vessel, letting her long keel dig deep into the waters, as the full sails made the most of the strong trailing winds.

By morning he was entering the Bay of Biscay, catching sleep every two hours in the master double berth, having been woken by the alarm from the countdown timer on the GShock. He spent the next two hours awake at the helm, now avoiding any kind of radio contact or close encounters with other vessels. As Cynthia progressed down the coast of France, Stewart followed the three developing news stories on the BBC World Service.

The standoff between the governments of the developed and undeveloped nations over the Magog free energy generators had intensified. Nearly a million people were now acting as a human shield for the transportation of a single Magog generator overland from Switzerland to Palestine. Maelstrom elite forces were acting on behalf of the developed nations and the United Nations, to try and prevent the progress of the convoy. Several violent clashes had occurred, resulting in deaths and injuries for the largely peaceful protesters. Public opinion was clearly turning against the developed nations and numerous celebrities were now taking every public appearance as an opportunity to voice support for Nissa Ad-Dajjal.

The ongoing search for "terrorist mastermind" Tavish Stewart continued, with intensive house to house searches taking place in West London, and increasing fears voiced from the Maelstrom executives, who were now providing leadership to the UK's law enforcement and intelligence agencies, that the fugitive may have already left the UK.

A challenge from back benchers to the leadership of Simon Brinkwater, after leaks from an unknown source showed enormous undeclared payments from Maelstrom to the Prime Minister, was growing in strength. Brinkwater was downplaying the allegations, and called for an urgent investigation by the Intelligence Services to identify the unknown source of the leaks. Stewart smiled grimly, as he had a feeling that the "unknown source" was only just getting started.

Although he had experienced far worse, the cooking and washing facilities on Cynthia were cramped, and the novelty of canned food soon faded. Stewart focused on the greater goal, settling into a routine at the end of each day, using a pair of Nikon Prostaff 7s 8 x 42 Binoculars from the Emerald, he took Cynthia's course closer to the French coast, so he could make visual checks of landmarks and compare them to his large-scale paper map, carefully plotting his position after each observation, before taking the boat back away from the coast line. Keeping to this discipline of two hours on and two hours off for sleep, he made his way along the coast of Portugal, round Cadiz and three days after leaving London he entered port in Tangier, where he knew from past experience cash could answer even the toughest questions.

The commercial port of Tangier shelters behind a long thick stone harbour wall of relatively modern construction and is split into three main sections. The outer, by the Route de la Plage Mercala, is for container traffic, the middle, behind the Avenue Mahomed VI and Grand Mosque, is for public and private vessels, while the final area within the Baie de Tanger is a public beach, where the once famous Cafe Panorama now rubs shoulders with a MacDonald's. The ancient port can trace its roots back to the Phoenicians, and its white buildings and ancient skyline make it look like an oasis paradise from the sea.

Stewart entered using the diesel engines and, passing the main ferry docks, made his way slightly further into a smaller harbour for a range of private vessels. The sides of the moorings were four or five boats deep, with vessel after vessel tied to its neighbour. In amongst this thick mass of floating crafts, Stewart guided Cynthia until he was opposite Restaurant Hadiya, which had only four small tables set outside and served a variety of fish dishes, the catch coming fresh every day from the nearby Ste Isibag Fish seller. After having tied up Cynthia to what resembled a floating village, four vessels deep, Stewart crossed over the boats in between and, after paying 100 times the going rate for someone to watch his yacht, reached the restaurant dockside. He sat at one of the wooden tables, passed a twenty euro note quietly to the young waitress and asked if he could speak to the owner, who turned out to be a tall dark haired middle-aged woman with four fully grown sons, all of whom worked in various capacities in the port. After some lengthy discussions prices were agreed for fresh supplies, a handheld GPS, the painting of "سينثيا" (Sinthia) on the Jeanneau's hull and papers registering the boat in Tangier.

In the early morning, after a busy overnight refit of Cynthia, she was now flying the Moroccan flag, and heading out of Tangier. The national symbol, of a pentagram on a red background, struck Stewart as having an odd synchronicity with the occult nature of his mission. As he passed through the straits of Gibraltar, Cynthia was stopped by a 426-foot-long Admiral Gorshkov class frigate, called the Admiral Kasatonov, that was looking for ships attempting to break the international blockade preventing the a transportation of Magog generators.

As the Russian marines inspected inside Cynthia, a grey Kamov Ka-27 helicopter, which Stewart recognised by its NATO designation "Helix", hovered overhead ensuring compliance with the stop and search instructions. Despite the inconvenience, Stewart was relieved to have been stopped by the Russian navy as they were not looking for British fugitives.

After leaving Gibraltar and the Russian warship behind, Stewart settled back into his two-hour work and rest schedule, the warmer weather and calmer seas making this leg of the trip much more enjoyable. Two days later he finally arrived at the Italian port of Ostia.

The tourist marina is located to the right of the mouth of the river Tiber, and has a double layered entrance that looks like a giant crab reaching out into the sea. Stewart passed Cynthia through the crab claws and steered the yacht slowly to a vacant spot on the right, near the marina's post office and central offices.

After paying for a private mooring with a number of his euros, Stewart undertook some essential shopping along the seafront, before entering the Barcelo Aran Blu hotel, where he told the concierge he was meeting his lover and wanted to be discreet about registration. After yet more euros changed hands, Stewart had a room.

Minutes after checking in, the Scotsman was on the roof terrace with a bottle of iced S. Pellegrino and a cheap blue Nokia 130 telephone, fitted with one of the three "pay as you go" CoopVoce Sims that he had purchased in the marina's CoopAdriatica supermarket.

Knowing that Stewart's showroom in Rome would most likely be monitored by Maelstrom, he dialled a memorised private number in Istanbul, where the deep baritone voice of Mohammed Sek answered.

FOLIO 4 – THE MAPS OF DESTINY

CHAPTER 22 - GODFATHERS OF THE NIGHT

"Old men are dangerous: it doesn't matter to them what is going to happen." - George Bernard Shaw

35°31'42.9"N 25°13'37.0"E
Aboard the 283m "Tiamat" Migaloo M7 Submersible-Yacht,
Sea of Crete, 50 Nautical Miles North of Heraklion, Crete
13.20HRS, 30th July, Present Day.

The bridge of the Tiamat was a clinically clean, fifty-five-foot square workspace at the front of the ship's superstructure, located just underneath the large domed SAMPSON AESA and S1850M static radar arrays. The control room was fitted with brushed steel surfaces and large high definition screens, displaying every detail of the vast vessel and giving views of the ship and the ocean around it from a multitude of different perspectives.

Schematic diagrams of the ship's many systems were displayed on some, while others streamed split screen CCTV coverage of the main work areas, ranging from the engine room to the galley. The clean-up and repair work caused by Jeffery Sonnet's flooding could be seen to be still ongoing.

Displays also showed external images of the vessel from ship based cameras, and some computer augmented "birds-eye" views from a "Zephyr" high-altitude, long-endurance (HALE) autonomous unmanned system, flying in a holding pattern some twelve miles above the Tiamat. This ultra-lightweight carbon-fibre drone weighed just 66 pounds and its fifty-five feet long wings were composed of solar cells that allowed it to remain flying high above the world for months at a time. This particular Zephyr acted as the Tiamat's personal communications satellite and reconnaissance system, relaying super high definition aerial images in visible and infrared spectrums, superimposed onto radar identified icons of every vessel and aircraft around the ship.

Long range active and passive radars were complemented by sonar and ultrasonic devices, providing the control room with the ability to track up to 2,000 vessels and aircraft for 250 miles around them. These complex systems were also fitted with "backdoor" access codes that allowed so called "Remote Weapons Telemetry" (RWT), the capability to take control over any compatible electronic weapons systems on military ships, aircraft or land bases within range, effectively giving the Tiamat devastating offensive and defensive tactical abilities that were totally deniable.

The bridge floor space was laid out with three white leather seats, the central Captain's chair being slightly raised to allow clear visibility of the forward observation windscreens and the main consoles. The other two seats were placed to permit operation of two large control panels to the front of the Captain's seat which, right now, was occupied by the beautiful owner of the Tiamat, Dr Nissa Ad-Dajjal. Her black silk Hermes trouser suit fitted her slim tall figure with a perfection that could only be achieved by bespoke tailoring. Her left sleeve fell carelessly revealing her gold Rolex GMT Master II chronometer. She glanced at the time.

"Since our departed guests... are both British it would be appropriate that their demise should be an embarrassment to that nation." Declared her silky-smooth voice.

She sat looking at a high resolution augmented reality display from the Zephyr's ARGUS-IS 1.8-gigapixel video surveillance platform and SAMPSON radar systems. On the detailed satellite image, a small blue grey Robinson R22 helicopter with orange landing floats was seen flying low over the ocean, heading directly towards an uninhabited island north of Crete, labelled "Dias Irakleiou" on the map. Beside the real-time image of the aircraft, superimposed over the blue ocean, information was displayed giving the call sign of the helicopter, its speed and latitude and longitude.

The senior of the three men standing before her, all dressed in identical gleaming white uniforms, was Bjorn Jersson, a tall Scandinavian with short salty grey hair and beard, who had over thirty years' experience working in the shadowy world of mercenary and military sea operations. He had been the skipper of the Tiamat since she had been commissioned two years ago and, prior to that, had worked for Government agencies in Europe and the Middle East.

Programming the ships systems by selecting a filter to show only British tactical assets, the display focused down to two possible weapons platforms. Bjorn's deep voice with its distinctive accent, described the two possible RWT options for dealing with the fleeing helicopter. The predicted outcome of each was being shown in an animated projection on the large screen before them.

The first option was a British Royal Navy Type 45 destroyer, HMS Daring, located off the Turkish coast near Antalya, North West of Cyprus, some 233 miles away. Fitted with SAMPSON AESA and S1850M, that were a perfect match with the Tiamat's own telemetry, meant that the billion-pound destroyer's Sylver Vertical Launching System (SVLS) A70 could be deployed.

As Bjorn spoke, the two men who had been standing to attention beside him moved to work on the consoles to the right side of the Captain's chair, initiating backdoor synchronisation with the British warship. The animated projection of this particular scenario showed the deployment of a Block 1NT Aster 30 missile. These sixteen feet long 992 pound intelligent missiles were capable of striking down multiple air or surface threats hundreds of miles away. With the flick of a single switch on the Tiamat bridge a thirty-four-million-dollar missile would accelerate to Mach 4.5, soaring to the edge of space before descending and vaporising the small helicopter in mid-air. Covering the 217 miles in less than six minutes after being launched, it would leave no trace beyond the rocket's own heat signature which would be identified as coming from the British warship.

The second RWT option was to divert an existing drone mission by a "Taranis" Unmanned Combat Air Vehicle (UCAV), that had taken off thirty minutes earlier from Gaziantep on the southern Turkish border near Syria, and was now over the ocean some 186 miles to the East, preparing to turn and rapidly pass over Lebanon into Syrian airspace. This UCAV was an eight-tonne black stealth delta-wing combat aircraft, forty feet long with a thirty-foot wingspan. Its high speed and ability to operate extremely high G manoeuvres had caused this class of UCAV to be misidentified in numerous UFO sightings during its decades of development. Now in full operational use within NATO for "Black Ops" deniable high-risk missions without risking personnel, this British aircraft was remotely controlled from RAF Boulmer in Northumberland, the UK's Air Surveillance and Control Systems Force Command.

Nissa Ad-Dajjal took in the two possibilities and shook her head, causing her long black hair to cascade slowly. Both deaths were too quick, Sonnet had caused her personal loss and his end should be equally personal.

She smiled and pulled a brushed steel Porsche design smartphone from the front pocket of her silk suit. Her long red fingernail scrolled down through some contacts and she initiated an encrypted call to an 0030 28340 prefix number that designated Zoniana (Ζωνιανά), a small village of less than 2,000 inhabitants in Crete.

Once famed for its shepherds and fierce resistance against the Nazi's during the second world war, the village had since moved on from simple livestock farming and is now known to international law enforcement as part of "The Devil's Triangle", a grouping of three small towns that form the centre of European drug production and organised crime, whose leaders are simply known as "The Godfathers of the Night" (νονοί της νύχτας).

In the 1960s and 70s the region became associated with small family based crime clans, who became renowned for cultivating and trafficking marijuana from drug plantations in fields near Malades. Limited by their family size their activities were largely focused on Crete and the Greek mainland. However, since the unification of Europe, the Cretan drug lords had expanded their business activities to include human trafficking, prostitution, kidnapping and illegal arms sales. The European Union's closer integration with former Soviet states in the late 1990s introduced a synergy between them and the Albanian Mafia who, in return for providing foot soldiers for the most violent and dangerous tasks, got an exclusive Eastern European criminal franchise for the Godfather's of the Night's activities.

Ad-Dajjal's call was received on a simple silver iPhone that buzzed loudly as it lay on a plain wooden table set in a small courtyard, where a grey-haired man in his late forties was sitting in the sun enjoying a strong black coffee from a plain steel mug held in his right hand. He was dressed in a black short sleeved open necked shirt, which revealed a thick gold chain and cross that highlighted his coarse grey chest hair.

His left arm revealed a variety of old knife scars as he reached over and pulled the phone to him.

"Ναί." (yes)

His thick and heavily accented voice spoke in a practiced tone that indicated the relaxed and indifferent attitude of someone who was used to being obeyed. On hearing the voice on the other end of the line his right hand involuntarily spilt some of the hot black coffee over his Armani suit trousers. Reaching down with his right hand he placed the metal coffee cup on the cobblestones at his feet and extracted a grey and white handkerchief from his front right trouser pocket which he used to try and dry some of the worst of the spill, as he listened to the phone held in his left hand.

"Nickos, thank you for taking my call," said a sultry voice.

A light layer of perspiration started to form on the man's face, the heavily tanned lines showing considerable stress. His right hand moved from mopping the spilt coffee to wiping his forehead.

"I have a slight problem that I would like you to solve for me," Ad-Dajjal continued.

"Two people… undesirable people... have taken one of my helicopters and are heading towards you…"

She paused as she checked the current projected course of the helicopter.

"They will probably arrive near the beach at Ammoudara, West of Heraklion. It would be most helpful if you could arrange a final, a very final, reception for the two of them. I will have photographs and details of the two-people emailed to you right now, so there are no mistakes."

The iPhone buzzed as an email arrived with attachments documenting Jeffery Sonnet's details as a retired Civil Servant, now an Antiquarian, and Ms Helen Curren, a forty-two-year-old lawyer.

"One of them, the male, does not look it but may be a challenge to deal with, so do not use those Albanian Allushi "blunt instruments". In fact, I would prefer if you kept this within your family, maybe even oversee the reception personally. I will be most grateful if you take care of this for me."

"Πότε." (At what time)? He asked simply.

Ad-Dajjal paused, again checking something.

"In around fifteen minutes. I know that does not give much notice, but I am sure you will manage in that," again she paused consulting some of the high-tech systems before her.

"Lovely new black BMW 750i... and with your talents for dealing with such things you will soon be back on your terrace to finish that coffee."

The old man's face frowned deeply as he looked into the clear blue sky above him.

"Thank you, Nickos. I trust your expertise in dealing with such problems." The line went dead.

Nickos Papais spat a curse at the floor before rising from his chair to reveal the back of his black cotton shirt, soaked with perspiration. A well-worn leather gun holster was just visible, attached to the waistband of his Armani trousers, the hilt of a 9mm black polymer Turkish built Canik TP9-V2 protruding in the middle of his lower back. This modified clone of the German Walther P99 was popular in the Mediterranean underworld because of its ease of availability, reliability and large eighteen round magazine. When combined with the Greek Mafia's use of Allushi clan members from the Kurcaj region, some of the Albanian underworld's most ruthless groups, and their weapon of choice, the AK47, it was easy to see why law enforcement preferred to accept a bribe to look the other way.

The heat from the strong Greek sunshine was magnified inside the small Perspex cockpit of the Robinson R22 helicopter as it flew low and fast, always following the "South" reading on the small display in front of the joystick. Sonnet ignored the extreme heat and kept his altitude at the very borderline of safety, skimming just above the water. As they approached a small island, he scanned the ground for any signs of habitation, especially roads, railways or ferry ports where he could set down and continue their escape. But it turned out to be just a small desolate outcrop, inhabited only by birds, so he flew rapidly over it and continued his path over the sea, pushing the small aircraft as low and fast as he dared over the rolling blue waves. He knew that red lining the Lycoming O-360 four-cylinder engine for such a long period would destroy its bearings and gaskets, but he was intending to ditch the machine once he landed, and all that mattered was maximum speed and the hope that his pursuers were using older radar systems, that might not be able to track him while he flew so close to the horizon. He looked to his left and checked on Curren, who was clearly still suffering from the after effects of whatever drugs she had been given. She lay slumped and semi-conscious beside him, mumbling odd words in an unrecognisable language, none of which made sense to Sonnet.

The fuel gauges in the small craft were starting to become a concern, but Sonnet could not risk lowering his speed as he tried to maximise the distance between them and the ship. He could have got a better long-distance view ahead if he had gained more height, but instead he kept to within fifteen feet above the sea level and maintained the 130 knots speed that he could get from the engine. After ten more minutes of open ocean, suddenly he could see a much larger land mass rushing towards them. He reduced his speed so he could take better stock of his surroundings. To his left was a large sports stadium and directly ahead was a long beach made up of a mix of dirt, sand and stones. To his immediate right were three large trees, which provided shade for a number of old caravans, and directly in front of him was an empty dirt car park some five yards from the shoreline. This section of the beach was empty, because of the much rougher waters where several rip tides mixed together.

Sonnet eased up the joystick, slowing the helicopter even more and stirring up the fine beach dust into a localised blizzard. He looked from side to side, seeking to guide the small aircraft down safely to the dirt carpark, in front of a group of twelve feet high grey breeze block walls and their matching grey two storey dwellings that lay beyond. A large black BMW saloon car came barrelling down the small alleyway that led to the beach, creating almost as much dust as Sonnet was generating with his own landing. The car spun in a classic handbrake turn, stopping dramatically. Two figures emerged from the rear, walking purposefully towards the helicopter, each carrying an item that it was impossible to identify due to the whipped-up cloud of sand that filled the air. As the two men approached closer, bright flashes of light became visible in the middle of the dust storm, and the thick Perspex cabin around Sonnet and Curren began to shatter, as numerous Kalashnikov AK47 rounds began passing clean through the small helicopter cabin space and into the surrounding fuselage. A mix of dark and clear fluids began flying into the space inside the cabin and a strong smell of gasoline filled the air. It was clearly only a matter of moments before one of the bullets struck either of the occupants of the helicopter with deadly effect.

In the midst of the unrelenting hail of high velocity 7.62mm ammunition, Sonnet swore loudly at the two men and then violently twisted the controls, making the cabin rear high up into the air and the tail dip, so low that it broke off the orange flotation landing gear as it bumped across the sandy ground. In a series of hops and tail impacts, the small Robinson 22 spun around 180 degrees straight into the two gunmen. Thumping one of the men backwards six feet, it sliced the second man into shreds, with such force that the rear rotor blade shattered into a hail of high velocity shards that embedded into the front side doors and windshield of the parked BMW. The grey sand around the cockpit had by now turned blood red. The second shooter recovered enough to resume spraying bullets at the copter, clearly enraged at the death of his colleague.

Sonnet's eyes narrowed and he pushed the joystick even more forcefully, this time forward, causing the Robinson to tilt down so that it stuck the ground repeatedly. Sonnet and Curren were bumped violently forward, ending up hanging suspended in their safety harnesses, as the main rotor began to make direct contact with the ground in front of them, dragging them slowly up the beach towards the second man and the parked black BMW.

The AK47's thirty round magazine ran dry, just as the main rotor blade thumped into the sand in front of the cockpit, with such force that it hacked the second man into small pieces, drenching the sand with a gory mix of blood and shredded flesh. Moments later, the main rotors completely disintegrated and the remains of the Robinson R22 slumped motionless into the sand. There was a profound silence after the chaos of the last few minutes.

Sonnet took a moment to cut himself and Curren free from their nylon safety harnesses, with his small 420 stainless steel Bowen belt knife. As the two of them hobbled from the wreckage, a single figure emerged from the driver's seat of the black BMW.

Nickos Papais was having a very bad day, he had just witnessed his two sons killed in some kind of freak encounter, where a retired civil servant had turned a small helicopter into a weapon capable of taking out two AK47s. He was not going to underestimate this barefoot man, even though he was very bedraggled and carrying an unconscious woman. He drew his Canik TP9-V2 from its holster in to his right hand, slowly and deliberately used his left hand to pull the slide to put a 9mm round into the chamber, and then lined up the tritium sight onto the centre line of the man's chest.

But, in the time he had taken to load the round, his target had already dropped to a kneeling position and launched a knife into Papais' gun arm. The burning pain of the deep cut made the strength fail in his fingers, causing the Cretan to drop the weapon. Undeterred, Papais spat at the ground, drew a wicked six-inch stiletto blade from his left trouser pocket and advanced on Sonnet. If this was going to get personal then so be it. Knife fights were his specialty, and by the time he had finished his work, this man would literally beg for him to end his wretched life, like so many before him.

Sonnet took in the experienced way that the large man in front of him was handling both the knife, that he had drawn in a modified saber grip with the stiletto tip or "scanso" ready to execute the "scherma di stiletto siciliano" (the deadly art of Sicilian stiletto fighting), and how he was reacting to the vicious wound he had just received from Sonnet's Bowen. Most men would have backed away after such an injury, but this one just became more aggressive. Throwing the Bowen had saved Sonnet from a lethal gunshot wound, but now he was left unarmed in a knife fight with an extremely dangerous adversary.

As the two men squared off, Sonnet kept his eyes on his opponent and pulled the surgical stainless-steel Tag Heuer watch from his wrist. Opening the extending diver's folding link in the bracelet, he wrapped the watch like a knuckle duster around the centre of his left hand, with the dial facing outwards and the case back against his knuckles.

Each time Papais's deadly blade thrust forward, Sonnet executed a perfect "quarto tagliata" and diverted the attempted stab with the steel Tag timepiece, producing a jarring sound of metal on metal that caused sparks to fly into the air. On the third strike, the watch's sapphire glass took a direct blow, shattering into fragments that fell into the sand and cut into the skin on Sonnet's bare feet with each step of their deadly dance.

As the Greek smiled wickedly at the sight of his opponent's blood, Sonnet took the initiative and delivered a lightning fast low Mawashi-geri roundhouse kick, the ball of his right foot striking his opponents left knee and irrevocably shattering the joint. As the crippling pain brought Papais to his knees, Sonnet's left hand delivered a series of repeated thundering full body strikes to his opponent's temple, with the broken Tag Heuer diver's watch. The force of the blows from the solid one-piece surgical stainless-steel case shattered the temporal, sphenoid and zygomatic bones of the skull, penetrating the frontal and temporal lobes, rendering Papais unconscious with the second strike. The fight was over.

Exhausted, Sonnet made his way over to the black BMW and sat in the driver's seat, looking through the items that had been left in the front of the car for anything that might be useful. Suddenly, his attention was diverted by a series of gunshots, and he looked up to see that Curren had recovered consciousness and was pumping two rounds from the Canik TP9-V2 into Papais.

Slightly disconcerted by her actions, but not wanting to waste any more time, Sonnet leaned out of the car, looked at the carnage that had been caused by the rotor blades, and called to Curren to hurry up, "Come on, Chop! Chop!"

CHAPTER 23 - LIKE LAMBS TO THE SLAUGHTER

"Know this dread secret, on the physical plane there is no magic stronger than those of the Dugpas (Left Hand Path Esoteric Buddhists)." - Notes from the Inner Group of the Esoteric Section of the Theosophical Society, 1890-1891 Handwritten MS.

Ammoudara Beach,
Gazi 714 14, Crete, Greece
14.10HRS, 30th July, Present Day.

The plume of smoke, from the combustion of aviation fuel and fuselage components, rose from the wreckage of the Robinson R22 helicopter high into the air above the small beach. The prevailing North Westerly wind rapidly pulled the smoke into a long trail out into the Gulf of Heraklion, making it look like a giant arrow pointing to the crash site when viewed by the Tiamat's Zephyr ARGUS-IS surveillance platform, twelve miles above Crete.

Dr Nissa Ad-Dajjal sat looking intently at the high definition screens in front of her, having watched the confrontation between Sonnet and the men who had intercepted the small R22 helicopter. She showed no emotion throughout the encounter, even when the two survivors dragged the remains of the three Greeks into the wreckage and set fire to the debris.

She waved her right hand dismissively as she rose from the Captain's chair.

"No matter, have Nickos' men wait for those two at the Papais villa and detain them. They may yet prove useful as hostages in an exchange for Stewart's emerald tablet. After we have the tablet we will send a wet team to eliminate all the loose ends."

Captain Jersson interjected, "Domina, how do we get…"

Ad-Dajjal smiled wickedly as she interrupted, "I will see to it that our two former guests deliver themselves willingly, like lambs to the slaughter."

With that Ad-Dajjal walked purposely from the bridge, her Christian Louboutin stilettos accentuating the length of her long legs within the elegant dark silk Hermes trouser suit. After she had left, the air in the ship's control room retained an intoxicating musky scent from the rare Ghost flower of the Mojave Desert, distilled exclusively for the billionaire by the Sultan of Oman's own perfume house, Amouage.

Back on the beach, Sonnet and Curren were sweating from the rigorous activity of the past minutes. Having got the BMW engine running, so that they could make a quick getaway if necessary, Sonnet joined Curren on the beach. Concerned by her un-characteristically violent behaviour, but assuming it was just due to the stress of the situation, Sonnet had gently taken the Canik pistol from Curren and had encouraged her to work with him, pulling what remained of the three dead bodies into the Perspex cabin space of the R22 helicopter. They collected up the men's wallets, watches and other personal possessions in a pile on the stained sand just outside the cabin.

The only body with clothing that could be reused was the older male. Nickos Papais had been slightly larger than Sonnet, but his dark Armani suit looked less conspicuous than the badly distressed clothes which Sonnet had been wearing since the conflict at Gordon Square and throughout the rescue on the Tiamat.

Curren's white linen robe could at least allow her to pass for a tourist, but Sonnet needed a change of clothes if he was not to attract considerable attention. The evidence of the gunshot wounds and the tear in the fabric on the right shirt sleeve from Sonnet's Bowden were visible on Papais' black shirt. But, by wearing the suit jacket that had been left in the BMW, no one would notice. The single Apple iPhone they had found in the sand turned out to also belong to Papais, and Sonnet had undertaken the ghoulish task of using the dead gangster's finger to gain access to the phone and disable the security features, so they could examine the contents at their leisure once they were away from the scene of the incident.

The two AK-47 machine guns turned out to have four spare thirty round magazines in the boot of the BMW 750i, so Sonnet replaced the spent mags on both guns and placed them in the floor foot well behind the front seats.

As his final task before setting fire to the wreckage, Sonnet carefully surveyed the assortment of personal possessions they had accumulated from the three men, throwing most of them into the small helicopter cockpit, along with the shattered Tag Heuer that had served him so well. Curren watched him and noticed he was only keeping a single cheap white-faced Timex, some keys, three remote door opening fobs, credit cards, cash and a single blue BIC lighter.

In her darkened private chambers Ad-Dajjal disrobed, washed her face, hair and hands with clean water from an undecorated silver bowl, drying herself off on a new white linen cloth which she threw into a bin after its single use. Having ritually cleansed herself she took a single lighted taper from a tall black candle, situated in an ornately carved ebony wall alcove, and moved purposefully in an anticlockwise direction around the perimeter of her sacred space, lighting three, two feet high, cones of kyara, one of the finest agarwood incenses, made specially for her ritual work by Akiyoshi Tshami, grand master of Tachikawa-ryu, an eleventh century left hand, black magick school of Mikkyō, esoteric Shingon Buddhism.

Successive purges by the Christian Church during the sixteenth to eighteenth centuries, and by Communist and Western regimes in the nineteenth and twentieth centuries, had systematically extinguished esoteric lineages from the European, American, Indian (Vāmācāra and Dakṣiṇācāra) and Tibetan (Nyingma, Kagyu, Sakya and Gelug) traditions and from China's own Esoteric Buddhist school, the Mìzōng. As a consequence, the Japanese Mikkyō, are the only tradition remaining who can claim intact esoteric initiatory lineages. Ad-Dajjal's own lengthy study and subsequent initiations at the Mount Koya and Mount Hiei temples, placed her among the most powerful left-hand adepts of the Tachikawa-ryu school.

There have been so many books written about magick, and yet for all the volumes that sit gathering dust on shelves, all the television programmes and movies that glorify the topic, and all the people who study obscure grimoires and practice secret ceremonies, very, very few have any real understanding or ability. Because magick, real magick is not about books, spells, or exclusive secret societies, it is about understanding and mastering the self.

It would be an understatement to say that Dr Nissa Ad-Dajjal understood. In fact, it was the terrifying depth and clarity of her understanding which led her to seek to create a new heaven and earth, in her own likeness. The asylums are full of mentally ill people who believe they are God. Unfortunately for all sentient beings, Dr Ad-Dajjal was very far from insane.

Practitioners of Right Hand Path esoteric Shingon Buddhism engage in Hogo meditations with practices such as Nembutsu, where they perform meditative awareness of past enlightened masters, called Bodhisattvas, to share their wisdom, compassion and peace. It is believed that such enlightened beings continue their consciousness beyond our limited understanding of death, and can even project their consciousness into new bodies at will.

Left Hand Path variants of Nembutsu attempt to commune with past masters of the darker aspects of existence. Ad-Dajjal's personal Nembutsu practice exhibited both her profound ability and the depths of the darkness that lurked within her being.

The three incense cones glowed in the dim light of the room and illuminated a small oak table, that stood within a gleaming brass circle that had been inlaid into the wooden decking. Ad-Dajjal approached the table and bowed to a human skull, covered with gold leaf and engraved with Sanskrit, which rested alone on the table. The thick incense began playing tricks with the light and made it look like the empty eye sockets of the infamous Dharmadhātu skull were animated with a dark intelligence.

The skull became the single focus for Ad-Dajjal, as she began a series of well-practiced tantric mudras and deep chants. Her long fingers formed the ancient hand shapes that manipulated the vital life energy called Chi within her body. When combined with a specific mantra the vital energy became converted into a very rarified form, called Uḍāna, a combination of sound, energy, vibration and the focused intent of the mind.

Although it can take a lifetime to fully master, ritual focus on Uḍāna energy provides the mechanism for consciousness to gain total control over the Chakras of the body. These Chakras, which normally convert energy internally into the physical form, can also create physical forms or forces externally and separately from the body.

Such forces are the building blocks of our existence on the physical plane and, once tapped by an adept, can cause, as an infamous magician of the twentieth century once said, "Change to occur in accordance to the will…". In a word, magick. It was not an exaggeration to say that this ancient ritual not only expanded Ad-Dajjal's consciousness, but placed the very fabric of existence under her conscious control.

As the mantra reached its climax, Ad-Dajjal's will started to exert control over the physical reality around her, so that the incense smoke started to twist and coil, spreading ever closer to the centre of the table, until the long tendrils poured through the empty eye sockets of the decorated skull.

The sizzling sound of the incense transformed itself into the basic rasping elemental noises of speech. An ancient language filled the air with obscenities that praised suffering, pain, loss and disease in a Sanskrit sutra attributed to the Bodhisattva of Despair.

Ad-Dajjal's skin glistened and she sighed with ecstasy as she entered into one of the 109 forms of blissful communion with Dakini-ten, the Principle of Darkness involved with the Skull Ritual of Tachikawa-ryu.

1035 miles away, having completed the uneventful journey from the sanatorium, the three priests were sitting in the office space of the Chief Exorcist. Suddenly, Fr Chin Kwon abruptly stopped in mid conversation, clearly losing motor control, his body beginning to shake, his arms and legs twitching uncontrollably. With a look of surprise, he dropped his paper coffee cup, spilling its contents, and was clearly in distress. With an extreme effort, he started forming his hands into a series of mudra forms that looked strikingly similar to those being performed by Ad-Dajjal so many miles away. His body continued to twitch in large uncoordinated jerks as he fought against some unseen force.

"What on earth is happening?" Demanded O'Neill to Verchencho, as they looked at the panic-struck Kwon desperately fighting some hidden influence.

"I do not know for sure, but I think somewhere, someone is literally raising Hell." Responded Verchencho.

"What can we do?"

Hugo Verchencho answered by kneeling and began speaking in a language that O'Neill recognised as Aramaic.

"Abwûn (Oh Thou, from whom the breath of life comes)
d'bwaschmâja (Who fills all realms)
Nethkâdasch schmach (May Your being be experienced)
Têtê malkuthach (Your spiritual light manifest)
Nehwê tzevjânach aikâna d'bwaschmâja af b'arha (Let Your Will be in the spiritual just as it is on the material on earth)
Hawvlân lachma d'sûnkanân jaomâna (Give us wisdom for our daily need)
Waschboklân chaubên wachtahên aikâna daf chnân schwoken l'chaijabên. (detach the fetters of faults that bind us to destiny like we let go the faults of others)
Wela tachlân l'nesjuna (Let us not be lost in superficial material things)
ela patzân min bischa (but let us be freed from that what keeps us from our true purpose)
Metol dilachie malkutha wahaila wateschbuchta l'ahlâm almîn (From You comes the life force that beautifies all and renews itself from age to age)
Amên. (I confirm with my entire being)"

The tendrils of incense flowed from the eye sockets of the skull and into Ad-Dajjal's own nostrils, blending the dark entity's primal evil with her own life force. She inhaled deeply, further activating the energy channels called Nadis which flowed down her spine. As the smoke concentrated in the three main Nadis it combined with Ad-Dajjal's own life force, creating an intertwined snake shape (Caduceus) which rose up from the base of the spine to the top of her head. Flowing around her, the shadowy essence formed itself into the dark cobra shaped hood of the legendary Naga left hand path master adepts. Ad-Dajjal's eyes opened and her face glowed, as she exhaled thick smoke through her nostrils. Her lips opened and a guttural male voice continued the sutra of the Bodhisattva of Despair in the same ancient dialect of Sanskrit, but now issued in the first person.

"I am the all-consuming Rage!

The betrayer of Trust,
The Hater of all living beings,
The bringer of Suffering, Desolation and Pain.
I was there when Lucifer fell,
I was there in the Garden when Eve gave Adam the fruit,
I was there with those who wept as the Ark sailed and the waters came,
I was there when the Christ was betrayed with a kiss,
I was there when Pilate washed his Hands,
I was there when the Carpenter's Son lost hope,
And I held the ladder as My Apostle felt the rope burn his neck,
Embrace Me, Bringer of darkness and the loss of all hope…"

Ad-Dajjal's own voice interjected into the obscene liturgy.

"Grant me the power to slip from this body to another, so I may sow discord where there is hope… in the pursuit of the great work of reordering heaven and earth into darkness, pain, hate and despair!"

On the beach, Curren stumbled slightly as she headed to the BMW car. She dismissed the clumsiness as a side effect from the drugs she had been administered on the Tiamat, some hours earlier. As she climbed into the front passenger seat, Sonnet smiled and passed her the iPhone.

"See if you can find anything useful on that as we drive."

Curren cleared her throat and responded in a slightly gruffer voice. "If we are lucky, I may be able to track the location of the home of the thugs who attacked us. Any idea why they picked on us."

"I would guess they were working for that crazy woman on the ship."

Curren coughed, and again noticed that her left leg and arm were twitching more strongly. "Those drugs just do not give up do they?"

"Just be thankful we escaped. Speaking of which, we should find somewhere to hide before more of those goons come looking for us." Sonnet engaged reverse and pulled the large car backwards, avoiding the wreckage that covered most of the beach around them.

As he drove down the narrow alleyway that connected the beach to the main road Curren coughed more strongly, noting that her breath smelt of a smoky mix of camphor, pine and mint. She put it down to the fumes from the fire that was now raging behind them. She tried to distract herself from the side effects of the drugs and the smoke by searching the gangsters phone. They were in luck, as Papais had made use of the GPS feature and with it they could track the BMW's starting point. After some discussion, they agreed it was worth checking if the gangster's home could be a viable location to hide, since it was possible that the house might now be empty.

As they drove through a large Carrefour carpark, Curren gave directions from the iPhone, interspersed with more coughing which grew more intense until she was bent double in the front passenger seat, and Sonnet was forced to pull over on one of the narrow roads off the Leof. 62 Martiron. As suddenly as the coughing and twitching had started it ceased completely. Apart from a sheen of perspiration over Curren's face, she now looked totally calm. Her movements became relaxed, smooth and fluid. Her voice was deeper, with a sensuous tone that Sonnet had not noticed before.

As they continued to drive, Curren began to look around the car like she had never seen the interior before. Her instructions to Sonnet were highly competent and, at times, he wondered if she was even checking the GPS. Evidently, she was because soon they arrived at the destination on the Epar.Od. Agiou Silla-Axounear road near the small village of Zoniana. Home for the gangsters was an isolated two storey villa, with white walls and a flat roof, that was approached by a long driveway. The BMWs broad sports tyres made considerable noise on the rough stone road surface. At the end of the long drive, their progress was halted by a set of two massive wooden gates set into a sixteen feet high stone perimeter wall.

By a process of trial and error, Sonnet worked through the sets of remote control key fobs they had collected, and eventually the two large gates swung open to reveal a floodlit courtyard around 100 feet square. Waiting to greet them inside was a group of three men, two of whom were armed with AK47s, and the third was holding the leash to two vicious Rottweiler dogs.

As Sonnet went to pull the BMW into a violent 180 degree turn to escape, he felt the cold muzzle of the Canik 9mm pistol pressed into the side of his neck. He turned his head slowly towards Curren's face, which no longer looked like the Curren he knew so well. The structure and texture of the cheeks and chin were different, younger and filled with a darkness that was not there before. And her eyes were so odd, they looked like those of the malevolent woman he had seen on the yacht, as she smiled cruelly and motioned for him to drive forward into the courtyard.

CHAPTER 24 - AN UNHOLY ALLIANCE

"The enemy of my enemy is my friend." - Ancient Arab Proverb

Piazza della Città Leonina.
00193 Rome
10.46HRS, 5th August, Present Day.

Father Thomas O'Neill stood waiting impatiently on the pavement outside the small coin and stamp dealership that overlooked the tree covered piazza. To his right, breakfast was being served at a number of metal folding tables covered with blue and white checked tablecloths. He had already eaten a hurried meal of cereal and cold milk four hours ago, but the smell of fresh bread and strong coffee was causing him to wish they had time to enjoy brunch.

They were already late for their 10.45 AM appointment at the Vatican, the mysterious Father Chin Kwon had delayed them by insisting on visiting an odd assortment of shops on the way, the latest being this small numismatic and philatelic shop, where he was currently inside with Verchencho.

For what must have been the tenth time that morning, O'Neill glanced at the white tritium hands on his scuffed Nite MX10 watch and back at the small shop entrance, while their vital preparation time slipped away. Another few minutes passed and then Verchencho and Kwon emerged, the latter carrying a small tan leather drawstring bag, followed closely by the shop owner who was clearly only too glad to see them leave.

"Do not worry so much Hugo," the deeply distinctive English accent still appeared somehow unnatural coming from the lips of a Japanese priest.

"I am renowned for keeping the most careful of accounts. No one is being cheated."

"And," He added looking knowingly at the Archaeologist,

"My dear Thomas, we will arrive at exactly the best time. It is always more important to be properly prepared than punctual. Speaking of which, are you both sure you do not want to change into something more suitable? Our meeting does literally decide the fate of creation."

Kwon looked at Fr Verchencho's black vestment, that was creased and spattered with the remains of the meals that he had consumed over the hectic past days. O'Neill for his part, looked more appropriately dressed for an archaeological dig than a business meeting, wearing scuffed brown leather walking boots, khaki cargo pants and a white open necked fleece.

In contrast to his two companions, the Japanese priest wore an exquisitely tailored Sartoria Ripense grey pinstripe suit, that they had collected personally from a small shop hidden on the Via di Ripetta.

From the look on the Master Taylor's face he had been up all night preparing this handmade suit for its 8am collection. But, as with everyone who interacted with Fr Kwon, he seemed only too willing to undertake the most arduous of tasks without payment, either through some genuine fear or a simple need to please, O'Neill could not tell. What he did know was that Kwon was skilfully charming and had extremely expensive tastes.

Since their first meeting he had transformed from an aesthetic monk, who had survived on the bare minimum in an unfurnished cell at the Sanatorium of St Michael, to a cultured and immaculately dressed figure. Upon arriving in Rome in Verchencho's ancient 6.9 litre Mercedes, after a long and dusty drive from the Abruzzo mountains, Fr Kwon had immediately insisted on being taken to the Banca Monte Dei Paschi Di Siena on Via delle Fornaci, next to the Vatican City. It was dark when they parked the 450SEL on the right-hand side of the road, adjacent to a series of small restaurants. Verchencho and O'Neill ordered a late dinner at the Trattoria Perdincibacco, while Kwon crossed the road, skirted around the large pedestrian underpass and knocked on a tinted glass door, where he was greeted by two, armed security guards in camouflage fatigues. O'Neill expected the Japanese priest to be briskly turned away, as the bank was closed, but some moments later a dark suited middle-aged man appeared and ushered Kwon inside.

As the world's oldest bank, Banca Monte Dei Paschi Di Siena had numerous private accounts, identified and accessed only by unique codes, passed down through families and businesses over the centuries. By using one of the oldest access codes in the bank's archives, Kwon retrieved a lead sealed bank safety deposit box, that had last been opened at the close of the second world war in Sienna and left with written instructions for it to be made available at this address at 11.30 PM today. The young priest emerged some thirty minutes later from the bank carrying a leather saddle bag over his right shoulder. Once seated at the table with the two other priests, Kwon ordered a Domaine de la Romanee-Conti (DRC) Pinot Noir which he shared and, although he did not join O'Neill or Verchencho in eating, he insisted on settling the bill.

The next days had seen Fr Kwon transformed in terms of grooming, with his long black hair now in perfect condition swept back into a stylish ponytail, his wrist adorned with a white gold Patek Philippe silver dial Calatrava, and his feet seldom seen out of Frarelli Borgioli Treno laceless leather oxford shoes. His white handmade Egyptian cotton Marcello shirts were accompanied with red silk Gucci ties, held in place with a stunning Faberge twenty carat diamond pin. An unusual dark metal ring graced his right forefinger, with a flat stone set in the centre that was engraved with some ancient seal.

Ignoring the critical comments on their dress sense from the Japanese priest, O'Neill gestured to his Nite watch indicating that they were late, and the three men made their way to the end of the small piazza where they passed the huge archway that led into St Peter's Square, and turned right into a street with a wide cobbled pavement on its left side, and a long row of tourist shops next to a McDonald's golden arch on their right. The street was becoming crowded with a mix of different nationalities all heading to St Peter's, and the three priests became separated by the sheer mass of people as they worked their way towards Porta Sant'Anna, one of the entrances into Vatican City that lay some 30 yards ahead on their left.

As they passed by a marble sign, detailing the buildings construction by Pope Pius IV along Via di Porta Angelica, they came under the ruthless scrutiny of a group of pickpockets, preying on tourists who passed this way. The affluent dress of Fr Kwon attracted the thieves' attention, and he was rapidly surrounded by two rough looking men in their thirties and one elderly woman, with a face that was a mass of wrinkles, bent almost double under a thick grey blanket that was coated with a mix of food remnants, that made Verchencho's stained vestments look pristine. The tan leather bag in the young priest's hand drew their attention, as did the diamond tie pin and large ring on his forefinger. Their eyes began to follow the items like hungry dogs.

Kwon did not seem concerned, instead he simply looked at the three-people closing in on him and said in perfect Romany,

"Droboy tume Romale." (Greetings).

The two rough men looked momentarily shocked, that this well-dressed stranger could speak their language so perfectly, but the older one of the two overcame his surprise and approached even closer, opening his dirty grey Adidas jacket to show the four-inch blade of a well-used hunting knife, which he drew and pointed towards the money bag, at the same time grinning with a mouth of rotten and missing teeth. Kwon returned the smile, and taking a step even closer, he tilted his head slightly and began to look intently at the man who was threatening him. Unseen to those looking from a distance, up close the young priest's eyes were inhuman, unblinking, like the narrow vertical slits of a large serpent. The eyes regarded the robber with a disinterested amusement, as one might regard something that was too insignificant to be a threat or large enough to be a meal.

The area immediately around this strange priest emanated an icy chill that made the pickpocket's breath steam and caused his body to shiver uncontrollably, not just from the unexpected bitter cold but also from a deep feeling of unexplained panic that came from the very core of his being. He was vaguely aware of a warm wetness flowing down his right trouser leg. Something primeval in his subconscious mind evaporated the courage from the hardened street robber as he backed away, dropping his knife, before turning and grabbing his friend forcibly and then running wildly down the pavement towards St Peter's square. As they fled, the pair knocked other pedestrians flying, shoving them aside so they could get away.

The old woman was left alone, gazing into the priest's face with its terrifying eyes and aura of penetrating cold that made the very air sting the lungs and throat. She gasped in horror, crossing herself as she fell to her knees weeping for mercy, while offering the well-dressed priest the money she and her two fellow robbers had stolen that morning. Kwon brushed slowly past the woman, deliberately scattering the coins, watches and assorted banknotes across the sidewalk, as he calmly walked on towards the massive Porta Sant'Anna gates that lay ahead on his left.

Father Verchencho and O'Neill were already standing there, waiting beside two armed Swiss Guards in their distinctive blue "night duties" dress, that is always worn at this specific threshold to the Vatican City state, due to an eleventh century prophecy by Saint Malach, Irish saint and Archbishop of Armagh, that in the twilight of days the Devil himself would enter through the Sant Anna gate. Verchencho looked expectantly as they approached the boundary to the Holy See. Kwon smiled knowingly.

"Do not worry, Hugo. I have passed through these gates more times than you."

Away from the mass of tourists who had filled the Via di Porta Angelica, the three men walked beside each other along the deserted Via Sant Anna, towards a small security checkpoint on the left side of the road, some eight yards inside the main gates. Once there, Hugo Verchencho presented the copy of an email invitation to a meeting in room B1c in the Vatican Library basement. After being issued with Catholic clerical yellow visitor badges, a dark suited man escorted the three along the entire length of Via Sant Anna towards the impressive Cortile del Belvedere, where they passed through the mass of cars parked inside the courtyard, before turning right and entering what was known within the Catholic Church simply as the Vat.

Although formally established in 1475, the Vatican Library has existed under other names right back to the foundation of the Roman Church. The Bibliotheca Apostolica Vaticana is one of the oldest libraries in the world, having subsumed and assimilated texts from famous collections that preceded it, including extensive acquisitions taken from the Imperial Library of Constantinople during the fall of that city in 1453. Since this famed Byzantine library was known in its turn to have rescued numerous texts and manuscripts from the previous great libraries of antiquity, the Vat is believed to contain the most significant documents from the ancient world.

Inside the grand La Galea entrance to the Vat, their dark suited guide took them past a large statue of Hippolytus and towards a set of grand stairs that led down to the first level basement with its private meeting rooms, set amongst the papyrus room and storage areas for manuscripts.

Conrad De Ven, head of Vatican Security, sat alone in front of a black Polycom Sound Station speakerphone, that had been placed in the centre of a long dark plastic topped metal table, next to a jug of water and some blue drinking glasses. The black Gucci jacket from his dark suit rested on the chair back and the sleeves on his crisp white cotton shirt were turned up, as a concession to the lack of good ventilation. Any investment in climate control in the Vat was focused on the books, not on the human visitors.

The small rectangular room was dominated by the table with its eight wooden backed chairs. A long window in the wall directly in front of De Ven was glazed with a semi opaque pane, that allowed an indistinct view of people passing by but did not permit clear identification. The other walls had a mix of white legal notices on procedures in case of fire, displaying the closest evacuation routes, and on the wall facing the door was a large plaster rendering of the Papal seal, showing the gold and silver keys of Simon Peter and the three crowns that symbolize the triple power of the Pope as "Father of Kings", "Governor of the World" and "Vicar of Christ". Lighting came from two fluorescent tubes that had been added, without any attempt at elegance, to the ornate plaster ceilings. The flooring was a red tile that had seen generations of cleaning and was now in bad need of a new coat of paint.

He had been sitting in the small basement level meeting room for nearly fifteen minutes, waiting for three low level clerics with the most unlikely of cases. Under normal circumstances, they would never have met and certainly not here, in the library. But these were not ordinary circumstances. The intense media focus that was now directed towards the Vatican, after the revelations of widespread corruption within the church, meant that the central offices were practically impossible to reach, so he had to make do with this makeshift space. And, of course, there was the subject of the meeting that had been requested by Fr Hugo Verchencho, the emerald tablet that had been traded and subsequently been the cause of so much current distress and embarrassment to the Church. A meeting between the Head of Vatican security and the Chief Exorcist was unknown in the two thousand years history of the church and, to be honest, would not have occurred even now except for the extraordinary context of the request from Hugo Verchencho, and the mention of an ancient prophecy that described the destruction of the Church as one of the steps towards the end of the world. De Ven remembered how the prophecy had been discussed, and promptly dismissed, at the meeting of the church council but now, in the aftermath of the media release, the demise of the Church did not seem so far-fetched and, if that was possible, who knew if the end of the world was such an absurd notion. Given the antiquity of the topic in question, De Ven was not surprised that Verchencho was accompanied by a member of the Pontificia Accademia Romana di Archeologia, but he was disconcerted that they were bringing with them a psychiatric patient from the Sanatorium of St Michael, known to be where the Church placed some of the worst cases of psychosis or just plain spooky obsessions. What had once been core beliefs, back in the middle ages, were now regarded as dogmas that held the Church back from being accepted by younger generations in the developed world. The letter from Verchencho had used an ancient clause related to his office as Chief Exorcist, demanding an audience with the Holy Father when an esoteric matter threatened the continued existence of the Church. De Ven mused that if this memo could only have come some days earlier, the Church might possibly have avoided the shame and calamity that threatened to reduce it to a shadow of its former self. The Holy Father and his entire council had withdrawn into hiding, avoiding all meetings due to the very real concern that a journalist would make their way into the crisis discussions.

The paparazzi had taken great delight in exposing some new smear concerning the Church leaders on a daily basis, causing a sustained drop in confidence in the Church and its members that was unprecedented in the long history of the Vatican. With no Pope to receive the ancient demand from the office of the Exorcist, the Head of Security took it upon himself to respond to it, in the hope that there might be some method to undo the damage that had been done. It was not so much that De Ven believed in the supernatural, just that he was desperate enough to try anything. As he mused about the meeting ahead, and prepared himself to hear what was undoubtedly going to be a bizarre story, he noticed the corridor lights outside dim unexpectedly and the basement suddenly began to feel colder. A knock on the door was followed by one of De Ven's own staff opening it and ushering in three men, each so very different in appearance from the other. One looked like he was on a hiking holiday, another like a Swiss Banker and the eldest looked like a red-haired Rasputin, dishevelled but with the powerful energy of a zealot. If he had not already known, he would have thought Verchencho was the psychiatric patient. As the three priests entered the small meeting room, the two fluorescent lights began to flicker, and De Ven noted that someone must have left one of the environmentally controlled storage rooms open, as a very distinct coolness filled the small room, along with a musty smell of something ancient being exposed to the modern atmosphere.

The attendant who had guided the men to the room introduced Fr Verchencho, Dr O'Neill and Fr Kwon and then shut the door and stood on guard outside, to see that they were undisturbed. De Ven gestured to the men to sit opposite him, with their backs to the corridor window, and waited expectantly.

"You no longer have it!" The statement came from the elegantly dressed priest and the words were filled with a barely concealed exasperation.

De Ven did not care for being subject to criticism, especially from someone who was, according to the personnel records, suffering from chronic delusions. He regarded Kwon and decided that taking the offensive might be the best strategy.

"So, you claim you are the Devil?" He said with a derisive tone.

"You have said so." Responded Kwon calmly.

"How dare you give me the response of Christ to Pilate! I am not looking for anything from you, the fact is that you,"

He gestured to the three of them,

"Are coming to me with some preposterous theory and request for Papal approval."

De Ven held up the letter from Verchencho that had described the need to protect the emerald tablets and which had prompted the meeting.

"The absurdity of listening to your crackpot theories about avoiding the apocalypse is clear to me now. You are clearly just wasting my time. Get out!" He thundered as he stood and gestured to the door.

O'Neill and Verchencho rose, preparing to leave. Kwon smiled but remained seated, looking at the powerfully built De Ven across the table from him.

"Oh, such a wonderful temper, for a mortal. I promise I am not wasting your time..."

The lights, which had been flickering since the three priests entered, suddenly emitted a sizzling noise as they dimmed, casting the room into a darkness that was broken intermittently by bright flashes of light as the bulbs blinked on and off in a strobe like fashion. In the moments of darkness, Fr Kwon's unblinking eyes appeared serpent like and unworldly, glowing like a night predator caught in a car's headlights. Kwon turned his gaze to the table and the water inside the clear plastic jug began to move of its own accord, swirling slowly at first and then churning more violently as it changed colour to an ink like black. A thick dark mist rose from the boiling surface creating long vaporous shapes in the frigid air around them, malevolently circling above the four men. While the fluid in the plastic jug darkened and bubbled, in contrast, the water in the glass in front of Conrad De Ven began to frost over and then it froze violently, bursting with a loud crack as the plastic beaker shattered into fragments over the table top.

As the room continued to become colder, the windows and walls started to run with dark condensation, causing strange patterns to appear as the stained water ran down the plaster and glass surfaces. Although De Ven was no occult scholar, he recognised some of them as classic sigils from the Lemegeton, the Lesser Key of Solomon. Others were unknown to him, but clearly were from more ancient Grimoires of the Goetia.

The condensation intensified on the surface of the Papal seal, causing the colours of the triple crowns to run and merge with the gold and silver of the two keys of heaven, forming dark rivulets that flowed into the shape of an inverted cross.

"Good God!" Exclaimed the Head of Vatican Security, as he sat back in his chair clearly shocked.

"Not your God..." Smiled Fr Kwon, as he gestured to his two colleagues to resume their seats.

CHAPTER 25 - THE MAPS OF DESTINY

"All creatures tread across the rubble of ruined civilizations." -- Rita Mae Brown

Basement meeting room B1C
Vatican Library
00120, Vatican City
Rome
11.34HRS, 5th August, Present Day.

After Kwon's demonstration of the existence of a darker reality beyond the normal physical senses, Conrad De Ven sat quietly and listened to Verchencho and O'Neill explain in more detail about the legends related to the emerald tablets. Culturally and historically, separate ancient prophecies, from the Middle East, China, Africa and South America, all spoke of four sacred tablets, texts or objects that, when united in a specific esoteric rite, would spark the "End of Days" spoken of in the apocalypse legends of every ancient civilization, including those of the Catholic Church contained in St John's Book of Revelation.

The four tablets had been kept safe during recent centuries by a series of scholars and enlightened leaders, until they were spread to the four corners of the earth at the fall of the Holy Roman Empire, in a deliberate attempt to prevent their misuse. But now there was an individual, with great influence and intelligence, who was gathering the tablets with the deliberate intention of initiating the ancient ceremony that was known as the final secret or forty ninth call or invocation. De Ven interjected and described how the Church council had been manipulated and misled, into passing over the tablet that had been left in their care, by a woman and her accomplices. The four men then speculated that this woman must indeed be the person seeking to reunite the four tablets but, without any clear evidence as to her identity, the only viable alternative was for them to track down the remaining three tablets and keep them safe.

Fr Kwon spoke with an eloquence and intellect that clearly surpassed his colleagues. He argued that the Principle of Evil was not clearly understood by the general population and even many in the church did not understand that the Adversary was simply a role, rather like a prosecutor in a human court. The Church played the part of the Advocate, attempting to guide and support the human soul in its life. In contrast, Evil was the way of testing faith and providing meaning to existence. In such a context, the role of Adversary could be assumed by many different entities depending on the circumstances. Hence the Adversary was known throughout its recorded interactions to call itself Legion. Kwon continued by proposing that every existence had a destiny to fulfil, so even the Adversary did not desire a premature end to creation until all had fully played out their role. The rise of an individual, who was seeking to unite all the tablets and prematurely end the current creation, was not in the interests of anyone in the current existence, so the young priest proposed that, just this once, the ancient enemies work together until this threat was addressed, and their normal roles of Advocate and Adversary could then resume.

The emerald tablets, he informed the group, had had many names attributed to them over the millennia, and were mentioned in the most ancient of creation texts, from all of the earliest civilisations, as the cause of a War in Heaven that had seen former angels cast into the darkness of the material world. At one time, he said with emotion, one being had been entrusted as custodian of the four tablets that had been used by the creator. This being had studied the items that had been placed into his care for eons, until he understood that there had been many gods and many creations, each originating with a single specific ceremony, that used the energy from an existing creation to form a new heaven and earth in the image of the being that initiated the process. Quite literally the consciousness that initiated this ceremony became the supreme creative being in a new Cosmos. This was the knowledge that had set the seed for the fall of the angels and the long history of magic, since all sorcery was derived from the secrets held within the four emerald tablets, and that this was the long-standing association between the Devil and the supernatural.

Conrad De Ven listened carefully, asking questions when he did not fully understand any aspect, until he finally interrupted to ask about the specifics of how they could retrieve the Church's emerald tablet, and what the Prophecy said would happen next.

Chin Kwon responded by asking De Ven to request a copy of the original sources for the prophecy from the Vatican library, along with the notes related to the original donation of the emerald tablet to the Vatican in 1806. Hugo Verchencho and Thomas O'Neill indicated their agreement.

The security head's request to access these rare source documents prompted a rapid phone call back from Dr Antonio Abatescianni, Cardinal Archivist, and it was he who personally supervised the delivery of the items to the small room some forty minutes later. He joined the four of them pouring over the documents, as O'Neill made copious observations in a small moleskin note book with the Pontificia Accademia Romana di Archeologia logo embossed on its dark leather cover.

Unseen to the others during the wait for the manuscripts, De Ven had also instructed one of the medical team attached to his security unit to discreetly meet him in the room next to B1c, to take a blood sample from his left arm and to check for traces of hallucinatory or hypnotic drugs. He also had the water jug, with its strange dark liquid, removed and sent for laboratory analysis.

The group carefully examined the oldest manuscripts, each wearing the white cotton gloves that Abatescianni had provided. The prophecy was mentioned in three separate sources and, given the resources of the Vat, they had two of the original documents and an eighth century hand written copy in Arabic of the third. All three sources talked about a knight, a priest and a fallen angel, who together would be all that stand against the end of days. There was little doubt among the group that the "Fallen Angel" could only be Fr Chin Kwon. The eighth century manuscript described a Priest of Rome as "one who dug up the bones of dead kings", so it was to be assumed that O'Neill must be "The Priest". Kwon confirmed that he had been waiting for Dr O'Neill to become drawn into the prophecy, as a consequence of his investigation into the ill-fated Finster expedition in Iraq.

The identity of the knight was more difficult to determine. Verchencho and Abatescianni proposed that it might be Conrad De Ven, since he was descended from crusader knights, but he did not fit the detailed description given in one of the Assyrian texts engraved on a small dark ceramic tablet. Kwon assisted O'Neill in the translation of the cuneiform engravings, and although there were some sections that O'Neill found confused, such as mention of riding a tiger to the ends of the world, it was clear that the knight was a peerless leader who was undefeated in battle, with a courage that came from the blood of kings that flowed in his veins. Also, it was said that he possessed one of the four emerald tablets and that the attempts to take this from him would bring him to directly confront the great enemy in the final battle.

They concluded that they had yet to encounter the knight, but Chin Kwon felt the warrior would travel to Rome if he knew that the Vatican's tablet was missing, since the knight might believe that this journey would bring him closer to identifying the person collecting the emerald tablets. De Ven and Abatescianni agreed and quickly organised for a press release appealing to antiquarians to be on the lookout for the relic. O'Neill, for his part, said he would try and trace recent purchasers of similar items from long held collections in Prague, as that might also give them the identity of the mysterious knight from the North.

The source documents related to the donation of the Vatican's own emerald tablet, Article TG345, were much more recent than those from the prophecy. Dated to August 5th 1806, there were a series of letters related to the apparent ancient provenance of the four-inch emerald stone with its strange carvings, along with some very detailed lithographic representations of the stone and the silver setting in which it had originally been housed.

The stone sent to Rome was one of a set of four, each with different inscriptions or engravings on their surfaces. The silver setting and first of the four tablets was to remain in a secure archive in Prague. The Vatican was to look after the second, and the third tablet would be placed in the care of the Eastern Church in Constantinople, now called Istanbul after a name change in 1923. The first three stones were to be protected by "the hand and will of man", however the fourth and final stone was to be protected "by the very sands of time", in what was variously and vaguely described as the "citadel of the Djinn", "Holy and Ancient city", "Agharti" or "Agartha" along the Silk Road.

Abatescianni and De Ven looked at Dr O'Neill expectantly, for some indication of the location of this mysterious sounding city. Meanwhile, Hugo Verchencho looked instead at Kwon and asked directly,

"Surely, you know where it is hidden?"

Kwon cleared his throat, "We know all that is known in the

consciousness of man, but when something is deliberately forgotten and lost to every mind, then it is beyond even my knowledge."

O'Neill interjected "Well, if you wanted to lose something, then the plains of Asia are an excellent choice."

Abatescianni nodded "The old Silk Route passes through some of the most desolate places on earth. The ancient kingdoms of the region were some of the richest empires the world has ever known. If legends are correct, there were vast cities that have now been swallowed under the howling wastes of the Gobi Desert."

Kwon agreed. "Indeed, beneath those sands lies gold, jewels and art of a refinement unknown in the modern world along with..." the young priest paused, clearly wondering how much he should reveal.

"...evidence of a civilisation that would radically overthrow the existing historical record. The prevailing winds move the Gobi Desert constantly from East to West, so that with a regular periodicity of 120 years these vast empires are briefly revealed to the light of day, only to be swept back under the sand again for another interval hidden from the sight of man. Interestingly, the next exposure will occur in less than one lunar cycle from today."

O'Neill looked sceptical but Kwon continued.

"There was once a vast inland sea which extended over the whole of Tibet, Mongolia and Shamo, which you now call the Gobi. Rich cities sat on the edge of this inland ocean, just North of the current location of the modern Himalayan ranges. To the South of this inland ocean lay an ancient vast continent."

Abatescianni sighed, clearly disbelieving everything that Fr Kwon was describing.

Fr Kwon regarded the others and continued, "Within this region existed a civilization as advanced as yours, which prospered until the last great glacial period, when there was a massive cataclysm which raised the Himalayan mountains and swept the waters of the large inland sea away. The rising sea levels caused by the melting glaciers sank most of the huge ocean continent beneath the waters, in the same way that the civilizations of Shamo sank beneath the sands, but with a much slower progress. A few survivors of this advanced civilization retreated to remote mountain regions and others to a fabled city, that was constructed on an island in the ancient sea that is now the Gobi Desert."

Kwon stopped and looked at O'Neill, gesturing for him to continue.

"Yes, Asian scholars know the legend of how the "Sons of Will and Yoga" survived the destruction of the Lemurian civilization in a secret city. This city has many names depending on different sources. The Tibetan legends speak of Shamballa, other traditions talk of a city stronghold called Agharti that was supposed to be located underground, which might fit with a city designed to withstand a cataclysm."

"You do not mean you believe a word of this nonsense?" Abatescianni exclaimed.

"In the last week, I have learnt to become much more open minded about what is possible." Responded O'Neill.

"Besides, if the people who were trying to hide the fourth emerald tablet were looking for "The City of the Djinn" on the old Silk Road, I would assume that they had heard the same legends. If we are going to locate the city we need to think like those who went before us." "What ancient cities do we know about in that region, Thomas?" Asked Verchencho.

O'Neill started drawing a rough sketch in his notebook, positioning the pages so everyone around the small table could see what he was drawing. He started with a small turret which he labelled Erdene Zuu.

"The Erdene Zuu Monastery is built on the ruins of Genghis Khan's capital and it is usual for rulers, like the Khans, to adopt good regional sites that have some established history, roads, water sources or rivers. So, they tend to build over the remains of previous cities."

He marked another turret which he labelled Ordu-Baliq.

"Ordu-Baliq, meaning "city of the court", was known to be built on the site of the former Göktürk imperial capital Kharbalgas. Also known as Mubalik and Karabalghasun, it was the capital of the first Uyghur Khaganate, which existed for centuries before being destroyed by the Ming Army in 1372. Kharbalgas means "Black City" in Mongolian, and was situated roughly..."

O'Neill drew a river which he labelled Ezen.

"On the east bank of the Ezen River, near the middle of the Gurvan Saikhan mountains, on what could well have been an island if the rest of the Gobi was once an inland ocean, as Kwon has said."

Conrad De Ven regarded O'Neill 's rough sketch and turning to Abatescianni asked,

"What Thomas said, about trying to think like the people who would have hidden the last tablet, sounds very sensible. In order to do that we need to know what sources they would have used to locate such a lost city. What ancient maps could they have used?"

The Chief Archivist paused and then picking up the black polyphone called a few numbers. They were rapidly joined by a short rather plump blonde-haired woman in her thirties, who Abatescianni introduced as Ms Dertinz, the Cartographic Archivist for the Vatican collections.

Dertinz listened carefully to the mandate of looking for the oldest maps that reliably described the location of cities along the ancient Silk Route. She opened her MacBook and with a few keystrokes had pulled up a digital image showing a very early hand drawn map, that included a black horned and winged figure blocking the progress of a king along what looked like a well-established route. Cities were shown as realistically as the demonic forms that emerged from the desert landscape.

The young woman explained that this was a representation of Alexander the Great on part of what was a well-established trade route even in 323 BC. It was suspected that many of the earliest geographically accurate representations of the Western sections of the Silk Route and its cities were based on those created by Alexander. For example, even as recently as the sixteenth century an atlas was known to be based largely on his campaign maps.

Dertinz added,

"If we are restricting ourselves to accurate geographical representations then we must look to the records left by ground breaking explorers, such as Marco Polo. The 1450 Fra Mauro map of the world is thought by many scholars to be based on the maps brought back from Cathay by Polo. Like the early Chinese and Mongol maps of that time, it shows South at the top of the map and North at the bottom."

"Do we have a copy of Polo's map or the Fra Mauro in our collection?" Asked Abatescianni.

"Although Polo never produced a map to illustrate his epic journey, after his death his family were known to sell maps of the routes to Cathay. We do have two of these in our restricted collection signed by Marco's three daughters, Fantina, Bellela and Moreta. Although not generally acknowledged, I am sure that the Cardinal could provide you with copies." Said Dertinz.

Abatescianni nodded.

She continued, "The Fra Mauro map is held in the Museo Correr in Venice. Any remaining materials from Polo's estate would also be in Venice at the Biblioteca Nazionale Marciana (National Library of St Mark's) where they were deposited in 1324 on Polo's death. Another map that could be of interest to you might be Johannes Schnitzer's from 1482, that has a striking similarity to what you have sketched there." She pointed to O'Neill's rough sketch, showing what Kwon had described as the location of the legendary continent of Lemuria, stretching out into the Indian Ocean.

"Schnitzer's map shows Africa connected to Antarctica, separating the Atlantic from the Indian Ocean. It has always been assumed to be an example of a lack of geographical knowledge, rather than a representation of ancient cartography."

Kwon smiled enigmatically.

Before thanking Abatescianni and Dertinz for their help and letting them return to their duties, they confirmed their need for facsimiles of the documents they had consulted, and the rare maps that were held within the Vat. O'Neill also indicated that he would like the Vat to acquire facsimiles of the exploration field notes from Sir Francis Younghusband's expeditions into the region of the Gobi Desert in the mid nineteenth century, since he felt they might provide some insights into how the location could have looked when the fourth tablet was deposited in the lost city.

De Ven concluded the long meeting by saying that he would contact his opposite number in the Eastern Orthodox church, and arrange for the group to travel to Istanbul to safeguard the third tablet, after they had visited Venice to study the Fra Mauro map and Marco Polo's records in the Library of St Mark's.

Forty minutes later, seated at the left rear corner booth in the busy AngryPig Birretta e Porchetta on the Via Tunisi, the short blonde woman was breathing heavily after having hurried through the busy rush hour traffic. Seated opposite her was an elegantly dressed man in an open topped white seersucker shirt and dark linen trousers. His hawk like features were partially hidden behind mirrored glasses. As Ms Dertinz gratefully drank the cold beer that had been provided for her, she passed over copies of the documents and maps that had been requested by De Ven, O'Neill and Verchencho. She thought it odd that he was wearing latex gloves.

"And you are sure they are heading to Venice before Istanbul?" Enquired the man.

"Yes, I guided them exactly as you told me." Dertinz replied.

"Excellent. You have done well, my dear."

He looked closely at the eyes of the woman in front of him, smiling as he noted how the pupils were already dilating and her body was sweating heavily. He carefully gathered up the papers she had brought with her, rose and walked away. Several moments later, a passer-by shouted for an ambulance, as they discovered a young woman slumped unconscious over her table.

CHAPTER 26 - ALL ROADS LEAD TO ROME

"Fate whispers to the Wolf, you cannot withstand the Storm… and the Wolf whispers back, I am the Storm!" - unknown

Barcelo Aran Blu Hotel,
Lungomare Duca degli Abruzzi, 72,
00121 Lido di Ostia
Rome, Italy
06.00HRS, 6th August, Present Day.

As the sun began to rise over the ocean in the bay of Ostia, Sir Tavish Stewart, VC, KT, was being watched by an amused group of hotel staff as he danced barefoot, dressed only in white cotton pyjama bottoms and a white T shirt, on the Tramonto rooftop terrace of the Barcelo Aran Blu Hotel. In his bare hands, he slowly waved a thirty-nine inch long wooden pole that he had acquired from a bemused cleaner, moments earlier, relieving it of its small brush head before commencing his exercise.

Knowing that his barefoot dance was attracting the attention of an increasing number of the hotel staff, he smiled and bowed to them in an exaggerated manner, attracting laughter and a small round of applause.

Having acknowledged his audience, Stewart's strange dance began to become more complex, the makeshift bokken making wide arcs in the air at different angles around his head, as his legs twisted and turned so that the weapon moved in all directions around a central point, which corresponded to the alignment of Stewart's hips with each turn. An expert observer would note that the wooden broom handle remained loose in Stewart's hands during his odd dance and, if it had been a blade, that it was being expertly guided along its cutting path, termed "Hasuji" by Japanese sword masters.

What started as an entertaining diversion to the hotel staff, became less amusing as the dance became faster and more focused. Stewart's slow warm up ended and he began his Suburi sword strikes in seriousness, transforming the slow movements into their full speed of execution. The broomstick began to make a sharp whistling sound, what the Japanese call "tachikaze" or "sword wind", which grew louder as Stewart's circular motions covered 360 degrees around his body with a technically perfect striking action, making the bokken appear as a blur of motion surrounding the Scottish knight.

By the time Stewart completed his practice, he was soaked with sweat and when he looked to where his amused audience had been gathered none remained, the deadly intent of the practice no longer being an entertainment. He cooled down with some slow Yoga stretches, by which time the restaurant staff had arranged some of the tables for those guests who wanted to have breakfast "all'aperto", watching sunrise over the Tyrrhenian Sea.

Stewart sat at a small table on the Southern corner of the roof looking over the bay, enjoying a large glass of ice cold freshly squeezed orange juice. As he waited for his breakfast to arrive, he reflected on his phone conversation with Mohammed Sek the previous evening. The news was disturbing. The Rome showroom was closed, Mario was missing, and there had been no contact from Jeff or Helen, so their whereabouts were also unknown.

Prima colazione (breakfast) consisted of freshly baked brown rolls, with an intensely flavoured thin-cut marmalade made with organic Avemaria Seville oranges finished with Aperol, to enhance both the flavour and the rich orange colour, accompanied by a strong black espresso using freshly ground beans from Hausbrandt of Trieste. Towards the end of his second cup a young man, wearing heavily worn black motorcycle leathers, appeared on the roof terrace and, scanning the clientele, noticed Stewart's distinctive dress, consulted a small scrap of paper, smiled and approached.

After signing "Patrick Smith" on the electronic receipt, Stewart tore open the paperwork showing the 225 euro fee for the Istanbul to Ostia overnight express courier, and revealed the interior of the small FedEx box which contained a used Samsung smart phone with battery removed, a set of keys, two pairs of latex gloves, several prepaid Visa credit cards, an international driver's license, a very convincing Canadian passport for a Mr Patrick Smith, who had more than a passing resemblance to Stewart, and the silver folio, which he had posted to Sek in Istanbul before his ill-fated SBS raid on Foster's residence in London. After using the passport to legitimise his stay at the hotel, he left it along with the credit cards and emerald tablet in the hotel's safe, and posted the safe deposit receipt in a self-addressed envelope in the Poste Italiane box at the Port central office back to the hotel where, if he was still alive, he would collect it later.

Stewart emerged from the small hotel foyer wearing black Ray-Ban Wayfarer sunglasses, a grey baseball cap with an "#Ostia" tourist slogan, and an unbranded blue cotton short sleeved Oxford shirt worn loose over light-coloured chinos, both of which he had acquired at Cynthia's safe house storeroom. On his feet, he wore a pair of brown Timberland heritage leather moccasin shoes which he had purchased in the seafront shops, selected because of their lightness and superior grip compared to the heavy walking boots that he had been wearing since leaving London.

Around his left ankle he wore the black Cordura ankle holster with the small .38 Colt Cobra. He distributed the three speed loaders, each holding six of the Hydra Shock rounds, in the left and two rear trouser pockets, while his Cold Steel Scimitar lay concealed in his front right pocket. Over the past week he had practiced intensively with these specific weapons, so their use had become second nature to him.

He would have preferred more firepower, more manpower and more options. So far, his opponent had consistently had the advantage, and past experience on the battlefield had taught Stewart that if he was to have any chance of survival against an enemy who was establishing such a pattern of dominance, he needed to take radical action to change the existing dynamics. The only advantage he had was that his opponents would not be expecting his next actions, and he intended to maximise that initiative to force them to make unintended errors.

Just outside the hotel, Stewart took a number one bus to the Lido Centro station. Inside the grey concrete two storey building he pulled the brim of his cap low as he purchased a single ticket on route FC2 to Porta San Paolo station. At San Paolo, he passed through the long underpass to Pirámide underground train station where he emerged and switched to a bus from Cave Ardeatine. He exited the number thirty Bus (Clodio) at Senato and walked towards Stewart's showroom at Via dei Coronari.

Positioning himself at a table in a pavement restaurant at the junction of Piazza delle Cinque Lune, Stewart could see that the narrow Via dei Coronari was crowded with tourists, who were struggling to pass a badly parked black Fiat Ducato Passenger Transport van on the left of the narrow lane, roughly opposite Stewart's shop front on the right at number 222. The unmarked black van had mirrored glass on all its windows and, based on the two large men who looked like nightclub bouncers who were entering and leaving the vehicle, it was involved with surveillance work.

When Stewart noticed two Polizia (civic police) heading on foot patrol towards Via dei Coronari, he pulled the used Samsung smart phone from his shirt pocket, inserted the battery and after checking that the GPS was functioning, he called Mario's office. As he expected, based on his conversation with Sek the previous evening, his call went straight to the answer phone.

In his message, he indicated that he was coming to the Rome office imminently with Mohammed Sek and that, due to the likelihood of the place being under Maelstrom surveillance, they would be disguised as police officers. Immediately after hanging up, Stewart called the emergency terror alert number for the Central Rome Carabinieri (military police), reporting that two Polizia had been kidnapped by armed men in a black Fiat van on Via dei Coronari and read off the Ducato's registration plates.

Terminating the call, Stewart jogged through the traffic jam and rapidly caught up with the two Polizia officers, telling them he had just found a phone and handed them the used Samsung. Just as the police took the phone they received an urgent radio alert on their earpieces which made them usher Stewart away, as they drew their 9mm Beretta Model 92FS pistols and ran towards the black van. Simultaneously, three men dressed in black paramilitary combat fatigues emerged from the shuttered doors of Stewart's showroom, one of them looking at a GPS tracking device, the other two carrying black polymer Glock 17 9mm automatics with long magazines that protruded well beyond the grips.

The two police officers called for the men to drop their weapons, but their attempts at an arrest were cut short, as the sliding doors of the black van slid back to reveal two more Maelstrom operatives armed with 9mm Heckler & Koch MP5 sub machine guns, surrounded by a mass of electronic surveillance materials crammed inside the van. The two officers slowly lowered their weapons and placed their hands on their heads. The man with the GPS tracker approached them and, after an exceptionally rough search, pulled a used Samsung smart phone from the jacket pocket of the shorter of the two policemen.

The bolder members from the crowd of tourists started to question the detainment of the police, and several of them were clearly making phone calls while others used their phones as cameras. Two of the gunmen fired a short burst of fully automatic fire from their H&K MP5 machine guns into the air, forcing the gathering crowds to run in all directions.

Black cable ties were fastened around the wrists of the policemen but, as they were in the process of being bundled into the black van, the sounds of screaming sirens filled the air and two jet black Alfa Romeo 159 sedan cars approached at high speed from both ends of the Via dei Coronari, placing themselves directly in front and behind of the black Maelstrom surveillance vehicle.

Above the rooftops, the sky was filled with the drumming sound of rotors as a dark blue Carabinieri AgustaWestland AW109 helicopter hovered above the scene. At the far end of the road, civil police officers deployed thick spike rolls across the road surface of the small lane, making escape by any wheeled vehicle impossible.

The heavily armed Gruppo di Intervento Speciale (GIS) "Special Intervention Group" counter-terrorism tactical response unit members were dressed in a similar manner to the Maelstrom team, with ceramic plate body armour, except they were wearing rank and branch insignia on their uniforms and instead of the H&K MP5 submachine gun these commandos carried the much smaller and shorter Steyr TMP (Taktische Maschinenpistole/Tactical Machine Pistol), a select-fire 9mm Parabellum calibre machine pistol that looked similar to the Israeli army Uzi.

Just as it looked like the situation would escalate into a fully automatic fire fight, the Maelstrom team members slowly exited their van with their hands on their heads. Within moments the GIS Carabinieri had all five men restrained with cable ties, lying them face down on the cobblestone street. Over the next hour, various branches of law enforcement came and went, until three very slow cappuccinos later Stewart could see that the street was clear, the Maelstrom men and their surveillance van removed.

No doubt various high level diplomatic interventions were underway that would see the five men on a plane back to the US within twenty-four hours, but for now Stewart had access to the Rome

Showroom. He tipped his waiter, crossed the road and headed down to number 222 on the right-hand side of Via dei Coronari. Approaching the shop front, he pulled on a pair of latex gloves and, using the key sent in the FedEx package, carefully opened the shuttered glass door.

Inside the showroom it was dark and the air was filled with the strong smell of blood, which grew significantly stronger as Stewart went cautiously up the narrow stairs to the right of the elegantly furnished store. Persian carpets hung from the walls, vases and Roman figure heads filled the display spaces. The snub-nosed Colt smoothly found its way into his right hand from his ankle holster, as he ascended to the top of the stairs and reached the ninety degree turn leading into the long and narrow first floor office, that was dominated by a large table in the middle of the room.

Stewart held the snub nose revolver in his right hand very close to his chest with the barrel pointing over his bent left arm. Sitting at his desk, with his back to the darkened window was his old friend Mario. His arms and legs were strapped tightly to the office chair, and blood had clearly flowed copiously from his fingers which were now just bloody stumps, having had their fingernails forcibly removed. A deep cut was visible at the throat and four vicious gunshot wounds had destroyed the knee and elbow joints. By the look of Mario's body, he had been dead for some hours.

On the large table beside his dead friend were a mass of A2 sized photocopies, that on closer inspection were a mix of maps and ancient documents marked with the Vatican Library seal. There was also a small A6 sized notebook that was open, containing some handwritten lists, which was placed next to some Alitalia tickets to Heraklion, Crete, an annotated map and two police mug shot pictures of Jeff and Helen.

Stewart walked slowly towards the documents and, as he did so, the window blinds were opened and a male voice commented.

"Well done with the diversion outside. Impressive for an old man."

Stewart moved his body so the Cobra's two-inch barrel pointed at the young man, who he recognised as the same skateboarder who had collided with him at Kings Cross station several days earlier. Dressed in a dark blue long-sleeved shirt and grey cargo pants it was only his beaded hair strands and facial scratch that remained from their encounter in London.

"No longboard?"

"Oh, you are sharp," sneered the young man.

"But clearly not that sharp, or you would have fired when you had the chance. But your misplaced code of honour will not let you shoot an unarmed opponent, will it? Now be a good boy and drop that little peashooter."

Behind Stewart, another man had approached silently, holding a Glock 17 in his right hand, his arm outstretched so the muzzle of the 9mm pressed into the back of Stewart's neck. The moment the gun barrel made contact Stewart became a blur of motion, rotating left so his arm brushed the Glock aside, and at the same time he fired the snub-nosed Colt up under his attacker's chin through the skull, avoiding the heavy Kevlar body armour and killing him instantly with a single shot.

While his back was turned, the long boarder struck Stewart with an expanding steel baton he had produced from his waistband, first across Stewarts kidneys and then on the right arm holding the small revolver. The Colt clattered to the floor and Stewart rolled away from the onslaught of blows.

The young man grinned as he approached closer, sensing victory.

"Tell me where the emerald tablet is and I will make it easy and quick for you."

"Like you did with Mario?" Stewart gestured towards the mutilated body tied to the desk.

The young man reached behind him and drew out a long wicked twelve-inch David Anders custom Bowie knife, smiling.

"Not me… but it was a blade like this that finished your friend. And now you will experience the same fate…"

"Except I am not tied up." Responded Stewart, as he pulled the Scimitar out into his uninjured left hand.

The young man openly laughed at the four-inch blade of his opponent and launched forward into a lunge, intending to cut open Stewart's stomach, so the intestines would be exposed, leading to a slow, agonizing death. The Scotsman brushed aside the lunging arm and countered with a deep stab under and into the young man's right arm pit. The attacker stumbled back, not sure if he had been hit, until he started to notice his knife hand shaking and blood dripping from his arm. He switched hands and lunged again, this time more wildly.

Stewart blocked the attack easily, and countered with a series of draw strokes on the wrist and elbow joints, causing the long-wicked Bowie blade to drop from the young man's bleeding hand. As his blood dripped onto the floor, the long boarder pulled a small single shot pistol that had been concealed in his right sleeve, as he sneered.

"Only one of us will leave here alive."

"That is the most sensible thing you have said yet." Stewart replied coldly and, using his left leg in a blindingly fast inner circular kick, diverted the direction of the small pistol away from his body.

Stewart attacked for the first time in the encounter, with a series of two stabs with the four-inch curved blade of the Scimitar knife. The first strike was lightning fast and went between the ribs of his opponent on the left side, causing the heart to be pulled much closer to the front and centre of the body as the lung deflated.

The second stab took full advantage of the movement of the internal organs, going into the solar plexus up under the sternum and penetrating the heart. As the young man fell back against the wall behind Mario's desk and sank slowly to the floor, still clutching his gun, a mobile phone began to ring from somewhere on the body. Stewart searched and found it.

A heavily accented male voice on the other end of the line asked,

"You are ready?"

Stewart replied, as he looked at the documents and notebook on the desk,

"Not completely, but I am catching up."

There was an angry curse in Arabic on the other end of the line, and the call was disconnected.

CHAPTER 27 - A DISH BEST SERVED COLD

"An intelligence officer's duty is to assess the validity and importance of the information coming across their desk. A field officer's task is to encourage foreign nationals to pass on information that may be of strategic value to Great Britain. Our work is based more on the intellect than the blunt violence and deception that you have seen in the movies but, of course, there are always exceptional situations that require exceptional responses." -- Welcome to the Secret Intelligence Service. Preface by Dame Cynthia Sinclair, Director General SIS.

Victoria Embankment Bus Stop
London SW1A
14.00HRS, 6th August, Present Day.

The large balding man was sweating profusely as he pushed through the crowds and squeezed his corpulent frame through the folding doors of the red AEC Routemaster London double decker bus. His blue pin stripe jacket was open, as was the collar on his white Savile Row shirt, his striped Eton school tie pulled loose from its usual Windsor knot, but these concessions did nothing to ease his discomfort from the combination of the summer heat and his considerable nerves. Years away from the field, in his role as Ministerial Liaison for Her Majesty's Security Services, had made Henry Brown go to seed. His MI5 derived field craft skills were never sharp but were now lost through lack of use, and his body was more suited to expensive lunches at the Dorchester Hotel than clandestine meetings, like this one.

The past five years had been extremely lucrative for Brown, with a series of consulting contracts to help the international security corporation, Maelstrom, gain exclusive outsourced provision of the UK's primary security services. First, there was the reallocation of close protection duties for the Royals and Cabinet Ministers, which had been taken away from Special Branch, further isolating those in power. Then the intelligence services, where the traditional roles of GCHQ, MI5 and SIS were being phased out to be replaced by a single Maelstrom "telepresence" support team based near Langley, Virginia in the United States. Given that most major UK intelligence activities since the Second World War had largely been US driven, having the same outsourced intelligence provider as the UK's primary ally reduced wasteful duplication, or so it was argued.

Recently, the Cabinet had approved Brown's latest plan for the outsourcing of all of the UK's elite "special forces", the 22 Special Air Service Regiment, the Special Boat Service, the Special Reconnaissance Regiment, the Special Forces Support Group, 18 Signal Regiment and the Joint Special Forces Aviation Wing. All were to be replaced by the guarantee (within conditions of course) of a twenty-four-hour response by specialised global Maelstrom "rapid reaction" teams, saving the UK the cost of having to train and equip large numbers of highly specialised troops who were, to be honest, seldom used. All these combined outsourcings promised to save hundreds of millions of pounds in defence and intelligence spending each year and, it was hinted, that Brown could expect to be included in the coming New Year's Honours List. The best of the specialised police, intelligence and military staff who were being laid off were being immediately rehired by Maelstrom, to do their original jobs but for higher salaries. His masters at the American security corporation were very pleased, not only could they "cherry pick" from these specialised employees, but their loss from their respective British government agencies would mean there would be no remaining expertise, so the outsourcing contracts would have to become permanent arrangements. So, what if the security, intelligence and military abilities of the United Kingdom were now effectively in the hands of a foreign corporation who could sell British interests to the highest bidder? Prime Minister Brinkwater was making more than enough from selling away every other aspect of the nation, Brown felt it was only fair that he took his own share of the action.

Another year or so and Brown would have accumulated enough money to leave this declining "has been" country and have some of the good life. He could disappear, to take up the new identity that Maelstrom had promised him, which would save the expense of a messy divorce that was now the norm in Britain. Maybe he would take Suzette, that sweet blonde intern that Frank Foster had so kindly introduced to him at their last "planning retreat" at the Gleneagles resort. Thinking about the distasteful way he had been summoned, by one of his own old "activation" codes back from the days when he was a field agent, he decided he had earned a treat. When he had dealt with this stupid meeting he would call Suzette. See if they could have dinner at his London flat. In fact, the more he thought about it, his status was now so above such summonses he would tell the idiot who he met at this liaison that he would personally make sure that their career was over. Big time. Henry Brown was too big a fish to be summoned like a common field agent.

He gasped, as he pulled himself up the small winding stairs that led to the open upper deck. His fat pudgy hands fumbled to straighten out the Classified ads section of yesterday's edition of the London Evening Standard, with a specific advert circled in blue ink which was his prearranged contact recognition code. The moisture from his sweating palms made the black ink from the news type spread stains over his fat fingers, and those stains spread in turn to his white shirt, as he clumsily checked the enormous new 10mm SIG Sauer P220 Elite Combat Pistol, tucked between thick folds of belly fat, in a shiny new leather belt holster around his fifty-four-inch waist. Brown glanced furtively around the upper deck looking for his contact, preparing to give some young recruit the benefit of his full repertoire of caustic putdowns, threats and insults. To his disappointment, there was no one who looked like a handler or agent. Just families, miserable parents with crying small children, and loud complaining teenagers all crammed into the upper deck under the blinding summer sunshine.

Fortunately, he located an empty double space near the front, that was opposite a single seat containing a distasteful looking old woman, who must have been on her way from cleaning jobs as she smelt of bleach, wore rubber gloves and carried an assortment of well used sponges and cloths, all in tattered Poundland plastic carrier bags. He pushed his way through the arms and legs that blocked the narrow galley way, and settled his large frame down with a grunt as he filled the double seat. The cleaning lady turned towards him revealing old fashioned thick black NHS glasses and a beige scarf that covered her head and obscured her face. She was wearing a stained nylon overall, with the "Acme Cleaning Company" logo of a mop and bucket, worn jeans and scuffed white Lonsdale trainers. On the left upper side of her overall was an embroidered name that simply read "Martha".

With a start, Henry noticed the old woman was also carrying a copy of yesterday's Evening Standard with an advert circled in yellow marker. It was the same classified as was highlighted on his own copy of the paper.

"Jack Russell Terrier Dog, last seen at 2pm at bus stop on Victoria Embankment. Reward given. Answers to the name "Hercules". Badly missed."

The phone number that was provided was in fact a verification from that day's TS (Top Secret) flash codes, that had been sent to the Home Office Security Desk Officer. The flash meant a high-level sleeper operative needed some vital information. "Hercules" was the identification code for Brown. Before he could react, the old woman moved the newspaper towards him and revealed a black metal suppressor attached to the business end of a 9mm Walther P5 hand gun.

"Easy, baby." Said a quiet voice that did not match the appearance of the woman before him.

Brown recoiled back into his seat exclaiming,

"Are you insane!? Do you know who I am?!"

"The real question, honey, is does anyone know what you have been doing?"

She reached very carefully into one of the tattered Poundland bags and produced Credit Suisse bank statements for Brown's numbered Swiss account, showing the transactions from Maelstrom for his services.

"How the hell did you get those? Only Maelstrom..." Brown started sweating even more heavily, and his face acquired a redness that looked most unhealthy.

The woman interrupted calmly, "It makes for interesting reading Mr Brown, especially when combined with these..." the second worn Poundland bag revealed sets of emails between Maelstrom and Brown.

The fat man finally let his temper loose,

"I do not know who you are, but I do know that you are extremely stupid if you think you can blackmail me. I can have you erased. Literally. I am untouchable!"

With that he reached forward, snatched both bags of documents from her, and, standing up, he loomed over the woman who cowered back, as Brown clumsily drew his SIG Sauer 10mm pistol and pointed it threateningly with his right hand, while his left held the two plastic bags, clearly intending to leave with the incriminating evidence.

"To think you could ever touch me. You are stupid. Really stupid!"

"Not as stupid as someone who draws a loaded gun on a central

London Bus." Replied Cynthia Sinclair, from her cleaning woman disguise.

There was a metallic thump sound as a London Transport Police undercover counter terror marshal discharged a suppressed laser sighted 9mm Glock 17 into the large gun wielding terrorist, who was clearly posing an immediate lethal threat to passengers. The specialised low penetration round entered just above the neck, fragmenting and expanding into a wound cavity that obliterated the cerebellum, before being stopped in its deadly trajectory by the occipital bone of the skull, killing the Ministerial Advisor instantaneously. He fell to the floor and the incriminating papers from the two plastic bags cascaded around him rapidly becoming edged with crimson.

Moments later, everyone had been evacuated from the double decker. Police forensic teams were beginning their painstaking examination of the thwarted terrorist incident. As the small crowd of traumatised passengers waited for stress counselling and medical assistance, no one noticed a shambling old cleaning woman walking slowly away along Victoria Embankment.

Seven hours later, in the electronically shielded second floor office at 10, Downing Street, Prime Minister Simon Brinkwater looked aghast at the five national newspapers for the following day that were spread out on the large mahogany table before him. The headlines were all the results of leaks from the London Transport Police enquiry into the terrorist shooting incident at The Embankment earlier that afternoon. Now the press had copies of the documents, that had been found with the body of Ministerial Aide Henry Brown, there was no stopping the story.

"Massive Security Corruption Scandal Rocks Brinkwater's Government." Said the Times.

"Wholesale sell out of British Security." Ran the Telegraph.

"Sir Tavish Stewart framed in elaborate Maelstrom/Government plot." Stated the Independent.

"Yanks Own Us after sell out by Greedy Government." Exclaimed the Mirror.

Brinkwater paced back and fore in front of the ninety-inch

conference display, which showed the skeletal face of media fixer Gerald Seymour, who was looking considerably less composed than usual.

"How could this happen? You promised me that everything would be taken care of and that no one would ever know?" Demanded the British Prime Minister.

"It is unfortunate. Our best people are on it, finding out what happened." Responded Seymour's deep Californian accent.

"Unfortunate?!? Un-fucking fortunate?!" Screamed the panic stricken Brinkwater.

"This is MY fucking future going down the fucking plughole. Don't sit there and tell me it's unfortunate! Don't you ever think I will not take all of you down with me. So, the question is Gerald, what the fuck are you going to do to sort this mess out ?!"

Seymour sighed like he was talking to a small child throwing a temper tantrum.

"These things happen, Simon. It is part of political life. You are a big boy and you knew that the risks were as big as the rewards. Remember all the other disgraced politicians, even war criminals, live well. You know we always take care of our own. After the few weeks of press coverage this will all die down, and we will find you a new leadership role on the world stage." Seymour consulted his notes,

"Maybe something in the UN. But you must sit tight and ride the storm."

Brinkwater exploded with rage, thumping the desk with the newspapers.

"You can fix it. Issue denials, remove the sources. I mean really remove them. You have done it before. Do it now. Now, or I will call a fucking news conference the like of which you have never fucking imagined."

Seymour nodded, sighed gravely and began typing at his keyboard, "If that is the way you feel, Simon. Yes, we will fix it."

"Good. Now!" Exclaimed Brinkwater.

At the far side of the darkened conference room Amanda King, the Prime Minister's Personal Assistant, nodded to some private message that had come through on her iPhone. She pulled down the hem on her skin tight blue bandage dress as she stood, her matching electric blue mini heels clicking on the polished wooden floor, as she walked slowly over to the soundproof double doors. Opening them, she checked the long narrow stairs and landing corridor outside. Both were empty, apart from a single elderly female cleaner who was working an electric floor polishing machine, while listening to music on in ear headphones and singing 1960s Motown hits off key at the top of her voice.

The noise from the polishing machine and impromptu karaoke performance was perfect cover, and King slowly closed and locked the double doors behind her. Back inside the dark soundproof conference room, Brinkwater's beautiful Personal Assistant and mistress walked to the rich mahogany and steel drinks cabinet in the corner of the room and slowly poured two large glasses of Hennessy Paradise Imperial Cognac, from a distinctive pear-shaped bottle with a polished metal neck and stopper.

The room's diffuse lighting highlighted the rich subtle auburn tones of the liquid in the large Bormioli Rocco bowl shaped glasses, as they released the notes of jasmine and dried fruits that had developed in the Cognac's 150 years of careful aging. Unseen by any but the most careful observer, Amanda King's left hand dropped a small pellet into the drink held in her right, which she offered to Brinkwater having approached him slowly across the room. He took the glass gratefully and downed it in a single swig.

Amanda King reached out and affectionately brushed the Prime Minister's ruffled light blonde hair from his eyes. He pulled her close to him and held on to her tightly like a child would, as he broke down and began to sob softly. The cries grew less frequent as the drug began to enter his system and, within minutes, King started slowly guiding the increasingly disorientated Brinkwater to the seat at his desk. Once he was positioned in the rich brown leather chair, she adopted her customary pose, raising her silky smooth left leg so her four-inch heel rested between Brinkwater's legs, causing him to giggle like a school boy. As her dress rode up it exposed her perfect thigh, along with a black lycra Can Can Concealment garter holster containing a tiny titanium two shot 9mm Heizer Defense DoubleTap derringer pistol.

Amanda King smiled as she pulled the beautifully engraved gun from her thigh and showed it to the bemused Brinkwater. He clearly thought it would form some part of one of their sexual games, as he grinned expectantly when King playfully pulled a set of latex gloves from the garter and after having fitted them on her hands, placed the three-point nine-inch gun in Brinkwater's unsteady fingers and put the short barrel into his mouth. He smiled stupidly and said "Bang" in a slurred voice.

"Yes. Bang." Replied King in a sultry tone.

The single shot rang out, violently shaking the pistol back with a ferocious recoil, breaking two of Brinkwater's front teeth and spreading his brains over the Turner painting on the wall behind the desk.

After the deafening pistol discharge, there was a strange unreal silence. The room reeked of cordite and fresh blood. King's heavily made up face was smeared with gore as she turned slowly, removing her latex gloves to find the double doors to the conference room open and Cynthia Sinclair standing next to Clive Basildon, Head of MI5, both armed and clearly having witnessed the cold-blooded murder without attempting to intervene.

Sinclair had removed the scarf and thick glasses from her cleaning lady disguise but was still dressed in the dirty cleaner's overalls, holding a 9mm Walther P5 fitted with a long black suppressor, that was pointed expertly at the blood spattered blonde assassin.

Amanda King reacted instantly, crouching to use the desk as cover, as she pulled the 9mm Heizer pistol from Brinkwater's dead fingers and discharged a round, which had Clive Basildon clutching his stomach and slowly falling to the floor. The small Defense DoubleTap derringer then turned towards Sinclair, but instead of another deadly round there was only a loud click.

"That's a Heizer, honey and you've had both your shots."

With that Sinclair's gun spoke twice, sending the beautiful blonde jerking violently to the floor at the feet of the dead Prime Minister.

CHAPTER 28 - BREAKFAST AT BABINGTON'S

"Of all the things you choose in life, you don't get to choose what your nightmares are." - John Irving

35°31'42.9"N 25°13'37.0"E
Aboard the 283m "Tiamat" Migaloo M7 Submersible-Yacht,
Sea of Crete, 50 Nautical Miles North of Heraklion, Crete
03.00HRS, 7th August, Present Day.

The woman's flawless body lay partially covered by a thin white silk sheet, her long dark hair flowing over the white satin pillowcase around her head, like a Pre-Raphaelite Rossetti painting. The long red manicured nails of her right hand dangled carelessly over the edge of the mattress on a large white oak four poster bed, that was the single item of furniture in a wooden floored room that occupied the entire width of the massive ship.

The port and starboard walls of the bedroom were open to the ocean, and a gentle sea breeze caused the semi-transparent white curtains that hung around the bed to gently billow from side to side. As the woman shifted in her dreams, a long green gemstone was exposed hanging on a thick silver chain around her neck. The surface of the emerald was engraved with a mix of strange symbols that glimmered as they were caught in the moonlight that poured through the open starboard side of the Tiamat.

In her dream, Nissa Ad-Dajjal was sitting on the top of an ancient hill next to an eleven-and-a-half-foot tall wooden post made up of sections of cedar, olive and pine wood. The top half of the post was covered with dark stains, a mix of blood, sweat and vinegar, while the very top of the post, where a thick cross beam had been removed, was left with its unstained wood exposed.

Ad-Dajjal was dressed in a long white linen robe, the emerald tablet still in place around her neck, but now with a cord attached to its base that frayed into fine strands, spreading away into the distance, down into a city that lay before and beneath her. The sun was setting and the dying rays caught the familiar outline of Vatican City. The long shadows showed the multitude of silver filaments covering the Holy

See, wrapping themselves around the buildings like a spider's web, cutting off all the sunlight.

Inside the smothered remains of what was St Peter's, numerous human figures, priests and nuns were huddled together making a pathetic whimpering sound as their faith and hope slowly faded out of existence.

As the darkness became absolute, the wooden post beside Ad-Dajjal issued a terrible groan, and cracked apart into its respective sections of cedar, olive and pine, revealing as it did so, large black birdlike talons within, which with a low scratching noise slowly started to enlarge the tiny hole that had formed in the very fabric of existence.

As the focus of the dream changed, Ad-Dajjal found herself back on her yacht lying safe in her bed but, as she listened for the comforting sounds of the moored vessel and the surrounding ocean lapping at its sides, she instead heard the unmistakable tread of soaked wet feet walking slowly across the wooden floor, towards her bed.

Pulling herself upright, Ad-Dajjal drew Frank Foster's gold-plated colt 1911 automatic from under her pillow and, in a well-practiced motion, released the safety and pulled the slide action to load a 230 grain .45 full metal jacket round. She rose silently, like a cat, from the right side of the bed, holding the massive gleaming gun in a double handed grip, pointing the muzzle towards the unfamiliar noise.

In the moonlight, she could see that there was a dark form walking around the far side of the bed. The figure began talking in an indistinct rasping voice, but Ad-Dajjal could hear enough to recognize that it was intoning an Egyptian curse from the Book of the Dead, intended to render suffering on the living.

As the ancient curse came to its climax, a strong breeze blew the curtains wide and Ad-Dajjal expertly fired a double tap where she could see the dark shape moving. The powerful .45 Automatic Colt Pistol (ACP) bullets burnt through the silk curtain leaving two closely grouped black stains, before clearly passing through the figure, which continued its slow walk. As Ad-Dajjal followed round the bed to get a clearer line of fire, she could see a water trail leading from the port side of the boat.

No matter how quickly Ad-Dajjal advanced, she could not seem to get close enough to take a clear shot. Then, just as the silk curtains blew away to provide a clear line of sight, the dark figure loomed directly in front of her, grabbing her shoulders in unnaturally strong hands, with the bloated fingers of a body that had been in the sea for days. Ad-Dajjal instantly reacted by discharging the remaining five rounds from the seven round .45 automatic magazine point blank into the figure, as it continued to hold her tightly. The gunshots were deafening but the moonlight showed the bullets had no effect, instead the soaked figure appeared more clearly defined. Dressed in a blue Metropolitan Police evidence suit, with vicious wounds in her stomach, heart and forehead, stood the late Miss Elizabeth Fitz-Glass.

Looking at Ad-Dajjal from clouded dead eyes, a smile formed on the spectre's disfigured features and she spat directly into her murderer's face, exactly as she had done at the moment of her death. Only this time where the fluids made contact with Ad-Dajjal's flawless features, the skin slowly melted into a mess of putrefying flesh, leaving only a grinning skull.

Ad-Dajjal woke, feeling her face with genuine dread. As four, armed security guards rushed into the bed chamber, the overhead lights came on to reveal her standing in a cloud of cordite, as she looked at a trail of wet footprints that circled the bed and led to the port side of the ship.

Seven hours later and 930 miles North from the Tiamat, three gleaming jet-black Audi RS6 TFSI Quattro saloon cars kept in close formation through the multi lane rush hour traffic, each car constantly moving, to place itself tactically in relation to their colleagues and other road users to pre-empt any offensive manoeuvres against them. To an outside observer, the only distinctive feature of the three vehicles, apart from the spatial judgement of their highly trained drivers, was the unique sound made by their nitrogen filled steel and Kevlar tyres as they rumbled over the recently cleaned wet cobblestone streets.

The car's twin-turbocharged 4.0-litre V8 engines barely registered the effort of their progress through the busy morning traffic and complex one-way systems, that make up the centre of Rome's small street network. The unmarked cars were the operational vehicle for the little known "Corps of Gendarmerie of Vatican City" (CGV), the Vatican's secret intelligence service. The exterior of the Audi A6 saloon could go unnoticed in most of the city's locations but, if needed, it's modified 597 horsepower engine allowed it Ferrari like acceleration (0-60mph in 3.7 seconds) which, combined with exceptional handling due to its Quattro four-wheel drive, made it the CGV's vehicle of choice.

Inside the luxurious burgundy leather interior of the middle vehicle in the three-car convoy sat Conrad De Ven, engaged in an audio conference with colleagues from the CGV about the current progress on tracing the emerald tablet, and identifying who had undertaken the ruinous blackmail of the Roman Church. Sources from the main international intelligence services were proving exceptionally unhelpful, leading De Ven to the unsettling conclusion that the single coordinating commercial intelligence platform used by most Western Governments, Maelstrom, might in some way be connected with the recent blackmail of the Holy See. Consequently, he had initiated CGV to explore the governance and ownership of Maelstrom, and had found layer upon layer of shell companies in offshore jurisdictions such as the Cayman Islands, Ecuador, Panama and the British Virgin Islands. Following the paper trail of directors' details and sources of funding in these layers of misdirection, had eventually led to a group of Swiss holding companies, that were directly or indirectly involved within the deepest layers of the "Russian Dolls" of the multinational corporate deception.

The core board members on each of these Swiss companies included representatives from the five major investment banks, media companies and, surprisingly, the charitable organisation UNITY, that was currently being mentioned on every news channel due to its high-profile confrontation with established economic powers over its MaGoG free energy generators. On paper, such a confrontation seemed inexplicable, since UNITY was also shown to hold controlling interests in the main investment banks, multinational media empires, Maelstrom and the four main European and US armament corporations.

As Conrad De Ven and the CVG colleagues pondered the possible implications from these revelations, they also discussed the disturbing scanned materials that had been emailed to De Ven's office late last night, which included copies of the rare maps and manuscripts that had been the focus of discussion in his confidential meeting at the Vatican Library yesterday. The source of these documents claimed to be none other than the man who had been so publicly hunted by Frank Foster,

CEO of Maelstrom, in London, Sir Tavish Stewart.

Normally, the Vatican would not associate themselves with international criminals but Stewart had been publicly exonerated of all charges against him, as a result of documents found on the body of a high ranking civil servant who had been secretly working for Maelstrom's interests within the highest levels of the British Government. The full ramifications of these documents were still working their way through the UK establishment, but already it had been announced by Maelstrom Media that the British Prime Minister, Simon Brinkwater, had resigned and totally withdrawn from public life. Overnight the world's press had been focused on the implications of these findings, with every paper raising questions about the need for safeguards against corrupt civil servants. Significantly, none of the major news networks had questioned the role of Maelstrom in the security and military affairs of the UK and other Western powers.

As De Ven's audio conference came to an end, the three, black armoured Audi's closed together into a single file formation, turning into the narrow lane of Via Di Propaganda, with its elegant stone fronted four storey buildings on either side and ground floor shops that offered antique books, ecclesiastical clothing and high-end cafes. When they reached the end of the one-way street, the three cars circled carefully around Giuseppe Obici's Column of the Immaculate Conception, each taking up strategic positions in the small Piazza Mignanelli, so that they controlled the main entrances and exits. After their humiliating failure to track the emerald tablet from St Peter's Square, the Vatican security services were not taking any chances with future operations.

De Ven exited the rear of his car, which was parked opposite the horned statue of Moses at the base of the column, simultaneously with six other men from the other cars in the CVG convoy. Each one of them wore an earpiece that was carefully concealed by their dark grey Boggi business suits, allowing them to remain in a coordinated formation as they walked past the Keats and Shelley memorial house, and began to work their way through the mass of tourists who had gathered at the base of the Spanish steps. Conrad De Ven looked to his colleagues to confirm everyone was in place and, seeing black Audi saloon cars parked at every intersection into Piazza di Spagna, he turned right into a small tea room at the base of the Spanish steps.

The entrance to Babington's tea room was relatively compact, with glass display cases on both sides showing an assortment of cakes, while exclusive jams and preserves were presented on the top of the old-fashioned glass countertops. A young waitress, with her blonde hair tied up into a tight bun under a white paper hat, took in De Ven's shaved head, security earpiece and elegant dark Armani two piece suit, cut from Loro Piana Tasmanian Super 150 fabric, with a smile and efficiently escorted him towards a four person table at the far rear of the café, where an elegantly dressed and immaculately groomed middle aged man was already seated, clearly enjoying Babington's signature English Breakfast while reading an assortment of the international newspapers.

After dispatching the young long boarder with the knife yesterday, Stewart had done some rapid tidying, erasing his own phone message on the answering machine and, after opening Mario's safe, he had scattered 500 euro notes over the desk in place of the notebook, photographs and Vatican library documents. Placing the Colt Cobra in the hands of the long boarder and the Cold Steel Scimitar knife in the hand of the dead Maelstrom operative, he dressed the scene to look like both had died in some financial disagreement. Then, after saying a farewell to his old friend Mario, he walked to the Portrait Roma hotel on Via Bocca di Leone, where he was on first name terms with the owner. Using the complementary ensuite iPad in his room, Stewart had photographed the Vatican documents and then Googled Vatican security on the tablet's browser, before emailing the scanned JPEGs from a newly created Gmail account. After an exquisite dinner, Stewart found an email waiting and from that contact he had initiated the meeting with Conrad De Ven at Babingtons the following morning.

Noting De Ven's arrival at his table, he stood. Both men looked into each other's eyes.

"Sir Stewart, a pleasure."

"Likewise." Said Stewart with a genuine smile.

Each man exchanged the firm, short, dry handshake which marks the unexaggerated strength of a classic gentlemen, someone who has no need to prove anything to anyone and who believes, along with the anthropologist Paul Friedrich, that "The highest praise that one can give a man is that he is capable of doing harm, but chooses not to." Both men sat with their backs to Babington's rear wall while viewing the entire cafe, its clientele and its entrances and exits. De Ven ordered an espresso and the two began to slowly exchange information about a common enemy.

Stewart summarised the armed raids on his home and warehouse in Edinburgh, his subsequent discovery of the legend of John Dee's emerald tablet and the very resourceful and ruthless adversary who clearly would do anything in order to obtain it. De Ven described the blackmail of the Church, the loss of the second tablet and the recent meeting with Verchencho and O'Neill, that had provided the Vatican Library maps and manuscripts that Stewart had discovered in the Stewarts Rome office. Neither man dwelled on the alleged esoteric nature of the case. Instead both noted and agreed that Maelstrom was the single common thread throughout the events related to the emerald tablets.

After De Ven had heard Stewart's description of the individual who had chased him from the raid on his family home and directed merciless automatic fire at him and the Scottish police, De Ven passed him a grainy still photograph from the CCTV footage from the Angrypig Birretta e Porchetta café, where Vatican librarian Ms Dertinz had mysteriously died from unknown causes. The picture showed a smiling hawk faced man walking from her table.

Stewart tapped his finger on the glossy photo, "That's him!"

De Ven nodded and provided some further higher resolution pictures taken from inside St Peter's, showing the same person but now dressed in a priest's cassock.

"This is the cheeky bastard collecting the Vatican's emerald tablet."

"And these show his identity…" De Ven pulled some more formal front and side images of the man, this time some twenty years younger and minus the dark glasses and overconfidence.

"Issac bin Abdul Issuin", forty-three years old, born Cairo, Egypt. Egyptian army trained where he advanced to special duties. Recruited to Bulgarian intelligence in the late 1990s. His special skills rapidly brought him to the attention of the Russians, who took him under their wing, so to speak. Then he went freelance and was implicated in numerous high-level assassinations.

Stewart regarded the pictures carefully, noting the man and thinking of the brutal murders of Hamish and Mario. He said with a cruel smile, "I would very much like to meet him."

De Ven nodded, "Then we have a common goal."

"Do we know who he is working for now?" Asked Stewart.

"My sources indicate that he has replaced Foster as the head of Maelstrom." Said De Ven.

Stewart did not seem surprised.

De Ven continued, "Frank Foster seems to have vanished from the scene. So, we can only conclude some kind of take over."

"Hopefully hostile." Commented Stewart, as he passed Conrad De Ven the smart phone that he had taken from the long boarder at the Stewarts offices, adding,

"I believe Abdul Issuin is the last caller to this phone, maybe your staff can learn something about his movements from the call logs."

"Thanks, I will share whatever I find. How can I reach you?"

"My Istanbul office." Stewart gave the phone number.

"Is that where you are going next?" Enquired De Ven.

Stewart shook his head. "Two of my friends are being held on Crete. I have to help them first."

"Maelstrom will be watching all the flights, so maybe you will allow us to help you?"

Stewart indicated his gratitude, and with that De Ven reached into his left jacket pocket and pulled out a small parcel the size of a long narrow jewellery box. The object was inside a sealed plastic bag. "Before we go, I have something to pass to you."

Stewart took the parcel from his new colleague and looked at it with the eye of an Antiquarian. It was clearly very old and was wrapped in leather parchment with a single large red wax seal that had started to crack with age. There was an indistinct spider like handwritten script in Latin on the outside of the small package. Fortunately, someone had added a typed catalogue note that Stewart recognised as being an inventory record from the Vatican Secret Archives. The typed cardboard note was aged and had the simple message, "To the Knight of the North who will appear at the Church of Rome at the End of Days". Deposited by Dr John Dee to Robert Southwell, Jesuit Priest, for transmission to Papal Library, London, 1590.

Stewart wiped clean one of the breakfast knives and carefully broke the 400-year-old wax seal, peeling back the leather wrapping which had taken on the shape of the container inside. Lifting the lid of a small rosewood box, the Scotsman found a nine-inch-long single piece of dark stone that had been sculpted into a short-handled dagger. The hilt was engraved with similar characters to those on the emerald tablet, while the blade had been expertly cut like a precious stone, so the facets caught the light, creating the optical illusion of a fine beam emanating from the tip of the blade. He tilted the box, showing it to De Ven and then, after some thought, closed it and placed it in his jacket pocket. No doubt he would discover its use in due course.

FOLIO 5 - THOSE THAT LIVE BY THE SWORD

CHAPTER 29 - SEE VENICE AND DIE

"Underneath day's azure eyes, Ocean's nursling, Venice, lies..." - Percy Bysshe Shelley

Garage San Marco,
Via Galileo Galilei,
30/1, 30173 Tessera, Venezia VE, Italy
11.00HRS, 7th August, Present Day.

If the air conditioning system in the ancient 450SEL 6.9 black Mercedes had ever worked, it showed no sign of doing so now on this scorching August day. The thick velour seats, that were so fashionable in the mid-1970s when the car was built, now only seemed to make the interior warmer and released a mix of stale odours from the numerous substances that had been absorbed into the fabric, accumulated over the forty years it had served as the Chief Exorcist's vehicle. The original light beige colour of the upholstery was now thickly covered with nicotine stains from Verchencho's habit of smoking high tar Turkish cigarettes when he was stressed which, as O'Neill had observed, was pretty much whenever he was working.

Although the Vatican had offered, on numerous occasions, to replace the car with more modern and efficient alternatives, the 450 SEL had, in some mysterious way, acquired what the Church calls "The Gift of the Holy Spirit" and become part of the Church's armoury against Evil. As such, it was now formally supported by an indefinite arrangement with Mercedes-Benz Vertrieb (MBVD) in Berlin for its ongoing maintenance.

During the five-hour drive from Rome to Venice, the 6.9 litre beast of an engine consumed the distance as effortlessly as it devoured gasoline, requiring four full seventy-five litre tank refills along the A1 and E35 toll roads through Florence to Venice. As the morning progressed, the heat had increased and O'Neill had discovered that having the AC off, the interior fans on full and the windows down helped cool the cabin and reduce some of the odours, but only while the big car was moving. Now that they had become stuck in the slow-moving traffic on the long modern road bridge, edging onto the small central islands that make up Venice, it was sweltering inside the forty-year-old limousine.

Both Verchencho and O'Neill were sweating profusely as the car crawled past the Via della Libertà railway station on their left-hand side. The only person who seemed unaffected was Kwon, who looked cool and composed sitting in the front passenger seat.

"Remind me again why we have to wear these ridiculous relics?" Demanded O'Neill, as he gestured to the full length black nineteenth century Roman cassocks, that all three of them were wearing at Kwon's request.

"And why do they have so many buttons?"

The thirty-five-degree Celsius temperature inside the car, combined with eighty percent humidity and the thick smoke from Verchencho's chain smoking, was clearly pushing the Archaeologist towards irritability.

Kwon sighed, "Thirty-three buttons for each of the years of His life".

In the short time that the three had been together, it was noticeable how the young priest scrupulously avoided referring to Jesus by name.

"And please, just trust me. These relics," He gestured to his own cassock, which somehow looked considerably more finely tailored, even though all three robes were identical, "will save your life before the end of the day."

"No talk of violence," cautioned Verchencho, "Remember, today is just a trip to the library and museum. Any sign of trouble and we leave, understood?"

O'Neill nodded and Kwon smiled, as if he knew some secret from their future.

As they drove off the highway bridge, they entered a small piazza with a coach station on the left and a tall grey concrete multi storey car park on their right, called Garage San Marco, which they entered. The huge black Mercedes struggled to fit within the narrow lanes of the circular drive up through the floors, but eventually found a free space on the roof. Verchencho carefully locked the enormous square edged car and the three men crammed into an uncomfortable small Perspex sided lift, that smelt like it doubled as a urinal, which took them down to the ground floor.

As they emerged from the tall building, they became the focus for a mass of tourists flocking to the tour boats moored just beyond the coach area, many of whom took pictures of the three priests dressed in the traditional full-length Roman Catholic soutane. O'Neill produced his iPhone and began to access the GPS to guide them but Kwon interrupted him, "Thomas, relax. I have spent much of my time here. Come."

With that the young priest set off, leading his two companions across the coach station forecourt, over a wide modern concrete footbridge and then through a maze of streets, filled with eighteenth century houses, narrow canals and even narrower passageways, that seemed to reveal a church at every turn. As they walked, it was clear that Kwon saw much more around him than just the swarms of tourists and expensive shops. His eyes looked carefully into the shadows that were cast by the overhanging roofs.

"What do you see?" Asked O'Neill, as he regarded Kwon looking intently into an empty space, that was being unconsciously avoided by the mass of tourists, under a thick archway that had been bricked up linking two fine houses.

Kwon regarded O'Neill, "I see the suffering that funded these fine constructions," he gestured his arms expansively around them. "Slavery, War and the betrayal of the Eastern Church, all for the profit of Venetian merchants."

He reached over and touched the Archaeologist's shoulder. Verchencho looked suspiciously at the young priest but let him continue, focusing instead on opening his third packet of Camel Turkish Royals.

O'Neill shuddered as he began to see men, women and children dressed in rags, huddled in the chains of slavery, whimpering, while dark shadows loomed over them.

"They are white!" He exclaimed.

Kwon smiled "But of course. Long before the seventeenth century African slave trade to the American plantations, there was huge profit to be made selling Europeans to the Persians, Sultans and Caliphates. The very word slave comes from the nation of Slavs."

O'Neill pulled back as he looked further into the various courtyard gardens that were now expensive cafes, "Are those bones? And that foul smell?"

An enigmatic smile spread over Kwon's face. "There also was

profit to be made selling and reselling plague-ridden merchandise to the unsuspecting. Helping the spread of the Black Death was good business."

As they walked on, they reached the church of San Giacomo di Rialto. Here O'Neill could see men and women sitting in rags, crying in desolation in front of the ancient church.

"More plague?" Enquired O'Neill.

"No, one of mankind's greatest achievements," replied Kwon, "After this church was rebuilt in 1071 the Rialto market was formed, in this spot." He pointed to the small courtyard where they stood. "It was here that the Bill of Exchange and the delicious concept of credit was created. You know, I often consider debt to be the most exquisite of Evils. Nations can be brought to their knees, with almost limitless suffering for their people, with just a slip of paper and a signature."

As the three priests crossed the Rialto Bridge (Ponte di Rialto), the young priest stopped, clearly waiting for something. The other two looked puzzled.

"Now what?" Enquired Verchencho, who was unimpressed and growing increasingly impatient to reach the Museum and Library.

As they watched, a blue suited woman carrying an umbrella above her head walked past, followed by a string of twenty people. After they had moved on, Fr Kwon bent down and picked up three unused vaporetto (public water ferry) tickets.

"Really? The Prince of Hell needs to steal tickets?" Exclaimed the Exorcist.

Kwon seemed almost amused, "Hugo, surely you did not expect me to BUY tickets. Besides, we will not have time to queue."

O'Neill walked on saying, "Chin, it is a lovely day. I cannot see why we would need to take the ferry back to the carpark."

"As you say..." Responded Kwon, as he followed behind O'Neill and Verchencho. They walked past the elegant merchant's houses beside the Grand Canal, decorated with the elaborate sculptures, friezes, columns and capitals that typify the fondaco houses of patrician families.

While most who passed were awestruck by the finery around them, all the entity controlling the young priest could feel was the exquisite sorrow of the betrayal by the Venetian led Fourth Crusade, that had sworn to protect Constantinople, and the suffering that Christian had inflicted on fellow Christian during the sack of the Byzantine city in 1204, which had provided all the fine decorations around them.

As the three priests walked away from the Grand Canal towards the Teatro Malibran and Marco Polo's house, located just behind the old theatre building, a thirty-foot-long jet black "Top Gun" cigarette boat cruised to the jetty along the Riva Ferro, rapidly depositing three dangerous looking men ashore. Each was dressed in black Interceptor Body Armour with Maelstrom insignia adorning their paramilitary uniforms.

Instead of the standard commando weapons, attached to each man's wrist was a black Streetwise MIL-Force Rechargeable Baton with Triple Stun Technology (TST). This military crowd control weapon is renowned for its deafeningly loud twelve-million-volt discharge, making it one of the most intimidating and effective non-lethal weapons available.

Before engaging its dual 600 HP Mercury Racing 600 SCi inboard engines, to get back into the flow of traffic on the Grand Canal, the remaining two-man crew on the cigarette boat launched a Hubsan FPV X4 Plus Quadcopter reconnaissance drone, which flew high above the rooftops. The leader of the jetty side operatives adjusted the rotating time bezel on his black carbon Luminox "Maelstrom" watch, with its discrete but highly distinctive whirlpool logo on the dial, and the three commandos jogged slowly to catch up with the priests.

Both Verchencho and O'Neill had passed through the small "sottoportego" passageway, that cut through what would have been the ground floor of a building in the Corte Seconda del Milion, and stood waiting as Kwon insisted on another of his irritatingly inexplicable pauses to their progress. This time, it was to purchase three red, black and white helium filled balloons, painted with comic devil faces, from a street vendor.

After some minutes, the young priest joined his two colleagues, but only after struggling to pull his balloons free from the overhanging passageway roof, which had snagged the ridiculously long strings that he had insisted were tied to the comic devil heads by the balloon artist.

O'Neill looked at Verchencho for an explanation, but only got a resigned shrug. Kwon clearly was enjoying causing puzzlement.

Marco Polo's house was rather nondescript and would have been easy to pass by without the small plaque that announced that this was thought to be his family home. As Verchencho and O'Neill looked up at the second-floor balcony, Kwon coughed and announced that the interior had been gutted by fire and rebuilt several times since the 1300s, when the Polo family had resided there, so there was no point in entering.

"Then why the hell did you drag us all the way here?" Demanded O'Neill, who was clearly becoming exasperated with their possessed partner.

"Balloons, of course!" Responded Kwon as he walked back through the "sottoportego" dragging his precious purchases behind him, and began guiding them towards St Mark's Square.

"Hugo, I always thought Satan was supposed to be supremely intelligent. What is going on? It is like going for a walk with a clown." Enquired O'Neill, as they walked a few paces behind Kwon through another maze of streets and canals.

"At first, I thought he was having some fun with us... but I am beginning to suspect otherwise." Replied Verchencho, as he quietly gestured to the Archaeologist to note the three men dressed in paramilitary fatigues, who were behaving like sheep dogs behind them, while a camera drone hovered above, filming their every move.

O'Neill hurried up closer to Kwon, who nodded with a smile at the three commandos stalking them, and hurried them towards St Mark's square, his three devil face balloons providing the Maelstrom operatives with an easy task of tracking them.

Meanwhile, in another part of the city, a second black "Top Gun" cigarette boat pulled alongside the waterfront at the Riva degli Schiavoni, near the two Columns of San Marco and San Todaro. It rapidly disembarked two men dressed in dark business suits, who cut through the heavy crowds into the square, and made their way towards the museum at the Western end of the UNESCO World Heritage Site, Piazza San Marco.

Approaching the North-Eastern corner of the square, the three priests pushed deeper into the crowds of tourists that filled the narrow Merceria Orologio street, fronted by numerous watch, handbag and money exchange shops. The sheer density of people now completely obscured their distinctive dark cassocks and the only way the following Maelstrom operatives could track their progress was by monitoring the red, white and black devil head balloons on their long strings, that bobbed high above their targets.

The HD camera on the Hubsan Quadcopter drone flying 1000 feet above St Mark's square, detected the distinctive balloons pausing for twenty seconds, then changing direction from the Museo Correr towards the Riva degli Schiavoni, losing one of the three balloons in the process. The drone controller, issued a warning over his throat microphone that the targets could be making a dash towards the water taxis. In response, the three commandos who were tracking the priests began pushing violently through the crowds, clearly intent on heading off their quarry before they reached the possibility of escape at the waterfront.

The single drifting helium balloon rose rapidly into the summer sky above St Mark's square, it's long trailing string making it look like a kite, as it floated in front of the midday sun. From the perspective of the drone operator, the rising devils face loomed larger and larger, until it filled the entire camera frame. As the balloons snaking cord became systematically entangled around each of the four propellers, the drone drifted in ever increasing angles away from its intended target and finally plummeted down in a wild trajectory that brought it violently into contact with the terracotta tiles on the roofs and ornate parapets of the buildings that framed the Northern edge of St Mark's square, where it crashed down, along with half a ton of dislodged masonry, into the canal beneath. The avalanche of bricks, tiles and Hubsan drone remains smashed directly onto the first cigarette boat, shattering the thin fibreglass and graphite hull and scattering brick debris for a dozen yards all around. As the dust settled, all that could be seen floating above the remains of the sunken speedboat, tethered to one of the crew, who floated face down in the canal, was a balloon devil face, that bobbed and grinned macabrely above the two corpses.

The three other Maelstrom operatives, who were herding the priests and making sure they could not backtrack to the carpark, ignored the commotion from the drone crash and instead continued their violent charge through the thick crowds, to reach and cut off the two remaining balloons that danced tantalizingly some ten yards ahead of them. All three commandos arrived at their target simultaneously and, violently pulling away the tourists who blocked their access, they drew their military crowd control stun batons, initiating the Triple Stun Technology (TST) in anticipation of finding the three escaping priests. The air around was filled with the hideous crackle of twelve million volts arcing, causing bystanders hair to stand on end and violently bursting the two remaining helium balloons.

Instead of the three-frightened clergy they were expecting, the Maelstrom commandos found themselves looking into the terrified faces of a group of disabled children in wheelchairs and on crutches, who were being escorted by six Direzione Investigativa Antimafia (DIA) (Anti-Mafia Investigation Department) agents taking the child victims of organised crime on their annual outing.

As intimidating as the former special forces Maelstrom operatives were, in their black Interceptor Body Armour and wielding twelve-million-volt riot control weapons, the Anti-Mafia agents were some of the toughest law enforcement specialists in the world and were clearly unimpressed, simply drawing their 9mm Beretta 92F pistols and demanding that the Maelstrom men surrender, immediately.

Within moments, the confrontation was over and tourists swarmed past, taking pictures of the three men dressed in black paramilitary fatigues lying prone, face down, as handcuffs were applied to them.

CHAPTER 30 - THROUGH A GLASS DARKLY

"We must remember that Satan has his miracles, too." -- John Calvin

Museo Correr
Piazza San Marco,
30124 Venezia, Italy
13.20HRS, 7th August, Present Day.

The Western end of St Mark's Square was much less crowded, the main bulk of the tourists focusing more on the area by the Doge's palace and the columns by the waterfront. With fewer people around them, Verchencho, O'Neill and Kwon's distinctive full length black cassocks could be more clearly seen, and they began drawing attention from passers-by, many of whom asked to pose, for a variety of religiously themed selfies, beside the classically dressed clerics as they queued for the Museo Correr.

"Well done shaking off those three goons who were following us!" Verchencho patted the shoulder of Kwon appreciatively, as the three-stood together, shoulder to shoulder, behind a group of Japanese tourists who were trying to steady a "Hello Kitty" themed iPhone on a six-foot long selfie stick, so they could capture the shot.

Once the photographic distraction was over, the red haired Verchencho expertly stubbed out a half finished Turkish Royal with his fingers, before placing it in a leather smokers pouch, for later enjoyment.

"I say we check the Fra Mauro map as quickly as we can and then make our way to the Library, before we get more unwelcome company. I doubt our pursuers will fall for the balloon diversion a second time."

With that, the Exorcist approached the entrance kiosk and, in an uncharacteristically generous act derived from his current good humour, the wild haired priest paid for all three of them to enter the museum. Inside, the lavish interior made it feel as if they were in a palace, with room after room having been renovated to look as it would in the height of the eighteenth and nineteenth centuries. Each was sumptuously decorated in golds and reds, with long tables laid out, as if in expectation of a formal dinner. If there was a plan to the layout of the exhibitions, then it was not clear. Some rooms could have been relocated from Versailles or The Hermitage, while others contained archaeological remains of Egyptian mummies in giant Perspex cases, Greek sculptures on white stands, and still more were hung with paintings by Bellini, Cima, and Carpaccio.

After wandering rapidly from room to room for nearly thirty minutes, they found what they were looking for in the final room of the Sale Monumenti. The Fra Mauro map was presented in a large golden frame that visitors could approach, as bulletproof glass protected it. The exhibit had four small compositions, related to cosmology and navigation in each corner and, inset within the larger square frame, was a smaller circular gold surround that contained the earliest known accurate representation of the earth.

The fifteenth century map showed the world as a sphere, orientated with South at the top, so it took a while for O'Neill to identify Greenland, Europe, Africa, India and China. Once he found his bearings, he pulled out his log book and made notes, as he began to examine the detail around the old Silk Route for cities or indications of ruined sites. Occasionally, he used his iPhone to take a picture through the thick glass.

As O'Neill and Kwon looked closely at the place names on the 600-year-old parchment, Verchencho read from the information leaflet which described the sources Mauro acknowledged for his map. This included Venetian merchant and traveller Nicolo de Conti in the 1420s, and Marco Polo some hundred years earlier. There was also mention of an earlier map constructed by Albertinus de Virga around 1411, which mysteriously disappeared on the 14th of June 1932 before it's intended auction in Switzerland, along with the map's wealthy Jewish owners. Rumours persisted of this missing map being of great interest to a European esoteric organisation called the Thule Society ("Thule-Gesellschaft"), a German occultist group in Munich.

O'Neill pulled up short from examining the map, looking incredulously at Verchencho. "The Nazi's were looking for this city of the Djinn?".

Kwon overheard and laughed.

"You have been watching too many Hollywood movies, Thomas. But, speaking of authoritarian secret police…"

The young priest nodded towards the two glass exit doors on their right that led into the museum shop, where a dark suited man, with a short haircut and a Maelstrom whirlpool pin badge on his jacket lapel, was showing the receptionist a set of three grainy head shot photographs.

Noting the concern on his two colleagues faces, Kwon continued, "…Our time is running out. Let's get going to the library to examine the Polo family bequest."

Before either of the two priests could ask how they were supposed to pass unnoticed through the length of St Mark's square, Kwon led them rapidly away from the Fra Mauro Map room, back through the previous exhibit, and to a fire exit, bringing them out into the sunlight of the world-famous square in time to hear the clock striking three pm.

Their exit coincided with a procession of the Catholic Order of Theatines (the Congregation of Clerics Regular), who were marching the length of St Marks to commemorate St. Cajetan's day on the 7th of August, and the founding of a Hospital in Venice in 1523. The Theatine priests were dressed in the long formal Roman cassock that perfectly matched the robes worn by Verchencho, O'Neill and Kwon, allowing them to blend seamlessly into the procession that headed from outside the Museo Correr to a space between the two Columns of San Marco and San Todaro, easily recognizable by the statues mounted at the top of each. On the left-hand column stood a Lion, denoting St Mark, although the figure was originally designed to represent a middle eastern Chimera, and on the right, the Byzantine Holy Warrior, San Teodoro, that was originally a statue of a Roman Emperor.

Verchencho smiled once again at the Japanese priest, "Trust you to get us to parade for the Patron Saint of gamblers."

Kwon smiled, adding "And bankers."

As the long procession of priests continued its slow progress up the full length of the square, the dark suited undercover Maelstrom agent had exited from the museum shop and was joined by a similarly smartly dressed colleague. The two athletic looking men stood outside the eighteenth century Caffè Florian and looked suspiciously, through identical mirrored Oakley aviator sunglasses, at the long procession of Theatines, whose leaders had turned right, past St Mark's Campanile, and were now approaching the Colonne di San Marco e San Todaro, the only place in the city where Venetian law once permitted gambling.

While the procession made its way, and began to gather by the columns, Kwon quietly led his two colleagues into an unlocked side entrance that led into the Biblioteca Nazionale Marciana (National Library of St Mark's) and, approaching an elderly female librarian, the young priest asked, in a perfect Venetian Italian accent, for the materials he had booked in the name of the Vatican Library for private viewing, which formed part of Marco Polo's estate deposited at the library in 1324. After a phone call and other formalities, which included signing an electronic register, they were led up a flight of stairs to a long corridor that ran the entire length of the building and which led to numerous small study rooms.

Private viewing room B was filled with leather bound books in shelves on every wall and had only one window which looked out into the square, which was shuttered to reduce the light damage to the ancient documents. In the centre of the bare wooden floor of the room, there was a single dark mahogany table, on which rested an assortment of scrolls, ledgers and a single shoe box. The elderly female librarian passed the three men a cellophane wrapped pair of white cotton gloves each and then excused herself, leaving them alone with the objects that had been deposited by the Polo family.

O'Neill put on his gloves and began reading from a Latin inventory, that predated Marco's birth, and described the business activities of Niccolò and Matteo Polo, who were travelling merchants during the mid to late 1200s, involved in trading with Constantinople and Sudak in the Crimea. Later, the brothers took the young Marco on many of their trips, in preparation for his taking over the family business. It was one of these trading trips that formed the basis for Marco Polo's epic story, and which established the Polo family within Venetian society as the source for maps to reach the legendary Cathay, or as we know it today, China.

As O'Neill worked his way systematically through the ledger, he became more and more disappointed because there was no mention of any of these maps. All that was left of the belongings from the Polo family was one of the earliest examples of Venetian glass work. Although a separate hand-written note, added by some unknown source in the late twentieth century, claimed that this object was in fact much older, and had probably come from Baghdad in the eighth century, based on the brown colouring of the glass and the heavy patterning of the mercury amalgam, which was unknown in Venice until the fourteenth century.

A further search through the scrolls revealed nothing more than itemised sales of glass beads, skins and silks over a 200-year period in a variety of locations, including many ports within the Byzantine empire. After an hour of diligent reading, the three men were left only with the old shoe box and its contents, a small handheld metal mirror, that was so badly stained and discoloured, that one could barely make out one's reflection.

"Useless," proclaimed O'Neill, "you could not even shave with it."

"But it is all that is left from Polo…" Pondered Verchencho.

Kwon smiled at his two colleagues and, making his way to the single window, he pulled open the blinds. Gently taking the ancient mirror from O'Neill, he walked back to the window and positioned it, so that its surface reflected the afternoon sunlight onto the bookcase on the opposite side of the room.

"So?" Enquired O'Neill, squinting his eyes as he tried to look at the sunlight reflected from the ancient mirror.

Kwon sighed. "Not here, there!"

The Japanese priest gestured towards the image that was projected onto the bookcase on the far side of the room. The outlines of Europe, India and Asia were clearly visible, along with the routes and cities that ran the length of the vast ancient Silk Route, from Constantinople to Cathay. Deep in the Mongolian desert the lone ruin of a vast city was marked, "Metropolis Diaboli".

Before any of them could make any further comment regarding their discovery, the wild haired Exorcist brought them back to the cold reality of their current situation.

"Now we have the map, I suggest we leave as quickly as possible and make our way back to the car," said Verchencho, as he began rapidly returning dozens of old manuscripts and ledgers back to their BNM (Biblioteca Nazionale Marciana) labelled cardboard lever arch files, "I have no doubt those ruthless men will not have given up looking for us."

On opening the thick wooden door leading out from the private reading room, the three priests almost stumbled over the body of the old woman librarian who had guided them earlier. She was dead. Lying in a pool of her own blood, with three ugly holes in her chest, where high velocity rounds had callously robbed her of her life. Numerous books of different sizes were scattered wildly around her body on the floor, clearly cast there as the elderly woman had desperately tried to escape from her killer.

Sitting coolly, at one of the long wooden reading and reference tables, beside the dead body, pointing a six round Smith & Wesson Bodyguard 380 semi-automatic pistol with a steady, deadly hand towards the reading room door, was the dark suited man from the museum shop.

"Successful day, gentlemen? I trust you found the map giving the location of the lost city?" He gestured with his empty left hand, clearly expecting to be handed a paper map or some notes.

Kwon ignored the demand, instead he looked at the body of the dead librarian. He commented coldly,

"That was unnecessary."

The young priest's gaze then moved from the prone body of the elderly woman with her surprised face, to the window at his right, and outwards from the library towards the red brick of St Mark's Campanile, the bell tower of St Mark's Basilica. Unseen by the Maelstrom agent, but clear to both O'Neill and Verchencho, the ten-foot-high golden statue of the Archangel Gabriel, that formed the weather vane atop the 320-foot-high bell tower, slowly rotated to face the Basilica, a classic Venetian sign that a wicked Sirocco wind and sand storm was rising, driving the ocean through the narrow, shallow Adriatic Sea, flooding the Venetian lagoon and bringing with it the dreaded acqua alta. The clear afternoon sky began to turn dark, obscuring the sun, and revealing a magnificent full moon, that hung low in the heavens. At that precise moment, The Renghiera, one of the five ancient bells of St Marks rang, just once, filling the square with a deep and highly distinctive, but disturbing tone.

O'Neill shuddered involuntarily, and said under his breath.

"The Maleficio, traditionally rung to announce an execution."

The killer smiled, looking first at the dead woman before him, and then towards the priests standing in front of him, saying,

"Remember, priests are just as easy to execute as old ladies. Now hand over the maps."

Verchencho and O'Neill were about to refuse, when Kwon pre-empted them,

"What you need is beside the Doge's Palace... allow me to guide you."

The assassin smiled again, "That is better, see how easy things are when you cooperate?"

He pointed with his gun towards the emergency exit to their left, and guided the three priests down a white metal spiral staircase to the public area, where the second well-dressed Maelstrom agent had been keeping watch so that no one disturbed them on the upper floor of the library building.

The two assassins expertly hid their black snub nosed .380 automatic pistols inside their suit jacket pockets, with the deadly barrels pointed towards the three classically dressed priests, as they guided them through the glass exit doors and out into the Piazza San Marco.

By the time they emerged, the storm foretold by the shifting golden Archangel wind vane had broken. Hail stones rained down harshly on St Mark's Square, as the acqua alta waters from the Grand Canal surged over the pavements, sending tourists scurrying away to find dry ground inside buildings or to form enormous queues, standing in tepid ankle-deep water, at the San Marco ferry terminal on the Riva degli Schiavoni.

Outside the library building, O'Neill could feel the warm air from the Sirocco wind blowing tiny sand particles into his hair and eyes, partially blinding him, but also reminding him vividly of his numerous archaeological digs in the desert and, most recently, his visit to Southern Iraq some months earlier. The violent hail, that had rattled heavily against the glass roofs and street side awnings ended, being replaced by numerous heavy, thickly pigmented water drops, stained by the red desert sand that had been picked up by the Sirocco winds over North Africa, causing what the locals call "blood rain" to begin to fall. The drops increased in frequency, soon becoming a downpour that turned the rising tide water, that now covered the entire expanse of St Mark's Square, into a deep opaque red, that looked like the rich arterial blood that had surrounded the elderly librarian's body.

Kwon seemed completely oblivious to the extreme weather conditions and the fast-flowing water, that was by now knee deep, making the full-length cassocks worn by O'Neill and Verchencho billow like sails and catch in the strong current of the rising flood waters, so that both priests made excruciatingly slow progress along the Riva degli Schiavoni, past the Colonne di San Marco e San Todaro, and beside the front of the Doge's palace. In contrast, the two Maelstrom agents, dressed in their soaked black business suits, strode easily through the knee-deep water, and were soon some yards ahead of O'Neill and Verchencho, closing in on the figure of the Japanese priest, who was standing next to the jetty beside the Ponte della Paglia bridge, clearly waiting for the others to join him.

O'Neill was about to shout a warning to Kwon, that the thick blood red flood waters would be obscuring the edges of the jetty, when both Maelstrom agents, who had started walking to where the young priest was standing, violently dropped from view, falling into the surging flood waters that were flowing rapidly down the Rio de Palazzo o de Canonica, past the Doge's palace, leaving the solitary figure of Fr Chin Kwon clearly standing above the pounding waters beneath his feet. As if to emphasize the moment, the Maleficio bell tolled twice, its deep resonance mixing with the screams of the two Maelstrom men, as they were swept away in the torrent of blood red water flowing under the legendary Ponte dei Sospiri (Bridge of Sighs).

The rain and wind, that had been pounding Venice, ceased as sharply as they had arisen. The dark clouds cleared and the flood waters receded, leaving a few long bands of red sand on the glistening wet paving stones of the Riva degli Schiavoni as the only evidence of the flooding. Kwon walked calmly towards O'Neill and Verchencho, offering the ferry tickets he had picked up earlier on the Rialto Bridge. In stark contrast to the soaked and dishevelled appearance of his two companions, the young priest looked immaculate, even his Frarelli Borgioli Treno shoes looked bone dry.

"Did he just…" Murmured O'Neill.

"Don't ask." Interrupted the Exorcist, as the three men walked to the San Marco ferry terminal.

CHAPTER 31 - L'IMPERATRICE

"Do what thou wilt shall be the whole of the law." - Aleister Crowley

35°31'42.9"N 25°13'37.0"E
Aboard the 283m "Tiamat" Migaloo M7 Submersible-Yacht,
Sea of Crete, 50 Nautical Miles North of Heraklion, Crete
11.00HRS, 8th August, Present Day.

The enormous walls of the sleek minimalist office were configured into their super high definition display mode. All of the world's major news channels were covering the gradual arrival of just over one million people at Istanbul, escorting a single Magog generator carried by a convoy of massive white Volvo FM Methane Diesel Trucks, on its slow overland journey from Grindelwald, Switzerland to Hebron in the Palestinian Authority.

Some of the news coverage discussed the many challenges, as the Turkish city struggled to accommodate such a mass of people. Other commentators were informing their viewers that, never before, had so many ordinary people acted together to demonstrate their peaceful commitment to a cause. The hashtag #MagogForPeace was dominating the world's social media, with intense and deeply personal coverage of the experiences of those who had given up their normal lives to voluntarily offer themselves as a human shield, in order to protect the Magog generator and to act to fulfil Unity's promise to free the poor from their economic slavery to Western energy corporations.

Many of the social media stories included harrowing details of violence and intimidation from representatives of the western coalition of nations, who had placed an embargo on the movement of the controversial Magog systems and who closely monitored the entire operation, often attempting to block roads and arrest the Unity crews who coordinated the transportation.

As if to underline the harassment message, the TV screens showed a series of short clips of heavily armed NATO grey Bell Boeing V-22 Osprey Helicopters. Some were overflying the tent city, others were tracking the long trail of people that continued to flow into the makeshift camps and, most worryingly of all, there were scenes of

Western Alliance V-22 Ospreys deliberately flying into the path of Mi-26TC Unity transport helicopters, that constantly ferried back and fore with the vital supplies that kept over one million volunteers housed, fed, washed and clothed on their long journey.

The current tent city was located just alongside the modern "Medipol Mega Hospital" where, as most of the news channels discussed, several hundred of the human shield volunteers were undergoing a variety of emergency medical treatments in the 280,000-square foot, 470 bed institution, at the personal expense of Unity CEO, Dr Ad-Dajjal.

A number of births had also occurred in the massive tent city during the weeks of travel, and news channels of all nationalities continued to show proud parents, who had named their male children Magog or their girls Nissa, in honour of the free energy initiative or the charismatic Ad-Dajjal, whose popularity ratings now showed her to be the world's most admired and influential figure, with over eighty percent of people acknowledging that she was their guiding principle towards making the world a better place.

Seated in a luxurious white leather chair, in front of her Murano venetian glass desk, the beautiful raven-haired woman allowed a smile to pass momentarily across her perfect features, as she was described in such positive inspirational terms by every news channel.

Turning off the displays and setting the walls to an opaque white, she turned to the tall and athletically lean man who stood silently by the right side of her desk. He was dressed in an elegantly cut black linen Desmond Merrion Supreme Bespoke two-piece suit, with a small solid gold whirlpool pin on his right lapel, denoting his current role as CEO of the global intelligence corporation Maelstrom.

"Is everything ready?" She inquired, in a soft but authoritative voice, looking directly at the elegantly dressed assassin.

"Indeed, Domina. The required ordinance has been confirmed on the inventories of several nearby US warships, and the Nimitz class aircraft carrier USS Ronald Reagan has been confirmed as leaving Port Said, on its way to Istanbul."

The hawk faced Issac Bin Abdul Issuin made a deferential bow with his head to avoid direct eye contact.

"And the vaccine stocks?" She smiled at the utter submission of the man standing before her, recalling the exquisite pleasure she experienced during the lengthy process of breaking so many of the world's influential, powerful and dangerous figures to her will, through the expert application of chemical, psychological and occult techniques.

"As you instructed, the entire stockpile has been systematically replaced with our special version over the past two years, by Unity owned pharmaceutical corporations who deliberately underbid when the contract was outsourced."

"Excellent." Ad-Dajjal smiled, as her total control over the utterly ruthless international terrorist made him whimper quietly at her single word of praise.

"Begin vaccinating our list of those who will be needed, including yourself, my dear, as my work for you is far from over."

She rose, walked slowly and sensuously from her desk past him, laughing as Abdul Issuin recoiled in a perverse combination of fear and pleasure, when her long red Rouge Louboutin coloured nails gently stroked down the length of his right cheek.

The impossibly long smooth legs of his tormentor were expertly highlighted by a thigh high split in a bespoke white silk Alexander McQueen robe, as she strode across the wooden floor and out through a concealed door, that opened before her and then closed, leaving the hawk faced Abdul Issuin with nothing but his orders and the intoxicating musky scent from her Amouage Mojave Ghost flower perfume.

Alone inside her private sanctum, Ad-Dajjal disrobed without any apparent awareness of the flawless nature of her body and pulled a full-length dark purple silk initiate's robe over her head. Her long dark hair flowed down the back of the gown and gathered around her shoulders, in a manner that looked like it should have taken hours of careful professional styling.

The gown was marked with Kabbalistic symbols, all related to the sphere of Kether on the Tree of Life, denoting her rank within several of the left-hand Western Esoteric schools as that of Ipsissimus (10=1), the highest initiatory level. Reaching into one of the pockets in the gown, she unwrapped a gold ring from a black silk handkerchief. The ring was clearly of great age and many of its engravings of ancient words and symbols, set around a five-pointed star, were worn away with use. Kissing the ring, Ad-Dajjal placed it deliberately on her right ring finger, so that the pentagram was inverted, indicating that her Magickal Intent was the subjugation of the spirit by matter, the so called Left Hand Path (LHP).

Being a follower of many dark paths, Ad-Dajjal had outfitted the Tiamat with a number of ritualistic spaces, each best suited to specific esoteric practices. For her current purpose, she chose the Western Esoteric Tradition (WET) temple room, a twenty-foot-long space with high resolution digital image walls that could project a wide variety of different esoteric banners and symbols, depending on the intent of the ritual. Today, they portrayed a series of crude Thelemic wall murals, that matched the stained wooden floorboards which had been carefully relocated from a small derelict villa near the city of Cefalùe, located on the northern coast of Sicily, Italy. The wood had been so carefully arranged that the original Magick Circle and Solomonic Triangle, that had been carved by hand in 1920, were still visible, along with the infamous six, claw like gouges that defaced the borders of the triangle, that were purported in occult lore to have been made by none other than the Enochian "Dweller in the Abyss", Ch...r...nz...n.

Approaching a small wooden table that was laid out before a ritual altar, she paused to arrange a set of four elemental wands into their specific positions, before commencing the ceremony. Standing within the circle, she first intoned the Kabbalistic cross, before flowing into a flawless performance of the Lesser Banishing Ritual of the Pentagram, using her right hand instead of any of the ritual weapons preferred by lower grades. Her intent flowed effortlessly through the ancient rituals, first to banish and then to invoke the elemental essences of the manifested universe.

Having completed her preparations, she sat at the simple oak table, where she opened an ornate 15th century Italian silver box, and removed a set of large cards that had once belonged in the legendary Visconti di Modrone collection. This ancient Tarot deck was unlike its more modern versions in having eighty-six cards instead of seventy-eight, two additional court cards, including a female knight and female page (often called the mounted lady and maid) and instead of the Pope, Star and Popess cards had Faith, Hope and Charity. In addition, this rare precursor to our modern Tarot, had no numbers or titles on the cards and although the Swords and Cups suits were represented, Wands were called Staves and the Pentacles were Coins. The images on the cards were faded with use, but the rich backgrounds and vivid colours were still testaments to the skills of the artist who produced them centuries ago.

Dr Nissa Ad-Dajjal closed her eyes to concentrate on her pending act of cartomancy, her dark MAC eyeshadow and Givenchy Le Rouge Rose lipstick highlighting her literally supernatural beauty in the semi darkness of the ritual temple. Hers was a physical perfection of form born not just to beguile the senses, but to lead humanity willingly to its own destruction.

Her long fingers expertly shuffled the 500-year-old Tarot and she exhaled slowly into the deck, releasing her essence into the controlled chaos of the re-ordering of cards, so that she could examine the unfolding nature of reality. Slowly, her blood red long nails cut the deck and then dealt the classic three card spread that showed the past, present and future.

Her first card was L'Imperatrice (The Empress), denoting a supremely powerful female dominating the world around her, with a smile that told of secret influence and the successful acquisition of every desire. Ad-Dajjal's right hand grasped the emerald tablet that hung around her neck on a thick silver chain, a smile of satisfaction, that matched that of the woman on the card, passing over her face.

The second card, denoting the present aspect, was the Cavaliere di Spade (Knight of Swords), showing the entry of a ruthlessly dangerous man into the current situation. The knight on the card was dressed in an unusual single piece of thick woven fabric, that was folded and wrapped around to cover the legs and body, in what was a fifteenth century Italian artistic representation of a traditional Gaelic filleadh mhòr or great kilt. Unlike the other three male Cavaliers represented in the antique Tarot deck, this knight lacked a shield, instead his hands grasped a very distinctive looking two handed long bladed sword, with a cross hilt of forward-sloping quillons that sported quatrefoil terminations, identifying it unmistakably as a Celtic claidheamh-mòr or "great sword", better known by its modern name of Claymore.

Ad-Dajjal's perfect deep red lips pursed into a playful pout, "Why, Sir Knight of the North, I wondered when YOU would arrive."

She ran her long blood red fingernails across the ancient card, tracing a diagonal cut that would sever the knights head from his body.

"I have been waiting so long for an opponent worthy of the game."

She smiled cruelly and drew the final of the three cards, depicting the future that lay ahead. Her card was La Torre (The Tower), violent and unexpected change, bringing chaos and destruction.

She paused, trying to intuit if the predicted destruction would be by her design or introduced by the intervention of the Knight of Swords. Her introspection was interrupted by a soft, insistent chime that rang through the hall from sets of Backes & Muller BM 100 speakers that were expertly integrated into the fabric of the large room. Her face turned towards the ceiling, where a hidden communication system had been fitted during the construction of the temple room.

"Yes? I have told you only to interrupt me on matters of the utmost urgency."

A female voice responded hesitantly, "Forgive me, Domina. TV Creta is running a news item about an auction of one of John Dee's emerald tablets, I thought that…"

"You thought correctly. Broadcast the channel into the WET Temple now." Ad-Dajjal brusquely interrupted, as she rose from her chair and strode over to the port side wall, as it transformed from a set of crudely painted heads into the local Crete news station's coverage of a Sotheby's auction, titled "Mystical and Religious Realms and Relics", that would commence tomorrow, 9th August, at the Creta Maris Convention Centre in Hersonissos.

The dark haired young female Greek TV hostess was seated on a bench in the atrium of the large modern convention centre building, next to a Sotheby's pull up banner that announced the forthcoming themed auction, and was mentioning some of the highlights of the items that would be presented. These included a last-minute listing from Stewart's Antiquarians, with items from a private Prague collection related to Western Alchemy and the Magic of the British Magician John Dee. The camera cut to a fit, sun bronzed middle aged man, with short cropped hair and beard. The news stations scrolling banner announced this was Sir Tavish Stewart, owner of the Prague collection that was to be put on sale.

"Sir Stewart, please explain what is so special about the items that you will be listing in tomorrow's auction." The hostess asked in broken English. A simultaneous translation into Greek text was presented on the screen.

Stewart smiled and, reaching slowly into his beautifully cut linen jacket, produced a long silver locket with four panels, that would have made up pages in a silver folio. Three of the silver panels were empty, but the first contained a large green gemstone that had been carved with numerous letters in a strange script. The strong light of the TV camera made the green jewel's engravings shimmer, looking like the carved letters were dancing across the surface.

"This is one of four rare emerald tablets that were magical ritual items believed to have been used in the 1590s by Queen Elizabeth I Astrologer, Dr John Dee, in his infamous Angel Magick."

Tavish Stewart smiled at the camera, as if knowing full well the effect the jewel was having on his adversary, fifty nautical miles away. For her part, Nissa Ad-Dajjal was transfixed, gazing at the image projected on the wall before her. The conversation between the TV hostess and the Scottish Antiquarian was lost to her, and she only regained her senses when the segment closed and was replaced with a local weather forecast.

Turning from the screen, she strode from the temple, still wearing her rich silk purple ritual robe, and walked back to her office, convinced that her destiny was unfolding. Soon she would possess a second of the emerald tablets and begin to break the great seals that hold our reality in place.

Back in the semi darkness of the ritual temple, powerful energies that should have been formally dismissed by a banishing ritual remained. Dust particles circled strangely in unnatural dances high in the air, and candle flames jumped, as random pockets of astral energy materialized into the physical realm. Outside the vast ship, the imbalance in energy was becoming equally apparent. Out of a totally calm sea, a single wave became evident in the distance and appeared to home in on the left side of the Tiamat. Gaining in height and speed as it grew closer, the centre mass of the wave contained the remains of a woman's body, face down in the water and dressed in a blue Police evidence overall. The freak wave hit the port side of the vessel, causing the ship to sway, and a sudden surge of seawater poured over one of the open side sections of the temple room, that had been left open for ventilation.

The surging water caused a large puddle to form, carrying with it a blue sapphire jewel that rolled noisily, like a child's marble, across the old wooden floor, leaving a thin trail of water behind it. The sapphire, that had once adorned the hilt on a silver Tantric Chakra dagger, moved directly towards the table where Ad-Dajjal had just read the fifteenth century Visconti di Modrone Tarot, and where the three cards remained as she had left them, on the leather table top.

The sparkling multifaceted jewel came to a halt when it hit one of the legs of the wooden Tarot table, causing the L'Imperatrice (Empress) card to flutter to the wet floor. The five-hundred-year-old pigments slowly absorbed the drops of twenty first century sea water, and began to bubble and bleed over the painted head of The Empress, grotesquely distorting the features on the left side of the exquisite face into a skeletal grimace, before mingling with the surrounding water, creating a blood red pool, which slowly engulfed the fifteenth century parchment.

CHAPTER 32 - THOSE THAT LIVE BY THE SWORD

"It is an advantage to choose the time and place for battle. Ideally a location which emphasizes your strength while limiting the strength of your opponent." - Thirty-Six Stratagems, Book of Qi.

Convention Center Creta Maris,
Port of Hersonissos
Crete 70014, Greece
15.17HRS, 8th August, Present Day.

Tavish Stewart spent the afternoon after his TV Creta appearance seated at a table on the light stone paved balcony of the Cretis Maris resort, overlooking the sparkling blue green waters of the bay of Malia, waiting for a reaction to his act of placing the emerald tablet on public auction. If his adversaries were as obsessed with the relic as he suspected, they would find such an offer irresistible and would make themselves known within hours of the announcement.

After his meeting with the Vatican Head of Security, Conrad De Ven, in Rome, Stewart had collected his belongings from the Aran Blu Hotel and booked a one-way ticket under his own name on the 07.15 HRS Iberian IB5078 flight to Crete, departing from terminal three at Rome's Fiumicino Leonardo da Vinci airport. He had deliberately seated himself in 2F, one of the bulkhead business class seats at the front of the Airbus A320, as it offered welcome additional legroom for his tall frame. As with most frequent travellers, Stewart liked to travel light and carried only two items of hand luggage, his Buckley Leather Duffel and black Swiss Army Lexicon 20X, opting to pick up any additional items he would need once he arrived at Heraklion.

During the two-and-a-half-hour flight, Stewart sat in the comfortable standard Airbus blue leather seat and made plans to free Jeff and Helen, using a brushed metal Google Chromebook which now contained digitised versions of all the documents he had discovered in Mario's office, together with some additional items helpfully provided by De Ven. By the time he landed at Heraklion, he had decided to make use of the Sotheby's "Mystical and Religious Realms and Relics" event, because the venue was close to where he believed Jeff and Helen were being held and, more critically, because it provided an environment where he hoped the numerical and weapons superiority of his opponent would be somewhat neutralised. In addition, to the auction on the 9th August, Sotheby's was hosting a week-long exhibition of priceless mystical items from around the world, which meant that the entire resort had been made into a "weapons free" high security zone for the duration of the event.

Thirty minutes after leaving the three storey white concrete N. Kazantzakis airport terminal building, Stewart was driving a brand new grey Volkswagen Golf 1.4 TSI rental car, which he had selected from the airport Avis based on its anonymous looks, automatic transmission (he knew from experience that gear changes could be difficult if injured), its ability to carry three people (two of whom could be unconscious) and its proven handling on small roads, while also having sufficient mass to cope with aggressive road behaviour (his own and from other road users). He paid in advance for a week, although he did not anticipate being on the island longer than twenty-four hours.

Coming out of Heraklion, Stewart headed along the E75 towards Sitea, stopping in the town of Lassithiou, where he had prearranged for the renowned father and son mechanics, Andreas and Dauid Antonakis, to make some modifications to the Avis rental car. The standard Rovelo 195/65R15 tyres were exchanged for Continental Self-Supporting Runflat (SSR) variants, while the windows and main body panels of the Golf had transparent Level #6 Polycast SMG SAR laminated film heat bonded to them, embossed with large AVIS "We try harder" logos, to provide a pretence for the lamination process. This specialist US made polycarbonate film provides protection against even 9mm submachine rounds, while adding only 180 pounds of additional weight to the vehicle. The father and son team also performed extensive remapping of the engine management ECU, modifying the fuel, air and engine mix performance to gain a short term additional sixty BHP and ninety NM beyond that conceived by Volkswagen at their design factory in Wolfsburg, Lower Saxony.

On his arrival at the Creta Maris resort, Stewart was relieved to see that the entire hotel and conference centre was ringed by a pair of temporary six and a half feet high double wire fences, patrolled by military trained guard dogs handled by specialised K9 handlers from the Hellenic Army base in Larissa. Having passed through the long two-lane entrance drive, the grey Volkswagen was thoroughly searched using underside mirrors and a rather excitable tan and white Springer Spaniel sniffer dog. Finally, before being able to check in to the Deluxe Sea View Bungalow he had booked from the aircraft, he was subjected to being screened by paddle metal detectors and undergoing an x ray examination of his two items of luggage. Stewart could only hope that his adversaries would encounter similar levels of security.

Arranging the TV Creta interview, to publicise the sale of the emerald tablet, was only a matter of a few calls to his personal contacts at Sotheby's and now, having made his announcement, he just had to hope that his gamble would pay off. As a veteran of many campaigns in varied theatres of war, Tavish Stewart had developed an ability to conserve his nervous reserves so, rather than worrying, he sat drinking iced tea at a circular wooden table shaded under a large umbrella, advertising a Belgian beer proudly proclaiming a fourteenth century heritage under its logo.

As a concession to the forty-one-degree Celsius temperature, he had placed his Canali linen jacket on the back of a chair beside him, along with his Buckley leather duffel that he had placed on the seat. The bag was open, revealing a USB C to A adaptor, a blue Nokia 130 telephone with three pay as you go CoopVoce sim cards, a black Bushnell 10x42 Legend Monocular, the Maelstrom notebook from Mario's office and a transparent plastic bag containing his toiletries. A mix of items that were, thanks to the constantly interfering security regulations, now excluding pretty much anything that could be useful against Maelstrom.

Due to the glorious warmth of the Cretan August afternoon, he had folded and buttoned up the sleeves of his white Craghoppers NosiLife shirt, wearing the UV 50 cool insect repellent fabric outside the waistband of his Incotex chinos, and had removed the socks from his Gifford suede loafers. Just as the digital display on the G Shock read 16.04, his wait was rewarded by the appearance of a very distinctive grey blue shape on the horizon, that grew larger and larger as it entered the sparkling waters of the Bay of Malia. Stewart took a picture of the vessel on the webcam on his Chromebook and, one reverse image search later, discovered that the mysterious new arrival was the Austrian built Tiamat, registered in Hamilton, Bermuda and owned by the Unity corporation who, he knew, from his breakfast briefing from

De Ven in Rome, was suspected as the controlling power behind Maelstrom.

Through his Bushnell Monocular, Stewart could see that, even before the vast yacht had completed its mooring far out in the bay, a classic wooden Riva Aquarama 191 motor launch was heading towards the resort's long wooden jetty. Stewart watched with satisfaction as three athletic looking men and a tall woman, wearing a fitted white linen Chanel trouser suit and a matching white Hermes scarf around her head, disembarked and were subjected to the same rigorous security checks he had encountered on his own entry to the resort, each being forced to surrender weapons to the three Greek infantrymen before continuing their progress up the jetty to the resort proper. As Stewart watched them disembark, he noted that there was something familiar about how two of the men moved, which he recognised from some period in his past but could not quite place.

By the time the Scotsman had paid his bill, and tipped the barman to keep his Buckley bag safe, he fell in some thirty yards behind the group of four people from the ship, as they entered the Sotheby's "Mystical and Religious Realms and Relics" exhibition on the ground "Zeus" level of the conference complex. Again, Stewart felt some instinctual disquiet about the two larger men, something dark and unwelcome lurked on the edge of his memory.

The massive Zeus Hall had been segregated into three large, twenty square yard areas, under the designation of North, West and East. Each room was dedicated to a specific type of artifact, with "Religious and Esoteric relics" in the West section, "Written Texts" in the East and, most interestingly from Stewart's personal perspective, "Mythical Weapons" in the North section, which was the first area that visitors encountered after entering through the double doors. Many of the artefacts on display had been loaned from museums and collections from around the world for the week-long exhibition, to maximise the numbers of people who would visit the auction and bid on the items that would be offered for sale on the following day.

The group from the Tiamat were clearly looking for a specific exhibit, as they hurried past numerous priceless and unique objects without giving them the slightest glance. Stewart's suspicion about the intentions of the four were confirmed when he heard a loud exclamation of frustration from the woman, as she stood in front of an empty display cabinet in the West section that had been allocated to the emerald tablet.

"I see you have noticed that it is missing…" Stewart remarked casually, as he approached the group of four people.

The tall woman removed her white linen jacket, dark Cartier sunglasses and white Hermes silk scarf, placing them on an adjacent glass cabinet, exposing a white Chanel sleeveless silk top that highlighted her toned bare arms. She turned, revealing piercing green hypnotic eyes and a luxurious mane of black hair that contrasted with her white trouser suit. She regarded Stewart with a look that could have been fear or anticipation, it was impossible to tell.

"Sir Tavish Stewart... we meet at last, I am Nissa Ad-Dajjal and…"

She paused, clearly enjoying the anticipation of what was about to transpire.

"I believe you know two of my associates. General Kolon Zeferski and Surgeon Major Seff Razsof. Both of whom I had brought here specially, as I knew they would be keen to see you again."

If Stewart was surprised, he showed no indication. He nodded at the two Eastern European men, who now had turned to face him with clear hatred in their eyes.

The larger of the two Serbians, Kolon Zeferski, stood six feet four inches with his grey hair cut short, and wore a loose Hawaiian shirt that failed to cover a number of poor quality red star tattoos on his neck, chest and arms. His Oakley aviator sunglasses partially hid a mosaic of deep scars on his face, while the belt on his khaki cargo pants displayed a pistol holster that was now empty, presumably surrendered on his entry into the resort. He wore no jewellery, apart from a well-worn Vostok Amphibia Dive watch, and Stewart noticed he was wearing a new pair of tan coloured Magnum Viper Pro boots. Based on the loose fit of his shirt and the empty gun holster, Stewart felt it was almost certain that the former General was still carrying some form of weapon.

Seff Razsof was a few inches shorter than Zeferski, with thinning shoulder length blonde hair. He wore a dark grey Ralph Lauren open neck polo shirt with dark blue Levi 501 jeans and a very new pair of Magnum boots, in his case a pair of black composite Stealth Force 6.0. Either both men shared an unlikely predilection for Magnum products or they had been outfitted in a hurry, which might mean they were poorly prepared. No watch or jewellery was visible on the bare arms of the infamous "Sadist of Sarajevo", whose unnecessary and infamous medical skills were the source of his barbaric name.

Ad-Dajjal continued, "And this is Haejoon Choi, a Sabomnim, or Master of the ancient Korean martial discipline and art, Taekkyeon." Stewart nodded at the heavily built Korean, who ignored the acknowledgement and simply looked at Ad-Dajjal, like a dog waiting for a command from its owner.

Choi was in his mid-thirties and clearly in peak physical condition, some four inches shorter than Zeferski and twenty years junior of the two Eastern Europeans. The Korean was dressed in a long sleeved black v neck cotton top and black loose-fitting cotton trousers, with a pair of ASOS black neoprene slider sandals on his feet, an unusual choice for an assassin. His hands were heavily calloused and, like the doctors, they were free from rings or other jewellery that, presumably, might get in the way of any performance of his deadly skills. Stewart's eyes scanned the martial artist expertly for any tell-tale signs of concealed weapons that might be secreted over his body, but found none, and then addressed the two men he had personally made sure stood trial at the Mechanism for International Criminal Tribunals (MICT) at The Hague, for their acts in the former Yugoslavia.

"Gentlemen, how careless of The Hague Hilton to let you both go before your War Crimes sentencing was completed. And, Dr Ad-Dajjal, based on your choice of associates, one can only guess at what interesting evenings you must have on that ostentatious yacht of yours. It is surprising, given your humanitarian work, that you have no problem employing these insane psychopaths, with convictions for Genocide and Crimes against Humanity."

Ad-Dajjal smiled at Stewart's attempt at provocation and gestured with her hand for the two men to stop their advance on the Scotsman.

"What a sharp tongue you have, Sir Stewart. Be careful it does not cut you. When I saw your TV announcement, I wanted to show my appreciation for your bold gesture, so I made a special effort just for you. Yes, I did have a role in liberating General Zeferski and Major Razsof from the Penitentiary Institution Haaglanden, but not with the intention of making them permanent employees. It was simply a business proposition. Their freedom in return for getting me your emerald tablet."

Stewart noticeably did not take his eyes off any of the three men, who stood beside the beautiful woman in front of him, as he conversed with her.

"Escaping multiple life sentences without hope of parole, in exchange for a piece of medieval hocus pocus? In that case, I can offer you a similar proposition. Helen and Jeff for the tablet."

Ad-Dajjal smiled cruelly. "Sadly, my associates have other plans for you and your two friends. Think of it as a reunion, where the Surgeon Major can let you experience his unique skills."

She glanced at her gold GMT Master watch and gestured to the double emergency doors at the right-hand side of the large stage that dominated the southern end of the Zeus West room. "In exactly... seven minutes an ambulance will arrive at that exit and you will begin what I am sure will prove to be an unforgettable end to the day… and your life."

She turned to the three men beside her, "I will let you catch up on old times. Just remember to get me the tablet before he... expires."

Turning to the Korean she added, "When you have him in the ambulance, bring my things..." she nodded at her jacket, glasses and scarf, "I will be outside."

"And, Sir Stewart, I do hope you will not disappoint Haejoon by surrendering without a fight, as he has so few opportunities to spar with other high grade martial artists."

Stewart eyed the Korean coldly, "Yes, I can imagine him dying to show off his Taekkyeon skills." Ad-Dajjal ignored the pointed comment, turned and walked purposefully through the exhibition rooms and out of the Zeus conference complex, her black Jimmy Choo heels echoing on the polished floor surface.

As the heavy double doors swung loudly behind her, the shorter of the two Serbian men looked intently at Stewart, like a butcher would regard a prime piece of beef he was about to cut, and pulled a blue coloured plastic box from his back jeans pocket. He carefully opened the side panel and, removing one of four semi-transparent plastic syringes, he moved towards Stewart's right-side grinning like some kind of insane demon.

"After your short ambulance ride, we will become much better acquainted. You will have to forgive me if I prove slightly rusty from lack of practice. Five long years in prison will do that to even the most skilful hands, but I will begin with your two friends and, by the time I come to you, I am sure I will have remembered enough to make your turn especially... rewarding. And while I work, we can discuss where your relic is hidden."

As the doctor was talking, Choi had silently removed his shoes, leaving his feet bare on the stone floor, and assumed what was obviously an attacking stance, his left foot leading and remaining straight ahead, with just the ball of the foot on the floor, while his right foot and leg formed a ninety-degree angle (a typical Cat Stance or goyang-i sohgi). He began to edge almost imperceptibly closer towards Stewart, while taking a number of deep breaths. His calloused left hand formed into the classic open hand in front of his body (sahnkal), in line with his leading left foot, while his right hand was held in a deadly fist beside his stomach.

Zeferski simultaneously moved to Stewart's left side and drew a wicked looking thin black composite dagger, that Stewart recognised as being a Cold Steel NightShade Boot Knife. Designed specifically as a single use stabbing weapon, it was made of a specialised resin called Grivory that was invisible to metal detectors, but still capable of inflicting a deadly attack to the neck, stomach or soft tissue.

Stewart instinctively grabbed Ad-Dajjal's scarf, glasses and jacket, as he rapidly retreated into the North room, away from the three attackers. But picking up the items cost him valuable distance and he was forced to collide violently backwards into one of the glass exhibits, in order to avoid a powerful crescent kick (bahndall chagi) from Choi's leading left leg.

The glass fragments of the case spilt onto the floor, exposing a long curved Japanese sword, the Honjo Masamune, believed to be the finest blade ever created by master swordsmith Masamune. It was lost at the end of the second world war, but re-emerged at auction in the US where it was purchased by the Smithsonian in 2016, who had loaned it for the purposes of the exhibition. Stewart smashed more of the broken glass in the exhibit case and swept the fragments with his right shoe across the floor, into the path of the advancing Korean master, but again the time taken to make the move cost him dearly, as Choi ignored the broken glass that cut his feet and launched into a high-flying side kick (goong jung chagi), that threatened to send the older Stewart flying into oblivion. It was only by means of a desperate sideways roll that the Scotsman managed to escape but he found himself right in the line of attack from the Grivory dagger, that was expertly held by Zeferski, close to his body, avoiding any possibility of deploying any of the standard knife disarming techniques.

Seeing his chance, the huge man committed himself totally into a lunge towards Stewart's stomach. In a blur, the two men collided and fell to the floor, as they both struggled to apply various arm and joint locks on their opponent. The two large men were well matched in skill and, for a moment, it was not clear who would succeed in overpowering the other. Then the Serbian General's face turned red and became distorted, as a Hermes silk scarf was pulled tighter and tighter around the huge man's bull neck. The powerful man struggled to get his fingers under the tight silk, but without success, and the fight faded from him as he passed out. Stewart slightly loosened the knot and rose from the floor, just in time to see the reflection of Razsof's syringe pass by his own exposed neck in the glass cabinet beside him. Only by twisting away and colliding with the display, could Stewart avoid the needle.

Now covered in smashed glass, which caused numerous small blood stains to begin to form on his shirt and trousers, Stewart rose from the floor and countered by breaking off the two temples (arms) from the Cartier sunglasses and plunging them, hinge first, into the soft tissue on either side of the sadistic doctor's neck. The force of the attack pushed the infamous Surgeon Major backwards, directly into the path of a thunderous reverse turning kick (bahndae dolrya chagi) from the Taekkyeon Master, that connected with the Serbian across his temple. The impact with the martial artist's hardened heel (dwi chook) made a sickening cracking sound that sent Razsof flying into the glass cabinet, containing the legendary Honjo Masamune Katana sword, that Stewart had damaged earlier. The gleaming wavy line (nioi), that followed the swords perfect blade edge (hamon), sparkled as it fell to the floor at the feet of Choi, who bent and picked up the sharkskin hilt with a look of wicked delight. Seeing his opponent was now armed, Stewart advanced throwing Ad-Dajjal's white Chanel jacket towards the Korean, who wasted valuable time slashing the silk fabric into ribbons.

Stewart meanwhile scanned the exhibition displays around him, as he retreated in desperation. Seeing the smashed glass exhibit case labelled "Sword of Saint Peter" (Miecz świętego Piotra), that he had broken when avoiding Razsof's syringe, he reached into the display blindly grabbing whatever lay inside, while keeping his eyes on the deadly Katana that was now pointed directly at him.

As Stewart pulled the weapon from the display case, Choi saw his opportunity and charged towards him, crying out a deafening Kiai and initiating a blindingly fast diagonal cut (Kesa Giri), that would have bisected the Scotsman from his left shoulder to his waist, had Stewart not blocked the strike. The thick rusting piece of iron, some twenty-eight inches long, which Stewart held in his grip, made an awful metallic scraping sound as Choi's extraordinarily sharp Japanese blade ran down the full length of the blunt and ancient iron sword. Having deflected the Korean's diagonal strike, Stewart instinctively began a counter, which successfully bypassed the small hilt of the Katana, striking the right hand and wrist of his opponent. But, his feeling of success was short lived, as the first century blade had lost its edge long ago and bounced harmlessly away, leaving nothing more than a bruise on the hardened hands of the Taekkyeon Master.

Choi smiled and moved into another attack, this time the classic direct overhead strike (Kiri Otoshi), that would split Stewart in two vertically, if it was successful. The rough and rusty old blade, which looked like a dirty machete, deflected the deadly blow, but the old iron could not match the tensile strength of the Masamune sword and broke half way down its length, as the two blades clashed. Stewart hurled the remaining rusting iron hilt at his opponent's face, to buy time, and retreated further backwards, almost colliding as he did so with a manikin, that was dressed in sixteenth century Spanish finery, complete with a short cloak, doublet, hose, a soft black felt hat and starched white linen ruff around the neck. Beside the figure, was a sign that proclaimed "Rapier, Toledo Steel, @ 1570 AD. Personal weapon of Spanish Sword Master Hieronimo de. Caranza, author of "De la Philosofia de las Armas.", 1569. Regarded by many as the founder of the Spanish School."

Resting on top of a plain wooden chest, was a three-sectioned wooden sword stand supporting a long fifty inch sword with an ornate basket hilt and a forty inch long thin double-edged blade. Stewart grasped the four-and-a-half-pound sword and, after his experience with the previous arcane weapon, he gently drew the edge of the blade over the skin of his left arm, smiling grimly as an area of forearm became shaved bare of hair. Before moving back to face his opponent, Stewart pulled the short black velvet cape from the manikin representing de. Caranza and held it in his left hand, while wielding the long rapier in his right.

Choi continued his advance and the two men stood facing each other, both just outside of their striking distance. For the first time, Stewart no longer retreated from the Korean's attacks but stood his ground, swaying slightly backwards and forwards, in the classic European fencing stance. The Korean was the first to move, launching his blade into a frontal strike towards Stewart's head, which the Scotsman countered by gathering up the Korean's weapon in the short cloak and manoeuvring the forty-inch razor sharp rapier blade, so that it pierced deeply into Choi's leading left knee. The Taekkyeon Master hobbled backwards, forcibly withdrawing his sword from the thick velvet cloak. Using his remaining sound leg, he lunged and slashed towards Stewart, only to find the cloak gathering his blade again and the merciless Toledo steel stabbing deeply into his wrist and leading right forearm. Deep red arterial blood began to drip to the floor from the two wounds on Choi's body and, for the first time in the confrontation, he looked frightened. Now only able to stand on one leg and hold the sword one handed, he hobbled backwards, but found himself trapped in front of a reconstruction of a mystical Roman gate from antiquity, labelled "Stone gates: Lapis Manalis or Ostium Orc" (the gates of Hades).

As the Scottish Knight advanced, the Korean made a last-ditch wild single-handed strike, which Stewart countered easily, tearing the Katana from his opponent's hand so it spun away to land on the floor, some sixteen feet away. The Toledo steel rapier tip found Choi's throat, but did not thrust. The Korean averted his eyes expecting the end, instead he heard the Scotsman's voice.

"Tell Ad-Dajjal that, if she wants the emerald tablet, she should bring my two friends unharmed to the Knossos palace at midnight."

With that Stewart walked away, pausing only to return the rapier to its stand, and then made a short phone call on his blue Nokia 130, before he proceeded to drag the unconscious bodies of the two Serbians, by their belts, towards the emergency exit.

Thirty-five minutes later, Stewart pulled up in the Mercedes-Benz 515 CDI Sprinter Ambulance into the courtyard fronting a large single storey building on the outskirts of Heraklion. The site was surrounded by a rusting corrugated iron fence with a pair of entrance gates, that hung loosely open. Exiting the driver's side of the ambulance, Stewart opened the rear doors and was greeted by streams of verbal abuse from the two War Criminals, who were restrained inside the van. As Stewart walked away, heading back towards the gates, numerous figures emerged slowly from the building. Some used crutches, some were missing arms, others wore eye patches. All of the men had long beards and the women wore head scarves. They congregated around the Mercedes and removed the two Serbians, both of whom began to scream for Stewart to return.

If the Scottish Knight could hear their cries, he showed no sign of recognition, instead he walked from the compound, past the faded sign beside the gates in Greek and Bosnian, proclaiming a Red Crescent refugee sanctuary for the victims of the ten-year Yugoslav Balkan Wars.

CHAPTER 33 - THE LABYRINTH

"They do not go to Crete as slaves. They go as food for the Minotaur."
- Plutarch, 100 AD

Minoan Palace of Knossos
Knossos 714 09, Crete, Greece
11.45HRS, 8th August, Present Day.

Lying immobile at the edge of a thicket of mature pine trees, hidden under a mass of tall grasses, mallow and crown daisies, Tavish Stewart was enjoying being serenaded by a large golden coated Tzitzikas, a Greek Cicada, 'Tibicen plebejus', that was resting on a nearby white mustard flower.

The Avis rental Volkswagen was parked some five yards away from him, on a small lane to the East of the 4,000-year-old ruins of the Minoan Palace of Knossos. Directly behind him, on the opposite side of a dirt track, was a pig farm, its distinctive smell cloying on the still summers night. A few of the occupants of the numerous small wooden structures in the field called out to each other, competing with the buzz of the Cicada.

Within the last seventy minutes, the North-Western side of the Knossos ruins had become a hive of activity, as a significant paramilitary presence was assembled in the large coach park, just off the Dedalou road that swept down the Western edge of the ancient site. From a vantage point high in one of the mature pine trees, Stewart had observed a large force of around 300 men efficiently setting up tents, portacabins and, ominously, several large metal holding cells, capable of detaining dozens of human beings for short periods.

Back on the ground, using his black Bushnell Legend Monocular, Stewart noted the arrival of three khaki ELVO (Hellenic Vehicle Industry) variants of the Austrian designed Steyr 12M18 heavy military transport trucks, which pulled up in the smaller visitor car park that directly adjoined the historical site. Two of these had then been opened to reveal three stand-alone Honda EM5000S portable generators and numerous PAGLIGHT POWERARC lights, that were rapidly set up expertly at specific locations, to illuminate all the main parts of the ancient site. The humming of the Honda petrol generators soon overwhelmed the more calming Cicada song and made movement in the undergrowth easier for Stewart. Parked strategically between the two Steyers, he noted, were two smaller grey Mercedes Unimog heavy series 437 all-terrain transport lorries, with their load areas converted to mobile command centres. The tops of these command units bristled with EADS (European Aeronautic Defence and Space) electronics communications systems and the sides of the van were decorated with the whirlpool logo, that Stewart recognised only too well.

The manpower for the operation arrived in numerous black Mercedes-Benz 6.X CONCEPT G-Wagon Light Armoured Patrol Vehicles. Stewart counted at least fifty men, some were technicians but most were dressed in the standard Maelstrom paramilitary uniforms, wearing similar body armour and carrying identical equipment to that which he had encountered in his previous interactions with Maelstrom in Edinburgh, London and Rome. The drivers of two of the square G-Wagons, and the remaining Steyr 12M18 heavy truck, exhibited a clear disregard for the history of the site. Powering up and over the Western side of the palace structure, crushing a large pine tree, the ceiling of a subterranean area, several archaeological signs and the barriers on the left of the main standing structure, they were parked on a broad plateau just beyond and below the highest point of the ancient site.

Emerging from the two military SUVs, that had pulled up on either side of the enormous Steyr military transport, one figure was clearly issuing commands to unload something from the massive vehicle. As the man turned, he became highlighted in one of the numerous arc lights that had been erected around the site. Stewart smiled cruelly, as he recognised the hawk like features of Issac bin Abdul Issuin through the lens of his Bushnell monocular.

A three-foot square mechanical shape, contained within thick, three-inch interlocking steel tubing, was slowly unloaded from the rear of the truck. It was clearly extremely heavy, as it shook the wheelbase of the massive Steyr when it finally rumbled onto the ground on a set of twin caterpillar tracks. Once it was on a firm surface, part of its central structure began to unfold through ninety degrees, revealing a set of cameras and sensors near the top of the raised section, and an array of different weapons systems in the main body. The camera section at the top of the unit rotated 360 degrees, taking in the trenches that surrounded the broad plateau where it had been unloaded. Suddenly, it's base pivoted and it rose onto the ends of the two caterpillar tracks, which clearly could double as legs.

Now it had assumed its bipedal form, Stewart recognised it as an updated version of a military prototype he had seen demonstrated some years ago at the MCB (Marine Corps Base) in Quantico, Virginia. That earlier version had required numerous power cables and a human operator to provide it with detailed instructions in order to control its actions. Clearly, someone in DARPA or Boston Dynamics had succeeded in developing an untethered autonomous version of their agile anthropomorphic robot, as this had no visible connecting power cables or human operator.

Given the six-foot height of bin Abdul Issuin, who stood nearby smiling wickedly at his new toy, this untethered bipedal robot was over seven feet tall and, based on the way it was tracing a small laser around its immediate surroundings, Stewart assumed it used this tool to build an image of its environment. Stewart's appraisal of the numerous weapons systems contained in this metal monster had to be put on hold, as he heard some activity in the road behind him. Turning slowly, he watched as a group of four Maelstrom operatives disembarked from a single black Mercedes G-wagon and worked together, fitting Claymore mines to the inside of the Golf's doors and the rear hatchback. Once that work was completed, three of them drove off in a Northerly direction up the farm track, leaving one man behind to scatter black metal three spiked caltrops over the road surface, remarking in German as he did, how "anyone entering the Golf would be spread into the pig's manure in the field nearby."

As the Maelstrom agent backed into the roadside foliage, making sure he cast tyre shredding spikes over the entire width of the mud track, Stewart emerged silently from the thick mallow, expertly placing his right hand over the operative's mouth to stifle any sound, as simultaneously his left hand guided Zeferski's black composite Grivory dagger to the left of the ceramic body armour back plate, up under the man's rear floating ribs towards the heart, killing him instantly and allowing the Scotsman to drag the dead body silently into the undergrowth.

Moments later, Stewart emerged wearing the Maelstrom operative's black Interceptor Body Armour and carrying his weapons, a long eight-inch double bladed Smith & Wesson knife, a Heckler and Koch MP10 (the 10mm version of the famous 9mm MP5) and a Glock 19, with the extended thirty-one round magazine, loaded with Speer Gold Dot 124 grain 9mm JHP +P rounds and, most important of all, an ARC X24 radio throat microphone and earpiece.

Stewart disliked the Glock 19 as a sidearm, it's lack of a safety catch meant you had one less protection against accidental discharge, and the fact that Maelstrom had selected the thirty-one-round mag along with the more potent 10mm HK machine gun, indicated they were expecting a significant fire fight. After walking to the Golf and disarming the Claymores, he put them into his newly acquired backpack and, using an improvised broom made from a pine tree branch, swept as many of the caltrops as he could off the small dirt road, before returning to his observation point under the heavy cover on the Eastern side of the temple complex. Inserting the ARC X24 earpiece, he also retrieved the Stanford Photonics night scope from the Maelstrom commando's backpack. Focusing the twin lenses, he then pulled them down around his neck so they would be ready once he had dealt with the arc lights.

While he had been dealing with the Golf, a five-foot-high, square tubular frame had been set up in the exposed central plateau of the palace, that had once been a courtyard, and two figures, Sonnet and Curren, had been tied by their hands to the cross bar of the frame that ran directly above them. Both appeared to have been heavily drugged, since they hung limply, unable to support their own weight, but they were clearly still alive as they tried weakly to keep a distance from the large robot that had approached the two of them.

Abdul Issuin had gathered fifteen of his men around him and was proudly showing off his "toy", as it walked jerkily around the Eastern perimeter of the plateau, its array of sensors exploring the edge of the palace site, looking for any signs of motion. Stewart listened carefully over the earpiece.

"What you see before you, gentlemen, is the future of infantry combat. The nine billion dollar Mobile, Intelligent, Nuclear powered, Outdoor-all Terrain, Automated, unTethered, Robot, or "Minotaur" prototype, is an eight-foot tall bipedal humanoid robot, based on the Boston Dynamics "Adam". As you can see, it is completely untethered and runs on a built-in hybrid fission power system, similar to those used by NASA for their planetary probes, so its combat missions are no longer dependent on battery packs, and can be practically unlimited in duration. It uses LIDAR, a technology that measures distance using laser light, to sense its immediate environment, and massive neural networks to control and plan one of its twenty thousand pre-programmed attack strategies, developed by some of the best first-person combat gamers in the world."

Abdul Issuin walked to the front of the Minotaur and, as he did so, it turned to regard him. Clearly not entirely confident of his own safety, Abdul Issuin took a step back, while he pointed to the numerous barrels of different sizes that protruded from the main body of the robot.

"Minotaur has a range of weapons, including lethal high amperage Tasers and super sticky fluorosulfuric acid foam (HSO3F) for close quarters work. Its prime weapon is the variant of Minnesota's Alliant Techsystems XM25 Counter Defilade Target Engagement System, which can detonate its smart 25mm high explosive grenades before or after a specific designated target, at a range up to 600 yards. This allows it to strike targets hiding behind walls or, in this case, trenches. But it's pièce de résistance is that its power system doubles as a tactical nuclear weapon, able to take out a whole city block. An unstoppable Minotaur can fight its way deep behind enemy lines, until it reaches a strategic target and then wreaks total havoc. As you can imagine, we have numerous Middle Eastern clients who would pay a fortune for what is the ultimate suicide bomber..." Abdul Issuin laughed loudly, as he looked at Sonnet and Curren, helplessly awaiting their fate.

"Once Sir Stewart has surrendered and given us the emerald tablet, we will have some fun and unleash Minotaur to finish all of them, to show how the future of infantry combat deals with the past. Having personally seen the simulations of Minotaur in combat against numerous professional gamers, I predict the Scotsman will be dead within seconds of his attempt to save his pathetic friends. But first we must motivate him to give himself up and hand over the relic..."

Taking a matt black Adastra MG-220D 30 W Megaphone from one of his men, Abdul Issuin turned to the East, where Tavish Stewart was concealed.

"Stewart, we know you are there, it was a careless mistake leaving your car so close. If you had proper training, you would never have made such an obvious error. It is time for you to give yourself up and hand over the tablet."

While Abdul Issuin was talking, three of his men had dragged an injured man from the leftmost Mercedes G Wagon. As the poor wretch was pushed to his knees, in front of the assembled Maelstrom men, his face was illuminated by the flood lights and Stewart could see that it was Haejoon Choi, the Korean martial art master he had spared at the Zeus hall earlier that evening.

"To provide you with some motivation to surrender, in thirty minutes we will begin rounding up people from the local area and executing a dozen of them each hour, until you come forward with the emerald tablet. I give you my word that, once you surrender, we will let you and your two friends go free... but do not think about rescue or escape, because we will carry out our executions with or without you, until we have the tablet. You do not want so many innocent lives on your hands..." Abdul Issuin gave a fake smile and continued, "They say do not shoot the messenger, but Maelstrom does not reward incompetence."

He nodded to one of his men, who pulled a Glock 19 from his side holster and shot the Korean in the right temple. Blood and brains oozed from the side of the head, as the body slumped sideways to the floor.

Up until that point, Stewart had planned to use the MP10 on single shot mode, to take out the numerous arc lights around the site, but after hearing Abdul Issuin's announcement he muttered grimly,

"OK, if that is how you want to play..."

Using the traditional iron sights on the HK MP10, he selected three round bursts, and targeted the group of fifteen Maelstrom men, who had been listening to Abdul Issuin's presentation, taking down four men cleanly, wounding five and sending the rest rushing for cover behind the nearby buildings and transport lorry. Having fired, Stewart moved rapidly sideways, heading North away from his location and, as he had anticipated, Minotaur tracked the origin of his muzzle flashes and unloaded a barrage of 25mm High Explosive Air Bursting (HEAB) grenades into the cover where Stewart had been hiding for the past hours. The whole area was illuminated by repeated explosions, sending clumps of earth, foliage and large limbs from the pine trees, twenty feet into the air. The Minotaur pressed home its advantage, by stepping clean over the five foot wide trench that separated the plateau from the trees, and continued spraying its air detonating 25mm rounds into the area.

Using the ensuing chaos as cover, Stewart scrambled down into the trench and found some excavation equipment, a rubber tarpaulin and three shovels. Taking two of the shovels, he spun them high into the air, so that one struck against the Northernmost Mercedes G Wagon, and the second shovel rattled against the windshield of the enormous Steyr military transport truck, both parked some fifteen yards to the left of Curren and Sonnet. As the shovels rattled against the jeep and massive truck, Stewart could hear over his ARC X24 earpiece panicked instructions for Maelstrom forces to retreat and regroup in the carpark. He smiled. The Minotaur spun around towards the Maelstrom vehicles and, thinking it had been surrounded, unleashed the full fury of its Counter Defilade Target Engagement (CDTE) System, nicknamed "the Punisher" by US forces in Afghanistan. Within fifteen seconds, the area where the Maelstrom vehicles had been parked contained just piles of steaming bent metal. Spent five round magazine boxes littered the ground around the robot. Finally, the firing mechanism repeatedly made the loud click dreaded by infantrymen everywhere. The monster had expended all its ammunition.

As the air calmed, Sonnet turned to Curren, "Stewart is here."

Curren smiled, "Yes, I had noticed."

The Minotaur stepped back and scanned the area for any evidence of enemy movement. Out of sight, Stewart started the countdown timer on his backup G Shock, that he had been wearing on his right wrist, and threw the black resin watch to the far end of the trench. Then he rattled the remaining shovel against the stone wall of the excavations and threw the rubber tarp over himself, just as the Minotaur jumped down into the trench, some five yards away from him. The robot's sensors scanned the entire length of the long dark stone corridor, looking for any movement. Detecting the beeping of the countdown alarm, it stomped towards the source of the noise. Once it had passed by Stewart, he risked placing his head above the rubber tarpaulin, only to find the Minotaur standing before him, with its sensors looking directly at him. The robot's systems responded immediately, by firing a 10,000-volt high amp lethal taser at its target. The four metal barbs struck into the thick rubber and discharged harmlessly. Sensing that its target was still active, the Minotaur then discharged a thick gummy acid foam, which spread over the exterior of the rubber tarp. Seeing his chance, Stewart threw the foam-covered tarpaulin over the sensor arrays, holding it tight against them, so that it covered the vision and weapons systems. Within five seconds, the foam had set solid and the rubber sheet was stuck fast to the front of the robot, its super acid burning away every exposed component on the nine-billion-dollar prototype.

Having lost its visual systems, and detecting that its weapons systems were inoperable, the neural net inside the Minotaur terminated its mission and it began to return to its base for servicing and repair. The robot frame folded down its legs into the two caterpillar tracks and started trundling down the narrow corridor, so it could exit the trench. Guessing its intent, Stewart jumped up onto its frame, so that he was riding on the robot as it crawled back to its service bay.

Opening the two, lead lined titanium access doors of the lower unit, with the Smith & Wesson HRT knife blade, Stewart was confronted with the DARPA hybrid radioisotope thermoelectric generator (RITEG) that powered the beast. The unit was covered in universal radiation symbols and warning danger signs, in several languages. Just like the NASA probe reactors, the main section of the exposed unit was eleven inches in diameter, fifteen inches long, and weighed approximately fifty-one pounds. However, unlike the NASA unit, surrounding the central area was a five inch wide Uranium-235 plasma band and separate central unit that contained, in Stewart's estimation, around eleven pounds of fission core material.

Looking carefully at how far the robot had to go until it reached the exit for the trench, Stewart pulled the temperature sensor off the unit and then, using the Condor Tactical gloves he had acquired earlier, gently pulled the three core rods free from the RITEG central unit, pressing the start on his Speedmaster chronograph as he did. Then he carefully installed the four M18A1 Claymores from his backpack, in a spherical pattern around the outer plasma band, and gently closed the titanium access doors. Removing the rapidly melting gloves, he wrapped the long thirty-one round Glock 19 magazine around the rods and cast them to the ground beside the moving robot, as he pushed himself off the Minotaur and out of the trench.

The searing heat from the three cooling rods reacted rapidly with the 124 grain 9mm rounds in the thin metal magazine and, within seconds, provided Stewart with the illusion of covering fire, as he ran at speed across the empty plateau, cutting Sonnet and Curren free from the metal frame using his Smith & Wesson HRT knife, and telling them both to move as fast as they could. Knowing their friend well, neither of them argued.

CHAPTER 34 - OPPENHEIMER'S DEADLY TOY

"Now I am become Death, the destroyer of worlds." - Dr Julius Robert Oppenheimer quoting the Bhagavad Gita.

Minoan Palace of Knossos
Knossos 714 09, Greece
00.35HRS, 9th August, Present Day.

Once they had left the flat surface of the palace courtyard, Stewart had to carry Curren, leaving Sonnet to stumble across the rough ground that had been exposed by the recent air burst grenades. When they reached the dirt farm track, Stewart helped his two friends into the rear seats of the Golf and drove the vehicle at high speed down the narrow lane, in a Southerly direction.

At the junction with Dedalou/Knossos road, they encountered their first automatic fire. 10mm rounds slammed into the front and side of the Avis rental car, shredding the bullet proof material that was only rated for lesser 9mm ammunition. Stewart began swerving from side to side in the narrow road, to produce deliberate oversteer, so that the rear of the Volkswagen impacted violently with the Maelstrom agents, who had situated themselves along the roadside verges, firing at the small car. Curren made involuntary grimaces with each impact and, soon, the outside of the rear passenger windows were heavily smeared with red and had cracked and formed a spider's web pattern from the glancing blows, as the heat-treated laminate held the shattered glass in place.

300 yards ahead, two Mercedes G-Wagons had formed a road block, facing each other with their bonnets together. Around ten Maelstrom men had grouped on the far side of the two large SUVs, and they sprayed the front of the Golf with fully automatic fire from their H&K MP10s. Realising what was about to happen, Sonnet reached past Stewart, who was intent on steering and, opening the glove compartment, used the spare Avis keys that were in the central storage bin to turn off the car's airbags, and then turned to Curren saying,

"Better buckle up!"

Stewart ignored the massive Hornady 180 grain submachine rounds, that were pounding the already shattered front windscreen, and drove directly towards the centre of the two SUVs that blocked the road ahead. Braking violently, from 70 mph down to 30 mph, as he reached both SUVs, he then suddenly accelerated back to 50 mph, so the bonnet of the Golf dipped and then rose at the precise moment it made a crunching impact with the two obstacles. Generating a lifting and pushing force, the Golf sent the two larger vehicles spinning out of the way, allowing the small saloon to drive through, while flattening several Maelstrom operatives who had not had the sense to get out of the way.

The speeding Volkswagen suddenly convulsed violently, shaking and sliding from side to side, as it rumbled over the road surface that had been covered in numerous sharp caltrops. After what seemed an eternity, they exited the thirty feet of road that had been sown with the spikes and the Continental Self-Supporting Runflat (SSR) tyres began to work flawlessly. The small car continued down the country lane, narrowly missing an oncoming bright orange BMW M3 driven by a couple of Greek Mafia members, who were using the back roads into Heraklion to bring in this coming weekend's supply of drugs to vacationing holiday makers. Cursing the crazy old fool in the Golf that had just missed him, the dark-haired driver of the BMW began braking wildly, to prevent destroying his wide Continental M3 sports tyres and precious nineteen inch alloys, on the three-pronged spikes that his headlights showed were littering the road ahead.

Issac bin Abdul Issuin was having yet another bad day, thanks to the same one man, Sir Tavish Stewart, who had been a plague to his every plan for the past weeks. What had seemed like an excellent opportunity to conduct a live fire test of the Minotaur prototype, against an armed human target, in a location that could not be more ironically appropriate, had gone catastrophically wrong. Not only had the nine-billion-dollar robot been defeated by a single opponent, it was practically destroyed, its sensors and weapons dissolved by its own super acid foam. Thankfully, the robot had disengaged before more damage could be done, and returned to its mobile service base located in one of the Unimog trucks, using a homing beacon. Right now, the technicians were assessing the damage, with orders to report directly to

Abdul Issuin, via their secure radio network. At least they seemed competent, unlike his so called elite operatives, who had let Stewart free the two hostages and escape in an Avis rental car which had, according to reports, just broken through a heavily armed roadblock and was, even now, being allowed to flee unchallenged from the scene. Still, Abdul Issuin reflected, soon his men would be rounding up and executing the locals, and Stewart would have innocent blood on his hands.

"As they say, if you want anything done, you have to do it yourself!" Reflected Abdul Issuin, as he sped away from the Knossos Palace down the narrow Dedalou/Knossos road, in a black Mercedes G Wagon. His headlights picked up the shapes of numerous bodies lying inert on either side of the road on the grassy verge.

"Imbeciles!" He snarled, as he passed through the wreckage of the road block at nearly ninety mph, only to find his tall SUV juddering and swerving wildly, as it passed over the caltrops. Its high centre of gravity made it roll over onto its right side, where it slid over the road surface generating sparks, before coming to a standstill in front of a bright orange BMW M3, that was highlighted in the overturned G Wagon's headlights. The two dark haired men in the M3 watched in surprise, as a tall powerfully built man in dark paramilitary fatigues, pulled himself from the wrecked SUV and walked calmly towards them. The hawk faced man tapped the tinted glass of the orange sports coupe with his knuckle and gestured for the two men to get out.

The driver of the BMW reacted angrily, pushing open his door he stood, pulling a massive chrome plated Desert Eagle .44 handgun from his inside jacket, and moved to point it directly into Abdul Issuin's face. The young Mafioso did not have time to realise what was happening as, in a single movement, his gun hand was bent ninety degrees flat, breaking the scaphoid, lunate, triquetrum and pisiform bones. The gun then moved another ninety degrees, this time in the hands of the hawk faced stranger, who fired four rapid shots of the Federal Premium Hydra-Shock P44HSA rounds, two into the central body mass of each of the young Greek men, killing both instantly. Leaving the second Greek man in the passenger seat, where he had just died, Abdul Issuin sat at the steering wheel as if nothing had happened. Turning the bright orange 430 horsepower sports car rapidly round, he switched off his own headlights and set off in pursuit of the rear lights of the escaping

Avis rental car, that were still visible in the distance.

Back in the Golf, Stewart was still driving with extraordinary skill, through the narrow winding country lanes. Taking a moment, he turned to Sonnet and Curren,

"You both ok?"

Curren smiled, "Yes, well apart from being drugged and kidnapped. And Jeff has shown me a new use for a helicopter."

Sonnet laughed, adding, "Helen was not herself for a while, but is now thankfully recovered."

He shared a knowing smile with Curren.

Stewart continued to drive hard, red lining the modified 1.4 litre engine.

"Mario is dead." He said it simply, but clearly, he was deeply angry about it.

"Shit. I hope you found who did it, and have sent them a clear message." Responded Sonnet harshly.

"It was Maelstrom. The same bastards who murdered Hamish. I am dealing with it right now," Replied Stewart, coldly.

Curren looked at the countryside flying past the blood-stained car windows, "Shouldn't we go back? I mean, we cannot let them begin executing innocent people..."

"Trust me, the further away we get the better." Said Stewart.

Sonnet looked incredulously at the Scotsman, "We must have covered two miles... I assume you left Maelstrom a surprise," he sighed, "How much explosive did you use this time?"

"I am not exactly sure, four Claymores and around ten to eleven pounds, I would guess." Replied Stewart.

"C4 or RDX?" Asked Sonnet, clearly doing some rough blast radius calculations in his head.

Stewart established momentary eye contact with Sonnet in the rear-view mirror.

"PU-239 and U-235 plasma."

Sonnet swallowed hard and, looking at the speedometer, just said "Drive faster," as he reached over and turned the air intake dial from "fresh" to "re-circulate".

At that moment, their car jerked violently forward as Abdul Issuin's pursuing BMW slammed into their rear. Without street lights, the unlit M3 had been able to make up the distance between the two cars, and was now aggressively trying to force the less powerful Volkswagen off the narrow road. Stewart executed a perfect counter clockwise 180-degree handbrake turn, thumping the left front wheel of the Golf into the right front alloy wheel of the M3, disintegrating the more finely tuned front axle and sending the BMW careering into the undergrowth of the right-hand verge, where it stopped dead.

Stewart then reversed and executed another 180-degree turn, so he could resume his rapid escape, although by now the whole left front side of the Golf's body work panel was dragging along the tarmac, only held in place by the shredded remains of the polymer sheets, that had been heat treated to the small car's body.

Pulling himself from his second car crash of the day, Abdul Issuin straightened himself up and began brushing off the white powder, that had covered him when the airbags had deployed. Seeing some lights approaching, he walked calmly towards a massive white oncoming twenty-ton MAN TGX 41.680 V8 truck, carrying machine parts for the Kastelli Airport. Minutes later, Abdul Issuin was behind the wheel of the 114 foot long rig heading South, when over his ARC X24 earpiece, he received an update from the officer in charge of the technicians repairing the Minotaur, in the large coach car park some way from the ancient palace.

"Sir, we have now examined the damaged prototype and we can confirm that the sensors and weapons will have to be completely replaced. We had a scare when we opened the power system, as Stewart had rigged Claymore antipersonnel mines inside the lead casing, but the old fool had all the "enemy this side" plates facing inside the power plant."

"What?!" Exclaimed Abdul Issuin, his fearful realisation almost making him lose control over the massive TGX lorry. "Are the core rods still in place?" He demanded.

"They must be... Let me just check..." The radio made a fearfully loud crackling, that forced Abdul Issuin to pull the earphones from his head. Back in the speeding Volkswagen, the ARC X24 earpiece, that Stewart had put on the front passenger seat, made the same piercing sound. Stewart looked at Sonnet and both men grimaced.

In a world where thermonuclear weapons are rated in terms of thousands of tons of TNT and millions of millions of joules of energy, Stewart's improvised fission device was very small, producing approximately the equivalent of fifteen tons of TNT, but it was intended to stop Maelstrom from carrying out its threat of executing innocent lives and give Nissa Ad-Dajjal a clear message, that she could no longer act with impunity.

Within the first milliseconds of the technician moving the core and triggering the fission reaction, the centre of the Maelstrom temporary camp ceased to exist, as a violent quantum wave disintegrated the atomic structure of everything within a ninety foot radius. The resulting 100,000,000-degree centigrade temperature created a plasma fireball, which engulfed the next 300 yards, leaving only the ionised shadows of the Maelstrom command portacabins and vehicles. Beyond the immediate atomic blast epi-centre, a 0.042 Terajoule (TJ) (0.015 Kiloton (KT)) energy wave then swept in all directions, flattening empty cafes, tourist shops, and every standing structure in the enormous coach parking area, that was fortunately located well away from the ancient palace or any densely populated area. Finally, a small signature mushroom shaped cloud rose some two miles above the site, glowing a dark red in the summer's night sky.

Four miles away, in the bay of Malia, the Tiamat was violently rocked as the sea shook around the massive ship. Onboard seismic tracking monitors sounded alarms and flashed warning radiation symbols on all the ships screens, as automated systems initiated emergency procedures to close all open windows and doors, so that the ship could begin to spray all of its exposed external surfaces with sea water.

Inside the Volkswagen, the car began to skid as the ground beneath the road began to shake, shaping the tarmac into ripples. Finally, the 1.4 TSI engine stalled, bringing them slowly to a standstill. There was total darkness as all electrical systems on the island blinked out and, just to complete the chaos, a nearby derelict farm building collapsed loudly, making Curren yelp in surprise.

The absolute silence was broken only when Stewart tried the ignition, on the third attempt the engine started. However, the car's instrument panel remained blank, and the headlights were burnt out, so their speed became limited, especially given the numbers of broken down vehicles that now littered the busy road to the Kastelli airport.

Isaac bin Abdul Issuin had not fared quite as well. His truck's electrical systems refused to allow him to restart the massive V8 engine, until he had disconnected and reconnected the battery. But, after that his systems worked, allowing him to thunder down the highway after Stewart, with hatred clear in his hawk like eyes, as they glowered through the truck's large windshield.

Twenty minutes hard driving, brought Stewart's Golf rental to the Western side of the one and a half mile long Kastelli airport. The site was in total darkness and clearly unable to operate, so Stewart took the small Northern approach road that snaked beside the starting point for take offs, on the shared military and commercial runway. A short drive over some scrubland, brought Stewart onto the runway itself, where a small, twenty-six feet long Cessna 172 stood with its Lycoming O-360 engine already running. Sitting in the pilot's seat was a grinning Conrad De Ven, who gestured for them to hurry to get on board. The reason for his haste became clear, as the full beam headlights of an enormous truck focused on the small Volkswagen and the Cessna. Ignoring the roads, the driver of the six-axle pan Technicon was heading straight across the rough open ground toward them.

Rapidly exiting the Golf, the polymer sheeting, that had been holding the car together for the past hours, finally gave up and the doors fell noisily to the tarmac, as Stewart helped Curren and Sonnet onto the small aircraft.

"There goes your no claims." Teased Curren.

"You think I had insurance?" Replied Stewart, with a wicked grin.

By now, the truck was closing in on them and would soon plough its enormous mass straight into the tiny wood and fiberglass airframe. Despite the imminent threat, and his companion's protestations,

Stewart insisted on going around the rear of the Cessna, before finally jumping on board and closing the door. It was always going to be a close-run thing.

Abdul Issuin had his foot planted firmly on the accelerator, taking the massive V8 engine to its limit, as he steered directly for the plane, intending to crush it and finally kill the supremely irritating man, who had ruined all his plans, Tavish Stewart.

The full beam headlights from the truck blinded everyone inside the small cockpit, as the single propeller pulled them slowly forward to the main runway. Now behind them, the massive truck was getting closer and closer.

Stewart turned to De Ven, "Got a light?"

De Ven sighed, "Is this really the time for a smoke?"

Stewart nodded and took the BIC lighter from the Vatican security head.

Just as it seemed nothing could prevent the twenty-ton truck from ploughing into them, Stewart pulled open the side door and, aiming at a growing dark stain that was pouring from the reserve fuel tanks of the Cessna, he threw the lighted BIC out of the plane, closing the door rapidly as the runway burst into a sheet of flame behind them.

The burning tarmac did nothing to slow Abdul Issuin. His foot remained pushing the accelerator pedal as far as it would go. The truck continued its progress, now with its entire length surrounded by dancing yellow flames. The twelve tyres began burning, sending a dark cloud into the air on either side of the massive rig.

"Jesus!" Exclaimed De Ven, looking behind them.

"Normally, I would say that prayer is always welcome. But maybe now, you should just concentrate on taking off." Retorted Stewart, with a grim smile.

Slowly, the small aircraft got lift, the nose started to rise and, as Abdul Issuin reached the back of the Cessna, it pulled itself above the height of the pursuing rig. Just as Stewart thought they had escaped, one of the truck's tall radio antenna caught the underside of the plane's left wing, trapping it for a long moment, before Conrad De Ven managed to manoeuvre them free. And suddenly they rose into the air.

Fuel continued to cascade from the aircraft, over the length of the Man truck and, seeing his prey escaping, reluctantly Abdul Issuin steered his burning rig off the flaming runway. He stepped down from the cab in time to see the small aircraft disappearing into the night sky, highlighted against the angry red mushroom cloud, that marked where his Maelstrom headquarters had been located minutes earlier.

CHAPTER 35 - ON A WING AND A PRAYER

"The danger? But danger is one of the attractions of flight." - Jean Conneau, 1911.

GQ SEH 187 Sky Express Air Crete Cessna 172
121 knots 1000 ft above sea level
37°28.'17.1"N 23°54'34.2"E
Near the Agios Georgios Island
Saronic Gulf
06.36HRS, 9th August, Present Day.

The pitch darkness of the summer night had hidden the severity of the fire damage inside the small four-seater Cessna 172 aircraft, but now the dawn light was starting to cast its rays over the distant horizon, transforming the ocean below from a colourless black into a deep aquamarine grey, the thick black carbon stains on the interior walls and ceiling of the cockpit, and the heat shattered instrument dials, were all too visible.

Being able to see the fire damage made the smell of burnt plastics and fibreglass seem stronger to the four exhausted occupants of the crippled plane. Although none of them said anything, there was a clear tension shared between them, their smoke darkened faces showing the strain of the past days all too clearly. Conrad De Ven's face was the most tense, as he cajoled the aged and broken aircraft to remain in the air, flying in a general Northerly direction by sight alone, since none of the onboard instruments functioned reliably after the electro-magnetic pulse and take-off fire. The cockpit clock showed the same time as his Swiss Army Chronograph, 03.20HRS, the time of the massive explosion at the Maelstrom camp in the Minoan Palace carpark.

Beside him, on his left side, Sonnet continued to try and bring the broken radio back to life, while in the rear, Stewart and Curren assessed the extent of the damage that had been caused to the left wing, where they had been caught on the truck's long aerial, during their emergency take off two hours earlier from Kastelli airport. As the light levels continued to increase, with the growing splendour of an Aegean sunrise becoming more evident, the white crests of the ocean waves that rushed beneath the low flying aircraft, became visible through numerous holes in the floor, where the runway fire had deformed and melted the airframe fiberglass. Since breaking free from the long radio aerial on Abdul Issuin's blazing truck, the small single engine Cessna had struggled to get above 1,000 feet. De Ven had fought valiantly to pilot the damaged aircraft around the massive mushroom cloud, which had dominated the Mediterranean night sky ahead of them, with its menacing radioactive glow and deadly fallout dust.

A habit formed over numerous years, had made De Ven start his Swiss Army watch on take-off but the chronograph sweep second hand simply bounced weakly without advancing, since it's circuits had burnt out during the EMP caused by the nuclear blast. A quick check by Sonnet, who had defaulted as the co-pilot, had confirmed that the Blackberry Passport, iPad mini, and silver HP envy laptop, contained in the Vatican Security head's Paradiver light Samsonite duffle bag, had all suffered a similar fate. Stewart had left his belongings behind in the rush to escape the wrecked Golf car, except for the emerald tablet, which hung around his neck, a long obsidian dagger, which he wore in an improvised leather belt scabbard, a notebook in his jacket pocket, and of course his battered old wind up mechanical Speedmaster watch which, apart from some smoke stains on the plexiglass, appeared to have survived unscathed from the events of the evening and so was able to measure the slow progress of their uncertain flight. Since the cockpit compass just spun uselessly, De Ven steered by using the Crete coastline as a rough guide until, finally, they were far enough away from the island that he could fix on the brightest star, Sirius in Alpha Canis Majoris, more commonly known as the North star. Once the sun had emerged over the horizon, Stewart's watch provided a check on their course, using the solar compass method that he had adopted to navigate the yacht Cynthia from the English coast to Rome.

The piston driven four-cylinder Lycoming O-360 engine, fitted to the small Cessna 172, has a factory rated time between overhauls (TBO) of 2000 hours, but that estimate does not include take-off through thick kerosene smoke, temperatures that were perilously close to the combustion point of the Jet A1 fuel flowing through the carburettors, or being exposed to a nearby thermonuclear explosion. As a result of one or all of these combined effects, the small air cooled 180 Horsepower engine was clearly unhappy from the moment it was airborne and continued to make disconcerting noises, with large variations in power, for the hours that it flew through the near darkness over the ocean, once they had cleared the Crete coast.

For the first hour or so, they had occupied the time in vain attempts to fix the radio and the compass, neither of which showed any signs of ever wanting to operate normally again. Then, once they had accepted that none of the cockpit systems were useful, the group began to exchange their experiences from the past days.

Sonnet described the hours from when he, Curren and Fitz-Glass, had been arrested by the police at Gordon Square, passed into the hands of Frank Foster and his Maelstrom thugs, only to be drugged, along with their captor, Foster, and whisked away on a helicopter. Sonnet went on to tell how he had woken in a specifically designed high security holding cell, on a large boat, that was moored around fifty nautical miles North of Crete. After breaking free from the cell, he tried to create a false trail by stealing and sinking one of the launches far away from the main ship, before returning to rescue Curren, who was subjected to a drug enhanced ritual, along with Frank Foster, in what looked like a recreated stone temple deep in the bowels of the enormous ship. Try as hard as she could, Curren could not remember anything that had been done to her but, based on her later behaviour on Crete, Sonnet assumed she had been subjected to some kind of brainwashing that had installed post hypnotic programming. Thankfully, Curren had rapidly returned to her normal behaviour, although they had spent the next few days tied up in a dark stone cattle-shed, while the mafia group awaited further instructions from the dark-haired woman that Sonnet had seen kill Maelstrom leader Frank Foster, in some kind of ritual in the recreated temple.

Conrad De Ven introduced himself and described his role in the embarrassing blackmail and hand over of the second emerald tablet to the hawk faced Issac bin Abdul Issuin, now head of Maelstrom, whose boss, Dr Nissa Ad-Dajjal, was believed to be the same dark-haired woman that Sonnet had described from the ship, and who Stewart had met face to face shortly before the rescue and escape from Crete. The Vatican Head of Security then described his encounters with the Chief Exorcist, Hugo Verchencho, along with a supposedly possessed priest, Fr Chin Kwon, and a Vatican Archaeologist, Dr Thomas O'Neill, who was on long term psychological sick leave. In spite of their less than inspiring personal backgrounds, De Ven knew first-hand the very real threat posed by Ad-Dajjal and Abdul Issuin and had become convinced that these two dangerous people believed the prophecy that had been presented by Verchencho's group, regarding the power of the four emerald tablets that had been spread to the four corners of the Earth in the early nineteenth century. Given the internal chaos within the Church, after the release of the blackmail materials, De Ven had taken it upon himself to deal with the situation and authorised the three-person team, led by Verchencho, to travel to Venice to recover any evidence from the Marco Polo estate which might lead to the lost city, where the last emerald tablet is supposedly located. Conrad De Ven had also informed his counterpart, in the Eastern Church in Istanbul, about the risk to the tablet in their possession, only to be told that the Eastern Church had surrendered it to state control in the 1920s. For his part, Stewart confirmed that he had seen Sonnet and Curren being taken away in an unmarked grey Airbus Helicopters X3, when he had arrived at Willow Manor on a rescue mission, shortly before being betrayed and captured by a corrupt SBS team on the payroll of Maelstrom.

He had only managed to escape with the help of Cynthia Sinclair, MI6 Chief, who had earlier been hijacked by members of the same SBS/Maelstrom team, while being driven to Chequers, the retreat of the Prime Minister of the United Kingdom. Stewart went on to repeat the full details of Sinclair's kidnapping, which she had revealed to him while they were both at the Griffin Park safe house, nearly two weeks earlier.

In the predawn early morning of the 29th of July, the same day as Stewarts ill-fated raid on Foster's London retreat, her two-car convoy, consisting of a Government Cars Agency Black Jaguar XJ Sentinel and a red liveried Metropolitan Police Specialist Operations BMW 530d, had been expertly intercepted on a tree covered bend, beside the St Peter and Paul church in the small village of Ellesborough. Four British MOD marked Land Rover Defender 110 V8 Wolfs, each rear mounted with Browning .50 Calibre Machine Guns, and a single Heckler and Koch Automatic Lightweight Grenade Launcher (ALGL) fitted on one of the two lead ambush vehicles, had positioned themselves across the small country road.

Immediately upon seeing the roadblock ahead of them on Church Hill, Detective Inspector James Fletch and Specialist Driver Sergeant Andy Cross in the lead car, attempted to charge through the two 110 Defenders that blocked the route ahead. However, they quickly came under a merciless barrage of .50 calibre rounds and 40mm MK285 smart grenades, that exploded around the lightly armoured cabin of the escort vehicle, easily penetrating the B4 level armour protection and killing both Royalty and Specialist Protection (RaSP) officers almost instantly. The charred wreck of the red BMW, lay motionless in the centre of the narrow road ahead, riddled with enormous holes, providing an ominous warning of the fire power and ruthless intent of the attackers.

Simultaneously, as his colleagues had ended their ill-fated charge towards the forward road block, Det Sgt Colin Wilson, driver of Sinclair's long wheel base armoured XJ Sentinel, began to reverse the enormous Jaguar, when two more 110 Wolf Defender Land Rovers burst from a concealed country lane on the right-hand side of the narrow Ellesborough Road, some twenty yards behind them. Blocking the only exit, they trained the long barrels of their .50 Browning machine guns on to the XJ Sentinel as it sped towards them, its rear reversing lights blazing in the early morning gloom. As Specialist driver Wilson began to redline the highly tuned Jaguar five litre V8 engine, the massive 4.4 ton limousine began to rock violently from side to side, the space inside the luxurious leather cabin filling with rough cuts of leather, seat stuffing and shattered fragments of armoured Perspex from the rear window, as .50 calibre rounds began to fly clean through the entire length of the car.

Det Inspector Allan Gordon, who was seated in the front left passenger seat, requested Sinclair to get down onto the floor, as he drew his police issued 9mm Glock 26 and discharged his entire ten round magazine through the open gap that was once the rear armoured window. Sinclair threw herself down into the specially armoured floor space, where she could feel the ceramic plates in the small refuge shuddering under each hammer like blow from the massive Browning machine gun bullets.

Gordon's bravery was short lived, as a further barrage of the massive .50 calibre rounds passed through the two front seats and the level three body armour of the two protection officers, lifting their two bodies forcibly up and through the reinforced front windshield. With the driver's death, the massive Jaguar's backwards charge to safety came to a standstill, and the thunderous .50 calibre gunfire ceased.

If the attacking force assumed the current Director General was a soft bureaucrat, who would surrender easily, they were in for an unpleasant surprise. Dame Cynthia Sinclair was a twenty-year career veteran, who had risen through the ranks of the Secret Intelligence Service from humble beginnings as an officer in the joint US/UK drugs enforcement agency, going undercover within the Caribbean and South American drug cartels. Due to her ruthless efficiency and outstanding performance in deep cover operations, she was recruited by the then 14 Field Security and Intelligence Company (internally known as "The Det" within British Forces) and served in field operations against paramilitary forces in Northern Ireland, before being transferred to the Secret Intelligence Service.

Dragging what remained of her black leather Hermes Berkin handbag from the rear seat, Sinclair mumbled,

"Merde!" in Creole, as she pulled out her own personal weapon, a battered old 1970s Beretta 93R, and a small metal keyring with what looked like a safe combination in its centre. With some practiced moves, she rotated the combination ring and depressed the central section. A small electronic beep began to be emitted from the keyring, as a variant of the aviation industry's 406 MHz ELTs Cospas-Sarsat emergency rescue system began a fifty-hour emergency broadcast, indicating an attempt to kidnap or assassinate one of a number of key designated British Government officials, in this case the Chief of the Secret Intelligence Service. Pushing the activated keyring into a concealed pocket in her skirt, Sinclair pulled back the chamber and turned off the safety on the ancient Beretta, as she listened to the sound of hard soled boots advancing slowly on the smashed bullet proof Plexiglass that surrounded the remains of the XJ Sentinel.

She silently shifted her body, so that her back was on the car floor and, using her hands, deliberately split open the left seam on her dark blue silk Prada skirt, revealing her gym toned legs as she braced them wide against the left side passenger door frame. She held the forty-year-old Italian pistol in the classic two handed extended grip, aiming towards the right-side passenger door, where the armoured window glass had been cleanly removed in the recent storm of .50 calibre rounds. When a gas masked face cautiously looked into the window space, Sinclair exhaled, squeezing the wide trigger on the Beretta, and felt it dance wildly in her two hands as it fired fully automatic three round bursts, at a rate of over 1,000 rounds a minute. Based on the classic 9mm Beretta 92 handgun frame, the 93 "R" ("Raffica" the Italian for "volley") was designed in the 1970s for Italian counter terrorism units, to defend nuclear installations and even the odds against superior attacking forces, with surprisingly fearsome firepower contained in such a small sized weapon.

Two of the three 9mm "Black Talon" Lubalox coated jacketed hollow point rounds from Sinclair's pistol, passed through the head of the masked attacker, sending his convulsing body falling to the asphalt road surface with a loud clatter. While his team members on the right side of the road threw themselves on the ground for cover, another charged for the left side of the car, assuming he would gain an easy access. As the specialist commando reached the Jaguar's left rear door, he risked checking the interior and heard a woman's voice growl,

"Malpwopte!"

as his left eye was pierced, through the broken car window, by a four-inch-high heel that shattered the tempered glass on his face mask, and penetrated two inches beyond his eye socket into his brain's frontal lobe. He staggered back, stunned and disorientated from massive brain trauma, holding his face as blood, tissue and eye vitreous poured down the outside of the rubber gas mask. Sinclair followed up on her devastating kick by emerging rapidly from the left rear passenger door, and let loose another burst of fully automatic fire with the 93R in her left hand, making the commando team approaching the rear of her car scuttle to a roadside ditch for cover. With her right hand, she grasped the neck webbing strap holding a Heckler and Koch MP5 on the wounded commando's chest, twisting his body round so the machine gun stock was positioned towards her, while her opponent's body rotated to face the men who were now advancing from out of the two Land Rovers that had originally blocked the road in front. Tightening the webbing strap around her upper right arm, so she effectively had a stranglehold on the wounded man, Sinclair used her free right hand to guide the barrel of the short HK MP5 machine gun over the top of his right shoulder, releasing its safety catch, and began directing short automatic bursts towards the group of men coming towards her from the front of the wrecked Jaguar, forcing them to scatter for cover, while being unable to return fire because of their wounded comrade held in front of Dame Sinclair.

Now shooting simultaneously with both hands in opposite directions and using the wounded commando as cover, Sinclair strode up the steep path to the churchyard that faced directly in front of where she had emerged from the car, her split skirt exposing her stockinged legs. Spent 9mm rounds cascaded from her two weapons, leaving a trail of red hot metal around her rapidly moving high heels. As she gained ground, on the approach to a pair of chest high wooden gates beside a tall hedge, her ability to direct accurate suppressive rounds at her attackers improved, giving her increased confidence that she might yet survive and escape this ambush attempt.

On reaching the gates, she allowed herself to break into a smile, as she saw some familiar faces, three heavily armed members of the Prime Minister's personal protection detail, who she recognised from her frequent meetings at 10 Downing Street and the nearby Chequers retreat. Behind them, she could see the Prime Minister's AgustaWestland AW159 Wildcat personal transport helicopter sitting in a clear space at the rear of the small churchyard.

Assuming they were responding to the radio distress beacon she had initiated earlier, Sinclair began to relax and, turning to keep the wounded commando between her and the kidnappers below, she retreated, guns still trained on the two groups of men, as she slowly edged backwards towards the Prime Minister's security team.

They, in turn, opened the wooden gate and two of the bodyguards came alongside Dame Sinclair, directing their deadly twelve-gauge combat shotguns at the two groups of men gathered below them at either end of the narrow road, but not yet firing. Sinclair was aware of the third officer approaching from behind and started to ease up her grip on the webbing strap, when her eyes widened in surprise, as she felt the cold steel of his gun muzzle against the back of her neck. She tensed, rapidly running through her options in her mind, but realizing any attempt at escape was futile when the two men flanking her turned and aimed their combat shotguns towards her. Cynthia Sinclair was captured.

FOLIO 6 - BEHOLD A PALE HORSE

CHAPTER 36 - THE FOUNDATIONS OF FAITH

"A great change will begin to come over the people of the world, as the foundations of faith tumble to dust." End of Days, paraphrased from The Holy Koran

Galaxy Rooftop Restaurant
Hilton Athens
46 Vassilissis Sofias Avenue,
Athens 115 28, Greece
20.26HRS, 9th August, Present Day.

The small group, of Helen Curren, Jeff Sonnet and Conrad De Ven, were seated around a four-person table on the long marble finished outdoor veranda of the Galaxy restaurant, that ran the entire length of the hotel's Western side, waiting for Stewart to join them. A glorious Athenian sunset was highlighting the 5th century BC Temple Monument of the Acropolis in the distance, making the danger and excitement of the past twenty-four hours seem like an unreal dream. But the cuts and burns each of them were suffering, hidden now under the numerous Betadine Wound Care plasters and gauze strips on their faces, arms, legs and hands, were real and so were the Hellenic Center of Disease Control and Prevention (HCDCP) stock 130 Mg Potassium Iodide (KI) tablets that each of them were now taking, washed down with copious amounts of bottled Theoni mineral water, as a precautionary measure against absorption of the radioactive dust. Seated around the small table, their conversation naturally turned to recalling their narrow escape in the small Cessna plane.

After updating Sonnet and Curren about the violent and treacherous kidnapping of Cynthia Sinclair, by officers of the Prime Minister's personal protection team, Stewart had told of his own escape from London, sailing to Rome and the subsequent discovery of Mario's tortured body, before the fortuitous meeting with De Ven.

Having recounted their individual journeys and, with the sun now higher in the sky, the group focused on establishing their position relative to the Greek mainland. Using the solar compass on Stewart's watch and the remains of a charred map of the region, they determined that the nearby land on the right side of the Cessna 172 was the uninhabited island of San Giorgio in the Saronic Islands, making them some twelve miles off the Greek coast and roughly thirty-seven miles from Athens.

The relief that became visible on all three smoke stained faces was short lived, as they were suddenly buffeted by a strong Westerly gust of wind, which deflected the airframe violently to the starboard and caused the small plane to make a loud groan, as the port side wing support struts suddenly collapsed, making the entire left-wing section drop. The Cessna lurched wildly and plummeted 800 feet before De Ven desperately regained control. The interior became drenched by the ocean spray, now mere feet away from them, as it seeped into the small cabin through the numerous holes in the fiberglass chassis. Stewart's smoke-stained face looked grimly at the broken wing struts and then he called to Sonnet to use the obsidian knife to begin cutting long sections of duct tape, from a roll they had found in the co-pilot's side storage bins. Hanging by his belt, which was grasped by Sonnet and Curren from the open door, Stewart pulled himself into the broken wing frame and, pushing with his back and legs, straightened the bent struts, binding them into shape with numerous strips of duct tape that made the fuselage look like some insane Christmas present. Finally, his work done, Stewart allowed himself to be manhandled back into the small Cessna and he lay laughing from relief with his two friends, who were by now equally exhausted.

Conrad De Ven however, did not share their good humour.

"If you three can please contain your enjoyment for a moment, I believe we have some," the rest of his sentence was lost, as two very large grey dart shapes streaked past either side of the stricken Cessna at over 800 knots, causing the small aircraft to shake wildly and severely testing the duct tape repairs just affected by Stewart.

The Hellenic Air Force Mirage 2000-5 Mk2 interceptors had been scrambled some sixteen minutes earlier from Tanagra, home of 114 Combat Wing, after civilian and military air traffic control had failed to receive any radio communication from a low flying unregistered aircraft, on a rough course towards the Greek capital. The two French designed Dassault Mirage jets assumed an escort formation around the much smaller Cessna, one fighter remaining at a fixed distance behind them, while the second came alongside to make visual contact.

De Ven and Sonnet used hand gestures to try and communicate that the Cessna had suffered a complete systems failure but, as they had failed to initiate the international protocol to indicate loss of all radio and telemetry systems, the fighter escort insisted that they prepare to ditch in the sea immediately, even though they could now see the coast a few miles ahead of them.

De Ven coaxed their air speed down and descended as low as he dared, cutting the engine just as they made contact with the ocean waves. The brave little Cessna shook violently and the airframe, which had withstood so much over the past hours, finally gave up its struggles and, after a few minutes, sank without trace beneath the swell. The intense heat of the fires at take-off had destroyed the buoyancy of the Cessna's life vests, so the four friends hung together for mutual support in the water, resting on their backs, interlinking their arms so their heads remained close enough to talk when needed and forming a highly visible star shape with their bodies while they floated, drifting in the strong six knot South Easterly current that ran down the coast near the port of Piraeus.

The two fighter jets continued to take turns to pass over them for some twenty minutes, before disappearing back towards the mainland, leaving them in silence and wondering if they had been forgotten and should perhaps try and make their way to the coast, that was just over one mile away. Eventually, they heard the distinctive rotor hum of a Makila 1A1 turboshaft engine from an orange search and rescue Eurocopter Super Puma AS332 from the Hellenic Coast Guard, with its distinctive cyan, white & gold livery painted on its tail, nose and side doors.

After being located, they were winched in by two search and rescue divers through the helicopter's massive sliding doors and given rough white towels, silver space blankets and warm sugar drinks, while being taken to Elefsis Air Base, West of Athens, for a detailed debriefing by Air Force and Athens Aliens Police Directorate officers.

Some phone calls to the Papal palace and the UK Foreign and Commonwealth office were needed before their story of escaping the Cretan Mafia kidnappers was grudgingly given some credibility.

Subsequent radiation precautions meant that all their clothes were confiscated for disposal, each of them having to complete several high-pressure showers and Geiger counter inspections, before they were provided with rough white cotton overalls and taken in an electric blue Hellenic Air force Ford Transit 100 minibus to the Athens Hilton, to recuperate and catch up on some much-needed sleep.

Several hours later, they had met on the hotel's famous Galaxy rooftop restaurant, having acquired a change of clothes courtesy of Antonio, the hotel's concierge. After the glorious sunset behind the Acropolis, the ancient temple complex of the Parthenon began to be illuminated by massive spotlights, although the group were more interested in the international news coverage being shown on a sixty-inch LG widescreen TV in the bar section of the rooftop restaurant, directly opposite their table.

The breaking news story was about a massive gas explosion near the ancient palace site of Knossos in Crete. Information about the blast was limited, as the explosion had also caused a power outage over the entire island, restricting rescue attempts and preventing live TV broadcasts. The coverage was therefore confined to showing stock pictures and short phone interviews with local eyewitnesses, who described a massive explosion in the early hours of the morning, followed by a complete loss of all electrical power on the island. There was no word yet as to whether there was any loss of life from the terrible accident.

The news coverage then switched to the ongoing confrontation between the coalition of rich nations and the supporters of the Magog free energy systems. A tense standoff had developed in Istanbul between the military forces of the coalition and the million-strong human shield of Unity supporters, who had escorted a single Magog generator by road from Grindelwald in Switzerland, and who now found their progress blocked by two coalition warships. The British Royal Navy Type 45 destroyer, HMS Daring and the USS Lyndon B. Johnson, a Zumwalt class guided missile destroyer, had taken up strategic positions in order to block the five large ferries, that had been hired by Unity to transport the Magog generator and its million supporters across the thirty-two mile wide Bosphorus straits.

The news showed coalition Boeing AH-64 Apache helicopters and low flying predator drones enforcing a strict blockade of one of the region's busiest shipping channels. The resulting loss to commercial interests was estimated to be several billion US dollars a day. The city's mayor and senior Turkish state officials came on screen, in a series of short segments, where they complained about this unwelcome unilateral interference in their internal affairs and demanded immediate financial compensation from the United States and Great Britain. The interview with Dr Ishmael Khan, the Turkish Prime Minister, was interrupted to cover a breaking development. Unity leader, Nissa Ad-Dajjal, was making a rare televised announcement to address the increasing tension between the Unity group and the military forces being deployed by the coalition of developed nations.

The camera showed the spartan interior of one of the tents in the huge temporary city that had grown to house and feed the million plus people who were now protecting the generator. Dr Nissa Ad-Dajjal was seated on the single item of furniture in the small tent, a worn canvas chair, and when she turned to face the camera it was clear that she had been crying. In her right hand, she held a simple wooden spoon which she was using to feed soup to a small sick child in her arms. Her normally flawless face was without makeup, but covered in dirt. Her trademark clean white linen trouser suit was crumpled and stained, clearly from days of wear. When she spoke, her voice sounded tired and she had to pause to take frequent sips from a canvas covered water canteen, that hung from one of the chair arms.

"My friends. I speak to you now to plead to the leaders of the developed nations to cease their blockade and harassment of innocent people. For pity's sake…." She held up the sick child, "for the sake of the sick… for the sake of the children… let us pass unhindered and peacefully. All we seek is a better future. For you and for everyone." Her voice broke at this point and she simply whispered, "Thank you."

Unseen by Sonnet or Conrad De Ven, Curren had become transfixed by the image of Ad-Dajjal when it had appeared on the TV screen. Curren's eyes became glazed and her face expressionless, as her lips repeated every word, clearly without any conscious awareness of what she was doing. As the video feed from the tent city faded out, Curren's senses abruptly returned. She blinked, shook her head and took a drink of the mineral water on the table, smiling at Sonnet and De Ven, completely unaware of her unusual behaviour.

Back on board the Tiamat, a camera crew pulled away from a mock-up tent and an assistant roughly took the baby doll in its swaddling clothes, along with the spoon and soup bowl, while others quickly began to dismantle the entire scene. Nissa Ad-Dajjal walked purposefully from the deliberately staged set to her private apartments so that she could remove the stained prop clothing and wipe the fake dirt from her face.

An hour later, Issac Bin Abdul Issuin was interrupted from his workout in the gymnasium, via the ship's intercom, and instructed to bring the Roman Church's emerald tablet to the "Holy Table", which was Ad-Dajjal's euphemism for the reconstructed Assyrian temple in the bowels of the Tiamat.

Entering the long dark hall, with its ancient stone frescoes depicting the most horrifying supernatural scenes, did not disturb Abdul Issuin but, as he walked slowly carrying the four-inch engraved emerald gem on a black satin pillow, he did note the unusual emotion of fear in his being. He had failed to acquire Stewart's emerald tablet on three occasions prior to the latest attempt in Crete, which had ended not only in the escape of the two hostages under his care but also with an explosion which had taken a brutal toll on Maelstrom's resources, all without leading them any closer to acquiring the Stewart tablet. He was only too aware that Dr. Ad-Dajjal did not tolerate failure in her subordinates and dealt with any form of incompetence with cold and often sadistic punishments. As Abdul Issuin drew closer to the central "Holy" stone table with its deeply carved Enochian symbols, he noted that, unusually, no one else was present in the temple. No handmaidens, guards or the intimidating priests, with their primitive but deadly axes.

Ad-Dajjal was standing in front of the Holy Table, dressed in a simple single piece white linen robe with a golden silk cord around her waist. Her feet were bare against the stone floor and, unexpectedly, she smiled, as she reached and took the emerald tablet from the silk pillow carried by her closest confidant. Up close to her, Abdul Issuin could see that the left side of Ad-Dajjal's face seemed slightly sallow and grey in comparison to the right, although makeup had been expertly applied in an attempt to disguise the change in her complexion.

If Nissa Ad-Dajjal was concerned about the failure to acquire the Stewart tablet, or the massive losses caused by the atomic explosion on Crete, she showed no signs of it. Instead she smiled enigmatically and, when Abdul Issuin offered to call one of the specially prepared handmaidens to act as a sacrificial communicator, she shook her head.

"That was when we were pleading for help from the forces of creation. With a tablet in our possession we need not ask, we command and creation obeys. Our opponents think they have bested us with their pathetic atomic fragmentation. Let us show them something of real power!" She raised the emerald tablet to her face, as if using it as a looking glass, and took a deep preparatory breath.

Enochian Magick is generally recognised as the most powerful form of all the Occult Arts, as it is the original esoteric instruction given by the Fallen Angels, and therefore is the essence upon which all other magick is based. Often referred to as post-doctoral conjuration, it's practice is expressly forbidden in many esoteric schools because it exists for one sole purpose, the destruction of all creation. Fortunately, the modern forms of Enochian Magick have been weakened by the deliberate burning of several key texts and instructions by Elias Ashmole, when he came into possession of Dee's Magical diaries in 1672. Still further alterations and deviations from the original forms of the practice were made in the late nineteenth and early twentieth centuries by notable Golden Dawn adepts such as Samuel Liddell MacGregor Mathers, Dr William Wynn Westcott, Aleister Crowley and Israel Regardie. When presenting the system to Dr John Dee in the 16th century, the Enochian Angels provided forty-eight calls but prohibited Dee from ever using the highest and most powerful evocations held on the four Emerald Tablets of Destiny, because the elements of this sacred forty ninth call begin the process of dismantling the pillars of existence. In literal terms, even reading one of the four tablets would begin breaking the seals described by St John in The Revelation and the Koran in its End of Days.

Nissa Ad-Dajjal's voice took on a strange vibration, as she began to intone the Enochian symbols engraved on the Emerald Tablet. As she spoke, the air around her shimmered like a heat haze in a desert and The Holy Table began to look as though the symbols that adorned its surface had become white hot.

A thousand miles away from Ad-Dajjal's evocation, on the Island of Malta, the Temple of Ggantija's massive rocks began to disintegrate to shapeless rubble. In Egypt, at the Temple of Karnak in Luxor, shrines that had stood for thousands of years fell to a disorganised mass of rocks. In the Egyptian museum in Cairo, the statues of Amun Ra (God of the Gods) cracked inside their glass displays. The Great Pyramid of Giza's foundations split into fragments, bringing the famous structure down in a spectacular but terrifying display of dust and rock. The massive upright megaliths of Stonehenge shook and toppled to the earth and, after a thunderous sound that could be heard for hundreds of miles in all directions, Mount Horeba (Sinai) in the Sinai Peninsula of Egypt collapsed in on itself, raising columns of rock and dust twenty miles high into the night sky.

Across the Atlantic, the Salt Lake Temple in the ten-acre Temple Square in Salt Lake City, Utah collapsed violently to its granite foundations.

The reconstruction of the Black House of the Church of Satan, including the remaining grottos, were engulfed in flames and reduced to ashes.

In Jerusalem, the Western Stone of the original Kodesh Hakodashim (Holy of Holies) and its famous wall, emitted an ear-splitting scream and inexplicably collapsed, along with the golden Dome of the Rock, while simultaneously, the Edicule within the Church of the Holy Sepulchre fragmented into a mass of small rocks and turned to sand and dust.

Thousands of miles away in the Mahabodhi Temple, Bihar, India, the Bodh Gaya shrine suddenly fell in on itself, leaving just a mass of brightly coloured stones. The River Ganges dried up, exposing an empty expanse were once the holy water flowed. In Rome, the structure of St Peter's was struck by a massive earth tremor resulting in its collapse, burying and destroying the foundations of St Peter's tomb. In front of millions watching on a live twenty-four-hour video footage, The Kaaba, located within the Masjid al-Ḥarām (Sacred Mosque) in Mecca, Saudi Arabia cracked and large segments fell onto the devout, who were circumambulating around the site, causing horrific injuries.

Throughout the world, the foundations of ancient holy sites disintegrated and fell into ruins. Crosses, crescents and other holy symbols of faith and hope fell from their places, Persian sacred flames extinguished, Taoist caves became buried under massive waves of rock, Shinto shrines sank beneath the ground and Tibetan lamaseries were swept from their mountain heights, as ancient graves and tombs broke open revealing the decayed remains within.

Standing before the Holy Table in the bowels of the Tiamat, Dr Nissa Ad-Dajjal ended her evocation, her eyes blazing with triumph, knowing the world would never be the same.

Back on the Galaxy Rooftop restaurant, Stewart, now dressed in one of his signature Ede and Ravenscroft light wool suits, that had been express couriered to the hotel along with a number of other items, joined the group and ordered a Glenfiddich, while he talked to Albert Goldberg, his stockbroker, on a new white Google phone he had acquired that afternoon from the concierge.

Suddenly, glasses overturned and bottles tumbled from the tables, as the entire roof top bar shook violently. The big glass windows in the bar area shattered as, in the distance, the floodlit Acropolis swayed, the iconic pillars of the Parthenon collapsing before their eyes. The bar television somehow still clung to the shaking walls as it showed similar scenes from holy sites around the world.

Conrad De Ven crossed himself. "Oh my God... it has begun!"

While the hotel roof shook violently, Stewart calmly steadied himself against a marble wall, holding his glass of single malt safe from the rocking tables around him. As he looked at the Parthenon, which was now just a pile of rubble, and the television coverage of similar destruction around the world, he took a slow sip of Glenfiddich and resumed his phone conversation, saying,

"…on second thoughts, Albert. Sell everything and buy gold..."

CHAPTER 37 - THE TECPATL

"And know that in those last days, even if the Knight of The North may carry The Tecpatl (Dagger of Destiny), he may not comprehend how he can use it to cut the Chinvat Bridge (Silver Cord or Bridge of Souls)." - Commentaries on the Jewish, Zoroastrian and Islamic End of Days.

Raffles Istanbul
Zorlu Center
Besiktas, Istanbul 34340, Turkey
08.45HRS, 10th August, Present Day.

Tavish Stewart sat alone at a single glass topped table, set out on the pool side terrace overlooking the timeless scene of the Bosphorus, drinking ice cold Abant Su mineral water sourced, so the label on the one litre glass bottle stated, from the Gölcük Geyiktepe springs, high in the Bolu Mountains some 140 miles East of Istanbul. Stewart was dressed in a long white Giza 45 Egyptian cotton robe, worn over a marl grey t-shirt, matching cotton jog bottoms and a pair of unbranded white rubber soled trainers, all acquired from the hotel spa that morning. Even though he had only had some four hours sleep, after arriving in Istanbul in the early hours, Stewart had risen for his customary morning exercises, just before the dawn Fajr Adhan echoed from numerous minarets throughout the timeless city.

After being admitted into the spa's empty exercise room, with its polished wooden floor and spotless mirrored walls, he completed thirty minutes of his own personal Iyengar Yoga and "Shinshin-tōitsu-dō" regime, followed by a traditional hammam oil massage, that one only truly experiences in the Orient. This was followed by an ice bath, that was so cold that it caught the breath and made his skin tingle. Now glowing and feeling more like himself, after days without proper sleep and exercise, Stewart had ordered a light breakfast and Kurukahveci Mehmet Efendi coffee, which he so enjoyed whenever he happened to be visiting Istanbul.

Since he was the only patron partaking of an early breakfast on the terrace, he indulged himself with the duty chef by asking for a Raffles custom cereal mix of rolled oats, ground ginger, cinnamon, sea salt, nuts, whole and flaked almonds, and assorted seeds, combined with maple syrup and extra virgin olive oil. The mixture was toasted to perfection in an open oven on the terrace, before being served at Stewart's table along with coconut milk yogurt and fresh fruit. As Stewart relished the unique taste of the toasted cereals and spices, he reviewed his overnight phone messages from Dame Cynthia Sinclair in London.

Although Sinclair had been reinstated to her office as Chief of SIS, with an official cover story of an attempted assassination, the removal of Prime Minister Simon Brinkwater had not reduced the extent of corrupt external influence within the British Government. If anything, it had revealed how deep the rot had set, as a strong Maelstrom supporter, Mrs Susan Merriweather, the former Defence Minister who had proposed outsourcing the nation's military services, was selected overnight by Lord Kenner, the ruling political party's Chairman, as Brinkwater's replacement, without any party consultation.

A long-standing infiltration programme by a secretive Cartel of investment bankers, media multinationals (led by Gerald Seymour) and major US corporations (including Maelstrom), had placed individuals in key advisory and non-elected Government positions, in return for substantial political donations that had proven vital for the election campaigns of successful candidates from all parties. The result was that every major political player was either surrounded by advisors supporting the agenda of this sinister external group, or was dependant for operationalising their policy on senior bureaucrats holding key state positions, who were former employees of organisations from within the Cartel.

Until recently, their agenda had been limited to actions obscured from public view, exploiting their hidden influence to divert the sovereign wealth of the nation, and future taxpayers' contributions, to their own projects and personal wealth accumulation. However, within the last twelve months, the Cartel's aspirations had evolved, from just being content with covertly controlling the finances of the nation, to subverting Government itself so it gradually surrendered all executive power.

Maelstrom was instrumental in this silent takeover, since it was assuming the key elements of the UK's national defence, security and emergency services, leaving the elected representatives as powerless pawns, only able to regurgitate a rhetoric of platitudes and excuses for their increasing ineffectual performance. So pervasive was the Cartel's malevolent influence, even within the Security Services, that not only did Sinclair despair at no longer having anyone who was actually loyal to the interests of the nation and its people, but she was also increasingly under threat herself from traitorous double agents within the Security Service, who were acting on behalf of the Cartel.

As Stewart read through Sinclair's messages on his Google phone, he reflected that Jeffery Sonnet, as a former SIS field officer and section head Moscow, was the obvious choice to help Cynthia in her vital mission. However, the removal of Sonnet would weaken their group further, especially since they had lost Conrad De Ven last night, when he was recalled back to Rome to help deal with the internal crisis now facing the Church, with the revelation that the Pope had been found dead, apparently taking his own life during a crisis of faith shortly after the collapse of St Peter's. De Ven had been directed to return at once to lead the investigation and to limit the scandal that would no doubt arise from the suicide of a Pope.

After the massive earth tremors had hit the Athens Hilton, the hotel management had insisted everyone vacate their rooms. Having only just acquired their new belongings, Stewart, Sonnet, Curren and Conrad De Ven ignored the emergency tannoy instructions to abandon everything and had instead quickly gathered up their items into white canvas hotel laundry bags. They met again outside the main foyer of the hotel, near a taxi rank that was busy taking extortionate unmetered fares from panicking holidaymakers rushing to alternative accommodation.

It was there, sitting on the raised concrete curb, that De Ven had revealed to the group that he had been summoned back to Rome. He had added that, after receiving the call from the Vatican, he had phoned his colleague, the Exorcist, Fr Hugo Verchencho, who was already in Istanbul, to arrange that he should meet with Stewart outside the showroom of Stewart's Antiquarians at 10am Further-eastern European Time (UTC+3) on the following morning, 10th of August. During the phone conversation, Verchencho had described the extent of the devastation within the ancient city and that it was his belief that they had witnessed the manifestation of the breaking of the First Seal of Creation, foretold both in St John's Revelation and The Islamic End of Days, the so called "Loss of Faith".

Hugo Verchencho's dark intuition echoed with some ominous truth, as De Ven had already been told that the College of Cardinals were struggling to find any candidates who professed sufficient faith, under the current situation, to act as the next Holy Father.

Recognising the growing urgency to make sure that they prevented Nissa Ad-Dajjal and her hawk faced associate, Issac bin Abdul Issuin, from getting the second of the emerald tablets, they piled into a battered old yellow Mercedes e300 estate taxi. De Ven, Curren and Sonnet went in the back while Stewart sat, rather uncomfortably, next to the driver in the front right side, after having had to remove a half-eaten meat kebab wrapped in greasy paper from the sticky leather seat. The grimy and balding young man driving the ancient Mercedes placed his hand over the meter and smiled as they all piled into the filthy cab. Brushing some dirt from the sleeves of his Ede and Ravenscroft suit jacket, which had accumulated just from entering the vehicle, Stewart reached over and pushed a generous two hundred euro note into the driver's hand with the request "Airodromio"

The driver smiled and shook his head as they pulled away at some speed from the hotel's taxi rank and the passenger doors locked with an ominous click. Looking at the quality of Stewart's clothes, the driver evidently thought he could extort considerably more money from this group and said, in broken English, as he pulled out the four-inch blade from a wicked looking spring loaded folding knife that had been concealed in his leather jacket,

"Today special rate, two thousand euros."

Without missing a beat, Stewart returned the driver's smile and responded,

"I always enjoy a negotiation..."

As he pulled the obsidian dagger with his right hand, from its waistband scabbard, in a lightning fast movement. The tip of Stewart's blade pointed directly at the jugular vein under the right jaw of the driver and, curiously, even without any contact between the razor like point at the end of the mysterious ritual dagger and the driver's flesh, it caused a trickle of blood to flow down his neck and stain the top of his collar a dark red. The driver gulped in shock, dropping his own knife, as he eagerly took the 200-euro note being offered by Stewart, quietly saying,

"efcharistó..."

"Probably no tip though. Hmm?" Smiled Stewart grimly, as he kicked the driver's folding knife into the passenger foot well and returned the dark obsidian blade to its leather sheath. The remainder of the journey was spent in silence and, as they were dropped at the airport departures terminal, the taxi sped away with considerable tire spin, the driver clearly not able to get away from his four odd passengers quickly enough.

Inside the terminal they said their reluctant farewells to Conrad De Ven, who was escorted by two of his own Vatican security team to a private Learjet 45 for his return to Rome. Stewart was also met by a uniformed Hellenic Police airport security officer who guided him, Curren and Sonnet to a private interview room, where two people were clearly expecting them.

The first was a nondescript middle-aged man with short black hair, wearing a rather worn linen suit, who answered to the name "Mr Smith" and who was based at the British Embassy in Athens. Acting on Cynthia Sinclair's instructions, Smith required a series of signatures, before he handed each of them a new British passport, issued through the Regional Passport Processing Centre (RPPC) in Paris with the observation printed inside "The holder is a member of her Britannic Majesty's Diplomatic Service".

Obviously not intending to make any small talk, Mr Smith closed his utilitarian unbranded leather briefcase and, after a brief handshake with them all, left the room, leaving them in the company of the second, much older man, Mr Boseau. Boseau was dressed in an immaculate black Savile Row suit and a pair of matching black dress shoes, that were so highly polished you could have used them as shaving mirrors. He was a Coutts bank representative, who also required their signatures, as he handed each of them a leather wallet containing a single credit card. The plain looking Coutts World Silk Card does not try to look as impressive as many of the black, gold or engraved prestige cards, used by the vain to impress the gullible. It does not need to. Unlike its numerous and more ostentatious competitors, you must have millions of dollars on deposit with Coutts to be issued with one of only one hundred cards in existence. World Silk Card holders include one Elizabeth Alexandra Mary Windsor.

Needless to say, the card brings benefits beyond those normally expected from any other credit card, one of the most useful to Stewart at this moment being the guarantee that all transactions and their locations were confidential, even from agencies like Maelstrom.

Once the cards were activated, Stewart used his new Google phone to make a secure call, asking his card's dedicated personal concierge to book them business class single tickets on the next available flight to Istanbul, which was the 22.25 HRS TK 1844 flight. Thanks to the express VIP booking, all three friends were able to sit together on a row of angled flat grey leather seats in the front of a relatively new Turkish Airlines Airbus A330, and discuss what they could do to prevent Dr Nissa Ad-Dajjal from obtaining her second emerald tablet. Clearly De Ven's church colleagues had already been in Istanbul for some days, so it was imperative that they find out what progress they had made to secure that tablet, before Stewart and his friends initiated their own plans.

They arrived in Istanbul airport just before midnight (Further-eastern European Time, FET) after a thirty-minute flight, their new passports allowing them rapid passage through the crowded airport, that was full of people fleeing the city after the recent earth tremors. By 12.30 AM they were all crammed in an old battered yellow Peugeot 406 taxi, that was so full of dents and honourable wounds from collisions that it was a wonder the wheels could still turn, but turn they did, and the old war horse of a car took them, without any drama, to Stewart's favourite overnight stay in the Turkish city, the Raffles Istanbul. There they booked into two separate Continents Suites, one for Stewart and a shared one for Sonnet and Curren, who had become a couple since their kidnapping.

As Stewart finished his second coffee, he was joined by Sonnet and Curren who looked well rested. While both ordered their respective breakfasts, Stewart updated them with the news from Cynthia Sinclair, causing them to exchange looks, and Curren gave assent to an unspoken question that had passed between the couple.

"T, let me go and help sort things out in London." Said Sonnet quietly.

Stewart nodded, but the look in his eyes told of his regret that they would now be so few, trying to protect the remaining emerald tablets. However, before Stewart could respond properly a deep booming,

"Tavish!"

filled the entire hotel terrace, and probably most of the hotel. The powerful voice belonged to an enormous thickly bearded man, with grey wiry hair and piercing black eyes, who somehow had managed to get his massive frame into a long red and gold "Cübbe" traditional Turkish robe. As this giant of a man strode onto the terrace, he was closely followed by three younger men in black leather jackets and expensive denim jeans, who silently took up expertly selected strategic defensive positions in the long outdoor restaurant. The three bodyguards had a striking facial resemblance to the powerful man now walking purposefully towards Stewart, confirming the preference he had for keeping his business within his own blood lines.

Mohammed Sek was in his fifties and, after a highly successful career in the Turkish military, had joined Stewart's Antiquarians to run the Istanbul showroom, which was like an Aladdin's cave of amazing rare objects from the Middle East and Orient, all obtained through Sek's network of extended family contacts.

Stewart had a deep fondness for Sek, after the two had worked closely together in October 1993, during a NATO humanitarian mission to evacuate a Red Crescent hospital, caught in the middle of the infamous Battle of Mogadishu in Somalia. Sek and Stewart had ended up alone together on the third storey hospital roof, laying down covering fire to enable Canadian Military Twin Huey Helicopters to evacuate the sick, against an offensive by hundreds of Somali National Alliance (SNA) militiamen. The eighteen-hour ordeal had made the two men develop a lifelong bond, that was clear to see as the two men hugged on the terrace that morning.

Sek fully occupied two of the six chairs arranged around the breakfast table, as he sat with Stewart, Curren and Sonnet, calling loudly for some more Turkish coffee to be brought. The hotel staff scurried like ants to accommodate the demands of the new guest, who was clearly well known to them. As they waited for the coffee, Sek pulled a large leather roll bag from his massive shoulder and, after undoing the retaining loops, unfurled it on the table before them.

"I hope these items will be close enough to what you requested." Smiled Mohammed Sek.

Resting inside the exposed leather sheet, was a set of supplies that the Scotsman had anticipated would help them with whatever might lie ahead for them in Istanbul and beyond.

First were three old brown leather British Military issue "emergency" belts, one for each of the three friends. Each contained fifty 7.32 gram 22ct gold sovereign coins sewn inside the lining, similar to the more modern versions Stewart had taken from the SIS safe house in London. These emergency "currency" belts had proven themselves over the decades to be critical in helping operatives when brute force had failed and no one was coming to the rescue.

Then there were two long bladed knives that resembled medieval daggers, one for Sonnet and one for Curren, complete with adjustable black nylon rapid draw ankle sheaths. These wicked double-edged seven-inch blades were complete with MOD broadarrow stamps, showing them to be genuine Mk1 Fairbairn–Sykes (FS) models, forged from the once legendary Sheffield Stainless Steel by Wilkinson of London. Developed by William Ewart Fairbairn and Eric Anthony Sykes, from their close combat experience in Shanghai, the knives were created in 1940 specifically for British elite commandos in World War 2. The dagger became so famous that it formed the regimental logos for both the SAS and SBS. Pre-empting the obvious question, as Curren and Sonnet took their FS knives, Stewart produced his obsidian dagger from an internal pocket within his thick cotton robe and placed it on the table in front of his coffee.

The next items were two used steel Ruger Super Redhawk Alaskan .44 Magnum revolvers with short two and a half inch barrels, stored in black nylon Blackhawk horizontal shoulder holsters, along with several boxes of 340 gr LFN +P+ Buffalo Bore Heavy rounds, that, according to the box, delivered over 1,500 ft./lbs of impact force, sufficient to kill a charging bull elephant with a single round.

Sonnet handled one of the massive 340 gr rounds and looked at Stewart and Sek with a grim smile. Finally, there were three large black carbon fibre Casio G Shock Professional Rangeman watches. Stewart grinned, knowing his two friends would have preferred their own choice of a Breitling Military Chronospace and a Jaeger Lecoultre Reverso respectively but sadly both of their watches had been destroyed in the explosion at Willow Manor. Stewart's own beloved Omega Speedmaster had flooded with sea water when they ditched the Cessna into the Aegean the previous day, and had been FedExed, by the Hotel's concierge, to Laing's on Frederick Street, Edinburgh to see if it could be repaired.

The Scotsman picked up two of the watches and passed them to Sonnet and Curren and strapped the remaining one on his left wrist. Curren looked at the enormous black watch with mock horror and regarded Stewart with a withering look saying,

"You shouldn't have..."

Sonnet added humourously, "And we really mean you shouldn't have..."

Sek shared their smile briefly, and then became very serious.

"I have some bad news, T. Last night our showroom on Nuruosmaniye Caddesi was attacked by a group of men."

Mohammed Sek clicked his fingers and one of the three bodyguards walked rapidly over to the table and passed his father a fine leather-bound iPad. Once open, the small screen showed some grainy CCTV coverage of a group of five men in black paramilitary fatigues, pulling up in a long wheel base Jeep Wrangler Unlimited outside a wide glass fronted building, filled with paintings, statues and other items of great antiquity and value.

Four of the men exited the vehicle and, with rapid military precision, smashed in the two front glass doors and threw in some flash bang grenades, before storming into the premises with a barrage of automatic fire, from what looked like the latest models of the Israel Weapon Industries Ltd. (I.W.I.) Uzi Pro sub machine gun.

For over a minute, the six wide glass windows of the shop front were illuminated by a series of very rapid machine pistol flashes, interspersed with brighter two shot bursts from a slower firing, but much larger bored weapon.

Clearly a fierce firefight ensued for, when the attackers exited the shop moments later, only two of the original four men were still alive. As these two men hurried across the street to their jeep, a huge figure emerged from within, filling the entire space of the two smashed glass doors and firing a double barrelled twelve bore sawn off shotgun from the hip.

As the retreating men reached the jeep, one of them was lifted clean off his feet and smashed into the side of the Wrangler by the sheer force of two, one ounce, twelve-gauge rounds hitting him simultaneously, from out of both barrels of the smoking twelve bore. The last of the attackers hurried around the far side of the escape vehicle, as the pursuing giant, who could now be seen to be Mohammed Sek, dressed only in a pair of white cotton boxer briefs and with a leather ammunition belt slung over his right shoulder, which he was calmly using to reload as he walked towards the Jeep and prepared to fire again.

Seconds later, the building behind Sek was consumed in flames from an incendiary device that illuminated the entire surrounding area and showed one of the men in the jeep, pulling off his black balaclava mask, to reveal distinctive hawk faced features which were highlighted even further, as he made a deliberate point of looking directly into the lens of the CCTV camera, as if challenging the viewer to respond, as the Jeep drove away at high speed.

"Yes, I already have unfinished business with this bastard!"

Snarled Stewart, as he froze the video and looked intently at the image, absentmindedly pointing his obsidian dagger at the screen. The ancient blade tip was clearly some inches away from the display, but made the iPad glass shatter and the frame violently deform, before Sek's giant hand gently guided Stewart's wrist so that the dagger was pointing away from everyone at the table, much to the evident relief of Sonnet and Curren.

"That is a most interesting weapon you have there..." Commented the now very thoughtful Mohammed Sek.

CHAPTER 38 - THE SILVER CORD

"When the silver cord is broken... the dust returns to the earth as it was, and the spirit returns via the Bridge of Souls to God, who gave it." – based on the original Hebrew Traditions of the Tanach

Beyazıt Tram and Bus Station
Yeniçeriler Cd.
34130 İstanbul, Turkey
11.05HRS, 10th August, Present Day.

Jeffrey Sonnet was dressed in a simple short sleeved white cotton shirt, which he wore under a classic cut grey linen jacket, teamed with a pair of stone coloured chinos and rubber soled tan leather moccasin shoes, all of which he had picked up from various street side market stalls as he walked from the Raffles hotel that morning. After a long discussion with Curren, she had reluctantly agreed that she would be safest staying with Mohammed Sek and his family in Istanbul, while he returned to face Maelstrom with Cynthia Sinclair back in London. Stewart, O'Neil and the odd priest would do what they could to prevent the Ad-Dajjal woman from acquiring the remaining emerald tablets, initially in Istanbul and then, if necessary, according to De Ven, somewhere in the forsaken wastes of the Mongolian desert. Given the inherent dangers in London from Maelstrom, who would view Curren as an ideal hostage to place leverage on Sonnet and Cynthia, and from Ad-Dajjal's followers seeking the emerald tablets if she travelled with Stewart, Curren reluctantly conceded she would be best staying with Sek and his family until the whole adventure was resolved, one way or another.

During his walk to one of the only remaining operational transit centres in the city, Sonnet had exchanged his white cotton Hilton laundry bag for a handmade leather duffle, which was now slung over his left shoulder. He joined the end of a long queue of people, waiting for one of the few taxis that continued to operate in the city centre amid the disarray caused by the combination of the massive earth tremor and the escalating tensions between the numerous Unity followers and the coalition military forces.

Maelstrom military police (MP) were examining the travel papers and possessions of everyone waiting to escape to Istanbul Atatürk Airport, whether by bus, tram or taxi. Turkish police were superficially included in the screening process but, it was clear, that they had effectively been rendered irrelevant by the heavily armed occupying foreign military forces.

Before leaving the others, Sonnet had handed Mohammed Sek back the Fairbairn–Sykes (FS) dagger, the powerful Ruger Revolver and exchanged the G Shock Rangeman for a white-faced Swatch, purchased from the hotel shop. Sonnet wanted to remain as anonymous and unmemorable as possible and, although the dagger, gun and G Shock GABC (gps, altimeter, barometer, compass) watch could prove invaluable especially in the Mongolian desert, they would be a hindrance to his ability to move unnoticed in more civilized settings.

His decision proved to be sound because, as he approached the end of the long queue for the airport taxis, he encountered a young soldier wearing a standard Army Combat Uniform (ACU) with a patch labelled "MP", in a subdued grey with black lettering, on his left arm, beneath his Maelstrom whirlpool badge. With his mirrored sunglasses, number one crew cut and a bad dose of arrogance, he dismissed Sonnet's British diplomatic passport with exaggerated disdain, tossing it to the ground at his feet. He then took great pleasure in pouring the contents of Sonnet's new duffle bag, his recently acquired toiletries and clothes, onto the dirty asphalt road surface in front of them, while staring directly into Sonnet's face to detect any sign of resistance to his authority.

After a few moments, without noticing any response from the middle-aged Brit, the young MP made a comment about the spineless English and moved to his next victim in the long taxi queue. Sonnet ignored the insults, slowly picked up the passport and refilled his bag, dusting off the street grime as best he could.

Directly in front of Jeffery Sonnet, were a group of extremely well-dressed priests with Catholic clerical collars and ostentatious golden crucifixes around their necks, clearly travelling together to the airport with a common final destination. They exuded an air of superiority and self-importance that, Sonnet speculated, must have been hard for them to subdue when they had been "inspected" by the equally officious Military Police officer.

In stark contrast to their elegance, they had been joined by an older man, with a shock of wild ginger hair, whose grubby old fashioned full-length priest's vestment was a mass of wrinkles and stains from heavy use. The older cleric carried a large old carpet bag in his left hand, while he chain smoked foul smelling Turkish Royal cigarettes, which he held in the other. The scruffy priest was clearly hoping to join his three "brothers" on their trip to the airport, but they were having none of it. The younger of the smartly dressed priests stepped closer to the dishevelled newcomer, pushed him backwards from the high curb and announced loudly enough that everyone in the queue could hear,

"No! You may not join us! I will have you know this..." He gestured to the older of the three smartly dressed men, who clearly delighted at being pointed out to the crowd,

"…is Cardinal Benedict, who is on his way to Rome to select the new Pope! He does not want to share his affairs with ordinary working priests, like you."

He then called out loudly to the MP who was some 12 feet away, inflicting his presence on a young Turkish family whose life possessions were contained in a few cardboard boxes that were now being brutally cut apart for "inspection" by the vicious seven-inch clip point blade of the young soldier's SOG Seal 2000 knife.

"Officer! Come back and deal with this disgusting man."

Just as the Maelstrom MP swaggered back, with a wicked smile on his face and his white crowd control baton drawn, ready to deliver some "justice", Sonnet stepped forward and indicated that the dishevelled older cleric was in fact travelling with him and had simply been confused about which group to join in the queue.

After the MP had left, the tall ginger haired priest stubbed out his Turkish Royal cigarette under a scuffed black leather dress shoe and extended his nicotine stained hand to Sonnet, introducing himself as "Hugo Verchencho" who, it transpired, had also been summoned to Rome, but clearly not supported by the same level of travel expenses as Cardinal Benedict's entourage. Recognising both the name and appearance of the man before him from De Ven's descriptions of the Vatican's Chief Exorcist, Sonnet could not help smiling at the coincidences of life. Later, during their shared taxi journey, Verchencho expressed his gratitude for Sonnet having come to his assistance and indicated that in the unlikely event of Sonnet ever needing a favour from his office, he should feel free to contact him in Rome.

Earlier that morning, after Sonnet had left the group to return to the UK, Stewart, Curren and Sek had walked together to the burnt out remains of Stewart's Antiquarian showroom at Nuruosmaniye Caddesi. As they passed through the streets of the ancient city it was clear that the population was in turmoil after the massive earthquake the previous evening. Although they had seen some damage when they drove into the city in the darkness of the early morning, in the daylight the extent of the chaos was starkly revealed. Various nation's military personnel, who formed the coalition forces, were occupying the streets using roadblocks to control access, trying to restrict the movement of over a million Unity supporters who were still camped out in the northern sections of the Turkish city.

The once elegant shop front of Stewart's was now just a charred wreck. The younger members of Mohammad Sek's extended family were busy digging through the rubble to retrieve any salvageable items, while the older sons and nephews stood on the higher ground, dressed in the now familiar black leather jackets and jeans, keeping careful watch with long double-barrelled shotguns trained over the street below them.

Standing directly across from the burnt-out shop front were two men, a middle aged European with short greying dark hair and trimmed beard and a younger clean shaven Asian, with his hair in a long black ponytail down his back. Both were dressed in identical traditional black full length Catholic Priests cassocks, but the younger priest's clothes exuded an intangible air of elegance and authority.

Sek took in the look of the two men and quietly teased Stewart about his new companions, as they walked towards them.

"A brilliant disguise, T. Two nineteenth century Catholic priests in central Istanbul. They are sure to go unnoticed…"

Stewart smiled but gestured for Sek to keep his thoughts to himself and, striding confidently across the street, introduced himself to O'Neill and Kwon. Since they could not use the shop for their meeting as originally planned, it was decided they would walk to Sek's home nearby in the Sultanahmet region of the city.

Number seven, Terzihane Sokak was a classic Byzantine villa, a stone's throw away from the ancient hippodrome in the centre of the old town. A stunning woman in her late thirties, dressed in a long dark blue abaya, greeted them when they knocked on the two, tall wooden double doors that faced onto the narrow street. She introduced herself as Zahra, Mohammed Sek's wife, and led them through the villa's paved central courtyard, with its gently flowing fountain, to a wide stone staircase that led up three floors to a large covered roof terrace, with a richly decorated mosaic floor and panoramic views over the remains of the seventeenth century Blue Mosque, that had sadly suffered extensively during the recent earthquakes.

The villa's own foundations dated back to 330 AD and, during its history had been a residence for Roman officials before eventually becoming a family home. It had been in the hands of the Sek family for hundreds of years and, as the group walked up the stairs, it was clear how much the huge man loved the old place.

The Archaeologist in O'Neil could not help examining the Doric Roman pillars, painted wall decorations and mosaic floors of the villa with a professional interest, as they passed up the well-worn steps. Evidently the recent earth tremors had caused some damage to Sek's home, because the North facing interior wall of the stairway had split open and revealed a disused stairway, with around fifty steep steps that led down beneath the current ground level and into one of the ancient city's many enormous water storage cisterns. There were clearly plans underway to make some urgent repairs to this damage, because the bottom of the wide stairway was partly filled with large plastic sheet rolls, electric sanding machines, rubber gloves and boxes of Pro3 FFP3 builders dust masks. As they passed the damaged section of wall, they could see that a narrow grey split hopper barge had sailed into the subterranean cistern through one of the waterway service locks that led from the harbour. The 100ft long boat had moored at the stone quay at the bottom of the ancient steps, some fifty feet beneath the level of the villa and had set up spotlights in preparation to making repairs to the shattered section of wall.

As the group sat around a long wooden table in the sunshine on the roof terrace, Zahra and her two daughters, Akila and Aygul, who looked like younger versions of their mother, brought trays with large silver dallah coffee pots full of dark sweet Turkish coffee, matching silver cups, two bowls containing sugar cubes and two silver trays of Turkish delight. These items were placed along the length of the table, with Mohammed Sek and Stewart seated at either ends, O'Neill and Kwon on one of the long sides and Curren on the other side opposite them.

Once each of them had completed the formality of appreciatively sipping from their ornate silver coffee cups, they began a round of introductions. Initially it was clear there was some reluctance to share information, but the sight of the ruined remains of the Blue Mosque was a powerful reminder to all of them of a common enemy, who potentially threatened the whole of existence. It was quickly agreed that they had to work together to locate Nissa Ad-Dajjal and prevent her and her associates from getting hold of the remaining emerald tablets.

Thomas O'Neil told of his experiences investigating the ill-fated Finster expedition in Iraq, of his attendance at Verchencho's seminars, his introduction to the priest, Fr Chin Kwon, their collaboration with Conrad De Ven, the ancient prophecies of a Knight, Priest and Devil and, finally the recent visit to Venice, where Maelstrom had attempted to capture them and Polo's Mirror, which showed the location of the lost city where the fourth tablet had supposedly been hidden. Thankfully, Kwon had been able to create a diversion near the Doge's palace, allowing Verchencho and O'Neil to escape. Under De Ven's instruction, the three had then travelled to Istanbul to locate the current keepers of the third tablet. However, their meeting with the Patriarch at St George's Church had been a serious disappointment.

After long delays, with numerous last-minute postponements, the Patriarch's private secretary had finally agreed to meet them at the grand high-ceilinged offices in Rum Patrikliği, only to reveal that the Eastern Church had been relieved of numerous artifacts, including the emerald tablet, by the Turkish State in 1922 during the establishment of a new Turkish constitution, when they confiscated numerous priceless relics that they claimed belonged to the people and not the Christian church.

After this disappointment at the Patriarch's offices, they had used De Ven's influence to initiate meetings with the Turkish public officers, who should have had responsibility for the tablet, rising slowly step by step and from meeting to meeting with ever more senior officials, each of whom denied any knowledge of the object, until they had reached the office of the Turkish Prime Minister, Dr Khan, where their requests for information and a meeting about the emerald tablet had finally been firmly rejected.

As the group discussed this impasse, Stewart showed his leadership skills by keeping them all positive and committed, suggesting they needed to focus on their next logical step, locating Nissa Ad-Dajjal, since she was certain to make a move to obtain the Istanbul tablet and they should be ready to intervene and stop her.

During these discussions, Fr Chin Kwon appeared increasingly uncomfortable, and kept looking behind and above Curren, who was seated opposite him, as though he could see something standing behind her. Eventually he spoke, addressing her directly,

"Helen, my dear, forgive me for staring, but unless I am mistaken you have recently been overshadowed by a powerful Magickal Will. Am I correct?"

Curren looked startled and glanced at Stewart, to check if it was alright to share her experience with the Ad-Dajjal woman and her own odd behaviour on Crete after escaping from the Tiamat with Sonnet. As she described what she had been told of her actions, Fr Kwon nodded grimly.

"I would suspect that Ad-Dajjal may be what Tibetan Lamas term a Sprul-pa mkyen-pa, a master of the art of transference, and has performed that act on many occasions and on many individuals. It explains the fanatical loyalty and fear shown by her close followers."

"Overshadowing? Transference? What kind of childish nonsense is this, T?" Laughed the clearly sceptical Sek, as he looked from his end of the long table at Stewart in confusion and amusement.

Kwon reacted with a look of irritation, that made O'Neill visibly flinch in his seat next to the young priest.

"With respect, Mr Sek, it is very far from nonsense... Did you but understand these phenomena you would comprehend the mechanism of life and death itself. If you dislike the ancient terms I can use the more modern interpretation "Tulpa" although, like all modern reinterpretations of occult phenomena, it has been grossly over simplified to cater for popular taste. Today Tulpa is understood, even by some of the most advanced magickal practitioners, as the use of the will and imagination to manifest thought forms into our visible reality."

Sek laughed,

"Thought forms? Father Kwon, also with respect, I have heard lots of tall tales in my long life... unless I see such things, they are just fairy tales."

Kwon smiled, "Indeed?"

While the two men locked eyes in their good-natured dispute, Curren gasped and pushed herself towards Stewart, while pointing at the shadows cast by the two tall silver coffee containers on the wooden table top. As everyone watched with disbelief, the shadows became visibly darker, until they were an impenetrable black that hurt the eyes, in the same way that mountain snow blinds in bright sunlight. The two pools of darkness then formed dozens of rivulets around their edges, that slowly transformed again, this time into thin crab like legs, permitting the dark shapes to lift themselves slowly up from the table surface and proceed to make a hideous scuttling noise, as they moved rapidly away from the base of the two silver dallah pots, knocking into and causing the silver sugar bowl to be violently overturned. As everyone except Kwon pulled away, the two nightmare shapes scurried along the full length of the table towards Sek, who recoiled in horror, tipping his chair backwards so as to escape from the two primordial crawling creatures and, drawing his steel FS dagger, he made ready to stab the nearest of the two animated shadows, whereupon the menacing shapes vanished, melting back into the table surface from whence they came.

Kwon smiled, "Forgive me, my friends, but it is imperative that you all appreciate the reality and scale of the challenges that we face. Modern esotericists call Tul-pa a mind-created apparition, the conjoined words come from the Tibetan "to build" or "to construct", but in fact it is only one tiny aspect of a much older forbidden magick, called Trongjug, the transference of consciousness and the animation of a body. The modern explanation of Tulpa as a thought form, is a deliberate blind by Tibetan Lamas, to distract from the real secret of Sprul-sku, a secret which is directly related to the well documented immediate reincarnations of the Dalai and the Panchen High Lamas of

Tibet."

"You seriously mean that the Dalai Lama uses this Trongjug magick to avoid death?" Asked O'Neill incredulously.

"And what has this to do with Helen?" Demanded Stewart.

"Looking at Helen's energy body, it is clear that she has been exposed to a highly specific form of Trongjug." Explained Chin Kwon, as he gestured for Curren to stand and turn so the group could observe her neck. As Curren stood and turned away from the table, the air around her head and shoulders began to shimmer, like a heat haze on a desert road. This shimmering effect grew stronger and slowly, like the way dusk descends on a summer's day, a series of three thin glowing silver coloured filaments could be seen emanating from the rear of Curren's head, her neck, and from behind her heart. Thickly wrapped around these fine three cords was a darker denser cord, that looked like it was choking the much finer fibres.

"What you are seeing," continued Kwon, "is the so-called Silver Cord, or Antahkarana, which is in fact a triple thread that passes from the immortal to the body's incarnate fragments. One fibre, called the Sutratma or thread of life, passes into the heart, another filament passes into the throat and is called the thread of creativity, while the final thread of consciousness resides in the Pineal gland in the skull. Combined together, these three filaments allow the soul to incarnate. In the normal process of death, the silver cord separates from the physical body, and provides what occult tradition calls "The Bridge of Souls" back to the immortal realm. The process of Trongjug allows an adept to substitute their own silver cord with that of another person taking over that person's body, either temporarily or permanently, in order to escape physical death when the original body becomes old, sick or injured. With Helen we can see, by the darker parasitic filaments surrounding her original silver cord, another has prepared her for such a Sprul-sku substitution."

"What happens to the original soul personality who has been removed from their body?" Asked O'Neil.

"The process can either be temporary, in which case the original personality stands to one side for a period of time, or it can be a permanent severance of the old soul body connection, leaving the original soul personality to face death, instead of the Trongjug adept who has taken over the body."

There was a long silence, while the group considered the full implications of what Chin Kwon had told them.

Stewart broke the silence, "Can you remove these dark Sprul-sku filaments from Helen?"

Kwon shook his head, "No, that can only be done permanently while the invading adept's consciousness has taken residence inside the host body. Then, if a suitable astral weapon,"

The young priest looked pointedly at Stewart's obsidian dagger,

"Is used to sever the invading cord, the Trongjug adept will be cut from their immortal principle, forced from the host body to return to their original body, or left to wander the lower realms for eternity."

O'Neil crossed himself, as he whispered a section from the act of excommunication,

"...to be cut from the grace of God..."

Fr Kwon nodded at O'Neill, and continued to address Stewart.

"But I can tell, based on the elemental imbalance in the fibres invading Helen, Ad-Dajjal is most certainly surrounded by salt water."

"The Tiamat!" Exclaimed Curren.

Some 730 nautical miles South West of Mohammed Sek's Byzantine villa, the Tiamat Migaloo Submersible-Yacht was cruising effortlessly at seven knots through the sparkling Aegean Sea on a general heading North.

Seated at her glass desk, facing a video conference link on one of the glass walls, was Dr Nissa Ad-Dajjal. Her once flawless complexion was now partially covered by a heavy dark red veil, which obscured the withering and blemishing that had started to consume the flesh on the left side of her face. She was wearing an opulent custom-made Stella McCartney gown, rich in purple, with scarlet highlights and adorned with gold thread, precious stones, and rare pearls. In her right hand was a golden cup, engraved with various goetic sigils and filled with a special brew of herbs and essences that she had concocted in her WET temple, to try and counteract the powerful influence which, she had finally conceded, was affecting the left side of her face, the result of Elizabeth Fitz-Glass's dying curse.

On the screen in front of her were the well-known features of the

Turkish Prime Minister, Dr Ishmael Khan. Nissa Ad-Dajjal's attempts at blackmailing the middle-aged politician, by revealing his links with extremist Islamic terror groups and his ordering the use of chemical ordinance against the Kurds, had failed. Instead of showing fear at the prospect of such information being revealed, Khan had just laughed, saying such acts were known to everyone and that she should go ahead and publish. No matter what, he and his nation would never bow to blackmail and would never hand over any item of their national heritage. Ad-Dajjal's voice took on an icy edge.

"Fool. Soon you and your whole nation will kneel before me and beg me to take it from you..." with that she clicked her long nails on the black remote-control unit, abruptly cutting the video link, and stormed from her office heading towards the Tiamat's control room.

CHAPTER 39 - BEHOLD A PALE HORSE

"Sadly, history shows, no matter how terrible the weapon, it eventually ends up being deployed by desperate, weak or wicked men... often just to see what it does." - His Holiness Pope James, Nobel Peace Prize acceptance speech.

35°46'04.6"N 24°55'01.7"E
Aboard the 283m "Tiamat" Migaloo M7 Submersible-Yacht,
Sea of Crete, 56 Nautical Miles North of Heraklion, Crete
14.00HRS, 10th August, Present Day.

Dr Nissa Ad-Dajjal's long purple and scarlet Stella McCartney gown trailed behind her, like angry thunder clouds before a tropical hurricane, as she stormed into the modern chrome and steel control room of the Tiamat. The speed of her movement caused her heavy veil to be cast slightly to one side, showing how the once perfect complexion was now darkened, the skin around the eye withered, and tissue damage had started to pull back her lips to expose the teeth on one side of her face.

When the results of Elizabeth Fitz-Glass's curse had started to show, Nissa Ad-Dajjal had tried to ignore it but, day by day, the effects became stronger and could no longer be camouflaged by makeup, veils, or her own magickal glamours. Slowly she was becoming resigned to enduring the condition for the limited time she calculated remained and, as an interim measure for public appearances, she had ordered a golden mask to be created to minimise the reactions her affliction produced. Whereas once her staff would sneak looks at her countenance when she entered a room now they all, without exception, looked at the floor, no one wanted to see the grinning skeletal profile of the left side of her face. Still, she reflected, in some ways the transformation was appropriate, given what she was about to unleash on humanity.

Sitting in the large white leather central bridge chair of the Tiamat, she issued a brusque order to the grey-haired Captain Jersson to set a course for Istanbul with maximum haste. The tall Scandinavian nodded and adjusted both the engine and reactor controls to level seven, causing the massive ship to shudder as it accelerated to its maximum speed of thirty knots and created a 165 feet wide wake in the calm seas behind them.

But Ad-Dajjal was dissatisfied, her eyes narrowing as she stood from her chair and reached forward with her long red fingernails, turning the two separate dials in front of her (one for reactor output and the other for engine speed) to their maximum extent, so that she also had to depress two mechanical locking safety switches in order to take both controls to the very limit of their red zones, labelled "Danger" on the console before her. Bjorn Jersson reacted with clear dismay at what Ad-Dajjal was demanding from his ship, and addressed her.

"Domina, this will risk damage, not only to the vessel and its crew but also the surrounding environment."

Ad-Dajjal glared coldly at the insolence of her Captain and pulled the veil from the left side of her face, staring him down. The tall grey-haired Scandinavian flinched and bowed his head, showing that his mental submission outweighed his concerns for the safety of his ship or crew.

"As you command, Domina."

Deep in the bowels of the massive ship, the Japanese designed General Electric Hitachi (GEH) twin reactors began to generate enormous amounts of radiation, as the limiting rods were removed from the cores and their fission reaction was pushed well beyond the safety threshold. The full thrust from the nuclear turbines caused the rear of the 283m vessel to push deep into the water, raising its prow high into the air and causing a massive 400-yard-wide wake to form, as the Tiamat exceeded its design limit of thirty knots, on a course towards the Dardanelles Straits and then Istanbul.

As the rear sections of the vessel became superheated, the Hitachi GEH design began emergency venting of boiling radioactive waste directly into the sea behind the ship. The discharge showed on the satellite infrared screen in the control room as a flowing deep scarlet wake spreading out behind the vessel, with more than a passing resemblance to the deep red gown worn by Ad-Dajjal on the bridge, reflected Bjorn Jersson grimly.

Back in the control room, Ad-Dajjal had ordered that the ship's control centre engage with the Unity "Zephyr" high-altitude, long-endurance (HALE) autonomous unmanned system, flying twelve and a half miles above them. Complex digital algorithms exchanged quantum "handshaking" encryption protocols and, slowly, the screens on the Tiamat bridge began to display real time tracking of all military vessels for some 250 miles around the ship.

As the various vessels stationed in the region had their full details displayed on the wall mounted screens of the control room, Nissa Ad-Dajjal's eyes carefully scanned each warship's weapons inventory, clearly looking for some specific ordnance. As her search became more refined she clearly focused only on US vessels and then, with a wicked smile, exclusively on the USS Lyndon B. Johnson, a Zumwalt class guided missile destroyer, sitting moored in the Bosphorus Strait near to Istanbul's city harbour.

Through the US warship's Aegis compatible combat computer, Ad-Dajjal linked the Tiamat's controls directly with the Lockheed Martin AN/SPY-3 telemetry and weapons systems. The combined electronic wizardry of the Tiamat and Zephyr systems permitted "Remote Weapons Telemetry" (RWT), the capability to take control over any compatible electronic weapons systems. Once she had acquired remote access into the Weapons Artificial Intelligence (WAI) of the US vessel, Nissa Ad-Dajjal's long fingers flowed effortlessly over the large touch screen, showing her expertise in respect of the capabilities and procedures of the Zumwalt class destroyer.

The first thing that the dark haired twenty-four-year-old Tactical Action Officer (TAO), Steve "Magnum" Hemmings, noticed was some unusual activity within the automated weapons systems linked with the AN/SPY-3 MFR, that were initiating the specialized lock out codes used remotely by strategic command when a US Warship has been compromised and taken over by hostile forces. By the time Hemmings raised the issue with Hank Sperring, Officer of the Deck (OOD), and he had in turn conferred with Tom Field, Executive Officer (XO) for that watch, the Tactical Action console had stopped recognising commands from the bridge. When Captain Alex "Cool Hand" Hammond arrived some seven minutes later, there was an air of rising panic as the bridge crew watched four specialised Boeing "E-Fog" RGM-84 Harpoon Block II+ ER cruise missiles being deployed, through four of the Zumwalts's eighty vertical launch tubes, by the automated weapons loading controller.

Hammond called for the Chief Engineer (ChEng), Tim Montgomery, to deploy an emergency weapons team to the forward weapons bay but, before the three-man unit could reach the front of the ship, the four modified RGM-84 missiles roared to life and the crew watched helplessly as the Harpoon cruise missiles soared off in each of the four cardinal directions, rising to a height of 20 miles above them. On reaching their target height, each missile terminated their rocket thrust boosters and deployed long broad wings at the front and rear, each with six large solar powered propellers that unfolded from hidden compartments and began providing lift to help keep the fuselage at a constant altitude.

Once each missile had stabilized into a holding pattern at their target altitude, a pair of thirty feet long wide gossamer like wings deployed from the middle of the fuselage and these began to transmit a sophisticated electronic "fog" that jammed all smart weapon guidance systems within a sixty-two mile radius, except for those on board the USS Lyndon B. Johnson, which were spared due to shared quantum encryption codes.

Almost immediately the E Fog broadcast had commenced, there were incoming radio messages from all military assets within the jamming range, querying what was happening. Not only did Communications Officer (COMMO) James Ubehert find himself unable to respond to these messages, due to his being locked out from his communications console, he became even more alarmed as he saw his ship issue what should be impossible, a Presidential authorised "kill command" to a specific series of thirty-two geostationary satellites, orbiting some 12,400 miles above the earth, bringing down the world's GPS systems.

All over the world, airlines and air traffic systems went into critical emergency procedures to bring flights down safely as quickly as possible. Internet routers and systems abruptly failed, crashing home systems and stock exchanges alike. However, these were the least of the consequences related to activating the Global GPS kill sequence, since both the allies and enemies of the United States shared the chilling knowledge that deactivating global GPS was the initial phase for a US first strike, deploying its extensive arsenal of weapons of mass destruction.

As Captain "Cool Hand" Hammond struggled to shut down the weapons systems on his vessel and abort the Global GPS kill sequence, little did he know that his day was just about to become far, far worse.

In addition to numerous conventional explosive ordnance types, a Zumwalt class destroyer has three categories, that are popularly termed "weapons of mass destruction", stored deep in its on-board weapons silos, designated C (chemical), N (nuclear) and B (biological), respectively. Over the last sixty years, the general public has developed a special fear of nuclear weapons, due in a large part to a campaign of propaganda intended to support massive arms spending during the Cold War. Although nuclear weapons have enormous destructive potential, measured in megatons and mega-deaths, the truth is that nuclear weapons are limited in the damage they can cause and the effects of their use can be modelled and predicted. Radiation is relatively well understood and somewhat treatable. In a similar fashion, chemical weapons, although terrible in terms of the suffering they cause to those exposed to the agent, are also limited in terms of the Kilo-death potentials of their warheads and the duration of their influence on the battlefield.

These kinds of limits do not apply to the third class of weapons of mass destruction, Biological. Bio-Weapons are typically the result of genetically enhancing the worst naturally occurring pestilences into forms that spread rapidly, are incurable, cause massive suffering and have a potentially infinite vector of destruction. The USA, Russia, France and United Kingdom have developed enhanced Pneumonic and Bubonic variants of the Black Death (Yersinia pestis), that killed sixty percent of the global population in the fourteenth century, and combined it with so called secondary and tertiary vector agents, that cause all animal and plant life to die simultaneously, leaving an infected region a desolate and lifeless place. Without access to vaccines, such tri-vector bio-weapons have the potential to spread exponentially, until they kill all complex life forms on the planet.

It was for these reasons that Hammond watched in growing horror, as the Presidential authorities for B (biological) designated weapons protocols were initiated and the automated weapons loading sequence was confirmed, by a pre-recorded male voice that echoed through the silent ship. Every man was now aware that they would be personally and collectively blamed for the horrors caused by an imminent biological weapons launch.

Some 5,230 miles away, in a concrete bunker 100 feet beneath the innocent looking sidewalks of Parsons Avenue in Washington DC, Captain Hammond's deployment of the Boeing E Fog missiles, the deactivation of the Global GPS systems and initiation of B class weapon deployment, had been noted with growing alarm. As numerous attempts to contact the USS Lyndon B. Johnson went unanswered, the decision was taken by Admiral (ADM) Peter G. H. Lorance to assume the Zumwalt class guided missile destroyer had gone rogue and needed to be terminated before she posed a clear and present danger to United States national security and broke just about every clause of the 1972 Biological Weapons Convention (BWC).

Central US fighter command and control (CENTCOM) at MacDill Air Force Base in Tampa, Florida, authorised the US forward base in Izmir, Turkey, to launch four Tomahawk cruise missiles at the rogue destroyer 250 miles away. Simultaneously, the USS Ronald Reagan, a US Nimitz class CVN-76 aircraft carrier at sea, 600 nautical miles away from Istanbul, was authorized to engage the errant war ship with a deployment of three Boeing F/A-18F Super Hornets that were already airborne around the Bosphorus Straits, maintaining air supremacy in relation to the confrontation between Unity supporters and the coalition forces.

Within ninety seconds of receiving the strike authorisation from CENTCOM, four Raytheon Tomahawk Block IV cruise missiles were airborne from the mobile ground launchers at Izmir airfield. Each one and a half million-dollar missile carried 1,000 pounds of RDX variant high explosive in its conventional warhead. The four intelligent missiles flew together in a close formation, always staying close to the ground and all adjusting their height for small hills and other ground features to avoid radar detection. At their top speed of 550 mph, it would take the four flying bombs some twenty minutes before they reached the USS Lyndon B. Johnson at its mooring in Istanbul harbour.

In contrast, the three Boeing F/A-18F Advanced Super Hornet fighter jets were able to engage with the rogue Zumwalt class guided missile destroyer immediately. Each of the three sixth generation fighters accelerated to Mach 1.8, turned to face their common objective, armed their coordinated telemetry and simultaneously launched wing deployed one point two-million-dollar AGM-84 Harpoon missiles at the rogue warship, that glistened in the harbour below them. The three "ship-killer cruise missiles" each carried close to 500 pounds of armament modified DESTEX high explosive at 500 mph, and skimmed over the harbour water, clearly targeting the fore, mid and aft sections of the Lyndon B. Johnson.

On board the Zumwalt class warship, state of the art automated defence systems registered the three Super Hornets taking up close attack formation, ready to strafe the ship with their 20mm M61A2 Vulcan nose-mounted rotary cannons, together with the incoming subsonic Harpoon cruise missiles. In response, what looked like a cloud of insects began to emerge from the eighty weapons bays on the ship. The USS Lyndon B. Johnson's Weapons Artificial Intelligence (WAI) had deployed two hundred tiny Perdix micro-drones which, under full "autonomous swarm intelligence" (ASI), separated into three clouds, forming a swirling pattern that resembled a biblical plague of locusts, and headed up into the sky towards the approaching fighter jets.

Simultaneously with the dispatch of the MIT designed Perdix micro-drones, the air was filled with abrupt loud roaring sounds and blinding flashes, as a series of white hot projectiles flew through the air from the warship towards the incoming Harpoon missiles. A second later, all three missiles had exploded and fallen harmlessly into the harbour, some 900 yards short from their target.

Before the three fighter pilots could even report the downing of the missiles, their General Electric F414-GE-400 turbofans started emitting deafening thumping noises as dozens of tiny 290g Perdix micro-drones deliberately flew into their engine intakes, causing immediate catastrophic engine failure. As the three pilots were forced to ditch their 100 million-dollar jets, they were left slowly drifting on their ejector seats into the waters of the Bosphorus.

Back on the USS Lyndon B. Johnson, the Weapons Artificial Intelligence (WAI) defence systems continued their relentless search for threats, and now detected the four incoming Tomahawk cruise missiles, some twelve minutes or 111 miles away from the ship's mooring in Istanbul harbour. The Raytheon "railgun" deployed on the Zumwalt class destroyer, which had already so effectively dealt with the three Harpoon missiles, requires twenty-five megawatts (enough electricity to power a medium sized town) to send its forty pound projectile at over one mile a second, to targets well beyond the visible horizon. The projectile requires no explosives or propellants, instead it relies on the devastating effect of its kinetic impact on its target.

It took less than ninety seconds for the railgun's deadly projectile to cover the 111 miles. The six million dollars of advanced weaponry contained in the four Tomahawk Block IV cruise missiles, were no match for the hypersonic impact that hit each of them with pinpoint accuracy and with over thirty million, foot pounds of force. The four radar signatures simply disappeared.

One would assume that the crew of the USS Lyndon B. Johnson would have been focusing their entire attention on the attacks being directed against their vessel. Instead they were absorbed in surreal horror, as a calm computer generated male voice confirmed each stage of a weapons preparation that was completely outside their control. Captain Hammond and his bridge crew listened in icy silence as MQ-8 Fire Scouts, unmanned autonomous helicopters developed by Northrop Grumman, were confirmed to be loaded with the so called "Triple B mix" tertiary vector agent.

The Triple B mix is a series of genetically enhanced bacilli and virus agents, developed by the U.S. Army Biological Warfare Laboratories (USBWL) Fort Detrick, Maryland, and other outsourced commercial facilities in Europe and Africa over the past sixty years, to exceed humanities darkest nightmares of infectious diseases. The micron sized droplets and ten nanogram direct freeze dried (lyophilization) particles are loaded with the so called triple mix of genetically modified Pneumonic/Bubonic Plague, Haemorrhagic Hanta virus and Anthrax, in optimised droplet and particle dispersion formats.

In desperation, Hammond had ordered the issue of small arms to his crew, who had now massed on the deck of the warship and were firing a range of ineffective rounds at dozens of armoured MQ-8 Fire Scouts, that were emerging from behind shielded take off bays and heading up and towards the ancient city.

In the streets of Istanbul, national and international TV news crews had been attracted by the ongoing weapons exchanges between three US Navy fighter jets and the USS Lyndon B. Johnson, moored in their harbour. Speculation was rife that an unknown military force, sympathetic towards the plight of Unity, had decided to intervene in the stand-off.

After the excitement of the three fighters ditching into the harbour (a sequence that was being replayed over and over on most news channels and social media), every network was now showing that the sky above the ancient part of the city was being systematically filled with small inflatable cigar shaped blimps, the classic US Navy logos clearly visible along their sides, that were being inflated and then deployed from larger unmanned helicopter drones.

Under each of these US NAVY six feet long helium inflatables was a long silver metal container, similar to a pressurised fire extinguisher that one might see in any workplace. Some of the extreme zoom footage of these canisters showed a fine aerosol spray was being released from 165 feet above the crowded streets of Istanbul.

The 3B mix was designed and developed to rapidly devastate an enemy, psychologically, logistically and finally, if they did not surrender, physically. The weapon has three human targeted vectors. The first vector is designed to immediately infect one in ten of the exposed population, with a violent and extremely rapid haemorrhagic reaction, with ninety five percent mortality within three hours, to inflict immediate terror in the enemy and overwhelm all medical and support resources.

The second vector is slower acting (eighty percent mortality within ten days), based on a highly refined version of the Yersinia pestis (Black Death), and is extraordinarily contagious, so that the population who flee spread the infection by inhalation, touch and bodily fluids to over ninety three percent of the people they meet, on what will be crowded mass transit systems. The third vector, an anthrax hybrid, spreads from the decay of the human and animal bodies infected by the first two vectors.

As the first haemorrhagic infections appeared in the crowded city streets, international news cameras relayed the full horror of the US biological attack to viewers worldwide. In the control room of the Tiamat, the grey haired Scandinavian captain Bjorn Jersson shivered involuntarily and felt his blood run cold, as he saw the scarlet woman before him smile and say to herself,

"And I looked, and behold a pale horse: and his name that sat on him was Death, and Hell followed with him. And power was given unto them over the fourth part of the earth…"

CHAPTER 40 - THE BLACK STAR SHINES

"The entire idea of a hypersonic space capable fighter bomber is a technical absurdity." - Spokesperson for the United States Air Force

John F. Kennedy Conference Room
1600 Pennsylvania Ave NW,
Washington, DC 20500, USA
06.40 HRS, Eastern Time Zone (15.40 HRS Further-eastern European Time) 10th August, Present Day.

Commander in Chief, President Wilson F. Jones, a tall, tanned athletic 65-year-old former Governor of Massachusetts, swept down the final uncarpeted steps leading from the Western end of the main hallway of the White House, turned left and entered a long, rectangular, low ceilinged basement room. The large 5,500-foot square windowless space was filled with a mass of uniformed people, most of whom had that pasty look from working long hours in a confined and artificially lit environment, where day and night passed without notice. The only mark of time here was the loud tick of twelve atomic synchronized wall clocks, and the changes of shift that occurred every day and night throughout the year, regardless of national holidays.

Dressed in his cotton pyjamas, wool slippers and a long blue fleece dressing gown, Jones carried a large white insulated coffee cup with "Best Granddad in the World" printed on it and looked, accurately enough, like he had just woken. The most powerful man in the world was surrounded by a team of six immaculately dressed Secret Service agents, wearing dark grey SAKS two-piece suits, with signature Maelstrom whirlpool lapel badges attached, Luminox watches, Ray Ban Predator II mirrored glasses and carrying FN 5.7mm side arms, with H&K MP5 short barrel 9mm machine guns hanging by the sides of the agents positioned on the two outer edges of the protection detail.

The specialised Presidential briefing room, known to the world as "The Situation Room", beneath the West Wing of the White House complex, included lead-lined cabinets near the reception area for the deposit of personal communication devices upon entry. Close by the entrance to the room was a set of glass-encased booths, that looked as if they had come straight from a 1960s-spy movie set, for secure and private telephone calls.

On entering through the heavily guarded door on the left side of the Situation Room, the President was met by Jessica Holmes, his middle aged Personal Assistant, who had followed him through the past twenty years of his political career. The depth of the crisis could be clearly seen in her eyes, as she made sure her boss's briefing notes and steel Parker pen were properly organised on his desk, before she left him comfortably seated at the head of the long conference table.

Beside the President's chair were eight 30-inch LCD screens set in a four by four array, and to his immediate left was a large US flag on a seven-foot-tall indoor flagpole. As Jones gathered his thoughts and prepared to call the meeting to order, he looked down the length of the single long table which dominated the centre of the room. Arranged along both sides of the dark wood conference table were sets of large and luxurious black leather office chairs, each with a dark grey desk pad placed on the table in front of them. Under the feet of the nervous looking men and women seated before him was a thick blue pile carpet, that contrasted with a lighter coloured wooden walkway, marking the space around the entire edge of the central carpet and the edges of the room. The walls were covered with a range of large and small video displays, each delivering different types of real time information from sources around the globe. Beneath these screens, a three-foot-high dark wood panel ran around the lower section of the walls, contrasting starkly with the ceiling which was white plaster board, inset with a mix of fluorescent tubes and circular lights to provide a variety of lighting levels. Jones reminded himself that sensors installed in the ceiling detected any cellular signals, to prevent unauthorized communications and bugging by mobile phones, personal digital assistants and other specialized listening devices.

Seated on the right side of the President, near the head of the table, was the skeletal Gerald Seymour in his signature black roll top. The world-famous spin doctor exchanged a,

"Good morning, Mr President." And looked the most composed of the dozen or so people who were gathered at this early morning emergency meeting.

On the President's left side was his Secretary of Defence, Jane L. Maskins, by her side CIA director Mark Pimms and then next to him a series of middle aged uniformed men, United States Army General (GEN) Jeremy "Jim" H. Orne, United States Marine Corps General (GEN), Louis M. Arnold and United States Air Force General (GEN), Cliff "Eagle" Smith.

Seated on the opposite side of the long table, next to international media "guru" Seymour, was a very tired looking Admiral (ADM) Peter G. H. Lorance, United States Navy. His uniform was crumpled, and he looked his years, after the worst night of his thirty-year career spent sitting in the USN control centre deep beneath DC, dealing with a four-billion-dollar rogue state of the art warship. After trying unsuccessfully to deal with the incident, he had not been given time to wash or shave and now, in the meeting, he was clearly being distanced by his colleagues from the other branches of the military and being allowed to "crash and burn".

The small bespectacled young man seated next to Admiral Lorance was, according to his visitor's badge, "Dr Horatio G. Numeberg" from SRI International Biosciences' Infectious Disease program. This unit had been discretely running US biological weapons research since the formal closure of the U.S. Army Biological Warfare Laboratories (USBWL) Fort Detrick, Maryland programme in the 1970s, after the US signed the 1972 Biological Weapons Convention (BWC).

The large array of screens beside the President showed a series of secure video conference links to the Pentagon, where the Joint Chiefs of Staff (JCS) were seated and waiting, ready for the meeting to begin. The JCS is a body of senior uniformed leaders in the United States Department of Defence who advise the President and, alongside them on the series of video displays today, was the Director of Homeland Security and the Director of the National Security Council, all of whom were located at their personal offices at the Pentagon.

Contrary to popular belief, the Joint Chiefs of Staff do not have any operational command authority, neither individually nor collectively. Since the Goldwater–Nichols Act in 1986 the chain of command goes from the President to the Secretary of Defence and from the Secretary of Defence to the Commanders of the Combatant Commands, all of whom were gathered around the presidential conference table, nervously avoiding eye contact with Admiral (ADM) Peter G. H. Lorance.

President Jones coughed, thanked the group for assembling at short notice and, without further formalities, asked for a briefing about the current status of the event that had caused this extraordinary unscheduled meeting.

As an indication of the power wielded by the media in the modern political and military world, all eyes turned to the White House Communications Advisor. Gerald Seymour began by giving a summing up of how the international media and general public were describing the event.

A US warship had made an unprovoked first strike against unarmed civilian targets, using a banned biological weapon of mass destruction, with hundreds of civilian casualties and injuries, all recorded and broadcast on live news channels around the world.

Further action by US forces, also recorded live on world news, had included unsuccessful attacks on the US warship by cruise missiles and fighter aircraft, all within a heavily populated city of a NATO ally.

There was silence around the table as Seymour continued by making his recommendations. He suggested that the immediate priority was to control and address public anger and fear. Especially since there was clear evidence that the US had tried to act to destroy the warship, with the subsequent loss of missiles and fighter planes and, most importantly, had been seen to have failed. Seymour concluded his presentation with a single simple PowerPoint slide that was shown on all the screens in the conference room.

"There was an immediate need to show decisive action and restore confidence in the ability of the United States to control the situation.

Recommend

- Overt show of force to neutralise the rogue warship with "shock and awe".
- Remove and destroy the biological weapon dispersal systems.
- Rapidly provide medical interventions to counter the effects of the Bio weapon and reinforce the image of the US as the undisputed world super power."

There was immediate and general agreement by everyone in the meeting, with both Seymour's assessment and recommendations. The skeletal advisor nodded his appreciation and returned to his seat. President Jones thanked Gerald Seymour and turned to the small bespectacled biological weapons advisor, asking for his prognosis about the biological weapons deployment.

Numeburg stood to his full five feet three inches, adjusted his thick glasses and then spoke slowly with a nasal New Jersey accent. His opening slide showed the Zumwalt warship schematic, alongside scale diagrams of the Northrop Grumman autonomous MQ-8 Fire Scout helicopter and the inflatable vector dispersal systems. The next slide showed details of the "Triple B mix" tertiary vector agent, made up of ten-micron particle-size droplets and ten nanogram direct freeze-dried granules containing genetically modified Pneumonic/Bubonic Plague, Haemorrhagic Hanta virus and Anthrax.

The small man's presentation took on a chilling tone as he displayed the results of the event, as predicted by the US DOD BioThreat simulator. Numeburg described the starting conditions for the simulation. Deployment of the tri vector 3B biological weapon had been into a coastal city with a population of fourteen million people, with a 3.7 mph NW breeze, temperature of 24c, barometric pressure of 1024 (falling) and humidity of ninety-six percent.

The simulation ran in an hour by hour and then day by day progression on the large wall displays, showing first the initial haemorrhagic casualties, calculated to be ten percent of the exposure population, all of whom had perished within three hours, creating an initial death toll of 1880 people. The vectors of infection then followed two separate growth patterns on the screens around the conference room, one rapid and designed to cause panic, and a second slower spread. This secondary contagion was deliberately designed to have a slower incubation period, so the infection would be spread by inhalation, touch and bodily fluids exchanged on crowded mass transit systems, whose passengers would then transport the infection to new regions world-wide.

From an initial mortality of 1880 within three hours of the deployment, the simulation ran showing the rising death toll and significant events that would be likely to be associated with that number of casualties in each geographical region of the globe. Within twenty-four hours, 100,000 people would die and the infection would spread overland into the nearby nations of Bulgaria, Romania, Greece,

Albania, Syria, Iraq and Iran. Small outbreaks would also occur in major transportation hubs in Europe, America, Russia, India and Asia. After forty-eight hours, the death count would reach 750,000, with infections reported throughout mainland Europe and major transit centres in the US and Asia. Five days after the deployment, twenty-one million people would have died. Africa, China, Europe and the US were all major infected zones. Seven days after the initial deployment, over one billion human beings would be dead, causing a world-wide crisis for all nations, with medical centres and services completely overwhelmed. Three days later, on the tenth day after initial deployment of the tri vector 3B biological weapon, it would have claimed the lives of over seven billion people. The room descended into a stunned silence as the simulation showed the entire globe infected with over ninety five percent mortality. Civilisation, as we know it, would be decimated.

General Jim Orne, US Army, interrupted, looking up from his own sets of rough notes taken from the presentation, to recommend an immediate coordinated series of thermonuclear strikes on the estimated perimeter of the infection zone. His calculations showed containment of the contagion could be achieved with five LGM-30G Minuteman III – Inter Continental Ballistic Missiles (ICBM).

Each Minuteman III ICBM could be launched within ninety seconds from central US silos and, with an in-air speed of nearly 18,000 mph, Orne estimated it would take a mere twenty minutes from launch to impact. The missile's Circular-Error-Probability (CEP) of 250 feet would, the General reassured everyone, provide a "surgical" removal of the threat. Each warhead had an explosive power of 475 kilotons (kT) and would be detonated at an altitude of 1500 feet above its target. The resulting fireball from the five coordinated explosions would effectively vaporize the entire threat zone and provide the "Shock and Awe" demanded by Seymour. The General smiled at everyone, clearly pleased with the simplicity and genius of his plan.

There was a shocked silence, then Gerald Seymour simply stated what everyone else in the room was thinking.

"It would be a public relations nightmare, Mr President. Fourteen million civilians killed by an unprovoked nuclear attack, hours after the US deployed a banned biological weapon. We would be better to focus on the vaccine. You do have a vaccine?"

The nasal voice of Dr Numeberg responded, "DARPA only contracted SRI to complete the necessary research to optimise the 3B weapon's potential, from a sixty to a ninety-five percent mortality rate. The final manufacturing processes for both weapon and vaccine were outsourced to BioSwiss/Unity AG in Geneva who, in turn, created a manufacturing facility in Mozambique, Africa. Under the terms of their contract they will have created stockpiles of the vaccine in central distribution centres in..." He paused as he consulted some notes, "...Paris, Manhattan and Manila."

"Might I then suggest that these stockpiles be immediately dispatched to the contagion zone, with a massive public media awareness campaign showing the airlift of the vaccines and US troops providing medical assistance to the public?" Stated Seymour.

President Jones nodded his assent to two Army officers, who immediately rushed from the conference room to execute the command.

Gerald Seymour was clearly satisfied, but then cautioned that the public relations damage from being seen to be unable to deal with the rogue warship would give America's allies and enemies a clear sign of weakness. There needed to be some show of undoubted force. Ideally an act commanding real "shock and awe" to counter any perceptions of weakness in the US.

President Jones considered Seymour's advice quietly and then addressed the combined group in front of him.

"You gentlemen mean to tell me we do not have anything that can deal with one rogue battleship? The greatest nation on Earth and we do not have anything that can show the world some real Old Testament Shock and Awe?"

There was silence. All the representatives of the military looked dejected, avoiding the eyes of their Commander in Chief. All except Mark Pimms, the director of the CIA, who coughed and smiled at the President.

"We do have options... Mr President. Something special from the Cold War, that we have kept in reserve in case we ever needed some..." He smiled as he paraphrased the President's own words, "Old Testament Shock and Awe."

The CIA director addressed the Commanders of the Combatant Commands and the others in the room, including the President.

"What's your security clearance gentlemen?"

"Level 5, why?" Replied US Army General Orne.

"Congratulations, you all just got upgraded to Level 7." Smiled Pimms, as he nodded to one of his assistants, who had been standing directly behind him during the meeting. A black suited man with a badge, that indicated he worked for the "National Reconnaissance Office", passed out two red coloured folders to each of the meetings participants.

The labels on the front of the red covers were marked in black bold type "FOR EYES ONLY DESTROY AFTER READING", and underneath that text each folder had a different title "TOP SECRET (MARAUDER)" and "TOP SECRET (BLACK STAR)". US Navy Admiral Peter G. H. Lorance looked at the folders and sighed.

"With respect, Mr Director, if you are going to put Cold War technology against the Zumwalt it will be a total no contest. The hypersonic speed of the railgun defence projectiles will prove too fast for any known weapons system launching an attack against the ship."

The CIA director smiled, "The operative phrase, Admiral, being any known weapons system."

Back in Istanbul, TV cameras continued to record the scene with remote robotic systems, directed from makeshift control rooms that had been set up by news and television stations at locations some distance from the immediate contagion zones. The cameras showed an armada of small airships continuing to dispense their deadly cargo over the ancient parts of the city. The streets were empty, except for the robotic TV cameras and the dead, who had been left without ceremony where they had fallen. Just as it seemed that one of the worst "friendly fire" incidents of the twenty first century was unstoppable, there appeared, to the observers and TV crews in Istanbul, to be a second sun in the sky, which grew in brightness until it outshone the original.

Ronald Reagan's 1987 allocation of 260 billion USD (close to half a trillion USD in modern value) spending on the Strategic Defence Initiative (SDI) produced many top-secret weapons, but none as exotic as the magnetized target fusion system, unofficially known as The Eye of Shiva (code name MARAUDER). Developed from the high powered pulsed power research device located at the Air Force Research Laboratory on the Kirtland Air Force Base in Albuquerque, New Mexico, this orbiting geostationary weapon was designed to create compact toroids of high-density plasma, that would be ejected from the device using a massive magnetic pulse, destroying supersonic missiles in flight or strategic ground targets. The project was officially scrapped in 1995.

22,236 miles above the earth, a geostationary 1,181 foot diameter jet black disc slowly sprang to life. Six huge nuclear fission reactors began charging the dozens of three point six terajoule capacitors. As sets of thrusters ignited, they guided the massive disc so that it lay twenty thousand miles directly above the rogue warship. A series of large fan like black covers retracted, exposing a massive twelve-armed wheel, that slowly began to vibrate and generate electromagnetic fields of over one hundred Tesla.

The USS Lyndon B. Johnson's fearsome twenty-five-megawatt Raytheon "railgun" is unbelievably fast, able to dispatch forty pound projectiles at over one mile a second within a 111-mile range, and each projectile lands with over thirty million-foot pounds of force. In contrast, "The Eye of Shiva" fires its plasma projectiles at 18,641 miles per second, 10% of the speed of light, and each plasma shot delivers 300 trillion calories of energy at a temperature of 200 million degrees Fahrenheit, four times the temperature found at the centre of the sun. It was, as Admiral Lorance had said, a total no contest but not in the way he had anticipated.

As the remotely controlled TV cameras focused on the curious second sun in the late afternoon sky, they recorded, what world-wide slow-motion replay would later show to be, doughnut shaped rings of fire and balls of lightning descending and exploding repeatedly against the entire 600 feet length of the guided missile destroyer. As this bizarre barrage began, TV cameras within 300 yards of the warship abruptly and simultaneously failed, as surges of electromagnetic and x-ray energy scrambled their electronics. Within seconds of the strange attack starting, the entire hull and superstructure of the fourteen thousand-ton Zumwalt class guided missile destroyer glowed white hot and melted, slipping quietly into the depths of the Bosphorus. The only trace of its presence was the steam rising from the boiling harbour water.

As "The Eye of Shiva" closed down its systems to resume its silent wait in space, an odd thumping noise filled the sky above Istanbul. The sound could be picked up on sensors as far away as the bridge of the Tiamat, some 340 Nm away, causing Captain Bjorn Jersson to re-calibrate the ships systems, disconnecting the remote weapons telemetry (RWT) and switching to high resolution surveillance using the unmanned Unity Zephyr drone, flying thirteen miles above them, to try and determine the source. Upon seeing the distinctive shape and speed of the incoming target, Jersson commenced an emergency "crash dive" of the vast Tiamat submersible. Crew members ran to their stations, as large metal screens closed over every opening and the enormous yacht sank below the waves, slowing rapidly from its thirty-knot speed. Nissa Ad-Dajjal grimaced and strapped herself into her leather seat in the ship's command centre.

Far above them, where the sky loses its distinctive refractive blue colour, an isosceles triangle shape descended at hypersonic speed from 300 miles above the already high-flying Zephyr, leaving a condensation trail in the clear sky behind it that looked like smoke rings on a rope. As this strange looking long black triangle descended, the thumping sound became louder, shaking the Zephyr surveillance drone in a series of powerful sonic shock waves, that are the unique signature of a scramjet pulse detonation hybrid engine (SPDHE).

The National AeroSpace Plane (NASP) project (code name BLACKSTAR), that resulted from Reagan's instruction to create a hypersonic space capable fighter bomber in his 1986 State of the Union Address, was a black budget project funded among NASA, DARPA, the US Air Force, the Strategic Defence Initiative Office (SDIO) and the US Navy. Boeing and the Lockheed Skunk Works were the funded commercial partners. The specification list of "Blackstar" made the NASA Space Shuttle, F-117 Nighthawk Stealth bomber and Lockheed Martin F-35 Lightning II fighter look like cracker toys. It was officially mothballed in 1995, although odd sightings continue to be reported near the Lockheed Skunk Works up to the current date.

The long body of the weaponised version of the Lockheed Martin SR-72 "Aurora" was composed of monolithic crystals of titanium wrapped in carbon fibre. The hypersonic bomber was traveling over sixteen times the speed of sound in its descent, and levelled at its weapons operational height of 120,000 feet above Istanbul. The space suited National Reconnaissance Office pilot, Col. Sepp G. Jones, based out of Groom Lake (Restricted Area 4808 North, R-4808N), locked his weapons systems on to the approximate location of the B3 bio-weapon deployment, with an icy calmness.

His action released a ten foot long black cruise missile, with folding fins which deployed on each side as it separated from a concealed port on the underside of the hypersonic fighter-bomber and fell down towards the city, twenty miles beneath them. Moments after confirming that the small Boeing cruise missile had successfully acquired its target, the Blackstar took off in a vertical ninety-degree climb, literally rocketing back into the stratosphere, accompanied by a series of sonic shockwaves and its characteristic vapor trail. As it disappeared into the stratosphere, NASA and the US geological survey issued simultaneous emergency warnings for an unexpected solar flare, that could seriously harm electrical systems and communications in the central Mediterranean region.

The 2,000 pound "CHAMP" (Counter-electronics High-powered Microwave Advanced Missile Project) electromagnetic pulse weapon detonated, not with a bang or flash, but with an invisible expanding series of very specific microwave frequencies. The effects varied depending on the distance from ground zero, which in this case was half a mile above sea level over the Western edge of the ancient centre of Istanbul. Within a 600 foot radius of the detonation, birds died in mid-flight, falling from the sky. 500 yards away, animals and human beings suffered first degree burns internally and externally. Within five miles every electrical system died instantly. The drones and biological vector dispersal systems fell from the sky, the microwaves and impact causing the fragile microorganisms of the B3 Vector agent to be irrecoverably damaged and cease to be biologically viable.

Twelve miles above the epicentre, the Unity Tiamat Zephyr drone's electronic consciousness flickered out momentarily, and then it's sophisticated Electro Magnetic Pulse (EMP) hardened systems rebooted. Shielded by over 1000 feet of seawater above them and some 340 nautical miles of distance, the Tiamat systems remained unaffected, apart from the momentary loss of data from the Zephyr, which rapidly re-established the complex cryptographic handshaking between the ship and its dedicated communications and reconnaissance centre.

CHAPTER 41 - THE MARK OF THE BEAST

"The Beast causeth all, both small and great, rich and poor, free and bond, to receive a mark in their right hand, or in their foreheads." - Revelation 13:16-18. St James Bible.

Mohammed Sek's Villa,
7, Terzihane Sokak,
Binbirdirek, 34122 Fatih,
Istanbul, Turkey.
03.45HRS, Further-eastern European Time, 11th August, Present Day.

Tavish Stewart lay sleeping. His strong hands gently clasped the emerald tablet and obsidian dagger close to his chest, making him look like some medieval knight in repose. Three layers of a thick, rough, grey sail cloth lay between his body and the cold, hard wooden floor of the cabin. Under his closed eyelids there were signs of movement, as a singularly vivid dream held his consciousness in a deep but troubled sleep.

Stewart dreamt of a beautiful dark-haired woman, dressed in a bright red silk gown. She was slowly walking barefoot in front of him, through thick wet grass in a heavily wooded glade, full of trees and flowers in full blossom. The scene was so real that he could feel the breeze on his face, smell the rich scents of the blossom, and the stirring of his own primal desire for the beautiful woman, as she swayed suggestively ahead of him.

As Stewart tried to move closer, he noticed there was something wrong. Something he could not immediately recognize, except as a deep unconscious feeling of cold dread, deep in his stomach. A sense he had felt before, in the middle of the battlefield when luck had deserted men and they had nothing but an acceptance of their fate.

Then it came to him. As seductive and sensual as this woman undoubtedly was, every living thing that she passed lost its vivid colour and scent to become a cold, lifeless representation of its former glory. All that was left in her wake was a forest of grey immobile stone sculptures but, for some unfathomable reason, it was hard to notice the effect. Almost as if his senses were being made to focus only on the seductive and sensual nature of the woman's physical form, and to ignore the dark influence she brought to this paradise. Slowly, by an enormous effort of will, Stewart pulled his perceptions free and became fully aware of the barren waste that followed the sensuous female form in front of him.

Just as he was preparing to retreat back the way he had come, the strangely compelling woman turned and made direct eye contact with the Scotsman. Smiling, as if she knew the effect she was having on him, her long red finger nails plucked a ripe green apple from the tall tree beside her and, as the tree turned to cold hard stone from her touch, she licked her crimson lips, as she reached out with her right hand and offered Stewart the apple, in a gesture that made him unable to think of anything, except her beauty and sensuous promise.

As Stewart slowly approached, like a sleepwalker, toward the fascinating woman her eyes left his and, in that moment, he became aware that her interest was not in him, but in something that was resting around his neck. In his dream, as he reached up and felt the strange carved letters on the cold surface of the emerald tablet, it's touch instantly cleared his mind from whatever spell he was under and, with a chilling fear, he recognised the dark-haired woman as Dr Nissa Ad-Dajjal.

With a wicked smile, that showed her indifference at Stewart's recognition, she slowly tore into the flesh of the apple and cast its broken sections to the dry and barren earth beneath her feet. Where each segment touched the soil, the earth crumbled away to reveal the tip of a skeletal bird's talon, which began to twitch and move as it clawed its way from the ground, tearing the earth apart, to reveal hideous winged forms emerging like monstrous chicks breaking through an eggshell, that was the skin of the planet Earth itself.

Stewart woke suddenly, to find himself soaked in a cold sweat, lying in semi darkness in an old boat cabin, with the vibration of a marine generator, the smell of diesel and the sound of two male voices just audible above the background noise of water cascading slowly over the thick plastic builder's sheets, that covered the small wooden cabin. Pressing the backlight on his Casio Rangeman he saw it was still in the early hours.

As his eyes adjusted to the gloom he first saw Mohammed Sek, who was sitting by a flickering candle set in a small chipped coffee mug, reading to his wife Zahra and his two daughters, Akila and Aygul. Sek's deep baritone voice was repeating a phrase over and over, as if repetition would empower his simple words.

"… There is none worthy of worship but He, the Ever Living, the One Who sustains and protects all that exists. Neither slumber nor sleep overtakes Him."

In the other corner of the small wooden cabin space, near the ship's wheel, in the dim glow of the GTLS (Gaseous Tritium Light Source) from his Vatican issued Nite Mx10 watch, Stewart could just make out O'Neill, who was kneeling, with his eyes closed in prayer with Curren beside him. The Archaeologist's quiet voice was almost lost next to Sek's deep intonation, but Stewart could just make out the cadence of the Catholic Kyrie invocation, in a version he did not recognize. He later learnt this was their original ninth century Latin form of the prayer that O'Neil had been taught by Verchencho.

"Kyrie, rex genitor ingenite, vera essentia, eleyson.

Kyrie, luminis fons rerumque conditor, eleyson."

(Lord, King and Father unbegotten, True Essence of the Godhead, have mercy on us.

Lord, Fount of light and Creator of all things, have mercy on us)

In the darkest corner of the small cabin, the only one of the group sleeping soundly, was the entity currently occupying the body of the priest Fr Chin Kwon, who lay on his left side. In the darkness, it looked as though the prone body was lying above and off the cold hard wood floor. After all Stewart had seen in the recent days, it would not have surprised him. Looking at the peaceful face of the young priest, it was hard to believe the events of the previous afternoon.

After Kwon's demonstration of Tulpa (thought form manifestation) on the roof top terrace of Mohammed Sek's villa, the group of friends drank more coffee while deep in thought, each of them trying to make some sense of what they had just witnessed. Sek eventually broke the silence, when a large black crow descended from the clear sky above them and landed on the table directly in front of the strange priest, intelligence clearly visible in the bird's dark eyes.

"Another demonstration?" Enquired the ever-mischievous wit of Sek.

"No, I think perhaps a message." Responded Kwon in total seriousness, as the large bird dropped a long thin section of blue ceramic tile from its long black beak on to the table, cawed loudly and then flew off, back into the sky. Picking up the small thin fragment, Fr Chin Kwon regarded it carefully and then asked to be excused for a visit to the washroom. Zahra guided the priest to the guest suite on the first floor of the villa and then returned to the group with some more coffee from the large kitchen.

On her return, she found her husband talking about hypnotism being the only rational explanation for what they had just experienced around the table. As Stewart listened to his host's increasingly desperate search for a rational explanation, he reached for the blue ceramic fragment that had been dropped by the crow, looking at it momentarily before passing it to Thomas O'Neil, who puzzled over the small flake of blue tile with its deeply etched characters before stating

"It is classic, Arabic, probably seventeenth century." O'Neill looked pointedly at the broken ruin of the once magnificent Blue Mosque, that lay clearly visible in front of them, as the obvious source of the tile fragment.

"Can you translate it?" Asked Curren. O'Neill nodded slowly,

"Hide yourself in the dens and in the rocks of the mountains; and say unto the mountains and rocks, fall on us, and hide us for today death itself is come and none shall be able to stand under the sky and survive."

Mohammed Sek sighed and exclaimed "The End of Times."

O'Neill started to cross himself, but Stewart stopped him and reassured everyone.

"That does not tell us anything we did not already know. Instead of sitting here like frightened children by a camp fire, let's find out what is keeping our magical friend away so long."

With that Stewart and the group rose from the table to commence a systematic search of the villa, after they initially checked and found the first-floor washroom unoccupied. They eventually located the young priest down in the ancient Roman water cistern, some fifty feet beneath the current level of the villa, looking critically at the old barge moored at the stone pier. Upon seeing the group descending the long flight of stone steps, Kwon nodded and approached them.

"I assume you have read the message? Sir Stewart, we must ask for your help in constructing a shelter."

Stewart looked critically at the high ceilings of the ancient Roman cistern, and the rusting barge moored at the small jetty before responding,

"I suppose it would be too much to hope that you can tell me what kind of threat we are up against? I do not have much experience making shelters against the powers of the supernatural."

Kwon smiled,

"No, Sir Stewart, today we need defences against the worst that modern man can devise to do to his own species."

Tavish's face went grey. "Shit. That is more challenging. Do you know roughly how long we have to prepare?"

Chin looked at his white gold Patek Philippe Calatrava watch. The roman numerals showed just ten minutes before noon. He shrugged.

"Not long. A couple of hours at the most before it begins. The event is still being formed in someone's mind, so I cannot be more specific."

Stewart looked around him and began directing preparations to create a shelter that might provide them with a chance to survive an NBC (nuclear, biological or chemical) attack. They took the rolls of plastic sheeting from the base of the stairs, created some makeshift sandbags with earth from the courtyard, and moved some corrugated iron sheeting to construct a makeshift curtain and doors over the gap in the north stair wall.

Using the remaining rolls of plastic sheeting they made a simple tent that covered the cabin space at the far end of the 100 foot long narrow split hopper barge. Once the plastic sheeting was in place, Stewart had Sek connect the outflow from the boat's bilge pumps to a thick blue plastic hose, and then attached that hose to the lifting rig so that it was positioned above the boat and could pump a constant water flow over the plastic sheets of the simple makeshift tent.

After finding an ancient Grundig Yacht Boy battery powered radio in the cabin of the barge, Stewart set to work repurposing a long length of thin iron, that originally formed one of the villas lightning conductors, into an extended radio antenna, but without connecting it directly to the boat. Stewart emphasized the connection would have to be done after any EMP, so they could stand a chance of hearing short wave news updates, should anyone still be able to broadcast after the anticipated attack.

Finally, all of them formed a long human chain along the length of the cistern steps, moving containers of drinking water, tinned food and a small Calor Gas camping stove to the plastic tent, that now obscured the entire rear section of the ancient barge.

Ninety minutes of hard work later, the boat was prepared for an unknown ordeal, and the friends regrouped on the roof terrace for a well-deserved break, sweet Turkish coffee, biscuits and, they hoped, an explanation. Instead, all they received from Stewart was a builder's dust mask, latex gloves and clear plastic goggles. Each of them looked glumly at these simple items and one could see in their faces the terrible thoughts that started to run through their minds, trying to imagine what might happen next and wondering if they would survive. Fortunately, or unfortunately, their wait was short.

Eleven minutes later, at precisely 14.00 HRS, they saw four missiles burst free, in a mass of flame and smoke, from launch tubes on the angular shaped structure of the USS Lyndon B. Johnson, moored on the opposite site of the Bosphorus harbour, which flew high into the summer sky above them. At that moment, they knew the nightmare that they had all been hoping was just a figment of Kwon's mind, was all too real. While Stewart directed everyone to put on their builder's face masks and make their way to the underground shelter, Mohammed Sek tried desperately to use his mobile phone to call and warn his sons to take cover in the basement of the burnt-out Stewarts showroom but, either the E Fog missiles had already locked down the area into a total communications black out or the sheer numbers of calls had jammed the local cell phone masts.

The rest of the long afternoon was spent going through the supplies on the small barge, at Stewart's insistence, to make a careful log of everything, although Curren and Zahra suspected it was intended just to keep everyone occupied.

At five o'clock Zahra, Curren and Kwon began preparing a meal of flat bread and a rich vegetable soup, followed by some meat and other assorted items that had come from Zahra's kitchen and would not keep without refrigeration. Considering their circumstances, the meal turned out well, and their spirits remained high enough for them to enjoy listening to stories from Mohammed Sek, about farfetched adventures he claimed he had shared with Stewart.

Eventually each of them made some preparations for a long night, Stewart set out some of the thick canvas sail cloth onto the floor and experienced a series of strange and vivid dreams, interspersed with moments where he woke and checked that the others were all safe.

Stewart arose at 7 AM to find Kwon cooking everyone a welcome breakfast of scrambled eggs, deep fried bread and strong black coffee. After the group had all finished eating, Stewart looked at Kwon and said,

"OK. Let's connect the long aerial and find out if there is anyone out there still broadcasting."

Stewart put on his makeshift NBC protection kit of the builder's dust mask, plastic goggles, and rubber gloves and, after a brief time outside the wooden cabin space but still within the plastic sheet tent, he returned, throwing his used gloves, mask and goggles into a black bin bag that he had placed by the wooden cabin door.

With the lightning rod now connected to the old Grundig Yacht Boy radio, Curren began slowly moving the tuning dial and pressing down channel selectors through the short-wave bandwidth. They eventually came upon an emergency news broadcast from a radio station in Athens, that was relaying the Russia Today (RT) English language news that described the situation. It was worse than they had ever imagined.

The female radio announcer emphasized that the current medical advice was to remain indoors, with all windows and doors sealed as securely as possible, and to avoid any form of contact with anyone who was not already inside a shelter with you. It was believed that inhalation of airborne microbes was the cause of the hundreds of violent deaths that had been witnessed throughout the Eastern

Mediterranean region in the past twelve hours, as a deadly illness spread rapidly from the epicentre of Istanbul, and that persons who exhibited a haemorrhagic fever were themselves spreading the disease to anyone who had close contact. After some minutes of this detailed medical advice the female announcer was replaced by a male speaker with a heavy Russian accent, who gave a summary of the latest world news.

Yesterday afternoon, a US Warship moored in Istanbul harbour, had launched an unknown biological agent into the heart of the ancient city. Over one thousand civilians died instantaneously from a violent haemorrhagic reaction and, in the mass evacuation that followed, the infection was transmitted to neighbouring regions and continued to spread in spite of attempts by authorities to set up quarantine centres and implement travel bans.

Estimates of the death toll now stood at over one hundred thousand people, with new reports of outbreaks of the "Red Death", as it was being named, as far afield as London, New York and Cairo. In the late afternoon, some three hours after the attack, the Pentagon acknowledged that one of their warships had initiated an unauthorized launch of infectious biological materials and that any further threat from this rogue warship had been immediately neutralized by the United States Military.

At a hastily called press conference from the White House, four hours after the attack, US President Wilson Jones took the unprecedented step of apologizing to the world and stated that this terrible event was thought to be an act of deliberate terrorism by an unknown group, who had taken remote control of the US warship. President Jones went on to assure everyone that the United States had a vaccine stockpiled for just such emergencies, that would be administered free of charge by trained US troops in critical key locations, beginning immediately.

However, tragedy struck shortly after, at a high-profile media event, where key dignitaries from Turkey, Greece, Italy and Romania were publicly receiving the vaccine on the White House press platform next to the President, when something went terribly wrong. As each nation's UN ambassador was injected, they rapidly exhibited the haemorrhagic reactions typical of the so called "Red Death". Despite intensive medical interventions by the US Army experts, all four dignitaries were rapidly pronounced dead on the scene and, after the

US President was hurried to a secure location, the entire White House was pronounced a quarantine zone. Subsequent announcements from the Centre for Disease Control and World Health Authority emphasized that on no account should the US Army vaccine be used and that any remaining stockpiles were being destroyed pending an investigation. The Russian radio announcer went on to state that several reports had also reached Russia Today that US troops had been found among the dead, so RT supported the latest advice to avoid the American vaccine.

The news summary continued by describing how one hour after the tragedy at the White House, Unity CEO, Dr Nissa Ad-Dajjal had called her own news conference, where she decried the hypocrisy of the United States and claimed that the "Red Death" was a deliberate biological attack aimed at her supporters. The unprovoked launch of biological weapons of mass destruction was made, she claimed, with the clear goal of preventing the Magog free energy generator from being transported to Palestine and, since it was no longer protected by the human shield, the coalition intended to take the generator so it could be reverse engineered for their corporate profit. Ad-Dajjal said, with tears coming from her eyes, that to prevent any further violence against innocent people, she had decided to destroy the Magog generator and to repurpose her organization. In future, Unity would focus its vast resources on the creation of a new peaceful world, under a single enlightened leader, devoted to rights for all and freedom from the corporate corruption that was exemplified by the Western Powers and its use of biological weapons against innocent people. But, Ad-Dajjal admitted, that before such a peaceful paradise could be created, the evils of this current corporate world order had to be confronted and defeated. Ad-Dajjal had therefore, reluctantly, called on the people of the world to align with her, in what she called the war of all wars, a clash of primary values and a fight for civilization against corruption and greed. She announced that she intended to use the coalition's own "Red Death" weapon as her method of conversion and salvation, working towards a better shared future. Knowing the evil of the corporate coalition, Unity had already made its own vaccine, one that cured and protected, instead of killing. Ad-Dajjal proceeded to make the nations and peoples of the world a very simple offer. Submission to her Unity movement, in exchange for the vaccine and life. Since her new world would be one of shared wealth, she said, every Nation or person seeking the vaccine would surrender their personal possessions and, in return, would receive the vaccine and a unique barcode on their right hand, so their loyalties to Unity would be forever known to all.

Within hours of Ad-Dajjal's offer, the pestilence had become so extreme in the regions surrounding Istanbul that at midnight, local time, the Turkish state announced that it would be submitting unconditionally to the Unity movement. Similar statements rapidly followed from the neighbouring nations of Greece, Italy, Bulgaria, Serbia, Croatia, Romania, Georgia, Syria, and Azerbaijan.

The response from Unity was a curt demand that the representatives of each of these "former nations" would present their unconditional submission in a formal ceremony at dawn, local time, at the ancient harbour in Istanbul, close to the site where the Roman Emperors had received the submission of conquered nations, in the distant past.

The radio transmission went on to describe how crowds, dressed in a range of protective clothing, from the professional Level Five Bio Hazard Suits worn by the representatives of the surrendering nations, to more makeshift improvisations of the ordinary people, were gathering expectantly in the predawn darkness at the site of the ferry terminal, awaiting the ceremony that promised to bring a cure to the "Red Death", and bring about a new world order.

Just as it seemed that this must be some form of cruel joke, as there was no sign of any Unity vehicles or personnel, a massive ship rose unexpectedly from the calm waters of the Bospherous, with the flags of the ten nations who had submitted their sovereignty, hanging lifelessly from ten flag poles on the front of the Tiamat.

Listening to the broadcast in the safety of the barge, Fr Chin Kwon spoke, and his words made everyone gathered around the old Grundig radio shiver, with a realization of the evil they were committed to defeating.

"And I saw a beast rise up out of the sea, and upon his horns ten crowns, and upon his heads the name of blasphemy."

CHAPTER 42 - IN THE FIELDS OF HAR MEGHIDDOHN

"The Antichrist shall perform such perfect deceptions that over half of the globe will embrace their rule; All hope becomes lost should the Knight of the North fall before he reaches the domain of the desert devils;" – The Emerald Tablet Prophecy

Mohammed Sek's Villa,
7, Terzihane Sokak,
Binbirdirek, 34122 Fatih,
Istanbul, Turkey.
17.25HRS, Further-Eastern European Time, 11th August Present Day.

The beleaguered group of Stewart, Curren, O'Neill, Kwon, Mohammed Sek, his wife Zahra and their two daughters, Akila and Aygul, spent the rest of the day alternatively sleeping, eating and listening to the shortwave Russia Today (RT) English language coverage of the current events unfolding in the world some 50 feet above their refuge, on the old barge moored in the Roman Cistern beneath Sek's villa.

The RT radio broadcast described the brief ceremony at the Istanbul ferry docks, where the Turkish Prime Minister, along with diplomats from Italy, Greece, Bulgaria, Serbia, Croatia, Romania, Georgia, Syria and Azerbaijan, had each received the "Red Death" vaccination and the Unity mark of allegiance, before removing their hazmat suits to cheers of delight and relief from the assembled crowds, who then eagerly queued for their own vaccinations. RT reported that tens of thousands had swarmed to the harbour after hearing about the successful vaccinations, gladly pledging allegiance to Ad-Dajjal in return for immunity to the "Red Death" or coalition plague.

In-between the hourly RT news bulletins, the Greek radio station provided coverage from the World Council of Religions in New York, where authorities from several of the world's faiths and a number of religious scholars, speculated that humanity was now experiencing the events that had been foretold in many religious texts related to the end of the world.

The short speech by Dr Nissa Ad-Dajjal, at the end of the day long mass vaccinations at Istanbul harbour, placed emphasis on the positive aspects of the acceptance by the ten nations to the beneficent Unity rule. Regional vaccination centres were confirmed by independent UN observers to have been set up throughout the ten submitting nations, and every citizen who now came under Unity's mandate was promised protection until, as Ad-Dajjal stated it, "the end of time", so they could enjoy a new life, free from the old corrupt corporate interference. With such a positive image of submitting to Ad-Dajjal's apparently beneficent leadership being projected to the world, other nations around the globe rapidly acceded to the Unity cause. Within five hours of the Istanbul harbour ceremony, over one hundred nations were formally under Unity's mandate, and were receiving vaccinations for their grateful populations. In the eight developed nations of the coalition, although the governments remained firmly in opposition to the Unity movement, a growing proportion of their people were choosing to visit Unity vaccination centres and take up Ad-Dajjal's offer, in preference to the incurable and horrific "Red Death". Around the globe, the tide was rapidly turning towards acceptance of Ad-Dajjal's new Unity world order.

In recognition of her growing power, at the close of the Istanbul harbour ceremony, Nissa Ad-Dajjal called upon the four billion souls, who by that point in the early afternoon had pledged themselves to her cause, to show their support against the wicked coalition who had unleashed the "Red Death". She announced that she was using the massive financial resources, donated by her billions of followers on taking their Unity pledge, to fund a mass peaceful gathering of her supporters at a place she had selected south of Jerusalem, near the ancient city of Megiddo, where the Unity followers would have a final peaceful confrontation with the corporate controlled coalition.

"Where the hell is Megiddo?" Asked Mohammed Sek, as the small group of friends crowded around the old Grundig radio in the gloom of the barge cabin.

O'Neill replied, with the serious academic tone he probably used in his lectures.

"Megiddo was a city in the territory of ancient Israel which, according to the Judges and Kings sections of the Old Testament, was where the most decisive Holy battles were waged."

Kwon nodded, adding.

"Including the one final great Holy battle that is yet to take place. The Hebrew translation of Mountain of Megiddo is 'Har Meghiddohn' or as you will know it, Armageddon."

"Christ." Whispered Stewart.

"No, Sir Stewart, not Christ, but the Anti-Christ." Corrected Kwon, and continued,

"Dr Nissa Ad-Dajjal clearly identifies with the role of the bringer of the end of days, and is carefully acting out the stages of the prophecy in exact detail."

Mohammed Sek agreed,

"Yes. Even her surname in Arabic المسيح الدجّال means "the deceiver", who is supposed to appear before Yawm al-Qiyamah, the Day of Resurrection. Forgive my ignorance of St John in The Book but, apart from assembling millions of people for some great final battle, what else does this woman think she has to complete? Maybe we can throw her game off by disrupting some aspect of the prophecy?"

Kwon considered carefully.

"The Magog confrontation over free energy is similar to throwing the money changers from The Temple. Somehow, she orchestrated to bring death to a quarter of the world, while making good on a promise of salvation by means of a vaccine, which must count as healing the sick. The Unity barcode is clearly the "Mark of the Beast". With this latest act of massing her supporters at the ancient site of 'Har Meghiddohn', I believe she only needs to have shown to have raised the dead, and she has completed almost all the main aspects of the prophecies related to the Anti-Christ and the End of Days."

"I hate to say what we are all thinking, but how exactly do you propose to disrupt "her game", if she IS the anti-Christ?" Asked a clearly discouraged O'Neil.

Stewart interjected.

"The first step is for us to accept that for all her power, wealth and influence, Nissa Ad-Dajjal is just a human being, who believes she is the anti-Christ. Mad houses and prisons around the world are full of people who share similar delusions."

"I understand what you are saying, Tavish. But I am the only one here to have had first-hand experience with this monster and, after having seen all the ancient holy sites collapse, I do not have a problem believing she is the actual Anti-Christ." Stated Curren.

"I am reluctantly inclined to agree. Verchencho said as much to me during our discussions, and that was his motivation to even contemplate beginning a collaboration with," O'Neill paused, and looked at Fr Chin Kwon,

"...a priest who is under extraordinary influence."

Kwon nodded his understanding at O'Neil's feelings, and addressed the group.

"The Anti-Christ is no more powerful than your Messiah and, as I recall, he was subject to temptation before being killed all too easily by a minor Roman provincial governor."

"How dare you!" Exploded O'Neil.

"Christ submitted to death only so he could save humanity from our sins."

A pitying look crept over Kwon's face.

"Calm yourself, Thomas. I intended no insult, merely to indicate that there are forces greater than Ad-Dajjal, even with her undoubted esoteric skills and knowledge."

Stewart quickly intervened to guide the discussion away from their growing differences, and focused instead on what drew them together.

"Whatever she is or is not, we will never stop her while we remain stuck in here. Now they have made the vaccine widely available on the streets above us, our first action must be to locate a stock so that we can inoculate ourselves."

After some further discussion about who should venture out from their shelter, the group agreed that at dusk, when they had less chance of being observed, Stewart, Kwon, Sek and O'Neill would dress in their improvised protective clothing, and leave their refuge to head to one of the Unity vaccination centres, that had been described on the radio as being located near Mohammed's villa. O'Neill would then return to the barge to inoculate Curren, Zahra, Akila and Aygul and remain on guard with them, armed with one of the massive Ruger Alaskan revolvers. Mohammed Sek would search for his sons at Stewart's showroom and, if he could find them share the vaccine with them, before going to keep a watch on the Tiamat to make sure that it did not leave port.

That left Stewart and Kwon to try and track down Ad-Dajjal, in case she had acquired the Istanbul emerald tablet.

Once this plan of action had been agreed, they shared a simple cold meal of beyaz peynir (a white feta-like goat's cheese) with bazlama flat bread and resumed listening to the RT news coverage on the old Grundig.

The female RT announcer, who they had heard when they first listened in the early morning, came back on duty as the sun set on the first day of Unity's rule over half the world's population. At 18.07 HRS, local time, the news summary was interrupted, to cover an impromptu press conference that had been called by Dr Nissa Ad-Dajjal announcing that she would personally lead a procession through the streets of the ancient city, concluding with a special multi-denominational service at an ancient site of worship that had been exposed under the ruins of the shattered Hagia Sophia mosque. She invited priests from all religions, who had accepted the Unity vaccination, to join her in a celebration of a new future, with the stipulation that those who took part would be required to renounce their old faith as the evening ceremony would mark the beginning of a new global religion.

As Ad-Dajjal's voice came over the radio, Curren's eyes clearly lost focus and her lips repeated Nissa Ad-Dajjal's every word.

"Our new faith will not be based on prejudiced and biased readings of questionable historical sources. Instead, it will be a faith that is better suited for a new world, free from the tyranny of profit accumulation and the use of religion as a weapon to further political agendas. Instead of corruption and empty dogma there will now be a focus on the spiritual principles that had been missing from organized religion for the past two thousand years."

The radio coverage of the press conference ended with a description of the route that the procession would take when it started in an hour's time.

"That is our cue." Said Stewart, as the four men quickly started putting on their builder's dust masks, goggles and gloves. O'Neill neatly folded his Catholic Priests cassock and hat into a blue BIM supermarket carrier bag for Stewart to use, so he and Kwon could join the procession after they had obtained the vaccine.

When the four men emerged outside the entrance to the Roman Cistern and into the open air, it was clear that only Kwon had no fear of suddenly contracting the "Red Death" and perishing, as the others exchanged frequent glances between them, checking everyone was still healthy.

Before they even had a chance to make a plan of action, the young priest had approached the blue fiberglass porta cabin on Isa Yusuf Park, located some fifty yards to the West of the double wooden gates of Mohammed's villa, and started to talk with the three Maelstrom operatives who were manning the deserted station. As one man prepared the computerized barcode procedure, taking down Fr Kwon's supposed address and bank account details, whilst at the same time relieving him of his Patek watch, Mohammed Sek walked quietly, or as quietly as a man of his size could, passing gently between the two other Maelstrom guards. As if intent on watching the vaccination procedure, swiftly grabbed each man by the neck and smashed their heads together in a blur of powerful motion, accompanied by a sickening thudding noise. As the two men fell to the ground unconscious, Kwon was dealing with the remaining Maelstrom male nurse, who had become extremely cooperative, unlocking the vaccine safe and helping O'Neill, Stewart, Mohammed Sek and finally Kwon inoculate themselves, before placing spare vaccine phials and syringes into two Maelstrom labelled Wenger rucksacks. They left the man wide eyed, in some kind of trance, on his seat at the entrance desk of the portacabin.

As the four friends emerged from the Unity Binbirdirek vaccination centre, Stewart was the first to remove his mask and take a deep breath of the evening air, the others quickly following suit. Within minutes, Stewart had removed all of his protective gear and put on O'Neill's cassock, which looked at least two sizes too small for him. The broad brimmed priests hat was the worst fit but, with some seams carefully loosened, it eventually fitted low enough on Stewart's head to partially obscure his face.

As Sek and O'Neill went their separate ways, each with a vaccine filled rucksack and one of the massive Ruger Alaskan revolvers, Kwon and the uncomfortable looking Stewart, who were now both dressed in classic Catholic priest's cassocks, walked calmly through the empty streets until they came across the Unity procession. Joining the long line of maybe four hundred priests, nuns, monks, rabbis, gurus and mullahs, they made their way in a slow rhythmic stride from Kennedy Cd, where the Tiamat was moored, North past the Marmara University building, then onwards besides the remains of the Blue mosque, where Mohammed Sek's villa was located, past the Dikilitaş Egyptian obelisk, through Sultanahmet Square and finally to the ruins of the Hagia Sophia.

When Stewart and Kwon finally arrived at the end of their mile long march, they were confronted by small groups of Maelstrom soldiers, dressed in black commando fatigues, who had gathered under sixteen foot high flood lights, set up next to three strategically placed Browning M2 .50 Calibre Machine Guns on large steel M2 mounts. The heavy machine guns all directed their lines of fire down the main approaches, away from the ruins, to defend the once great Hagia Sophia mosque.

"All this for us?" Whispered Stewart, taking in the fortifications and strategically placed sandbags, guiding the procession into clearly designated killing fields.

"I have yet to see a new religion that did not require military might."

Said the enigmatic Kwon, from under his broad black hat.

Stewart raised an eyebrow, as they passed through a set of gates fitted with metal detectors, and congratulated himself on his earlier decision to give the Ruger revolvers to Sek and O'Neill.

The closer they approached to the old mosque, the greater the damage they could see to the ancient structure. The remains of the massive stone dome had collapsed through the stone and marble floor, smashing it and exposing four hidden stairways, which lead down from the underground crypt to deeper forgotten subterranean layers, dating from before the original construction of the Shrine of the Holy Wisdom of God, in 537 AD.

As the procession made its way down these heavily worn stone steps, each fourth row of priests was handed a wooden flaming torch by a Maelstrom operative. From the light of these flickering torches, they could clearly see the walls of the stairwell that were now free from the layers of plaster and paint laid down over the centuries, the exposed original walls showing patterns of flowers and birds in precisely cut white stone, set against a background of black marble.

Massive sections of the dome had smashed their way deep down into the bowels of the ruins, and sections of the four- supporting piers (spherical triangular pendentives) were strewn alongside the fallen columns, surrounded by a mix of broken masonry bearing Islamic quotes from the Koran and Christian images.

As they continued to descend the narrow stairway with the throng of other priests, the yellow light from the torches revealed an ancient painting of an enormous six-winged creature, with long razor thin talons where its fingers and toes should have been. Its entire body was covered in dark shapes that could have been feathers or scales and everywhere, seemingly on every part of the body, were large predatory eyes, like those of a massive salt water crocodile.

"What the hell is that?" Enquired Stewart.

Kwon looked at Stewart and replied.

"A Hexapterygon." Then, seeing a lack of recognition from Stewart, he added.

"A six-winged Angel."

"It does not look like any of the Angels I remember from Sunday School, and certainly does not look like it is bringing peace and goodwill to all mankind."

Kwon regarded Stewart, and then the painting.

"Above him stood the Seraphim; each had six wings; with two he covered his face, and with two he covered his feet, and with two he flew. Isaiah 6:1–3." Quoted Kwon, as though that answered all of Stewart's questions.

"But why cover their face, if they have eyes everywhere?" Enquired Stewart,

Again, Kwon regarded his companion, as if he was surprised at his lack of knowledge.

"That is simple, Sir Stewart. They cover their face because no living thing can look upon them"

While Kwon and Stewart were discussing Angelic beings, and descending into the prehistoric chambers below the Hagia Sophia, their friend Mohammed Sek had reached the charred remains of Stewart's

Antiquarian showroom at Nuruosmaniye Caddesi. After climbing over the rubble, and using his phenomenal strength to pull away some of the wooden doors that had been piled over the shop's basement entrance, he descended into the darkness of the cellar, where he found his sons, Yusuf and Berat, who thankfully had survived by wearing two old rubber gas masks from the 1960s that they had found in the shop's underground store room. The joy of finding them alive was tinged with sadness at learning of the passing of their elder brother Ahmet, who had contracted the Red Death while helping their neighbours. His body had been buried, as best the two sons could manage under the circumstances, in the small garden space to the rear of the showroom.

After inoculating his two sons, and saying a prayer over Ahmet's grave, Sek explained to them the nature of the calamity that faced the world from Ad-Dajjal and the job he had agreed to perform with respect to watching that the Tiamat did not leave harbour. Naturally, Yusuf and Berat wanted to avenge their brother, so enthusiastically agreed to help. Sek then led the trio expertly through the back alleys of the city, making sure they avoided the Maelstrom check points that had been set up at every major intersection and cross roads within the city centre.

Eventually, at around 9.35 PM local time, the three arrived at the ferry terminal, where they were immediately approached by a group of smartly dressed men in white naval inspired uniforms with Maelstrom insignia. Using their assumed rights over the citizens of Turkey and with the added persuasion from H&K MP5 machine guns, they pressed the three new arrivals into service, along with a small group of other local men, to load large sacks of wheat, vegetables, casks of liquid, crates of live animals and general supplies, from the quayside up a large grey metal gangplank and to the storeroom deep in the bowels of the Tiamat.

The long line of people in Nissa Ad-Dajjal's religious procession eventually reached the bottom of the numerous flights of worn stone steps, where their flaming torches were extinguished by armed guards. The representatives from the numerous world religions were then guided into a large candle lit underground chamber, that had been carved into the bedrock, some 250 feet under the crypt of the Hagia Sophia. The chamber itself was 150 yards in diameter, with an enormous thirty-foot-high ceiling that had partially collapsed, leaving three massive stone blocks lying randomly on the central floor space.

Stewart pushed his way through the throng of people, who had gathered in rows four or five deep, around the edges of a rusted iron circle that was set into the otherwise solid stone floor, forming what was clearly intended to be the edge of a sacred ritual space. At one end of the chamber, a large temporary platform had been erected from massive sections of wood and, seated there, on a black carved wooden throne looking down on the gathering, like an empress, was Dr Nissa Ad-Dajjal. Looking around the mass of people through her golden face mask, she finally decided that the time was right and, clapping her hands, commanded that the ceremony began.

A group of thirteen dirty, unkempt looking men with long red beards, walked slowly into the ritual space, dressed in the distinctive black linen robes and tall felt hats of Left Hand Path (LHP) Mawlawīyya or Dervishes.

"Left hand path Semazen-s!" Whispered Kwon, as though this should mean something to Stewart, and then added, "No matter what happens next, stay close to me and do nothing."

"No problem." Said a bemused Stewart, as he wondered what could cause such a comment from Kwon.

One of the thirteen was clearly their High Priest, because he separated from the group and began a series of evocations in Arabic, that echoed around the enclosed chamber. This was taken as a signal to extinguish some of the lights, and for a group of seven men to begin playing on kiz ney and larger mansur ney pipes, with bendir and darabuka drums as accompaniment. The musical cadence started slowly, but gradually grew faster.

As the drumming beat increased in speed, all thirteen of the Satanic Semazen-s pulled a highly distinctive curved bladed Janbiya knife from their thick black leather belts and, rolling up their long sleeves and tying the material up with linen strips, proceeded to inflict deep cuts on their exposed skin. As the blood flowed down their arms, they began the distinctive rotating dance of the Dervishes, but in an anticlockwise direction. As the drums increased their cadence, the room grew cooler and the lights dimmed even more.

Stewart felt the hairs stand on his neck, and he could not at first believe his eyes but, as he adjusted his vision to the semi darkness, he could see shimmering forms appearing on each of the exposed bleeding arms of the whirling devotees. As these shapes consumed the freely flowing blood they grew more definite in their substance, until each man had what looked like a large leech or slug shape feeding on their arms.

Stewart turned to Kwon asking,

"What the hell are they?"

"Larvae." Replied the young priest and again, seeing this meant nothing to his Scottish companion, added,

"The remains of deceased astral forms, reanimated by the life essence of the living."

"Dangerous?" Asked Stewart.

"Only to those stupid enough to feed them, and mistake the reanimated astral shell for the immortal spirit." Responded the clearly unimpressed Kwon.

After the music reached a frenzy, twelve of the Satanic Semazen-s collapsed to the floor and, in the silence that followed, Stewart gradually became aware that, interspersed among the crowd that had formed around the edge of the ritual space, were not just the living, who he had marched alongside, but also shadowy figures of the dead, many of them still covered in the blood of their horrific demise from the "Red Death".

In a state of delight Nissa Ad-Dajjal, dressed in a robe of purple and scarlet silk adorned with gold, precious stones and pearls, raised her right hand in which she held a golden cup containing some of the Dervish blood, and proclaimed that everyone was now witness that she had raised the dead, as foretold in ancient prophecy.

At that moment, when Stewart felt things could not become any darker, a group of heavily armed men in Maelstrom paramilitary fatigues, led by a familiar hawk faced man, marched from a stairway near to where Ad-Dajjal was standing and passed to her a small green stone object, that Stewart recognized immediately as one of the emerald tablets.

Ad-Dajjal's face beamed with sheer pleasure, as she announced.

"You have all born witness to my power over the living and the dead, now I require a pledge of your own life's blood to flow into this cup."

Issac bin Abdul Issuin stepped down from the wooden platform, with the golden cup in his left hand and, walking to where the Satanic Semazen-s were still seated within the circle, took the long ritual Janbiya knife from the Dervish high priest. He then began systematically approaching each of the individuals who were gathered around the edge of the ritual iron circle, rolling up each person's sleeves before cutting them deeply, so their blood was first caught in "the golden cup of abominations" before overflowing onto the iron ring that marked the edge of the "sacred" space. The sheer number of people in the small temple area prevented any movement, so none could think of escaping the blood sacrifice demanded by Ad-Dajjal.

After agonizing moments, Abdul Issuin was rolling up Stewart's sleeve, when he noticed the distinctive large resin Casio Rangeman watch, and exclaimed.

"An odd watch for a priest..." and, pulling off the large brimmed hat, immediately recognized the Scotsman, exclaiming.

"Tavish Stewart!"

As the Maelstrom guards, who were positioned strategically around the cavern, covered everyone expertly with their composite H&K 9mm MP5 machine guns, Abdul Issuin dragged Stewart to the centre of the temple and roughly removed the emerald tablet in its silver folio from around the Scotsman's neck, holding it high in the air in triumph.

Nissa Ad-Dajjal's voice announced in a sneering laugh from the podium,

"I did not think I would be pleased to see you again, Sir Stewart. But you have brought me such a wonderful gift..."

Abdul Issuin pushed Stewart brutally to his knees and, drawing Frank Foster's gold Colt 1911 pistol, prepared to execute the Scotsman who had caused him so much frustration.

FOLIO 7 - THE KEYS TO CREATION

CHAPTER 43 - GIVING THE DEVIL HIS DUE

"The error made by every priest when preparing an exorcism is to overestimate the Church's power in relation to the Ancient Adversary. As the first born of creation, Lucifer is the only being able to survive in the direct presence of the Holy God. As "The Son of the Morning", he is a level above all other beings, in heaven and on earth, not only in appearance and power, but also in intellect, for he alone was created to understand the mind of Almighty God."
Subtexts on Satan, The Deliverance Handbook. Fr Hugo Verchencho, Vatican Press. Rome.

Sistine Chapel
Apostolic Palace
00120 Vatican City
22.50 HRS Central European Time, 11th August, Present Day.

The shattered fragments of Michelangelo's magnificent ceiling and wall frescoes lay, gathered methodically, in numbered transparent plastic boxes, that were stacked sixteen feet high on either side of the altar at the far end of the chapel, awaiting years of painstaking reconstruction. Thick metal scaffolding supported the fifteenth century building, and the few intact sections that remained of the frescoes had been treated with a resin to prevent any further damage, should there be more aftershocks.

Ironically, given current world events, Michelangelo's depiction of "The Last Judgement" on the wall behind the altar remained undamaged and provided a dramatic backdrop for the laying in state of his Holiness Pope James. The late Pontiff's body had been placed on a dais directly in front of the altar, under the exposed roof sixty feet above, which gave a view of the heavens that would have been beautiful under other circumstances. The shock of white hair, that had been the famous hallmark of the sixty-seven-year-old James, was visible beneath his mitre hat and his long thin frame was hidden within the white robes of office. At the other end of the chapel, near the tall entrance doors, was a mass of red, that denoted that the College of Cardinals had gathered in the world famous 122 foot long Papal chapel.

The emaciated body of the dead Pope lay with his head facing the altar and his feet pointing towards the most senior representatives of the Roman Church, or rather those who remained after the ravages of the "Red Death" and the recent media revelations of widespread clerical misconduct.

The remaining eighty-seven members of the two hundred and twenty-nine College of Cardinals were seated in two long rows on either side of the open roofed space. Most were elderly, with an average age of seventy-five years, and all of them looked frail and uncertain. With the church morally and structurally in ruins, the recent suicide of Pope James had been the final straw that had convinced almost every one of the frightened old men that there was no hope of the Catholic Church coming back from such a catastrophic series of setbacks. Already over seventy of the members had signed a declaration to pass control of the church and its remaining assets to Dr Nissa Ad-Dajjal's Unity movement.

Two figures sat alone behind the mass of red robes. One was a forty something athletic looking man with a shaved head, who was dressed in a black Armani suit that was doing a poor job of disguising the large calibre hand pistol in the shoulder holster under his jacket.

Seated next to him was a large man in his sixties, whose nicotine stained fingers nervously fidgeted with a battered Ronson lighter, an action that drew a seriously disapproving look from the Swiss Guard, who was making sure that no one interrupted this "Crisis of Faith" meeting to decide if there could be a new Pope.

At the head of the conclave, Dr Antonio Abatescianni, the Cardinal archivist, with his distinctive long hair and grey beard, looked quite different in his formal red robes. His wire framed glasses were perched on his narrow nose, as he stood alone, facing the two rows of elderly clerics, to lead the silent personal prayers for inspiration. The meditative silence was broken unexpectedly by agitated talking among the Cardinals, who were all looking and pointing at something behind Abatescianni.

As the Vatican Archivist turned, he saw that the prone figure of the dead Pope was slowly sitting upright, and was looking down the chapel towards the assembled meeting. As Abatescianni hurried to provide assistance to the Holy Father, he noticed that the chapel had become noticeably colder and a putrid stench had filled the air, making the Archivist cover his nose and involuntarily halt his advance towards the risen figure on the funeral plinth.

The Pope's eye sockets were white orbs and, when he opened his mouth, yellow mucus dribbled from his lips, as he made a disgusting rasping noise with each breath, that was a mix of a cough and a laugh. Even though, moments earlier, the great skill and care of the Papal morticians had made the late Holy Father look like he had just fallen asleep, now the exposed skin on his face and hands was blotched with the dark stains of post mortem bruising, giving him the look of a ghoulish apparition.

This horrific animated corpse looked around at the broken chapel and the frightened old men scurrying to the door and, in perfect Aramaic Nabataean dialect, rasped.

"How fitting, a broken church filled with broken old men, who have lost their faith. With the fall of the Knight of the North we, who are Legion, are compelled by prophecy to rise and seize control of the Mother Church in these final days..."

Seeing the mass of terrified Cardinals, frantically trying to get to the locked double doors, the dead Pope's eyes fixed on a thick stack of wooden benches, that had been placed to the left of the entrance, and immediately they slid violently over the marble mosaic floor. As the benches blocked the entire doorway they scattered elderly Cardinals to the floor in a mass of red robes. The rasping entity now spoke in a variety of accents and languages, all different, as if a dozen voices shared the same vocal cords.

"Don't go so soon, Brothers... we have so much to discuss... and clarify, for the future of the Mother Church in its final days. It has been so long a wait, until you became weak enough for us to rise unchallenged, to take control of the very thing that oppressed us for thousands of years. Your crisis of faith is a blessing, for now there is none of you that can stand against us. Kneel!" Demanded the thing that had taken possession of the body of the old Pope.

The command echoed in such a loud fearful roar that, as one, the gathered Cardinals fell to their knees in a clear supplication, born of blind terror towards this unknown, but clearly demonic, entity that animated the body of the former Pontiff.

Just as the future of the Roman Church seemed lost, a lone figure came striding through the centre of the gathering of kneeling Cardinals, towards the supremely confident seated figure of the risen Pope.

The fearless newcomer, who had been sitting hidden at the back of the meeting, was a complete contrast to the elegance and pomp of the Cardinals in their red gowns. His unkempt ginger and grey hair danced wildly around his frayed and worn collar, his vestments were scruffy and, in total defiance of the "Vietato Fumare" signs, he had lit a Turkish Royal cigarette and was exhaling a trail of thick tar ridden smoke, as he stormed down the length of the chapel towards the reanimated body of Pope James.

The foul creature which had taken over the Pontiff edged itself forward, so it was sitting on the end of the funeral plinth, the bleached and bruised skin of its legs visible, hanging from out of the bottom of its shroud. Pure hate manifested in the white reanimated features of Pope James and it snarled in sudden recognition at the Chief Exorcist, striding fearlessly towards it.

"Why, what is a lowly priest doing among all these enlightened Cardinals? If I recall, the regulations of the College of Cardinals only permit those with the ring of eminence to approach and talk to the Holy Father." Sneered the rasping voice. However, it's evil grin evaporated as Dr Antonio Abatescianni stood and calmly removed the thick golden ring from his own hand, placing it solemnly on Verchencho's right ring finger.

The entity animating Pope James growled,

"Even being elevated will not help you, Exorcist! As you well know, a suicide's soul and body become ours. No exorcism will remove me, or save the Church from its new path under my direction!"

Verchencho took a long deep draw on his Turkish Royal, and replied in a cloud of thick smoke.

"I do not dispute that the body is yours. But, I do admire your courage to manifest and possess it on consecrated ground… The slightest spark... and you would be consumed by the very fires of Hell... would you not?"

The slightest hint of a smile could be seen on Verchencho's face, as he took another deliberate deep draw on the remaining stub of his cigarette. As its tip glowed brightly, he removed it carefully between his second finger and thumb, before deliberately flicking it away with his first finger.

The flames consumed the figure seated on the edge of the funeral plinth with a height and intensity that defied rational expectation.

Verchencho stood his ground in the intense heat and remained watching until the final glowing cinder floated upward on the heat thermals, high into the night sky, leaving a set of dark scorch marks on the plinth's white cloth as a lasting record of the event.

De Ven pushed his way through the mass of Cardinals, who were now discussing the future with new hope and, standing next to Verchencho, said.

"I told you those Turkish Royals were killers."

Cardinal Verchencho nodded, as he slowly lit a new one with his old battered Ronson lighter.

250 feet beneath the ruins of the Hagia Sophia, in the prehistoric temple complex, Tavish Stewart's two patella bones throbbed from the violent impact they had sustained on the hard stone floor of the ancient temple. In semi darkness, with his head bowed in front of him, he was now simply awaiting the killing shot from the large gold Colt 1911 he had seen drawn by his hawk faced enemy, before he had been dragged to the centre of the ritual circle. In the silence that had descended within the underground Temple, he had heard the distinctive sound of the .45 chamber hammer being pulled back and was now awaiting the last sound of his life. Stewart did not fear death. It had been an occupational hazard for most of his adult life and, like many men of action, he had long ago accepted that his moment would come, but he wished that fate would have allowed him one more chance to face this hawk faced bastard with more even odds.

"Wait!" A female voice thundered through the small space, in place of the anticipated roar of the massive pistol.

"Instead of just shooting the Knight of the North, let us have his life blood flow and consecrate the emerald tablets, so they are washed crimson in his blood!" Demanded Ad-Dajjal. As she descended from the podium and approached closer, she took Stewart's silver folio from Abdul Issuin and fitted each of her own two emerald tablets into the silver clasps so there was now only one unfilled slot in the silver container. Looking at the three exquisitely carved stones resting together, back in their traditional home after hundreds of years apart, she pulled her steel Porsche design Blackberry smartphone from a concealed pocket in the front of the scarlet robe and took a series of HDR close up pictures of each of the carved emeralds, before returning her designer steel phone to its place. Turning to Issac bin Abdul Issuin, she explained.

"With these images, the staff on the Tiamat can begin the preparations for the next ceremony, which gives us time for something extra special here to mark our victory."

With that she took the ritual Janbiya dagger from Abdul Issuin, gestured for the bald-headed leader of the Left-Hand Path Dervishes, the High Priest Kellep Davrasi, to make the sacrificial cut, and carefully placed the silver folio on the floor in front of Stewart, so that his blood flowing over them would be the last thing he saw.

"Dedicate his life blood to the ultimate principle of evil that you worship, Davrasi."

The High Priest grinned and, taking the wicked blade from her, he waited beside the kneeling figure of Stewart, while Nissa Ad-Dajjal and Abdul Issuin returned to the platform to watch and savour the sacrifice that would break the prophecy, that a Knight of the North would prevent the Anti-Christ from fulfilling her mission of creating a new heaven and earth.

Kellep Davrasi began some incantations under his breath that were clearly leading to the act of cutting Stewart's throat, but his preparations were unexpectedly interrupted by a young Catholic priest walking calmly into the ritual space and stating quietly.

"There are two of us here."

Looking at the immaculate cassock worn by the innocent faced newcomer, Davrasi proclaimed loudly.

"Just as the prophecy foretold! A Priest of Rome and a Knight of the North. Both can consecrate the three tablets of destiny with their life blood! Such a sacrament may even evoke the ultimate principle of evil to visit and give us his blessing!"

"Be careful what you wish for..." Responded the newcomer, with a smile that caused Nissa Ad-Dajjal an unfamiliar sensation, which she eventually recognized as being a visceral fear deep in her stomach, but she rapidly dismissed the momentary distraction, thinking the young fool before her had a misplaced faith in his pathetic Christ.

However, as Fr Chin Kwon walked calmly straight up to where Stewart was kneeling and pushed himself directly into what would be the path of the killing stroke from Davrasi's Janbiya dagger, Nissa Ad-Dajjal became increasingly uncomfortable, especially as she found that she was unable to focus her Magickal Will on the young priest.

Unused to having anyone resist her, Ad-Dajjal performed the Cabbalistic Cross and then a more powerful elemental banishing but, even as she mentally traced the air with her pentagrams, she could feel her magick was being overwhelmed by some greater force and, instead of achieving clarity, she was finding herself increasingly off balance.

Nissa Ad-Dajjal finally recognized the source of the magickal disturbance, when the blurred face of the young priest came starkly into focus, returning her stare. At that moment, she felt a Magickal Will of such power that fear, combined with an instinct of self-preservation, overwhelmed her and she dashed from the platform towards the Northern exit stairs, leaving a bemused Issac bin Abdul Issuin to follow rapidly afterwards.

As Ad-Dajjal and Abdul Issuin ran up the stone stairway, Davrasi responded to the arrogance of this young Priest of Rome, with a well-practiced savage diagonal cutting stroke aimed at Kwon's exposed neck. However, instead of cutting deeply into the soft tissue, the priest's skin changed its texture, appearing as glistening scales, and the curved steel blade simply broke into fragments that scattered loudly across the stone temple floor, casting bright sparks into the air, like those that are seen when metal strikes metal.

Looking intently at Davrasi, the clearly uninjured Kwon tilted his head, like a raven regarding a morsel he was about to consume, and slowly raised his hands towards his face, palm outwards, deliberately covering his eyes, in a gesture that reminded Stewart of the stylized Angelic icon he had seen on the walls of the stairway during the procession down into the depths of the Hagia Sophia. As the priest's hands finally reached his face, the flickering lights in the temple made his whole body appear to have been transformed into a mass of glistening scales.

Something deeply sinister in Kwon's stance and apparent transformation, made Stewart remember the chilling comment about why the Hexapterygon covered their features, and he quickly grabbed the silver folio from the temple floor and dashed to the Northern stairway, where, after ascending two flights of stairs, he took cover in a small passing alcove that had been chiselled into the bedrock. Lying face down on the rough stone floor, he covered his head with his hands. As the candles in the stairway dimmed, the space became unnaturally cold, as thick ice formed on all the exposed stone floor surfaces. For the first time in decades, Tavish Stewart prayed with intent.

In the frigid semi darkness, there was the unnatural sound of wings and feathers unfurling, combined with the smell of something ancient coming into contact with fresh air. A deep voice filled everyone's head, but the words were not spoken. Instead, they were rather felt in the bones as vibrations that emanated from the space in the centre of the temple.

"Always such arrogance. To IMAGINE that a worm can summon the gardener."

The few remaining candles flickered wildly, in random currents of air that now filled the space, casting strange shadows that made Fr Chin Kwon look different. Radically different. Taller, darker and wearing a thick leather cloak that unfurled like a mass of dark wings, with hideous talons in place of his hands and feet. To those who had not already fled from the area, the dark figure seemed to be covered with glowing eyes that were everywhere. The underground temple now felt cramped, as the huge scaled and leathery forelimbs unfurled, filling the entire space and touching each person who remained, some feeling talons, some leathery wings and others the crushing embrace of a massive serpent, causing them to scream involuntarily as they were engulfed by the primal nightmares of humanity, from the very dawn of time.

Literature has portrayed Lucifer as the being responsible for the darkest aspects of human behaviour. The reality is that human beings do not need a supernatural entity in order to manifest evil. History shows we are more than capable of planning and operationalizing actions that bring terrible suffering to all species, including our own.

Real life demonic possessions are seldom as dramatic as shown in the movies, blasphemous outbursts are far more frequent than levitations, projectile vomiting or head rotations and, rather like past life regressions, every possession is by an entity with a predisposition to megalomania and exaggeration.

Comparative theology has shown that the names of our devils are those of the gods from earlier or competing religions, cast into the role of supreme evil for propaganda purposes. With this understanding, it is an understatement to say that the real Lucifer is far more complex and powerful than we have been led to believe by exoteric religions. Few people care to contemplate what being "The Light Bringer" really means, and certainly do not connect the first theological manifestation that issued from the primeval formless void, "Let there be Light" (יְהִי אוֹר), to be connected with an entity that they have been taught to consider as being synonymous with Satan.

In all ancient Assyrian and Hebrew cosmogonies, it is the "Architects", (in Hebrew the collective "Elohim"), not God the Unknowable (Ein Sof, אין סוף,), who fashion order from disorder, separate light from darkness, heaven from earth, subject from object and most significantly, for serious occultists, mind from matter and intelligence from consciousness. The absurdity of a mortal human thinking they could summon or control such an entity says all you need to know about the vanity of man, and the twisted sanity of the authors of the Medieval Grimoires.

The vibrations that forced the terrifying voice deep inside every consciousness in the subterranean temple continued in what was the most ancient litany in creation. Each verse caused the listener to cry out in despair from their personal encounter with an ancient terror that was beyond reason.

"I am the Darkness before the Light!
Know Me
I am the Chaos before the Order!
Know Me
I am the infinite Darkness that awaits Everything!
KNOW ME!"

Normally, the evil high priest Kellep Davrasi enjoyed looking into the eyes of the dying and seeing their despair, as they found their faith lost and they were confined to oblivion. Now, he felt a cold unlike anything he had ever experienced and, before him the baby-faced priest had transformed into a dark serpent manifestation, who towered as high as the vaulted thirty-three feet ceiling, with huge scaled wings covered with eyes that were filled with malice, as they glowed in the growing primeval darkness of Chaos, drawn from a time before the divine order of Theos or Kosmos.

Davrasi gazed into one of the unblinking serpentine eyes and screamed. A scream of a mind unravelling its conscious structures of reality. Chaos literally unfolded in the confined space of the small temple. Shapes, sounds, smells and formless things extended to touch and collapse the minds of all they encountered.

Since time and space ceased to have meaning, it is pointless to estimate how long the terror lasted but, what is certain, is that for those who directly experienced the touch of darkness, it lasted for eternity.

As the lights slowly returned, they revealed what remained of the worshippers, who had gathered to follow Ad-Dajjal. Human forms lay scattered, broken into impossible configurations, while those who were alive sat in their own excrement. Many simply rocked slowly back and forth sobbing, while others giggled and traced random patterns on the floor, as if they were the sublime secrets of nature.

In the centre of the room, like some hideous crystalline statue, was what remained of the high priest Kellep Davrasi, now a mass of melting salt that was slowly dissolving onto the dusty stone floor.

CHAPTER 44 - THE DUEL

"Of all the aspects of close quarter combat there is none filled with more nonsense than knife fighting. Let me summarize all you need to know: The best knife is the one you carry all the time. Everyone in a real knife fight gets cut. There is no way to train for getting cut and bleeding. Winning is defined as staying alive." – Close Quarter Combat – NATO handbook series, Col. T. Stewart

Northern stairway beneath the ruins of The Hagia Sophia
Sultan Ahmet Mahallesi,
Ayasofya Meydanı,
34122 Fatih
İstanbul, Turkey
00.12 HRS Further-Eastern European time, 12th August, Present Day.

Tavish Stewart sensed the manifestation was ending by the increase in temperature, the brightness he could sense in the alcove where he was sheltering, and something intangible beyond his simple biological senses. He carefully reached around him, his eyes still firmly closed and, by feel alone found the silver folio on the floor beside him. He placed it around his neck, using the same worn black nylon paracord he had originally fitted in Edinburgh.

Standing and opening his eyes, Stewart found himself face to face with the hawk faced Issac bin Abdul Issuin, who was returning down the stairway for the emerald tablets, that were now so clearly visible in the silver folio hanging from Stewart's neck.

Stewart smiled. "And they say, wishes never come true..."

Abdul Issuin did not waste time talking. He knew from bitter experience how dangerous Stewart could be and did not intend to give him any chances of survival or escape. Drawing Frank Foster's massive gold .45 pistol from his webbing waist holster, he aimed a killing shot between Stewart's eyes.

As if in slow motion, Stewart saw his hawk faced opponent raise the shining Colt 1911, and he instinctively used the only resource available to him as, hopeless though it appeared, he flicked the frozen fragments that clung to his fingers from the icy stone floor, directly into the eyes of Abdul Issuin.

Even the most highly trained fighters cannot completely override their body's natural defensive responses, and so it was with Abdul Issuin. As the tiny ice particles made contact with the white flesh of his sclera, they triggered an involuntary corneal reflex blink. In that instant, Stewart applied what at first appeared to be a classic pistol disarming technique, common to most modern military combat curricula, but which rapidly evolved into a traditional Japanese Ju-Jitsu move.

Stewart moved slightly to one side, pushing his left hand flat against the gun to make sure the barrel did not follow in his direction, and then simultaneously grabbed and pushed the gun side on with his right hand, twisting the pistol violently in a circular movement away from him. So far, his actions followed the standard disarming technique, except the Scotsman immediately followed this move by rotating his entire body counter clockwise, continuing to push against the barrel, so his entire mass applied a wicked twisting joint lock on Abdul Issuin's wrists. The irresistible circular force brought the Scotsman's armed opponent to his knees, with the gun pointing toward Abdul Issuin's throat.

For his part, Issac bin Abdul Issuin's black belt Krav Maga training sensed Stewart's intention from the initial movement of the ancient Jiu-Jitsu technique. Instead of resisting, he followed the circular motion and, from his final kneeling position, launched into his own reverse spinning leg sweep, which forced Stewart to respond by violently changing the direction of his momentum and roll against Abdul Issuin's leg sweep. The big 1911 gun was sent tumbling down the stairs, discharging a series of full metal jacket rounds into the stone walls and ceiling. Ricochets flew around the confined space of the stairway, and weakened sections of sharp masonry began flying through the air, cutting the exposed flesh of both men's faces, leaving tiny rivulets of blood.

As Stewart pulled himself up from where he had landed, he found himself grasped in a powerful front bear hug, with his arms pinned expertly by his sides and his breathing already becoming heavily restricted. As the two men gazed into each other's eyes with unconcealed hatred, Issac bin Abdul Issuin allowed himself the momentary pleasure of tormenting the older man, as he felt some of Stewart's ribs crack under the murderous pressure of the expertly applied crushing hold.

"You fight bravely, for such an old man. But do not let your lucky start fool you as to how this will end. Just like all your friends you will die… so why not just give in, and I will make your ending painless." Sneered Abdul Issuin.

Stewart knew that if he talked he would cause the bear hug to expel more precious air from his lungs so, instead, he let his legs go weak, pretending he was losing consciousness.

The hawk faced assassin grinned wickedly.

"Soon you will be with Hamish and Mario. Ah yes, your friend Mario. My, how he screamed. I never heard a man make so much noise..."

Stewart's body hung limply, very close to the ground, feigning being close to death. Then, just as he sensed overconfidence in his opponent, he made use of his low position to suddenly plant his feet wide and hard on the stone floor and launch both of his hands into the classic chicken head shape of "keitou uchi", with his pointed fingers (washide), striking hard into Abdul Issuin's exposed groin on either side of the genitals, penetrating deep into the nerve and lymph centres at the top of the inner thighs. Then he grabbed his opponent's testicles with his right hand, violently crushing and twisting them, first in a clockwise and then, after a momentary release, initiating a further savage crush and counter clockwise rotation. The combination of strikes into the major pelvic nerve centres, followed by two massive genital traumas, was expertly calculated to induce the most extreme pain signals possible within Abdul Issuin's autonomic and parasympathetic nervous systems.

The noise which emanated from Abdul Issuin's mouth was a deafening mix of a scream and a shout, as the femoral nerve and lumbar plexus generated neurological pain signals that completely overloaded the spinal column and forced an involuntary reflex that released Abdul Issuin's deadly bear hug.

Stewart took full advantage of his freedom by grabbing his attacker's shoulders with both hands and striking the hawk like nose of his stunned opponent with a perfectly executed head butt, that would have achieved universal respect in any run down inner city area.

As Abdul Issuin staggered backwards, with copious blood flowing from his eyes and badly broken nose, Stewart remarked.

"You do not scream badly yourself. I do not hold the death of

Frank Foster against you, that did the world a favour, but over the past months you have destroyed my home, my reputation, kidnapped and tortured two of my friends, and you have murdered two of my associates. I seldom make violence personal, but I am making an exception in your case."

Stewart was bent over double as he spoke, his hands on his thighs, as he tried to re-oxygenate his lungs while trying not to aggravate his broken ribs, all the time carefully watching his opponent struggle to overcome the groin trauma with the use of specialized Goju-Ryu Karate Kote Aite pain absorbing deep breathing techniques, and resetting his badly broken nose by feel alone. Both men were now injured, and watched for the other to make the next move, in what was a very evenly matched close quarter combat between two highly trained professionals.

"They deserved to die, just like all the others I have dealt with in my profession." Issac bin Abdul Issuin snarled, as he spat out copious amounts of blood from his mouth.

"Hand over the tablets, Stewart, and stop delaying the inevitable. We both know you are giving away too many years in this fight, and your traditional 17th century Bushido is no match for the 21st century Krav Maga techniques I was taught by the Bulgarian State Security, Service 7."

Stewart grimaced.

"Ah. The infamous Bulgarian Service 7, the psychopaths who helped create organized crime within much of Eastern Europe, when it was under Soviet control."

Abdul Issuin's hawk like eyes narrowed, as he responded to Stewart's insult.

"If you have heard of us, then you know that our fighting techniques are efficient and deadly, as I am delighted to demonstrate… Tell me, how does your Jujitsu cope with falling down stairs?"

Abdul Issuin launched into a powerful side kick, which forced Stewart to block with the hardened heel of his right hand against the attacking leg's upper shin bone, and then evade by moving backwards onto the descending stairs.

"Already on the lower ground and in retreat." Laughed Abdul Issuin, who then followed up with a lightning fast Krav Maga vertical front kick, aimed at Stewart's midsection, with the clear intent of sending the Scotsman flying backwards down the merciless stone steps.

Stewart responded by turning his body counter clockwise, using his right arm in an elegant scooping motion that diverted the force from the kick, trapping his opponents foot and, with a deep classic Ju-Jitsu circular turn, pulled Abdul Issuin's body high into the air and down the flight of stairs. Abdul Issuin twisted expertly in mid-air, like a cat, to avoid landing on his spine, but as he impacted with the stairs numerous back up weapons, syringes, poisons and a small .22 Derringer pistol became dislodged and cascaded noisily down to the bottom of the stairway.

The moment he made contact with the cold stone, Abdul Issuin extended his arms and legs to try and stop himself falling the entire length of the staircase then, ignoring the pain and bruises on his hands, face and knees, launched into a sweeping kick from his kneeling position, again with the clear intent of sending Tavish Stewart flying down the steps.

This time Stewart was in a superior strategic situation above his attacker and deliberately met the full force of the kick with the hard edge of his Magnum boot, coming down hard on the exact same spot on Abdul Issuin's upper shin where he had struck earlier. As Abdul Issuin pulled himself to his feet, for the first time in the exchange he exhibited tiredness in his normally impassive features. But this show of fatigue was a deception, as he lunged unexpectedly at Stewart in a classic one-two punch combination, which Stewart only just managed to avoid by moving sideways to his left, away from the line of the punch and, using both hands to trap his opponents arm, forced it into an over extension of the elbow joint. Abdul Issuin countered by altering his attack in mid technique and launched into a full body charge which, because of the small distance, neither man could bring to their advantage, and both crashed hard into the stone side wall of the stairway. The impact of the two men caused the walls and ceiling to begin to slowly dislodge, sending much larger fragments of rock and dust tumbling into the confined space.

Stewart's broken ribs sent violent stabbing pains through his diaphragm, making it hard for him to regain his breath and, on pulling himself upright, he noticed three of the fingers on his left hand had become dislocated. After bracing himself against the pain, Stewart pulled them violently back into their joints, and began looking for something to serve as a protection for his left hand. In desperation, he tore lose the long white clerical "dog collar" from his ripped vestments and wrapped it around the digits of his left hand, grasping the fingers around the mass of the cloth, hoping it would at least hold the injured joints in a fixed position, so although he would not be able to use his fingers he could at least deliver blows with the hand.

For his part, Abdul Issuin had quickly pulled himself away to prevent Stewart making use of Ju-Jitsu's fearsome repertoire of ground based holds and locks, but he had also acquired injuries of his own and, feeling inside his mouth, he removed two of the premolars from the left side of his face and spat more blood to the stone floor.

Looking at the two bloody teeth in the palm of his left hand, Issac bin Abdul Issuin exclaimed, "Ayreh Feek!" and decided it was time to end this nonsense. He had no doubt he would eventually win this brutal unarmed contest, but the cost in physical damage to his body was proving too high and he was running out of time. Ad-Dajjal had indicated the Tiamat would disembark, with or without him, at 00.45 HRS and, through the shattered crystal that had been damaged in the recent brutal combat, his Luminox "Maelstrom" watch showed it was already 00.15 HRS.

Reaching behind his back, he drew a wicked twelve-inch-long Damascus steel Bowie knife, that had been hand crafted for him by Master Blade Smith Lin Rhea in his legendary Arkansas workshop. As has been proven numerous times in modern conflict, no matter how advanced weapons systems become, the knife remains the final weapon after everything else fails. Taking in Stewart's injured left hand, half closed right eye, and clear difficulty in breathing, Abdul Issuin began advancing expertly towards the Scotsman, holding the long knife in a classic Sabre grip to maximize the reach advantage of the nine-inch-long razor-sharp clip point blade.

Stewart was perspiring and breathing heavily but, on seeing the hawk faced Abdul Issuin draw the custom Bowie and begin advancing toward him, the Scotsman forced his now tired and pain racked body into a slight forward stance, with his left leg leading and, using his one good hand, he drew his own nine-inch-long one-piece stone dagger from its leather sheath. Holding the weapon in a defensive reverse knife grip in his right hand, the engraved Enochian symbols on the hilt and carved faceting on the blade glinted strangely in the flickering candle light, causing the illusion of a fine beam of light emanating from the downward point of the seven-inch obsidian blade.

Abdul Issuin looked at the pre-historic weapon facing him, and said a sarcastic,

"Really?" Before launching his own deadly blade into a series of three well practiced lunging stabs, aimed at Stewart's knife hand, the injured left hand, and his leading knee. Stewart's obsidian dagger clashed twice with the incoming Bowie blade, successfully blocking two of the stabs, but missing the third that inflicted a glancing blow on his leading leg, which although not serious, caused the Scotsman to edge back.

Abdul Issuin followed up almost immediately, with a blistering series of slashing attacks, that were successfully countered by Stewart's downward defensive blade, but the longer reach of the Bowie was proving difficult for the shorter blade to counter, and several light cuts were in evidence on Stewart's right knife arm, his red blood showing through the slashes in the material of the long sleeve of the priest's cassock.

"First Blood!" Snarled the wild-eyed Abdul Issuin in triumph, as he could see that the older man in front of him was breathing ever more heavily, sweating profusely and now dripping blood over the floor at his feet.

"Throw the tablets at my feet and I will make your death easy…" Lied Abdul Issuin.

"Like Mario you mean… did you use that knife?" Queried the breathless Stewart.

Abdul Issuin smiled cruelly, looking at the expensive custom knife in his hand and, after a pause, he replied.

"No, but I did finish that hound of yours with it... she was brave until she felt the bullets, and then whimpered like a small puppy as I gutted her…"

During the previous knife parries and attacks, Stewart had been carefully observing the technique of his opponent and had noticed he was not defending his mid-section, relying instead entirely on his body armour, so he could focus on attacking without wasting attention on blocking.

As Abdul Issuin relished reliving the gutting of Stewart's beloved dog, Bella, the Scotsman saw he had a clear opening and, for the first time in the entire fight, he initiated an attack. Completely taking the hawk faced Abdul Issuin by surprise, he lunged forward with the primitive obsidian dagger, in a classic stomach thrust, and felt his knife hand impact heavily against Abdul Issuin's military body armour.

Abdul Issuin saw the attack coming, and tried to make a sideways evasion, but found his left leg unexpectedly buckling, as a consequence of the repeated strikes on the tendons beneath the knee made by Stewart earlier in the fight. Unable to evade the stab, his body rocked with the unexpected impact, causing him to lurch back a step, but he nodded dismissively at the stone age blade in Stewarts hand and gestured to his own heavily protective body armour saying,

"Kevlar and Ceramic."

Stewart looked at Abdul Issuin's increasingly blood-soaked midsection and replied.

"Looks more like blood and guts to me..."

If a scientist was to examine the Dagger of Destiny, they would describe its razor-sharp point as a "quantum anomaly", an area where space time was in a constant flux and the classic laws of Newtonian physics were meaningless. Stewart's instinctive knife thrust had pierced through the Maelstrom AR600 composite & ceramic plates like tissue paper, leaving a deep wound that was exposing internal organs and causing substantial arterial blood loss.

The wound trauma rapidly caused the colour to visibly drain from Abdul Issuin's hawk like features, as the blood loss began to force his body into shock. He instinctively staggered backwards and was only saved from a deadly upwards throat stab from Stewart, by a falling marble pillar and masses of debris filling the small stairway.

When the impenetrable dust cloud cleared, Abdul Issuin was gone, just leaving a long trail of blood leading up the stairway, disappearing into the thick clouds of falling masonry and debris. Before Stewart could follow he was intercepted by Kwon who, reassuringly for once, did not look immaculate, being covered in the thick dust that was falling in increasing amounts, as the ice that had formed during the manifestation melted and caused the entire temple structure to slowly disintegrate.

"Wait! Sir Stewart, this whole Northern section is about to collapse. Your time with that man will come again. We must make haste for the city of the Djinn, to catch it's once in a lifetime emergence from the desert sands. Even though we now have the three emerald tablets in our possession, it would be better for humanity if Ad-Dajjal does not get her hands on the fourth."

When Stewart and Kwon eventually arrived back at Mohammed's villa, they discovered that Yusuf, Sek's younger son, had returned with a message that his father and Berat, Yusuf's older brother, had hidden on the Tiamat as it left harbour. They would make contact as soon as they could, but Stewart, O'Neill and Kwon should make all haste to secure the final tablet, as Ad-Dajjal had already dispatched teams of Maelstrom operatives to Mongolia before leaving Istanbul.

As Helen tended to Stewart's numerous injuries, she insisted that she must accompany them to look after the Scotsman, since she felt he was not really in a fit state to travel. For her part, Zahra vowed to remain at the villa and wait, as she put it, for her man to return, but begged that, in spite of his injuries, Stewart should go to the lost city to finish the job, as Mohammed had requested. It was finally agreed that at first light the group would sail the barge out from the Roman cisterns, and begin the long journey to the city of the Djinn.

An exhausted and pain racked Stewart dozed on the layers of thick sail canvas, that formed his bed in the small barge, while the others examined the silver folio up on the roof terrace, and discussed what the strange engravings could mean on the three emerald tablets.

In his sleep, Stewart found himself back in the vivid dream of following the sensuous Nissa Ad-Dajjal through a beautiful woodland to a singularly large fruit tree. Stewart could see now that the distinctive apple tree lay at the centre of an enormous ornamental garden that was full of flowers, trees and animals of every description. The dream was almost identical to the one Stewart had experienced the night before, except for an unexpected and dramatic difference in the ending.

For this time, as Ad-Dajjal reached for the rich green apple, instead of plucking the fruit, a large black serpent, which lay concealed deep in the foliage of the tree, struck with blinding speed. Using its large fangs, it embedded its massive triangular head into the exposed flesh of Ad-Dajjal's shoulder, and then proceeded to coil rapidly and powerfully with its massive dark scaled body round the entire length of her arm, while unseen lengths remained anchored somewhere around the centre of the tree.

The extraordinary rapidity and violence of the serpent's attack continued, as its thick axial musculature rippled visibly and constricted with such force that Nissa's humerus, radius and ulna bones issued three hideous cracks, one after the other, as the enormous snake pulled Ad-Dajjal rapidly and irresistibly ever closer to the tree.

As Ad-Dajjal struggled ineffectually to free herself from the coils of this massive dark serpent, she issued a piercing scream of such ferocity that it shook the entire paradise garden. Stewart woke with a start, noticing that Kwon had joined him in the barge and had been watching him as he slept. The young priest nodded, as an understanding passed between the two men, Stewart finally acknowledging the true nature of the entity residing within the body in front of him. Kwon spoke.

"Understand, Sir Stewart, that on the physical plane, I am constrained to follow the terms of the ancient prophecy, just as Ad-Dajjal must. For all her occult power, she still has to physically gather all four of the emerald tablets in a single place before she can complete the forty ninth invocation. In a similar fashion, I can only operate within the limits of the prophecy, to assist the Knight of the North in preventing Ad-Dajjal from fulfilling her mission of creating a new heaven and earth."

CHAPTER 45 - THE SILK ROUTE

"The maximum specified air speed for a fully laden Boeing 747-400 is Mach 0.92. Exceeding this speed will invalidate your warranty and may seriously damage the aircraft." – Section C - Getting to know your 747 airliner. Boeing Commercial Airplanes (BCA)

39°20'02.2"N 24°48'51.7"E
Aboard the 283m "Tiamat" Migaloo M7 Submersible-Yacht
Aegean Sea, 250 Nautical Miles North East of Athens.
09.00HRS, 12th August, Present Day.

After spending the eight hours since the ship had left Istanbul hiding in the frigid darkness of the Tiamat's meat store, the huge figure of Mohammed Sek emerged slowly and silently, through a white steel and plastic door marked "Forward level 6, Cold Room - Keep Closed".

Finding himself in the much larger general storage area, that was sparsely lit by ceiling mounted red emergency lights, Sek quickly commenced a systematic search, walking quietly and expertly among the rows of tall blue metal storage racking that filled the enormous one hundred and seventy yard long warehouse noting, as he did, the range of goods and the positions of the CCTV cameras.

Finally, once he was satisfied he was alone, he returned the Ruger Magnum revolver he had been cradling in the crook of his left arm back to the Blackhawk horizontal holster, that he had concealed under the left side of his thick red and gold robes.

He then took the razor sharp seven-inch Fairbairn–Sykes double edged blade from his mouth, where he had been carrying it pirate style, carefully putting it back into a custom sheath attached to two thick red cordovan leather ammunition belts, that had been buckled together in order to reach around Sek's massive waist. Each of the sixty belt bullet loops, thirty on each belt, showed considerable strain from being forced to hold the enormous 340 gr Buffalo Bore rounds.

Sek began systematically rubbing his arms, legs and neck to warm his massive frame, while blessing the thermal properties of his traditional thick full length red and gold "Cübbe" Turkish robe. Chuckling as he brushed off the frost that had accumulated on his thick grey beard and hair, he turned and began a good natured vigorous massage and pep talk for his son, Berat, who looked frightened, uncomfortable and very cold. The younger man's fashionable black leather jacket and smaller frame had made him more susceptible to the vicious cold of the refrigerator store and, although he had experience on the streets of Istanbul, he was in no way as comfortable with being an unwelcome stowaway on a hostile ship as his father.

After searching through some of the wooden crates and cardboard boxes, that Sek himself had deliberately damaged during loading, he prepared an impromptu meal for the both of them, of raw eggs, long life milk, crispbread and some wax covered cheeses. Long experience with battlefield foraging had taught Sek that no one was ever surprised to find items missing from boxes that were already damaged so, for short periods, their food consumption would go unnoticed and the extra rations were essential after the hours of frigid conditions.

After they had eaten, the pair explored the row of controls and screens that Sek had located midway along the length of the massive warehouse during his initial exploration. It rapidly became clear from a set of schematic diagrams on the wall that, when the Austrian designers at Migaloo had built the Tiamat, they had created twelve separate small control rooms throughout the massive ship, so the numerous complex systems could be monitored and controlled in case of an emergency. What was more interesting to Sek, was that the owner had clearly overridden some of the safety features of the vessel, by specifying that two enormous spaces in the lower sections of the ship were not to be fitted with the watertight self-sealing bulkheads, that were so conspicuous elsewhere. Father and son were clearly in one of the two unprotected spaces at the front of the ship, the other large bulkhead free region was one level higher and towards the rear. It was not clear from the diagrams the purpose of the rear space, it was simply marked "Temple" but, based on the schematic, not only did it lack bulkhead protection but it also had a long passageway that led to one of the central stairwells. Pulling a small worn leather notebook and steel Waterman propelling pencil from his robes, Sek made some rough calculations, which showed that the two-large bulkhead free zones and long passageway amounted to just over thirty five percent of the ships total volume.

Narrowing his eyes in concentration, Sek then carefully studied the schematic diagrams. Identifying the thinnest sections of the Tiamat's steel double hulls he estimated the location of the weakest structural points within the two bulkhead free spaces, marking them exactly with the lead pencil.

Once Sek had completed his examination of the ship's structural weaknesses, he began exploring the numerous CCTV feeds that he could access from the four large LG 8k display screens on the wall above the consoles.

Surprisingly, most of the massive ship appeared empty of personnel. Evidently the occupation of Istanbul and the surrounding regions had required all available Unity forces. The crew quarters showed row after row of empty bunk beds, with the bedding neatly folded up at the foot of the mattresses. Even the mysterious large space in the lower rear of the ship, labelled "Temple" on the schematic, was in total darkness, the CCTV just showing outlines of a central table and, if the images could be trusted, the walls appeared to be lined with stone frescoes, adding considerably to the mass of the ship. Sek amended some of his rough calculations in light of the increased weight, evidently with considerable satisfaction judging by the wicked smile that crept across his face when he had finished his calculus. In contrast to the rest of the ship, which appeared to be manned by a skeleton crew, the video of the bridge showed three uniformed men, one of whom was clearly the Captain, whilst the other two younger men were so busy with the operation of the vessel that Sek relaxed, since it was unlikely they would be monitoring the other aspects of the ships complex systems, such as an intruder using one of the emergency control consoles.

Eventually, after scanning through over 127 feeds, the screen showed a white 120 feet square "clean" room filled with complex equipment, including state of the art graphics design workstations and a custom built Selective Laser Sintering (SLS) 3d printer, supplied by German manufacturer EOS, which dominated the room.

Mohammed Sek muttered "Maazallah!" as he saw the dark haired Nissa Ad-Dajjal, who was dressed in an exquisitely cut white silk trouser suit that was probably Chanel or Dior. She was standing facing away from the CCTV camera, with her hands on her shapely hips, looking at a 3d rendering on a sixty-inch 8K LG wall mounted display of curious letters that had been deeply etched into three separate large green stone surfaces. After a moment, Sek recognized with a sinking feeling that the images were a series of high definition renderings of the emerald tablets, meaning that Nissa Ad-Dajjal was only one tablet away from being able to complete her insane ceremony to bring about the end of the world. Noting his father's clear interest in the scene that was being displayed, Berat explored some of the console settings and suddenly they could hear as well as see what was happening.

"Idiots! Why am I surrounded by such worthless fools?!" Ad-Dajjal snarled in clear frustration, as she picked up three four-inch-long green objects from beside her and hurled them at the group of technicians, who were cowering behind the computers and complex EOS SLS 3d printer.

The most senior of the technicians, a serious looking man in his forties with short cropped hair and wire rimmed glasses, tried to appease Nissa Ad-Dajjal.

"Domina, I assure you these are perfect renditions of the objects you photographed, down to two microns and printed on synthetic emerald. I know you have been up all night attempting to use these replicas in the ship's Temple, but maybe there is something else about the original objects that empowers them?"

Ad-Dajjal dismissed his comments with a curt,

"Obviously!" And stormed from the room.

With some hurried coordination between father and son in the warehouse control room the CCTV feed followed the dark-haired woman, as she strode purposefully on a pair of towering black Jimmy Choo stiletto heels down a long undecorated white corridor, entered the gleaming chrome and brushed steel bridge of the massive ship, and demanded,

"I hope for your sake, you have some good news about him?" Addressing a clearly terrified salt haired man, that Sek had already identified as the ship's Captain. He bowed his head as he responded.

"Domina, they found him unconscious from loss of blood outside the Hagia Sophia during the evacuation. He was taken to the Maelstrom field hospital at Istanbul Airport, from where he was airlifted to the HUG University Hospital, Geneva. Overnight he has been treated by Professor Dr Stefan Zuch, the HUG's leading specialist on wound trauma. We have been informed that Zuch has performed surgery to remove shards of Kevlar that had penetrated a deep abdominal wound, replaced lost fluids with a massive transfusion and closed the wound. However, Professor Zuch recommends at least eight weeks rest."

"Impossible! "Ad-Dajjal retorted, unconsciously adjusting her long hair with her left hand, exposing her once beautiful complexion, which was now so withered into a skeletal form that it caused Berat to gasp with shock.

"He must be ready to return to Istanbul by 18:00 HRS, to lead the elite Maelstrom teams and catch Stewart with the real tablets, before they reach the ancient city. I expect you to personally coordinate the mission. I do not care what it costs, or what manpower needs to be reallocated. The best operatives must be sent, with the best equipment and logistics support. These two teams must reach the Gobi region within..."

She paused to consult her magnificent solid gold Rolex GMT Master II Chronometer.

".. thirty-four hours, or everything we have worked for will be lost!"

With that Ad-Dajjal sat expectantly in the Captain's chair with her arms folded and her long legs crossed, clearly waiting for her instructions to be obeyed immediately.

Having seen enough to know the current plans of his enemy, Sek turned off the CCTV feed, and instructed his son to explore what methods were available to transmit an undetected signal from the Tiamat. While Berat worked systematically through the digital user manuals, his father searched the inventory of the ship's stores and, finding what he was looking for, walked carefully back through the rows of tall racking, only to return a few minutes later with four dust covered disks, each roughly three inches thick and ten inches in diameter. They were evidently quite heavy, since Sek could only carry two under each of his powerful arms. Torn and stained cardboard sleeves around the mysterious objects were labelled "EPR 6.5", with a company address in Bari, Italy for "Tecnovar Italiana S.p.A".

Smiling at his son, he said.

"Keep at it. I am just going to distribute some gifts for our hosts. If I am not back in half an hour, download as much information as you can about the activities and plans of these murderous bastards and get off the ship. OK?"

With that Sek walked quietly to the warehouse entrance and, after carefully checking the corridor, stepped out and closed the large metal door behind him.

Tavish Stewart had woken on his makeshift folded canvas bed in the barge feeling stiff, sore and with almost every part of his body showing signs of cuts and bruising. Even his indestructible Casio GShock had suffered badly in the terrible fight of the previous night, its thick black plastic cover was ripped from its metal case in several places and the large LCD display was cracked, so it now only showed sections of the date and time.

Before joining the others for a breakfast of scrambled eggs on toast with a mug of strong Turkish coffee, Stewart had stripped off what remained of O'Neill's clerical vestments and dived naked into the bracing cold waters of the Roman cistern, completing some brisk lengths of the 330 foot long underground reservoir, before thoroughly washing and shaving with a bar of Wright's coal tar soap and one of Berat's safety razors, thoughtfully provided by Zahra the night before.

Dressing in a plain white cotton T shirt, Levi denim jeans and a worn black leather jacket, kindly donated from the collective wardrobes of Mohammed's son's, Stewart put on his own black Magnum boots, before stiffly climbing the flights of stairs to the roof terrace for breakfast, and to get an update on world events.

Overnight, so Zahra informed them, while she poured thick Turkish coffee into everyone's cups, more and more of the world's population had voluntarily converted to the Unity cause, in return for the vaccine. Where people had surrendered their belongings and their previous existence, in order to be transported to the Unity gathering south of Jerusalem, there had been a loss of critical workers and expertise. Factories and shops had been forced to close, and emergency and essential services had become so unreliable that people had given up and chose to join Unity, not just for the vaccine, but increasingly for security, food, clothing and accommodation.

In the coalition nations that had forbidden the use of Ad-Dajjal's vaccine, the death toll from the "Red Death" was unprecedented in recorded history. Cities, transport networks and even hospitals were deserted for fear of the contagion. All the world's smaller nations had now aligned firmly with Unity, against the remaining coalition members.

The narrow-split hopper barge's old diesel engines complained bitterly at being started, after resting for so many days beneath Sek's villa but, after belching clouds of thick smoke that filled the entire underground cistern, they eventually fell into a constant rumbling vibration that became almost comforting, as the old boat worked its way from beneath the network of Roman cisterns through four locks and out into the comparatively fresh air of Istanbul harbour. The sea outside was filled with coalition warships and a mass of smaller boats, ferrying desperate people both ways across the straits but, no matter how hard they looked, there was no sign of the 900 foot long blue grey Tiamat.

Stewart merged their narrow barge smoothly into the flow of large and small vessels, all heading north through the Bosphorus straits. From his expressions, as he steered the helm, it was clear that he was in pain, but he refused to take anything that might dull his senses or reflexes. His only reluctant concession to his injuries was in allowing Curren to wrap some bandages around his left hand.

As the morning progressed and the chugging barge continued its slow progress, Fr Chin Kwon became increasingly agitated, insisting that they must find some faster transportation or risk missing the single day and night associated with the one-hundred-and-twenty-year re-emergence of the ancient city, that would occur at the next full moon in three days' time, in the mountains of the Gobi Desert over 3100 miles away. Just as O'Neill was suggesting they commandeer one of the numerous hydrofoil ferries that were speeding past them, Stewart passed under an ultra-modern concrete and steel suspension bridge that spanned the entire width of the Bosphorus, and guided the slow-moving grey barge into a small harbour set into the Eastern (starboard) side of the Bosphorus straits, which O'Neill quickly identified from their map as "Poyrazkoy". It was a tiny settlement with small shops and single storey homes, all constructed from the same white concrete, gathered around the tiny inlet.

At the end of the long concrete jetty that enclosed the Northern section of the harbour, stood a battleship grey "Merlin"

Agusta/Westland AW101 helicopter, with large British Royal Navy markings. As they approached, chugging slowly along the 1000 foot long quay, Stewart could see that the soldiers from Three Commando Brigade of the Royal Marines had set up six light machine guns and four RPGs overlooking the straits, to defend against anti coalition forces.

After docking, Stewart walked slowly towards the guns, only to find that all twelve of the British troops were dead, clearly having administered themselves with the coalition "Red Death" vaccine. As Curren, O'Neill and Kwon joined him, Stewart pulled two bodies from the open hold of the transport helicopter, entered the cockpit and powered up the aircraft systems to check the fuel levels. Satisfied with what he saw, he briefly surveyed the cargo hold and began coordinating the task of minimizing weight by removing every non-essential item from the sixty-foot-long Merlin HM1 Navy helicopter. As a final act, Stewart and O'Neill dragged the ten dead British soldiers together and, after a short prayer, poured kerosene over the bodies and set fire to them, leaving their dog tags hanging from a makeshift wooden cross.

Less than an hour later they were airborne, flying low at nearly 170 miles per hour, in a North Easterly direction over the Black Sea towards Russia, where they would hopefully stand a better chance of avoiding the search, that Maelstrom would have almost certainly started, for the emerald tablets that were hanging round Stewart's neck. None of them were surprised when Kwon volunteered that he could pilot a helicopter, and so for the next five hours Stewart and the young priest took turns flying. The further they got from Istanbul, the fewer ships and aircraft they encountered, until after three hours they were completely alone, flying over endless sparkling waters. O'Neill and Curren sat strapped in bucket seats in the large rear cargo area, wrapped in thick black thermal blankets, while Kwon and Stewart alternated between resting and piloting the large transport helicopter over the rushing waves of the Black Sea. As the Merlin's fuel empty light went from flickering to a steady red, Stewart begin trying to get landing approval from air traffic control at Gelendzhik airport on the Russian Black Sea coast, but there was no response, only an ominous static. How the Royal Navy HM1 remained in the air during the final minutes of their approach towards the very long runway, was a mystery. Still without receiving any radio contact, they landed the Merlin beside a small deserted single storey prefabricated terminal building, whereupon the engine promptly cut out, leaving only the sound of the hot engines clicking as they cooled, and gusts of wind blowing across the silent airfield.

Leaving the others standing beside the silent helicopter in the late afternoon sun, Stewart entered the terminal buildings, only to find them deserted save for the badly decaying bodies of tourists and a few staff members. Birds and other animals had already begun the grizzly task of consuming what remained, and the silence was only broken by the terminal doors slamming back and forth, as the wind gusted from the ocean a few hundred yards away. The story was the same in the control tower, bodies lying where they had fallen, as if in a scene from a horror movie.

After twenty minutes, a grim looking Stewart returned to the group carrying a red plastic "Rossiya - Russian Airlines" clipboard, marked on the back with the text "Boeing 747-446 EI-XLD Serial #: 26360", and gestured for Curren, O'Neill and Kwon to follow him, as he led them out to a mass of parked passenger aircraft of different shapes and sizes, all covered in colourful logos and Cyrillic text.

Passing beyond the lines of aircraft, Stewart strode towards the distinctive shape of a 230-foot-long Boeing 747-400 at the far end of the airfield, with extraordinary red livery on the rear two thirds of the aircraft and a realistic rendering of a Siberian tiger's face (promoting their conservation), painted on the front. The giant tiger painting caused Curren and O'Neill to exchange glances, as they remembered and remarked that some versions of the emerald tablet prophecy foretold that the Knight, Devil and Priest of Rome would ride to the ends of the earth on a tiger.

Kwon chose simply to focus on more practical considerations.

"It is an excellent choice. One of the fastest civil aircraft, and with a range of over 6,000 miles"

"8,300 miles when fully fuelled, like this one is supposed to be." Replied Stewart, as he checked the details on the Rossiya clip board, climbed up the boarding steps, turned left and almost immediately began to complain at the complexity of the cockpit controls, claiming loudly that they made the space shuttle look simple.

At another airport, 621 miles to the West, a group of ten large muscular men dressed in Maelstrom commando uniforms were gathered next to a dark grey unmarked 150 feet long Airbus A400M Atlas four-engine turboprop military transport aircraft. The massive transport plane had been configured to carry fifteen personnel, along with two Oshkosh Defense Light Combat Tactical All-Terrain Vehicles (L-ATVs), six Kawasaki KLR 650 expedition motorcycles, and enough high-tech weaponry to overthrow a small nation.

The ten men were literally the cream of the elite world of special forces, headhunted from their various military units within the coalition nations, at short notice. Many of them had worked with each other before and exchanged stories of wives, girlfriends and recent operations. Others, who were less socially inclined, checked their personal inventories of GPS, ABCs, guns and knives, while covertly weighing each other up, and wondering which man they could rely upon in the critical situations that would no doubt lie ahead. Three of these exceptional men stood out from the others, a massive six-foot five-inch Japanese commando with a deep scar down his left cheek, named Suzuki, a six-foot bald-headed tobacco chewing US Army Ranger with a thick moustache, called Duke, and a five-foot six-inch blond haired Australian SAS officer, who everyone knew as "Croc". Each was used to leading their respective units, and they were collectively struggling to understand why they were being assigned a unit commander who, by all reports, not only had no special forces experience but was also seriously injured.

As time progressed well beyond the planned mission departure time, the three men began to comment negatively and pointedly look at the Suunto timepieces they had been issued specifically for this mission, at the same time as they were given their Scorpion W2 Desert Sand 500 pixelated camouflage uniforms and Dragon Skin Extreme silicon carbide ceramic body armour.

Their impatient waiting ended when a black Bell Boeing V-22 Osprey tiltrotor military aircraft came into land vertically, settling down within twenty yards of the airbus transport aircraft, its revolutionary design allowing the seventy-million-dollar plane to convert in mid-air from a seemingly conventional twin propeller aircraft, with a 300 mph cruising speed, into a twin rotor helicopter capable of vertical take offs and landings.

Within three minutes of touchdown, the front swing door to this unique aircraft opened, and a tall lean man descended, very slowly, down the short steps to the tarmac, his distinctive hawk like features hidden behind large mirrored Jawbreaker HALO wrap-around Oakley sunglasses, which only partially obscured the severe swelling and dark bruising that disfigured his eyes and long hooked nose. His left leg was clearly still suffering from the repeated strikes delivered by Stewart on the patella tendons, as he walked with a pronounced limp, and his left hand clutched what must have been an exceptionally painful abdominal wound. The ten men regarded their new leader with a mix of apprehension and repugnance. When Abdul Issuin stumbled on an uneven patch of the tarmac, Duke and Croc took pity on him and assisted him up the rear loading ramp seating him in one of the bucket seats in the rear of the Airbus Atlas. Thirty minutes later, all other air traffic from the busy Istanbul Atatürk International airport was suspended, giving the 81,000-pound military transport priority, as it soared East at nearly 500 mph into the cloudless sky.

Even with Kwon's innate aeronautical skills, it took nearly an hour of drill like practice with six-large red plastic A4 ring binder "Rossiya" manuals, that they had found stored in the left side cockpit locker, before Stewart, Kwon, O'Neill and Curren felt comfortable with the mass of confusing switches, dials and sliders that Boeing had seen fit to cram onto every available surface on the Jumbo's flight deck. This was followed by two aborted take-off attempts, before Stewart finally successfully coaxed the nineteen-year-old Russian airliner up from the long Gelendzhik airstrip, out over the Black Sea, which shimmered in the rays of the setting sun, and turned the 440,000-pound jetliner around 170 degrees to head South, South East, towards the pitch-black night sky and Southern Mongolia.

Stewart quickly discovered that the weight of the full fuel tanks meant that they could not rise above 35,000 feet and, without any air traffic control guidance, it was decided that Curren and O'Neill should take turns to keep a constant watch on the plane's close proximity radar, in case there was any other air traffic. All four friends remained crammed into the small cockpit and worked together to manage the confusing array of indicators and controls. They jointly decided to keep the airspeed steady at around 370 mph, so they could cope with any unexpected events, and it was only after three hours without spotting any other planes or raising anyone on the cockpit radio that they relaxed enough to consider using the autopilot, rising to the plane's cruising altitude of 45,000 feet and keeping their leisurely but safe speed of 370 mph.

Once the big plane was flying itself through the pitch-black night sky, they focused as a group on trying to determine a location on the onboard navigation system map that could match the image that was projected dimly onto the cockpit cabin door, by shining the aircraft's emergency torch directly into Marco Polo's mirror. The challenge, they discovered, was that the ancient map image was so indistinct, and the modern digital images were so detailed, that numerous possible sites looked like they could be the location indicated by Polo's map. Eventually, after hours of debate and discussion, they decided on a scientific approach recommended by O'Neill from his archaeological surveys, looking for the nearest match for seven distinct typographical features they could identify on the Mirror map, that also occurred on the landscape of the Gobi Desert.

The best fit was a steep pass called Chötgör Shatny (Devils Stairs), that led from a glacial gorge shown on the navigation map as Yolyn Am or Valley of the Vultures, in the remote Gurvan Saikhan Mountains of Southern Mongolia. After setting the GPS coordinates (N43 32.980 E104 02.087) into the Boeing navigation system they took shifts to pass the night, two resting, while the two who remained on watch nervously monitored the flight navigation display, as it showed them gradually approaching the small seven featured valley in the long 10,000 feet high mountain range.

Dawn rose over ice covered mountains in the distance that sat on a massive plain of emptiness, that was the Gobi Desert. Seams of quartz and mica sparkled like diamonds beneath them, as the huge aircraft set itself into an automated holding pattern at 8,000 feet above the rocky desert floor far below. While the massive four engine jet steered itself gently round and round in an endless 25 mile wide circuit, Stewart, Kwon, O'Neill and Curren searched the areas beneath their flight path and cross checked it with the onboard navigation system, trying to identify the best place to put down, as there were no suitable landing sites indicated on the displays or visible on the ground.

They became so engrossed in this task that they missed a small blip on the close proximity radar, that gradually grew larger as it approached closer and closer, until finally they were startled when the massive 747 started shaking violently in a rattle of sudden impacts that could only be small weapons fire. Looking from their starboard windows, they saw a large unmarked grey four propeller military transport plane with its rear bay doors open, and a group of uniformed men, all standing on the lowered cargo access ramp, directing fully automatic fire towards the unarmed Jumbo jet.

As the Maelstrom commandos continued to shoot at them, numerous windows shattered down the left side of the empty passenger compartments of the 747 and the constant rattling noise from the numerous bullet impacts started to be lost in the roar of pressurized air leaving the plane. It was clearly only a matter of moments before the bullets would find some critical system, and they would plummet helplessly to certain death on the rock covered desert beneath them.

Curren began crying, and looked desperately at Stewart, hoping he would think of some solution. Stewart's eyes narrowed as he looked at the Maelstrom Airbus Atlas flying some 4000 feet away from them, noticing that the open rear loading bay was clearly causing the transport plane some stability problems. As Stewart climbed into the pilot's seat and buckled himself tightly in, he turned to Kwon and asked innocently.

"How fast did you say this thing could go?"

Kwon looked slowly from Stewart, to the wobbling military transport, and then back to the Scotsman, with a smile.

"Well, theoretically I suppose, a 747 could break the sound barrier... but I don't think anyone ever has..."

Stewart returned Kwon's smile.

"And what kind of sonic disturbance would a 230 foot long object weighing 440,000 pounds cause?"

"The biggest one you ever saw..." Laughed Kwon.

Curren and O'Neill looked at other with a mix of terror and excitement, as they buckled themselves into the rear facing flight attendants' seats, while Kwon strapped himself firmly in beside Stewart, as the Scotsman opened the four slide thrusters and took the massive 747 into a combat turn and climb, more fitting for an F-16 fighter, rising 10,000 feet, before directing the Tiger faced nose of the Jumbo back towards the Airbus Atlas, that was now below and in front of them. As they descended, Stewart opened the four Rolls-Royce RB211 engines to each deliver their full 60,000-foot pounds of force, and Kwon began to shout out the speed readings from the dash.

"Mach 0.9… 0.92… 0.95… 0.97…"

The ancient Jumbo began to shudder, as if they were riding over railway sleepers. The noise became so loud, Curren covered her ears and missed Kwon continuing the readings.

"0. 98.. 0.988… 0.994… 0. 999.."

the counting was drowned out completely by an enormous bang, which shook the aircraft and felt like they had flown through a brick wall.

Back on board the Airbus Atlas, the three pilots in the cockpit were laughing at the sight of the ancient 747 behaving like a fighter jet, banking and climbing at extreme Gs, and then turning and displaying what looked like a gigantic Siberian Tiger diving straight towards them, in what was clearly an airborne game of "chicken". Their laughter was cut short by the hawk faced leader of the commandos they were transporting, bursting into the cockpit shouting furiously.

"Idiots! He is not bluffing. Close the rear doors and dive…"

But the warning was too late.

Tavish Stewart did not intend to actually hit the Airbus Atlas, but his lack of flying hours and injured left hand, meant he brought the two aircraft closer than even he would have desired.

The massive sonic shock wave from the 747-400, ripped off the tail, three of the four propellers, and blew out the reinforced cockpit windows of the Airbus. The entire contents of the transport hold were instantly thrown backwards out of the open load doors, including the ten elite Maelstrom commandos. The men and equipment could be seen plummeting down to the ground some 8,000 feet below, with the severely damaged transport plane following rapidly down behind them in a cloud of smoke, before disappearing behind one of the nearby dunes with a thunderous explosion. In the trail of smoke left by the Airbus, four military parachutes could be seen to have opened.

Breaking the sound barrier had also inflicted serious damage to the ancient 747-400, which screamed down to meet the merciless desert floor of rock and quartz, that lay just beneath the peaks of the Gurvan Saikhan mountains.

CHAPTER 46 - TYPHON: FATHER OF THE WINDS

"No matter the might of your armies, the thickness of your walls or the knowledge that fills your libraries... everything will be swept away in the blink of an eye by the Father of the Winds." - Mongolian Legends of the Gobi.

Victoria Embankment Gardens
Villiers St, London, WC2N 6NS, UK
10.00HRS, 13th August, Present Day.

It was one of those typical grey overcast days that often interrupt an otherwise glorious British summer. Thick brooding clouds obscured the sunlight, enough to make the whole of the capital take on a miserable hue, but never delivered the wonderful release provided by a true downpour. A light drizzle, that had been floating in the air since dawn, had prompted those who remained in the city to don raincoats and hide under black umbrellas as they hurried about their business, bravely ignoring the "Red Death" as their great grandparents had the Luftwaffe.

A classic London Taxi Company TX4 black cab, adorned with posters for The Lion King complete with additional small stickers announcing "private virus filtered boxes now available", drove along Whitehall Place and pulled up next to the Embankment underground station. A beautiful woman, with the gym honed figure of a professional athlete, emerged from the rear left-hand door of the cab, wearing a light blue surgical mask which, when combined with her tinted Dior cat's-eye sunglasses, obscured her face to such an extent as to make her unrecognizable. Walking from the TX4 cab she looked up at the grey sky, with its countless droplets of fine rain, and effortlessly took in the locations of four CCTV cameras as she joined a throng of people entering the tube station, each person showing, as was now the fashion, their style and status with a bewildering range of branded anti-viral protective masks and gloves.

After allowing herself to be swept along by the mass of hurrying people, the elegant woman swiped her Blackberry phone at the

Transport for London (TfL) turnstile, releasing the gates, but then sidestepped, apologizing to the young man directly behind her, who was wearing an Apple iMask, saying she had forgotten something. After allowing the man to pass through to the trains, she backtracked to the crowded entrance, pushing against the oncoming people, all the while looking carefully at the convex ceiling mirrors, checking that she was not being followed and that she was the only person going the “wrong” way. Once back out on the soaked pavement she kept close to the walls, avoiding the CCTV cameras, and made her way down to the North side of the Thames Embankment, near the Palace of Westminster.

Dame Cynthia Sinclair finally conceded to the fine drizzle by covering her head with a silk Hermes scarf, that toned perfectly with her Ralph Lauren dark pinstripe business jacket and matching pencil skirt, that could be seen beneath her Christopher Kane Leopard-print transparent raincoat. As her Gucci, black kitten heels clicked confidently on the wet pavement, she walked past a figure standing next to a lamppost on the busy A3211. The man was dressed in a Burberry honey coloured Westminster Long Heritage Trench Coat, similar to that made famous by Bogart in Casablanca, the top part of his body hidden behind an opened copy of the broadsheet version of The Telegraph, which proclaimed the collapse of the Stock Market under the headline “The end of Capitalism?”, and a secondary feature headed “New Pope – can he save the Christian Faith?”, which ran alongside a quarter page feature for Prada anti-viral wipes.

The large newspaper moved, to reveal Jeffery Sonnet, his eyes hidden behind lightly tinted black rimed Hugo Boss sunglasses, clearly loving every moment of working “cloak and dagger” again with his old boss Sinclair. Under his careful gaze, Cynthia Sinclair walked from the wet pavements of the busy A3211 into Victoria embankment gardens and stood in front of the bandstand, its famous flag shape awning hanging in front, today acting to block the fine drizzle instead of the blazing sun.

On stage, the Band of the Grenadier Guards from the nearby Wellington Barracks, played Irving Berlin’s 1936 hit "Let's Face the Music and Dance". Appreciating the synchronicity of Sonnet’s old regiment playing “There may be trouble ahead…”, Sinclair settled into the centre position on a long wooden bench to the right of the bandstand, crossing her shapely long legs momentarily to check that she had easy access to a hidden femme fatale thigh holster and its tiny five-inch polymer eight round 9mm Beretta Nano. Finally, she checked the time on her gold Cartier Tank watch.

Shortly afterwards, a six-foot-tall lean man, in a long classic grey Aquascutum raincoat, matching Gladwin Bond Fedora Trilby Hat and Ray-Ban Wayfarer Classic sunglasses, came and sat next to Sinclair on her right side, saying,

"Dame Sinclair."

"Director Pimms."

Cynthia nodded in approval,

"Glad to see you could dress appropriately for the occasion."

Pimms responded with his famous dry New England humour,

"Clandestine meetings between Intelligence Services Heads in London, traditionally do have a strict dress code." He continued,

"Unorthodox invitation by the way... you were lucky we still check the 1960s dead letter drops."

"I check that you check..."

Pimms smiled.

"Quite. Last time it was used your predecessor was telling my predecessor about Kim Philby. 1963."

He noted Jeffery Sonnet guarding them.

"We even have a Harry Palmer. I thought he had quit. Joined Stewart's antique business."

Cynthia regarded Sonnet, as he slowly advanced unseen towards another man, who was giving their meeting an unwelcome amount of attention, and responded,

"He is helping out with a spot of bother."

"From what I recall, he was rather good at that." Said Pimms, clearly intending some considerable understatement.

Some sixty feet away, Jeffery Sonnet had used the alternative park entrance to silently come alongside a familiar face, who was wearing Polaroid aviator sunglasses and a new Jasper Conran navy rain coat. Reaching his target, Sonnet pushed his 9mm Walther Police Pistol Quick (PPQ) M2 into the man's ribs, with the newspaper concealing the barrel, as he said.

"Colonel Lev Averbuch Bachrach of the State Security Agency of the Republic of Belarus… Fancy seeing you here."

Surprisingly, Lev looked genuinely pleased.

"Jeffery, what a pleasant surprise."

Sonnet reached into Lev's coat, and pulled out a heavy black metal 12 round Russian made .380 ACP Makarov PMM pistol.

"Still carrying these big old monsters? I thought you had all moved on to the Yarygin MP-443 "Grach" pistol?"

Lev grunted, "The Grach is such an ugly thing. I cannot bring myself to use it."

Sonnet nodded sympathetically, and nudging the Russian in the ribs with the concealed Walther PPQ said.

"Let's face the music..."

As both men approached the bench, it was evidently to the discomfort of the CIA Director.

"How the hell is he here?"

Sinclair raised an eyebrow. "He checks the same dead letter drops as you, my dear."

"And you knew?" Asked Pimms in disbelief.

"I was counting on it. And that it would intrigue Moscow enough to send him."

Jefferey Sonnet deposited Lev on the left side of Sinclair, who responded with a cheery,

"Well, isn't this cosy?"

As she nodded to Sonnet, who opened his worn tan leather Union briefcase and passed folded copies of the Telegraph to both men. Hidden inside each newspaper was an iPad mini with headphones.

Pimms became incredulous.

"You are sharing intelligence with the enemy?"

Sinclair responded coldly,

"Sometimes enemies are more reliable than friends."

With that the CIA Director and Head of Russian Intelligence, Europe, plugged the left earphone in, leaving their other ear with access to the real world, and viewed two video clips. The first segment showed video and audio evidence of Nissa Ad-Dajjal's role in the Remote Telemetry attack on the US Zumwalt class warship, and Unity's role in deliberately altering the US vaccine stocks so they contained live strains of the Red Death virus. The second series of clips showed Ad-Dajjal detailing, to an unknown third party, how Unity had, over a number of years, convinced wealthy countries of the supposed economic necessity of outsourcing their intelligence and national security to Maelstrom, with the ultimate goal of having the elected leaders so frightened by a manufactured threat that they would willingly allow themselves to be held in protective custody in underground bunkers, as Maelstrom assumed executive control for Ad-Dajjal. The last sections of the playback showed this final stage had been reached, the leaders of the developed countries were now voluntarily incarcerated by their nation's own elite forces, who were, in turn, now under the direct command of Maelstrom.

Director Pimms was the first to finish viewing the materials. Pulling the earpiece from his iPad he queried.

"Where did these come from?"

Lev was noticeably silent, as Sinclair answered,

"Broadcast from a Zephyr communications UAV above the Aegean Sea. Registered to Unity. The assumption is that someone was broadcasting from the Tiamat, Unity's floating HQ."

Sinclair then informed both agency heads that she had confirmed independently that the new British PM, Mrs Susan Merriweather, was currently under Maelstrom control at a bunker in Berkshire, with no communication possible. She added that she was no longer sure of her own people, which was why she had called this off the record meeting.

Pimms thought for a moment about the damming evidence he had just seen, and Sinclair's admission. He then reluctantly confirmed that outsourcing had led to the same situation in the US, where every critical executive operation was under the control of Maelstrom, even US special forces units now wore the whirlpool badge. The CIA Director concluded by admitting he too was isolated, and unable to know who to trust, just like Sinclair.

Lev remained silent. Unlike the Western nations, Russia had not outsourced their services, their leaders were always too paranoid about surrendering control. Finally, he stated,

"This Ad-Dajjal woman needs to be dealt with, and it pains me to admit it, but we need the Western leaders freed. Russia is too decimated by the Plague to act alone."

Director Pimms grimaced.

"It will not be easy. President Jones and the heads of the US military forces are all being held in the Cheyenne Mountain Complex, a military installation and nuclear bunker located in Colorado Springs. What is worse, is that the installation's 721st SFS Force protection (FP) has been augmented with a few hundred men from all divisions of the US special forces, Delta, Rangers, Seals, the best of the best, under the control of Maelstrom."

Lev smiled.

"Your American SF will be fiercely loyal to your nation, and, if faced with clear evidence that they have been misled by Maelstrom into imprisoning their Commander in Chief, they will most certainly release him. Therefore, we must disseminate these two videos far and wide so everyone learns the truth about Ad-Dajjal. Let me take this," the Russian indicated the iPad mini in his hand, "And let some of our Black Wolf hackers distribute these videos over social media."

It was hard to disagree with such a clearly logical solution from the Russian chess master, but they still needed to convince everyone that these videos were not just another fake news item. As they discussed the problem, they realized they had to have a figure in a position of moral authority, a world leader who would be listened to long enough to lend credibility to the evidence broadcast from the Tiamat. Looking at the headlines on the front of the two folded newspapers, Sonnet smiled as he indicated that he knew someone who owed him a favour.

As Director Pimms headed to Nine Elms Lane, Colonel Bachrach stood, aiming to return to his Embassy in Kensington Palace Gardens, when Sinclair put her hand on his arm saying "Lev, before you go… I have a favour to ask..." The Russian sat back down on the bench and listened.

As far as airline crashes go, it would not even have made the top 1000 on YouTube. The truth is that modern airliners, even twenty-year-old ones with Tigers painted on their nose, have been designed and engineered to endure exceptionally harsh landings. After a terrifying ninety second descent, where Stewart and Kwon wrestled with the yoke trying to escape from their high-speed nose dive, the Rossiya Boeing 747-446 levelled out just moments before it ploughed a massive six and a half feet deep, six-mile-long gouge into the flat rock-strewn desert floor, eventually coming to an abrupt stop, that left a towering two-mile-high dust cloud. The sudden silence after such violent shuddering, creaking and crunching, interspersed with numerous electronic alarms and announcements, warning them to "Slow Down", "Pull Up…" and finally "Brace!", felt unreal. The four of them sat stunned in their seats for some minutes, before Stewart asked,

"Everyone ok?" and began smiling, as he heard Curren complaining that this was his most expensive write off to date. He unclipped himself from the pilot's seat and stiffly walked around to check on everyone. Curren and O'Neill had fared well, being strapped in their backwards facing crew seats and, as expected, Fr Chin Kwon looked like he could have been attending an embassy party. Stewart asked Curren and O'Neill to work out how to open the side emergency exit slider, while he returned to the cockpit and searched inside the pilot's lockers for any items that might prove useful, eventually emerging with a pistol sized yellow tube marked along its edge as a three round "Pains Wessex Compact Distress Signal" flare launcher.

Exiting the aircraft, with the flare gun clutched to his chest beside the obsidian dagger and silver folio, Stewart came down the orange inflatable slide feet first, only to find himself beside a startled O'Neill and Curren, who were looking directly towards a group of four Mongol nomads dressed in thick furs, carrying old AK47s and curved long bladed swords. As Stewart looked closer, he could see that the men's animal hide robes were decorated with embroidered patterns of strange birds, silk tassels, mirrors, feathers and copper discs. Their heads were covered with pointed felt caps, that had been made to look like the antlers of a reindeer, and their fur boots had iron soles, that could be for providing grip on icy surfaces or perhaps for some unknown mystical ritual.

Just as Stewart was wondering how many of the four he could down with the Ruger Magnum pistol, Fr Kwon arrived down the 747's orange escape slide, and the fearsome looking Nomads collectively fell to their knees.

"It appears they were expecting you. Anything else you would care to share with us?" Said a clearly suspicious O'Neill.

Kwon ignored O'Neill and instead walked towards the four kneeling men, raising them to their feet and embracing each of them, before turning to Stewart.

"Our new friends are Sky Spirit Priests. Tengerism is the traditional

Mongol shamanic religion. They will act as guides in our journey to the city. Their leader is called Hujk." Kwon indicated a fit looking forty-year-old with a red felt cap and a noticeable lack of front teeth.

After a tentative series of introductions, where the shamans were clearly impressed with Stewart's knighthood and speculated how well he could ride or wrestle, the group set off towards the high mountain that filled the skyline before them. The four men carried a set of supplies and, with their old-fashioned kerosene lamps and hemp ropes, looked as if they were part of a 1920s Himalayan expedition. As they walked, Kwon engaged in an ongoing commentary, explaining these Shamans were guardians of the Gurvan Saikhan mountain, site of the citadel of the Djinn, and their families assisted each generation's seekers, who attempted to take advantage of the 120-year exposure of the ancient site.

The desert floor proved to be rough going, being made of rocks and blocks of quartz and mica. It may have looked like a giant smooth flat mirror from a distance, but up close it was a challenge for walking, needing constant vigilance to avoid injury from tripping over the sharp uneven surface. The mountain, which had looked so near when they started their trek, proved to be much further away, and three hours of steady walking left them with the 10,000 foot high peak still looking like it was only minutes away, but in reality, they were not significantly closer. As the sun began to cast shadows from the larger rocks on the flat desert floor, Kwon became increasingly agitated that they should pick up the pace, his mood not being improved when Stewart and Curren's GShocks began beeping with a warning of a massive pressure drop detected by their watch's barometers.

Two further hours of hard walking later, they began their climb into the foothills of the Gurvan Saikhan mountain range. The rocky ground transformed into low scrub, with the odd withered tree clinging to life, and they began to hear the sounds of running water, from mountain streams fed from glacial ice melting in the peaks towering high above them.

Passing a small reed filled pool, O'Neill began to tell Curren about one of the more colourful legends of the Gobi, the Olgoi Chorchoi or Mongolian Death Worm. Kwon translated what O'Neill was saying to the four Shaman, and they listened with increasing reactions of good natured humour.

O'Neill told of a ten-foot-long monster worm, that hid in the sands, looking like a super-sized lamprey. Weighing up to one thousand pounds, it could rise up from the desert, fire an electric death ray and spit a toxic venom, that was supposed to be able to kill a camel.

As the four Mongolians literally became weak with laughter, at Kwon's translation of O'Neill's descriptions of the "Death Worm", Hujk their leader began to explain about the true nature of the "Olgoi Chorchoi". Kwon translated. It was, in reality, only two feet in length, weighed less than ten pounds, grew to the size of a human forearm and was closely related to the catfish, which it tasted like when cooked. It lived near water courses and was most commonly found after heavy rains from May to September. It hunted for small prey using a very short duration electric shock, which although very painful was not lethal to humans. Furthermore, Kwon continued, its name did not mean Death Worm, instead it referred to its red colour and size, which made it look like a section of intestine.

By the time the explanation and increasingly friendly exchanges were complete, the group had reached the gorge they had last seen on the 747's navigation screen, known as "The Valley of the Vultures". They were then led by their four guides behind a large thorny gorse bush to a set of narrow steep steps, hewn from the rock, that would have been all too easy to miss. The partially over grown steps led up into the clouds, to the spot indicated on Marco Polo's mirror map, and to their long-anticipated destination, The City of the Djinn.

On the other side of the world, a tough looking US Marine Corps (USMC) Master Sergeant, was supervising the drill practice of a group of just under a thousand immaculately dressed men, who marched, turned and presented arms on a cinder covered parade ground, with a synchronized precision that spoke of thousands of hours of practice. Their boots, belts, shirts, trousers and guns gleamed, and in stark contrast to the Maelstrom commandos, who were all clearly individualists, these men exuded a clear willingness to live and die, with and for each other.

As the men came to attention, a short wheelbase Jeep Wrangler drew up beside the parade ground, and the base commander's Adjutant ran up to the USMC Master Sergeant at double time, informing him he was required at the CO's office ASAP. Saluting his men, Master Sergeant Jackson turned and entered the doorless Jeep, which drove off at speed under the long shadows of a Californian sunrise across Camp Pendleton, home to the 1st Battalion 1st Marines.

When Jackson arrived at the white two storey prefabricated building, located alongside the parade ground that housed the CO's office, the Master Sergeant found himself reporting not to his commanding officer, as he expected, but to Lieutenant general "Colt" Cobbin-Smith, Commander, U.S. Marine Corps Forces Command (COMMARFORCOM), from the Naval Support Activity Center in Norfolk, Virginia. "Colt" was dressed informally in a short-sleeved combat fatigue and was carrying, as well as his usual weapons, a camouflage coloured backpack containing an Amrel RF10 laptop and a sheaf of papers.

Placing the computer on the wooden desk, along with the documents, Lt Gen Cobbin-Smith started the machine up and, after instructing Jackson to stand easy, played the first of two video's which had been sent to Virginia that morning attached, rather unbelievably, to an email from His Holiness the Pope, which mentioned Jackson specifically by name, citing his previous involvement with the Vatican Archaeologist, O'Neill, on their mission to investigate the ill-fated Finster expedition. Despite their initial scepticism, the technicians at COMMARFORCOM had confirmed the source of the message and that the videos had not been edited or tampered with.

The evidence was clear. The U.S. Commander in Chief, President Jones, had been misled, along with the other leaders of the Western coalition, into placing himself under the direct control of Maelstrom.

The President was currently being held deep within Cheyenne Mountain, protected by 300 troops from the very best of the U.S. Special Forces, as well as the permanent Cheyenne Mountain staff and a smaller contingent of Maelstrom operatives who were controlling the situation, feeding false information to the President and his aides, whilst maintaining a communications lockdown with the outside world.

Cobbin-Smith closed the laptop and looked at Jackson. 'We need to get the President out of there, son. We can only use men that we fully trust for this. Do you think you can do it?'

Jackson's calm blue eyes looked at the detailed maps and plans of the Cheyenne mountain facility, and then moved to the list of names of the 300 US Special Forces men and women, unwitting participants under the control of Maelstrom, who were holding the US President.

Eventually, he responded,

'Yes, sir."

'What's your plan, son? And what do you need?' asked the Lt General.

'Just my winning personality, Sir. and a small amount of luck!'

Jackson leaned forward, and briefly stated his solution.

The Lt Gen nodded and, after gathering up the papers and placing the laptop in his rucksack, briefly shook the Master Sergeants hand. Jackson stood to attention, saluting smartly as Cobbin- Smith left the building, heading for a Bell UH-1Y Venom helicopter, waiting to return him to COMMARFORCOM in Norfolk, Virginia.

The Cheyenne Mountain Complex is a vast underground command centre located in Colorado Springs, Colorado.

Originally the base for the United States Space Command and NORAD, since 2008, after those units relocated to Peterson Air Force Base, Colorado, it had been redesignated as the NORAD and USNORTHCOM Alternate Command Centre. Prior to the "Red Death" crisis it had been manned by a mere 210 personnel, ten percent of the original staffing capability, utilising just 30 per cent of the complex, shut away from the world behind a series of 25-ton blast doors. Hollowed out of the mountain, with 2000 feet of granite pressing down on its numerous tunnels and chambers, it was built to withstand a 30-megaton nuclear explosion, has its own independent power plant and water supply and is equipped with filters capable of trapping chemical, biological, radiological and nuclear contaminants. But, as is the case with many high security installations, despite the high-tech infrastructure, it is a person who ultimately decides whether you gain access or not.

Jackson turned the Jeep Wrangler off of State Highway 115 and headed down the hairpin road toward Cheyenne Mountain, coming to a halt at the guarded entrance station about 1.5 miles away from the famous North Portal leading into the complex. Under normal circumstances, active duty forces for Cheyenne Mountain would be supplied by the United States Air Force, but these were far from ordinary circumstances and, with so many of the country's military already having succumbed to the Red Death, alternative troops were having to be deployed to carry out essential duties wherever necessary. Having checked the personnel manifest that Cobbin-Smith had been carrying with him, Jackson had noted that he had seen active service with many of the men and women listed there, all staunchly loyal to their country. The Master Sergeant was taking a calculated risk that the soldiers manning the checkpoint would recognise him and, hopefully, that any Maelstrom operatives would be located within the complex itself, ensuring that the President remained 'undisturbed'.

As the Marine brought the Jeep to a halt, a heavily armoured soldier, wearing a USMC uniform with the name 'Kerkhoff' embroidered on the lapel and carrying an AR15 assault rifle, exited the guard hut and walked toward the car, his gun sights aimed directly at Jackson. As he neared the vehicle, his face broke into a huge grin, and lowering his weapon, called out,

'Jacko! Hope you haven't brought any more of those Claymores with you?'

'Nope. But I do have something even more explosive!"

The Master Sergeant finally allowed himself to breathe a sigh of relief, knowing that his gamble had paid off.

It only took a few minutes for the four-man team on guard duty to be briefed of the latest developments, Kerkhoff vouching for Jackson to the other three men on duty, whilst they brewed a quick coffee and decided on a plan of action. As Jackson had suspected, the Maelstrom Commander, Brigadier Smeggett, an officious British Rupert (officer) who'd never seen any real action, was hiding deep inside the mountain with only a small team of true Maelstrom operatives, relying on the misplaced loyalty of the US service men and women under their control to keep the President where Maelstrom wanted him.

But the sheer physical size of the complex, with its massive blast doors and snaking tunnels, alongside its reputation for impenetrability, had also made the Maelstrom leadership complacent, so that there were only ever a handful of men guarding the President and the remainder of the service men and women were involved in the day to day running of the base, including time out for exercise and recreation. Especially today, when Smeggett had given permission for a charity NFL game, organised to raise funds for the widows and orphans of the victims of the 'Red Death', between the Dallas Cowboys and the Washington Redskins to be relayed to the facility, where a large number of the off-duty personnel would be gathered in the Rec room to watch it.

'On a Smart TV?' queried Jackson.

'65 inch!' replied his buddy.

Getting into the Cheyenne Mountain complex was surprisingly easy now that Jackson was wearing a security pass clipped to his chest and Kerkhoff was officially escorting him, under the pretence that Jackson had an important message for the C.O. Which was, the Master Sergeant mused, ironically quite true, although he doubted any of the Maelstrom team would be happy to receive it.

Having made their way through the approach tunnel to the North Entrance, the two passed unchallenged through the first of the blast doors, leading them into a curving passageway, designed to deflect any blast materials directly out of the South Entrance to the complex, and the second of the 25-ton doors. A rather incongruous awning emblazoned with the slogan 'Welcome to Cheyenne Mountain Complex' greeted them once they were through, when Kerkhoff turned off from the main passageway, taking them into a series of smaller colour coded tunnels and walkways leading to the various chambers and support areas.

As they approached the area designated as the gym, Jackson could already hear a hum of voices from the personnel gathered in the large rec space eagerly waiting to watch the football game, providing a touch of normality in an otherwise chaotic world. Slipping into the room, the Master Sergeant could see at least 150 service men and women, sitting on rows of plastic chairs, engaged in friendly rival banter, while on the large 65-inch Sony screen in front of them, a marching band warmed up the crowd at FedExField with a rousing rendition of the theme from Star Wars. Kerkhoff subtly pointed out Brigadier Smegett at the far back, standing unhappily behind the seating, clearly displaying no interest in the forthcoming game. 'Probably more at home on a polo pitch' muttered Kerkhoff, with clearly no love lost between him and his temporary C.O. The Brigadier was surrounded by half a dozen Maelstrom personnel, distinctively dressed in their black paramilitary fatigues, so that they stood apart from the rest of the service men and women that filled the room.

As the band on the TV exited the playing field, the conversation in the room died down and all eyes turned toward the screen. It was then Jackson made his move. Walking behind the huge Sony he stumbled and, tangling his feet in the power cord, disconnected it from the mains. With thunderous abuse raining down on him from the assembled masses, the Master Sergeant sheepishly apologized, reconnected the device, and quickly inserted a USB stick, given to him by Cobbin-Smith, which he had been wearing around his neck alongside his dog tags, into one of the three ports on the back of the Sony. As the screen came to life, showing not, as expected, 22 huge American football players facing off against each other, but Nissa Ad-Dajjal detailing her role in the destruction of the USS Lyndon B. Johnson and the duplicitous takeover of the Western Governments by Maelstrom, a huge Navy Seal Captain in the front row exclaimed,

'What, the fuck?'

And, as the images played on, every man and woman seated in the room, took out their firearm, and turned to face Smeggett and his goons, as the Seal said in a rather more menacing tone,

'SEAL Team six, escort The President from the complex. The rest of you detain these Maelstrom scum.'

The small group of Stewart, Curren, O'Neill and Kwon, led by their four guides, were soaked in sweat and gasping for breath in the oxygen depleted mountain air, as they approached the top of the steep rock hewn stairway that rose from sea level in the Valley of the Vultures to the unnamed 10,000 foot summit. For the final two thirds of the climb, they had been forced to cut their way through thick undergrowth just to be able to see the next rows of steps. The four Shamans took turns at the thankless work, hacking expertly with a long-curved Bolo machete that had to be sharpened several times during their ascent.

As they climbed, the sky had turned from a peculiar red to an ominous black. The wind had also started to grow in strength, chilling them to the bone, while also sending a blinding mix of earth and grit into their faces. When their guides offered each of them a pair of filthy leather wrap around goggles which, based on the deep brown staining and pungent fragrance emanating from the leather, must have seen generations of use by yak herders during long winters on the steppes, they were gratefully accepted.

At the end of the steep climb and the long trek in the desert, they all sat exhausted looking down at the sheer 10,000-foot drop before them and the magnificent Gobi Desert reaching out as far as the eye could see in every direction.

While Stewart, Kwon, O'Neill and Curren admired the setting sun, creating kaleidoscope patterns from the growing storm clouds reflected on the mirror-like polished stone desert floor, their guides set to work removing decades of undergrowth and trees within the eighty feet wide mountain top clearing, that gradually became revealed as an ancient camp site. As one of the Shamans repaired a three-foot-high dry-stone wall, which acted as a wind break, another used some of the drier wood sections to start a fire within an ancient stone range, complete with an oven and metal overhang for boiling liquids. Twenty minutes later, after some strong tea had been brewed from the melted glacial ice, Stewart, Kwon, Curren and O'Neill were led by Hujk towards a small opening in the side of the mountain, hidden behind layers of trees and thick ivy, that had to be cleared before anyone could gain access through the hidden doorway, into whatever existed beyond.

"This is it! At last the legendary City of the Djinn! Do you realize what this discovery could mean to my career?" Shouted an excited O'Neill.

"Don't you mean to the field of Archaeology?" Added Curren, winking humorously to Stewart.

"Never mind science and careers. We just need that damned tablet" Responded Stewart grimly.

Even in spite of such teasing, O'Neill was clearly unable to contain his professional curiosity as he eagerly pushed his way forward, only to pull up in surprise. Inside the door was a small twenty-foot square space, with a straw covered flat stone floor and artificially straight walls, that were covered in names and dates in different scripts and languages. As Curren and Stewart joined O'Neill inside the tiny space, followed rapidly by Kwon and then Hujk, it became very cramped and claustrophobic. Ignoring the graffiti, that covered almost every available surface, Stewart, Curren and O'Neill frantically looked for another passageway that could lead to a cave complex deserving of the legends.

Curren was the first to voice what everyone else was thinking.

"City? More like broom cupboard of the Djinn!"

Stewart was more pragmatic, turning to Kwon he asked pointedly,

"Chin, where is the final emerald tablet?"

The young priest, who had been so eager to get here, now seemed distracted. He looked blankly at Stewart. Understanding that the Scotsman expected an answer, he turned to the leader of the Shamans and, after an exchange, replied simply,

"Now is only for the Father of the Winds."

Looking less than impressed, Stewart sat with Curren and O'Neill to discuss the situation. Asking quietly,

"So, thoughts? Have we just been taken on the mother of all wild goose chases?"

"Well, Kwon IS a mental patient. Is it so surprising that we end up in a small cave instead of a legendary lost city, if we have been indulging some psychotic fantasy?" Speculated Curren.

O'Neill pointed to the walls that were covered in dates and names.

"I have been looking at these carvings. They are not just random graffiti, each is around 120 years apart, many with the same surnames repeating over and over."

"How far back do they go?" Asked Stewart.

"Hard to tell for sure," replied the Archaeologist "But, IF they are real, it would seem to go back thousands of years. If it is not a fake, maybe this is some kind of ritual site."

Stewart nodded "That would match with what Kwon just told me, something about now being the time of the winds."

At that moment, the three other Shamans came into the small shelter carrying wooden bowls of warm food, which they distributed and proceeded to eat, while seated cross legged in a small circle on the cave floor. Clearly the size of the shelter was intended to closely match the size of the traditional Yurt skin tents, as their hosts rapidly assumed a relaxed attitude, and it would have been easy to imagine them all in some nomadic camp on the steppes, if it was not for the sound of the growing storm outside.

The meal was a fatty meat gruel, that O'Neill said was probably reindeer, with some mashed-up vegetables that remained unrecognized, even as they sucked the residue from their fingers. It was warming and that was all that really mattered. After the meal, Hujk chose a clear spot on the cave wall and, by the light of a clay oil lamp, began carving the current date with a small bladed knife with a bone handle, asking, via Kwon, the phonetic spelling of their names.

"So, we are immortalized." Said Curren, who was clearly not looking forward to a night in such a confined space with seven very smelly men. Her very worst fears looked like they were going to be realized, when four large yak bladders were proudly presented, and a truly foul-smelling liquid was poured into wooden cups, and quickly downed by the four Mongolians.

Before Stewart could reach forward to try a cup, O'Neill exclaimed,

"Don't! That is the ritual soma of these Nomadic Siberian tribes. They force feed reindeer the hallucinogenic fungi amanita muscaria and then collect the urine to get a refined form of Muscimol. No wonder they think they come here to visit the City of the Djinn! A cup of that and you will be chatting with God alone knows what."

True enough, around thirty minutes later the four Mongolians began to sweat profusely, and after vomiting on the cave floor passed into trance states, where they clearly believed they were communicating with other beings.

In an effort to try and avoid the pungently overwhelming smells of soup, vomit and urine, Stewart walked close to the cave entrance and gestured for Kwon to halt his intended action of rolling shut the large circular stone door, stating,

"Leave it open, we could do with some fresh air."

Leaving the massive round rock for the moment, Kwon stood framed in the entrance, watching powerful lightning flashes flying across the entire width of the sky. Sensing Stewart was looking at the barometer on his watch, which read an unbelievable 650mb, the young priest turned and said.

"In your travels, I am sure you have heard desert peoples talk about "The Mother of Storms", the Haboob (هَبوب), an intense atmospheric gravity current that can bury tons of sand on cities in moments. Understand that the Haboob is nothing in comparison to this…"

the priest gestured to the mayhem unfolding outside the cave,

"… Typhon, Father of the Winds, is a once in a lifetime super storm, when a million square miles of desert rock and sand moves."

Stewart felt himself shiver, amid the constant rumble that sounded and felt like hundreds of locomotives shaking the very bedrock of the mountain and, as he looked out beyond the cave entrance, his mind slowly registered that the patterns before him were vast dunes of rock and sand rising into the sky like ocean waves. Lightning flashes lit up the desert to the very horizon and, in that moment, Stewart could see the massive 747 swirling round like a toy, within numerous thick funnel vortices that were dancing on the desert plain below.

Stewart nodded to Kwon,

"Let's close the cave door, and wait for dawn."

CHAPTER 47 - AGHARTI, CITADEL OF THE DJINN

"I have not told half of what I saw..." – deathbed confession of Marco Polo, Sunday, January 8, 1324 (Julian Calendar)

36°34'00N 21°8'00E
Aboard the 283m "Tiamat" Migaloo M7 Submersible-Yacht.
Depth -410 feet
Calypso Deep, Ionian Sea,
South-West of Pylos, Greece
06.00Hrs (Eastern European Time), 14th August, Present Day.

Located along the port side of the Tiamat's painstaking reconstruction of an Assyrian Temple, was one of Asia's more significant ancient esoteric artifacts. The "Sen No Yorokobi No Tēburu", or "Table of a Thousand Delights", had been constructed from a two thousand five-hundred-year-old fig tree, ritually felled during a dark lunar cycle, that had originally stood in the Mahabodhi Temple grounds in Bodh Gaya, India.

According to the many myths associated with the object, it had been assembled according to plans dictated by Dakini-ten, esoteric Shingon Buddhism's discarnate Principle of Evil, during the fourteenth century at the infamous Shinseina Iki monastery on Sado Island in Niigata Prefecture, Japan.

Although Japanese history reports that the table was lost, during the purging by fire of the accursed monastery in the late 1630s by Tokugawa Iemitsu, third shogun of the Tokugawa dynasty, in fact the artifact had been traded to Portuguese Jesuits, in the infamous "Niigata Exchange", for certain black magick relics acquired by the Inquisition. Many esoteric scholars think that this collusion was ultimately responsible for the Portuguese being expelled from Japan in 1639.

In the legends associated with the device, it was believed that the wood used in the construction of the table opened an unending pathway to truth, although sadly not in the same manner as Gautama Buddha achieved through his meditations under the famous fig tree, from which the infamous device was constructed.

When using the table, a human body was suspended by the arms, legs and torso from thick straps, stitched, it was said, from the tanned skin of the very monks who made the device, onto a rotating open frame that permitted movement in all planes of direction, enabling torture at any point or angle on the unfortunate victim.

Dr Nissa Ad-Dajjal stood beside this treasured possession, dressed in tight fitting red surgical scrubs that accentuated the curves of her perfect body. She was no longer hiding the withering of the left side of her face, instead she had deliberately accentuated it with makeup, so her appearance now matched her true nature, and was impossible to behold without a sensation of visceral fear.

Ironically, although she had finally embraced the transformation of her countenance, recent revelations in the news had forced her to withdraw from the public eye. The evidence showing her involvement in releasing the USS Lyndon B. Johnson's tertiary bio-vector agent, causing billions of deaths, and the deliberate contamination of the US vaccine stock piles, in order to force mass acceptance of her leadership and control, had turned public opinion dramatically against her. So much so that she had ordered the Tiamat to find deep water, and dive to a depth where they would not easily be identified. She now intended to avoid the scrutiny of the world, opting instead to wait until she had the four emerald tablets and could conduct the ceremony to which she had dedicated her life.

The headline of "Ad-Dajjal: Messiah or Pariah?" in the New York Times, had done nothing to help her dark mood, as this premature exposure had never been part of her original design. Decades of planning and work had been dedicated to the single purpose of providing Ad-Dajjal with the ultimate tribute to her dark Magickal Will, specifically, manipulating the whole of humanity into submissive adoration of her and her alone, before she revealed her true purpose. The old creation would be snuffed out moments after every man, woman and child knew the extent of their betrayal, and the new creation would emerge built from that despair. No other Left-Hand Path adept had ever contemplated such a dark abuse of all humanity, not even Aleister Crowley, let alone brought it so close to actualisation. She had no doubt that she would still complete The Ceremony of the Forty Ninth Enochian Key and bring forth a new creation in her image but, sadly, without the desolation she had intended to lie within the heart of humanity in its final beat.

Understandably, Ad-Dajjal sought to identify the source of her own betrayal, and for that reason she had arranged to have Media Mogul Gerald Seymour brought to the Tiamat to determine, using her unrivalled magickal skills, if he had leaked the recent revelations to the world's news.

Seymour's thin, flaccid middle-aged body lay naked, strapped to the "Sen No Yorokobi No Tēburu", his pale flesh glistening with perspiration, that reflected the flickering candles and many dark shadows in the Temple around them. Seventeen black, "Da Zhen" spikes, four inches long with one-inch diameters, had been hammered expertly into chakra and meridian points on the media mogul's spinal column, neck and skull. Each wound oozed a mix of clear and light red spinal fluids, that pooled within elegantly carved Sanskrit characters on the highly polished dark fig wood.

When Ad-Dajjal had acquired the legendary torture device, she had also procured a set of thirteenth century Chinese Jiu Zhen or Nine Needles, each with its own very specific torture pathway and each able to be coated with different traditional hyper-aesthetic compounds that, in contrast to anaesthetics, heightened pain sensitivity to levels unimagined by modern Western medicine.

For Seymour's experience on the Table of a Thousand Delights, Ad-Dajjal had selected the "Akuma no chi" compound, one of the most refined of the seventy hyper-aesthetics listed in the 9th century Shifuku no Mikkusu scroll, supposedly composed by Dakini-ten himself.

Gerald Seymour's consciousness floated in an endless sea of pain, that was beyond anything ever imagined. He had long ago told "The Voice" anything it demanded, in some futile hope that he could find some escape from the hideous experience which now eclipsed every other consideration. Over the past six hours, strapped to the table, his awareness of external reality had gradually eroded, until there was just "The Pain" and "The Voice", which became a disembodied Goddess, who offered the only way to end this unbearable existence. Whenever Gerald thought he had reached the furthest limits possible, before the merciful oblivion of unconsciousness would engulf his senses, "The Voice" showed him there was still a deeper suffering to be experienced. He heard himself, like he was a thousand miles away, pleading.

"I know nothing. I have always been loyal. Just let this end. Just let me die. Please."

"Yes, I can imagine that by now death seems the sweetest desire," responded Ad-Dajjal, with a voice as soft as satin,

"After six hours, you will have no doubt started to understand the more unique attributes of this special object? It sustains the experience of suffering beyond the normal limits of unconsciousness, madness and even death, allowing its inflicted pain to continue indefinitely. Your body, Gerald, would have surrendered to death some hours ago, but the relic has held your consciousness in its sublime grip, where you would remain for eternity, unless..."

Nissa Ad-Dajjal slowly reached for the yellow tanned straps that held the Media Mogul's body to the frame and untied the thick leather clasps, allowing what was once Gerald Seymour to land, with a wet sounding thump, beneath the legendary torture device.

"Released by your…"

Ad-Dajjal searched for the technically correct esoteric Tibetan term.

"Duḥkhakaṣṭa kō svāmī (Swami of Suffering) …"

She concluded with a smile, gesturing to one of the two female attendants, who had assisted during the last six hours, to take the small black hammer engraved with intricate eighth century man'yōgana characters from her right hand, and for the second attendant to recover the priceless thirteenth century "Da Zhen" spikes from the chakra points on the body of Gerald Seymour, that now lay motionless on the black stone temple floor.

While Seymour had been experiencing Ad-Dajjal's expertly choreographed journey, through the Akuma No Chi's seventy-two pathways of torment, down in the pressurized diving chamber in the bowels of the Tiamat, Mohammed Sek was checking that his son Berat remembered the correct procedure that was required to use the large orange submarine escape system they had just liberated from a red wall mounted emergency cabinet, located beside the double airlock doors to the diving chamber.

The RFD Beaufort SEIE MK11 Submarine Escape Immersion Equipment (SEIE) suit, came in three sizes and even the smallest was clearly too large for Berat, but still provided the best chance for him to survive the 400 feet of cold water, that lay between the diving chamber and the surface of the Ionian Sea above them. Sadly, none of the SEIE suits came anywhere near fitting over his father's huge frame, besides, because of a series of recent onboard announcements, Sek knew that armed guards were already carrying out a ship wide search for stowaways. If he was to delay the discovery of the revenge he had prepared for the "Cadı" (witch) in repayment for the death of his son, Ahmet, he knew that he had to remain on the ship and allow himself to be captured, hoping that Berat would be able to bring back help in time.

Once out in the water, Berat's suit would inflate and rise slowly from the depths, the inbuilt scuba tanks providing air until decompression was completed, when the life raft would automatically deploy itself on the surface, allowing Berat to be picked up by any passing vessel that detected the 406 MHz Emergency Position Indicating Radio Beacon (EPIRB). Satisfied that his son understood how the SEIE suit functioned, Mohammed Sek hugged Berat and made him promise to tell Zahra how much he loved her, before watching him plunge into the lapping ocean in the circular opening in the centre of the dive chamber, and vanish into the dark waters.

As the large figure of Sek emerged from the cold steel pressurized airlock doors of the chamber, he found himself surrounded by six Maelstrom guards, dressed in blue grey Tiamat uniforms and armed with non-lethal weapons.

Sek reacted with a humorous,

"They only sent six of you?"

Moments later, his thickly bearded face grimaced in pain, as two metal filaments lodged into his chest and left arm, each delivering 50,000 volts from military variations of the multi shot X3 Taser, fired expertly by two of the guards in front of him. After pulling the two barbs dismissively from his body, Sek stepped forward in what could have been an almost friendly gesture, but then reached for the necks of the two guards, who were by now retreating, and with his massive hands bashed their heads together viciously, sending the pair immediately to the floor. While his enormous back was turned, another of the Maelstrom operatives launched into a vicious Muay Thai axe kick, which landed with pinpoint accuracy on the back of Sek's thick neck, causing the giant Turk to rub the impact with his left hand, while turning to face his attacker with what looked like a casual swiping backhand slap, that lifted the Thai boxer clean off his feet and impacted his head against a metal bulkhead, causing the guard to fall to the ground like a sack of potatoes. Before Sek could continue his rampage against the remaining three guards, two large blue coloured darts stuck deep into his massive chest. He pulled one out and appeared puzzled at the label which read "fifty millilitres Carfentanil" and showed a picture of a sleeping elephant. Moments later, Stewart's fearless friend sank to his knees and then fell face forward on to the black rubber mats of the hallway floor.

Not even the four intoxicated Shamans slept well in the confined space of the cave. The raging storm's movement of the Gobi's sands and rock shook the enormous mountain range to its very core, causing constant noise and vibrations, that made it feel as though they were riding in a railroad baggage car. To make matters worse, the stale air was filled with the rancid smells of spices, flatulent indigestion, sweat and of course the odour of vomit, an unavoidable side effect of the hallucinogenic Muscimol, strong enough to prompt both O'Neill and Curren to experience the compulsion to join the Shamans in staining the reeds on the cave floor. It was therefore an enormous relief when the vibration and thunderous roar gradually began to decline and, by 04.32 HRS, the cave became still and silent, except for the sounds of the unconscious Mongolian guides, who continued to mumble incoherently, twitch and pass wind.

Even Kwon looked relieved when the massive circular door was rolled back, and a fresh breeze flowed into the dark and dank cave. Not sure what to expect, Curren and O'Neill let Stewart and Kwon lead the way out into the dawn light, which was blinding after so many hours confined in the darkness of the cave, illuminated as it had been by only two small reed lamps.

Curren stumbled gratefully into the sunlight, noting to O'Neill,

"A good night for the mushroom Djinn..."

"Yes," laughed O'Neill,

"I fear they…" he motioned to the unconscious Shamans,

"...will be the only ones among us with amazing accounts of their visit to the legendary lost city..."

His sentence remained unfinished, as he saw that last night's storm had totally transformed the environment outside their shelter. Oceans of rock and sand had been moved, and what was once a mountain had become a giant sand dune, with just the rocky peak left exposed to the morning sun. Beneath them the desert floor had been stripped to the bedrock, revealing what was once a set of enormous golden gates that had fallen open, showing a deep ravine in the valley floor that clearly formed an ancient passageway.

Before anyone could comment on the incredible sight, Kwon turned to the group,

"The Lost City of Agharti! It is a rare privilege, even for me to visit, but you must all take precautions to avoid becoming an eternal guest, when the desert reclaims its prize."

He then went on to recommend that both Stewart and Curren start separate twelve-hour countdowns on their Rangeman watches, so the group would be alerted when the sands were about to take back the city, and emphasized that each person leave immediately when they heard the alarm, no matter what they were doing, and to make their way back to the cave, even if they were alone.

It was very noticeable that Kwon was not including himself in these plans. Curren and O'Neill exchanged glances, both clearly wondering what that could mean, and then followed Stewart and the young priest down the 11,500 foot high sand dune, that led from the cave entrance down to the broken gates below.

When they reached the foot of the steep slope, the sheer size of the city's entrance way became apparent. The long passageway lay between two steep cliffs, just under 165 feet high, and the massive fallen gates would have once filled the entire end of the open ravine. O'Neill started taking detailed pictures and videos on his iPhone, there was no signal here but he had decided he could use it as a digital record of what they found, while his battery lasted.

As they continued to walk, they entered the tall ravine and could see detailed carvings on the walls of the various peoples who had visited the city. There were one-hundred-foot high reliefs of fierce Mongolian Shamans shown guarding the entrance, who looked very much like the four unconscious men they had left in the cave, then there were a series of friezes that depicted groups of different peoples, all in distinctive costumes, some of whom O'Neill recognized as Sumerians, Phoenicians, Yellow river people from Han China, Mohenjo-Daro people from the Indus Valley and the El Abra from South America, all exchanging gifts with some winged figures that O'Neill said looked like the God "An" in Sumerian and "Anu" in Akkadian mythology.

While O'Neill was occupied photographing the numerous friezes, Stewart made a more gruesome discovery, the floor of the 165 feet wide passage way was littered with human remains. The first that he uncovered were a group of skeletons dressed in well preserved leather light armour, each man had been carrying a short bow and a quiver of metal tipped arrows. The bones of these archers and their short-legged horses were mixed together into a tragic sculpture, created at the moment of death, as they had galloped at full speed around another group of dead bodies, dressed in Roman military uniforms with shields raised above their heads, which would already have been skeletons at the time the riders died so close beside them.

Deeper into the passageway Stewart came alongside Curren, who was looking down at a perfectly preserved skeleton dressed in a Roman Catholic cassock, similar to the ones that O'Neill and Kwon had been wearing when they first met in Istanbul. Curren speculated

"What do you think, T? Could he be the cleric charged with putting the final emerald tablet here?" Stewart nodded grimly.

O'Neill seemed indifferent to the tragedies so evident in the few hundred yards they had covered so far, remarking only on the amazing diversity of history on record, as his iPhone took picture after picture. Stewart was more measured in his reaction.

"This looks like a very dangerous place. Did you notice that everyone is trying to escape from something, when they died so rapidly?"

Kwon looked down at the cleric's body, explaining,

"It is simple. Everyone leaves their escape from Agharti too late. The returning sands claim them."

Noticing something glistening on the surface of the sand before her, Curren reached down and found an old brass compass with a smashed glass, but recoiled in horror when the original owner's bones protruded from the sand, still grasping the artifact. Stewart was less squeamish and, brushing aside the sand that hid the body, found a perfectly preserved pair of nineteenth century Meyers Pinfire Pepperbox Revolvers still in their red leather Gould Goodrich belt holsters, with some ancient Cartridge S.A. Revolver rounds, remarking,

"Mid 1850s. Impressive technology for the time. Clearly firepower is no match against the sands of Agharti."

As Stewart, Curren, Kwon and O'Neill made their way towards the end of the elaborate entranceway and passed through a large doorway some 100 feet high and thirty feet wide, cut into an elaborate frontage in the rock face that made the ornate treasury in Petra look plain, four camouflaged shapes emerged from expertly created hides in the sand, near the entrance of the long ravine.

Issac bin Abdul Issuin and his three remaining Maelstrom operatives had weathered the previous night's storm by fastening themselves to black diamond titanium "Deep Bore" Protex pitons and bolts on the sheer rock face, beneath a small overhang on the south side of the Gurvan Saikhan mountain peak. After watching Stewart's group enter the city gates, they used Military variants of the Apache wing suit to speed down the two mile dune slope to what was now the desert floor, where they rapidly deployed desert sniper hides and launched "Dragonfly" remote control micro-drones, with live audio-visual feeds, to follow the progress and activities of the Stewart party.

Inside the ornate frontage, the darkness was in such complete contrast to the glaring desert sunshine that it took some minutes for everyone's eyes to adjust, but eventually O'Neill, Stewart and Curren began to make out the details of fine carved stone work, forming ornate random geometric shapes on the walls, floors, ceilings and high doorways. The tragic theme recorded in the bones of the dead continued inside. Doors and passage ways were blocked by a mass of men, women, children and animal remains, of those who had clearly perished slowly after finding their exit blocked with falling sand and rock.

Stewart's old-fashioned kerosene lamp illuminated the remains of a man and woman embracing, with daggers pierced into each other's hearts, rather than face death by starvation in the endless darkness of this tomb of a city, making Stewart remark to the group,

"Jesus, this place is a death trap, let's get this tablet and get the hell out of here."

In contrast, O'Neill acted like an excited child, photographing and adding voice recorded notes on the architectural styles, and the origins of each new grisly discovery of human remains. Clearly the Archaeologist assumed that these sets of carved rock chambers were all that remained of the legendary citadel, as his voice notes started describing the total size and the probable ritual use of the site.

While O'Neill was preparing what he evidently thought would be an earth shattering archaeological announcement, Kwon moved to a dark corner of the furthest room and kicked away the straw that covered that section of the floor, causing the ancient dried grass to disintegrate into a fine dust over his Salvatore Ferragamo black leather shoes. He revealed a six-foot square stone trap door, with carved metal handles attached to numerous broken clay seals, etched with characters and dates in Sanskrit, Latin, Chinese and Mongolian.

Hearing Kwon cough and point his ancient kerosene torch at the trap door, O'Neill stopped his dictation and walked sheepishly to the exposed area in the floor and, after examining the twenty or so broken seals fastened to the handles, dismissed them as fakes.

Recognizing hurt pride, Curren cajoled the Vatican Archaeologist.

"Humour us Thomas, what would they mean if they were real..."

"They would show one hundred and twenty-year cycles repeating over and over, for roughly 2,500 years. It is just not credible." Responded a clearly hurt O'Neill.

Stewart shone his lamp further around the trap door, and noted more piles of similar clay seals that had been systematically discarded over time. With the hard work of Stewart and Kwon, using some of the Shaman's thick hemp rope, they raised the stone door and were confronted with clouds of dust and thick smoke rising from the opening in the floor, smelling of candles that had just been extinguished.

"How are candles still burning…" Asked Curren, only to be interrupted by O'Neill,

"It is a well-known phenomenon when opening airtight tombs." Said the Archaeologist dismissively.

The opening in the stone floor revealed around sixty neatly cut stone steps, descending around thirty feet to another set of rooms carved into the bedrock. O'Neill led the way down into the next subterranean level of what was clearly a complex of dwellings.

Unlike the rooms above, with their carved geometric patterns on the walls and floors, here there were just very orderly piles of dust particles and metal oxidation, leaving shadow like images on the floors and walls.

If these "dust shadows" were real, and O'Neill declared them as clever fakes, the rooms would once have been full of furniture and desks, indicating an office space that had long since decayed away.

"So, if this was real, how long would it take for objects to turn to dust shadows, like this?" Asked Curren, to the clearly uncomfortable Vatican Archaeologist.

"Tens of thousands of years. It is nonsense. Impossible." Said O'Neill, struggling with the evidence of his own eyes.

Then, seeing some text and pictures on a tall obsidian wall carved in Assyrian, Sanskrit and two other unrecognized languages, O'Neill clearly thought that he had found something to put this place back into a proper modern archaeological context. He announced,

"This looks like a form of calendar. You can tell a lot about a culture by the way it measures time. Hunter gatherers record herd movements. Agricultural societies focus on seasons for crop harvests, the more sophisticated, like the Babylonians, Egyptians, and Romans, recorded the simple movement of planets and constellations, and created the basis of our modern calendar."

"And what of your civilization, Dr O'Neill?" Asked Kwon pointedly.

O'Neill paused, and responded proudly,

"We measure everything from sub atomic processes, to the huge span of time needed for our own planet's development, from its origins in a dust cloud to the diverse ecosystems that make up our world today. Our measure of time is the year, how long it takes for the Earth to rotate around the solar system."

Fr Kwon smiled, as if he was leading a child to solve some maths problem.

"So, Dr O'Neill, what measure of time did these people use?"

O'Neill approached the obsidian wall carving, explaining as he did,

"Many desert based civilizations used phases of the moon, so I would expect to find lunar phases or even seasons and basic astronomical observations."

The Vatican Archaeologist went very quiet, as he examined the carving that described the basis of this civilization's time keeping. The wall in front of him showed a very exact spiral shape of a Galaxy, named in Sanskrit "Ganges of the Heavens" that we know better as the Milky Way, with its rotation clearly indicated as the primary measure of the passing of time. Under the detailed carvings of the central Galactic Bar, were the edges of the Norma, Perseus, Orion-Cygnus, Scutum-Centaurus and Carina-Sagittarius stellar structures and our own solar system, shown clearly in its 250,000 million terrestrial year rotation around the central Galactic bar, forming the so-called Galactic year.

With O'Neill now silent, and clearly not wishing to describe what was detailed in the list of timeline events below the Milky Way pictograms, Curren asked Kwon for a summary which, judging from his smile, he was delighted to provide. The young priest moved his light closer to the dark obsidian wall and pointed to four major historical events carved in the stone. Sixty galactic years ago showed four carved tablets and a massive explosion of light; fifty galactic years ago showed the birth of the Milky Way; twenty galactic years ago showed the birth of the Sun; one galactic year ago showed a massive earth impact, the so-called Permian–Triassic extinction event.

Curren looked to O'Neill who remained silent, and then back to Kwon, asking the Japanese priest,

"And what of these dates in the future?"

Fr Kwon put his finger against four future events that were carved below, one galactic year from now showed all the continents on Earth fused into a supercontinent; four galactic years from now showed all multicellular life had died out on earth; twenty galactic years from now showed the Milky Way and Andromeda Galaxy colliding and finally, 500 galactic years from now showed darkness, as the visible universe expanded beyond the cosmic light horizon.

Stewart turned to O'Neill.

"What kind of civilization marks all of existence in eight items?"

Kwon interjected, before the clearly stunned Archaeologist could respond.

"If we do not stop Ad-Dajjal from getting that final tablet everything will end much sooner than shown here. So please let us move on. The tablet will have been placed in the deepest part of the citadel and we do not have much time."

Kwon checked Stewart's countdown timer, which showed just over four hours remaining until the Gobi would reclaim its prize and bury them, along with all the other bodies they had found in the entrance.

The group of four moved forward from the obsidian wall with its complex carvings and, some ten yards further on, found a doorway sealed with clay to make it airtight. Without any hesitation O'Neill broke open the sealed doorway and they found themselves on a long high terrace above a large dark area, which stretched out well beyond the limits of their kerosene torches. Stewart pulled out the Pains Wessex Distress Signal that he had taken from the crashed 747, and sent the first of his three flares high into the air. The flickering light hung from a tiny parachute and revealed a small settlement of around twenty tall buildings, complete with sidewalks and wide roads filled with shops and metal objects that looked like street lights. But, as if in some nightmare, as they watched the whole scene began to disintegrate to rubble and then dust, as the fresh air made contact with the ancient materials and, within the space of five minutes, all that was left were piles of dust and metal oxide shadows similar to those they had seen in the first level.

"Look what we just did!" Exclaimed O'Neill in horror, holding his iPhone as he played back the loss of the entire settlement.

"We should avoid any more sealed doors." Stated Stewart, looking pointedly at the Vatican Archaeologist.

Since Kwon believed the remaining tablet would be found in the lower reaches, they continued down flight after flight of stone stairways, everywhere littered with skeletal remains, past five further levels of ancient inhabitation, including one large floor area that looked like an aircraft hangar, with a large 165 foot diameter opening in the high ceiling, which had long ago partially collapsed. On the floor were several sixty-six feet long V shapes formed from shadows of metal oxide, powdered glass and dark organic materials, looking for all the world like the outlined remains of a modern fighter jet. Kwon guided the group past these "distractions", and on to the stairs leading to the lower depths, explaining only that these objects were "vi-māna" (in Sanskrit "measuring out" or "traversing"). O'Neill looked even more stunned with the "vi-māna" flying machines than he had been at the obsidian wall, his iPhone taking movies as they hurried past.

Beneath the hangar space was the last of the seven levels that had been carved deep into the desert bedrock. It was a completely empty space leading to a vast stone precipice. Stewart stood close to the edge of the impenetrable darkness and, firing the second of his three flares, revealed a set of steps cut into the sheer rock face before them, similar to those they had encountered at the Valley of the Vultures, which led down to a vast underground expanse of water extending as far as the eye could see into the distance. The dark waters were filled with the sparkles of luminous creatures, bleached white in the constant darkness of the massive sea that once existed where the Gobi is today, but which was buried beneath the earth during a massive continental plate collision around 700,000 terrestrial years ago.

As each of them watched the flare drift slowly down to the ocean, Curren exclaimed,

"Look!" As a small island, just over a mile square, was revealed a few hundred yards out in the water. Twenty minutes later, at the bottom of the seven hundred and seventy steps, which O'Neill insisted on counting out loud as they descended, they found a small stone jetty hewn from the rock, and an ancient crossing barge made of volcanic pumice. The hemp rope pullies which operated the barge looked strong, and must have been replaced only 120 years ago when the unfortunate cleric had visited to deposit the final emerald tablet. After a brief crossing, where Stewart, Kwon and O'Neill had to work together like a tug of war team to keep the barge moving, they arrived on the small island which, unlike the rest of the underground citadel, was remarkably free from skeletal remains, instead being littered with rusted chain mail, shields and weapons from past ages, that had evidently proved ineffective against some unknown opponent.

As the four ventured further onto the small island, the light from their kerosene lamps revealed numerous openings, ranging from three to ten feet wide, like the holes in Swiss cheese, that surrounded the shoreline, and were especially frequent around the edge of the jetty near the water line. The sight of these strange regularly shaped holes prompted Chin Kwon to recount that one of the many legends of this place was of a network of tunnels extending out into the Gobi. Some even claimed these passageways connected as far as a secret sanctuary high in the Tibetan plateau, but such tales also told of monstrous tunnel guardians who delighted to feast on human flesh.

Away from the shoreline, the island was filled with statues of strange human bird chimeras with hideous talons and wings, which O'Neill said were typical depictions of the mythical Djinn. There were also sets of enormous obelisks, some as high as sixty feet, covered with carvings in a script that looked very much like the one on Stewart's dagger and the emerald tablets.

In the very centre of the island was a single storey stone temple, some 300 feet long and 100 feet wide, with a ritual Holy Table in its centre. The fourth emerald tablet was sitting in one of four carved slots on the table surface, that was clearly intended to be a repository for all four of the Tablets of Destiny. However, it was not the final tablet which drew everyone's attention, instead it was the terrifying dark stone wall frescoes showing hideous talons being summoned from what was clearly an image of the Holy Table, clawing through the very fabric of reality. The very same pictures that O'Neill had seen in Iraq, and that Curren vaguely recalled from a nightmare memory.

The recreated Assyrian temple on the Tiamat was an exact replica of the one on the small island beneath the Citadel of the Djinn, except the roof was lower and the air was filled with the smell of incense and something else, dead flesh. The candles flickered and illuminated the same hideous stone friezes that were fascinating O'Neill and Curren, showing demonic entities clawing through and tearing the universe apart.

Mohammed Sek was slowly awakening from the sedatives, finding himself bound to two chairs facing towards the Ad-Dajjal witch, who was dressed in a black Prada silk trouser suit, going through his belongings, which had been laid out on a small tray that was resting on the left side of the top of a large steel surgical trolley.

Nissa Ad-Dajjal noticed her stowaway was waking and remarked, while holding the massive Ruger Super Redhawk Alaskan .44 Magnum revolver.

"What an interesting gun…"

She made a show of removing all but one of the 340 gr Buffalo Bore rounds from their chambers, spinning the cylinder slowly before placing the short barrel to Mohammed's left knee, and pulling the trigger with an empty click. Looking carefully to judge her victim's reaction, she smiled.

"We can have fun with this later…"

Ad-Dajjal then started examining Sek's other items, the large Casio watch, FS daggers and finally a crumpled photograph of a twenty something male, smiling in front of Stewart's shop in Istanbul. Ad-Dajjal tossed the photograph back and turned her attention to a second tray that lay to the right of Sek's belongings saying, with a cruel smile.

"I promise you will find my toys… unforgettable," and as she ran her hand through a range of Chakra knives, electric cables, crocodile clips and syringes it was clear she enjoyed torture for the sake of it. She returned her attention to his belongings, adding.

"You can tell a lot about a person from what they carry."

Sek nodded his agreement, adding,

"If you understood what that old photograph tells you about me, then you would be afraid."

Ad-Dajjal laughed.

"Me? Afraid of you? Whatever for…? You were stupid enough to remain on board to get caught."

"Not exactly, madam, I came on board to exact revenge for your murder of him,"

Sek nodded to the photograph, "My eldest son Ahmet."

"And you failed..." sneered Ad-Dajjal.

"I have not finished yet, madam." Retorted the massive Turk.

"You look pretty finished to me…" Nissa Ad-Dajjal patronizingly patted Sek's left cheek.

He ignored the contact, instead focusing on the face of his Casio Rangeman, which was lying sideways on the steel surgical table in front of him, and smiled.

"Never underestimate a vengeful parent."

Seconds later an enormous explosion rocked the massive ship. The fourteen-pound Tecnovar EPR marine limpet mines, planted by Sek hours earlier, sent carefully calculated sonic shock waves through the vessel, disabling onboard systems and causing it to begin an uncontrolled dive. On the bridge, Captain Jersson looked at the displays with disbelief, as he struggled with the Tiamat's buoyancy controls, exclaiming.

"Damn, the bastard who planted those charges knew their stuff, and could not have picked a worst spot for a forced dive..." As he and his two officers desperately tried to steady the ship.

Back in the Temple, Nissa Ad-Dajjal regained her composure and reached for a syringe filled with acid, snarling.

"Fool, that will not have breached the Tiamat's double hull."

"I know... madam,"

Responded the now grinning Sek, just moments before there was a second massive explosion, which separated the multibillion dollar vessel's outer hull from the already breached inner hull, like a banana skin.

"But trust me… that one will…"

On the bridge, Captain Jersson looked at the control panels, which were now a mass of steady red lights showing the Tiamat was tearing itself apart from the pressure, as it rapidly headed down on a one-way trip. The salt haired Scandinavian sat himself stoically in the Captain's chair and methodically strapped himself into the seat, ready to die with his beloved ship.

Back in the recreated Assyrian temple, Dr Nissa Ad-Dajjal looked startled but not afraid. However, her attitude markedly changed when the first wash of incoming sea water ran over the stone temple floor, bringing with it three small round jewels, a red ruby, a blue sapphire and a green emerald, that had once sat in the hilts of Ad-Dajjal's own corkscrew shaped iron, silver and gold chakra daggers, but which now rolled slowly across the wet stone to stop at her feet.

As Ad-Dajjal stepped back, focusing only on the appearance of the three chakra dagger hilts, the temple wall behind her began to crack and then formed into a massive tear revealing the impenetrable ocean darkness beyond, caused by the pressure wave implosion from expertly placed charges. Matching pairs of carefully located breaches in the double hulls meant that, as seawater poured into the warehouse space, everything inside the temple was sucked out into the inky blackness.

500 feet under the Aegean Sea there was hardly any light, but as Ad-Dajjal and Sek were dragged towards the cold darkness, the huge Turk felt a massive shock wave flow through the water, as the Tiamat's twin reactors finally ruptured, thrusting out the remaining contents of the enormous ship into the surrounding ocean depths, along with enormous air bubbles that began floating up towards the surface hundreds of feet above. As Sek watched, some of the heavier items from the temple caught Ad-Dajjal's floating body, dragging her down into the dark cold depths of the abyss, where the African tectonic plate slides under the Aegean Sea plate, creating the Hellenic Trench.

CHAPTER 48 – AVARITIA

"For greed, all nature is too little." - Lucius Annaeus Seneca, 45AD

Agharti, Citadel of the Djinn
South of the Gurvan Saikhan Mountains,
Southern Mongolia.
10:25HRS (GMT+8), 14th August, Present Day.

The four figures moved in a fluid, snake like series of well-practiced manoeuvres, through the tall walled ravine that led to the ornate carved entrance of the subterranean citadel. Each man alternated seamlessly from leading, to covering the centre ground and then finally to rear point duty, scanning the terrain around them and the ravine edges above, looking not just for movement, but also for any signs of recent disturbance.

Where Stewart's party had paused to look at the historical grandeur buried and carved into their surroundings, these men were a blur of motion, halting only to check for possible threats. Their Scorpion Desert Sand pixelated camouflage blended so well with the colours of their environment that it was only when each man moved, to change their position in the formation, that they could be noticed. Their sand coloured polymer Heckler & Koch (H&K) MP5 machine guns were enhanced with factory fitted short suppressers, the numerous MOLLE (Modular Lightweight Load-carrying Equipment) Velcro straps and speed clips on their Dragon skin body armour were covered in diverse deadly devices, that ranged from gas and fragmentation grenades, to sets of thirty round 9mm MP5 magazines duct taped together, one up and the other down, to permit rapid magazine exchanges during intense firefights. Each of the three Maelstrom commandos carried a modified nine-inch Rockstead UN ZDP bladed knife, made from the legendary ZDP 189 steel, fitted on a tough silicon ankle sheath attached just above their Warrior Aqua Sand combat boots. Their hawk faced leader had opted to carry his Lin Rhea custom twelve-inch-long Damascus steel Bowie knife in a special quick draw sheath, worn across the rear of his lower back. The sand coloured Glock 17 side arms, on each of the operative's webbing belts, had odd looking thirty-two round magazines that extended well beyond the end of the traditional hand grip, a battlefield adaptation that proved vital in an extended exchange of fire.

As the four men reached the 100 foot high citadel entrance they paused to attach Silva Pro Line SL10 Red LED head lamps to their Kevlar helmets and check their modified US Night Vision (USNV) PVS-7 scopes, that were linked to the digital data feeds from COBRA (Covert OBservation Robotic Automata) drones. COBRA was a classified DARPA system, a three foot long mechanical tube that explored enclosed spaces, where the floor was filled with debris that would obstruct other forms of autonomous drone. The strange looking mechanical snake was designed to be deployed ahead of Special Forces (SF) troops before entering a cave or building. Using serpentine movements, its systems could explore the interior and deliver three dimensional images of the layout and structures of a building, along with the locations of any living being.

Only when the four men had halted, did it become clear that the three Maelstrom SF operatives were exhausted, the air crash followed by a hellish night nailed to a ten-thousand-foot mountain peak, where they had been constantly rocked by monstrous winds, had taken its toll on their mental and physical reserves. Their faces looked pasty, dark black shadows lurked under their red blood shot eyes and, behind their bravado, there was a growing unease about the way the mission was deteriorating, losing most of the men and equipment, having no radio communication, deploying equipment without replenishments from weapons caches and, worst of all, no discussion of an extraction plan. The whole operation was looking more like some personal adventure rather than a special ops mission, and the men knew it was on these kinds of unplanned deployments that entire platoons of the very best personnel became lost.

In contrast, the hawk faced Issac bin Abdul Issuin looked considerably better than he had the day before, the expectation of settling the score with Stewart, after his humiliating defeat beneath the Hagia Sophia, clearly invigorated him, as did the desert heat and brightness, which reminded him of his beloved Egypt. Issuin smiled as he dispatched two of the robotic COBRA devices from their backpacks into the darkness ahead of them, their snakelike appearance enhanced by paintings on the front of the drone simulating eyes and fangs, as was the fashion with so many weapons.

After receiving confirmation from the two ground based reconnaissance drones that the area ahead was empty, the four men synchronized their black ceramic Suunto watches, donned their modified USNV PVS-7 scopes and entered the pitch blackness. As each man raised his H&K machine gun and stepped over the threshold, the unease was clear on their faces.

At the furthest corner of the first level of the Agharti citadel complex, where Stewart and Kwon had broken the clay seals and raised the stone trapdoor hours earlier, two COBRA drones cascaded in a slithering mass of coils down the deeply cut steps and then separated to explore the lower floor space, their serpentine movements disturbing the neatly ordered debris patterns of the original office, that had lain undisturbed for millennia, into an unrecognizable chaos. In the level above the mechanized snake drones, the massive Japanese Commando, Suzuki, had sat down on the stone floor next to the intertwined skeletons of the lovers, that had so moved Stewart earlier. He casually prized the two daggers from the bodies, examined them in the red LED light of his helmet torch to assess their worth, and then cast them to one side, striking a match on the thigh bone of one of the bodies to light a large Arturo Fuente Opus X cigar, causing the ancient bone to crumble to dust, while his inhalation made the tip of his cigar glow brightly in the impenetrable gloom.

Standing nearby in the darkness, the increased humidity in the enclosed space had caused Duke to remove his Kevlar helmet and mop his face, brow and smooth head with a cotton bandana printed with a Skull logo and "Rangers lead the way" motto. While the American slowly chewed a wad of "Grizzly" tobacco, he assessed his Australian and Japanese team members. The short blond haired "Croc" appeared to be handling the humidity but, like Suzuki, he was clearly looking around for any "bounty" that might make this expedition financially rewarding. So far all they had encountered were old bones and, judging by the data feed from the COBRAs in his night vision goggles, there were only thick layers of dust in the level below them.

After getting the all clear signal from the hawk faced Abdul Issuin, the three men resumed their progress. Croc placed a blue Cyalume military ChemLight on the middle steps of the flight of stairs, just as he had placed others at regular intervals within the first level rooms, providing a clear line of lights in the darkness so the group could quickly retreat towards the exit, if needed.

Two levels deeper down in the labyrinthine citadel complex, the four men encountered their first sealed doorway, and the three SF commandos reacted as if they thought they were Howard Carter, opening Tutankhamen's tomb. Much to Abdul Issuin's annoyance, the three operatives insisted on examining the contents behind the plain sealed door labelled "ग्रन्थालय" (granthaalay or Library). After some minutes prizing the thick clay from the edges of the door frame with their Rockstead UN ZDP knives, and eventually smashing the door itself into fragments with the hilts of their daggers, they forced their way inside. The red lights from their head mounted lamps revealing a large room, 165 feet long and sixty feet wide, filled with row upon row of wooden racks. The nearest set were filled with large dried leaves covered with a fine black ink script in an unknown language, others were stacked with papyrus scrolls and still more with carved clay tablets. The disappointment was evident as Suzuki, Duke and Croc walked among the wooden shelving, roughly searching for anything of value, but finding nothing. Eventually the three men gave up, dismissing the contents of the room as worthless and they exited the library just as everything began disintegrating, leaves and papyrus turning to dust along with the wood in the racks, which cascaded to the floor, causing the remaining clay tablets to smash into tiny fragments on the hard stone behind them.

The lust for treasure grew worse as the men continued their progress downwards, every skeleton was broken apart in a search for gold and diamonds, and every set of human remains that failed to deliver some minor trinket was cast aside into the nearest corner with increasing callousness. The discontent grew with each disappointment, until Suzuki started openly questioning why so many good men had been sacrificed, in order to follow a small group of harmless civilians. They had all overheard the conversations of the Stewart party during their advance down the long ravine, they clearly were just Archaeologists and the huge Japanese commando thought they should forget hunting a harmless bunch of fools and focus instead on looking for treasure.

When they reached a dead-end corridor that led to a single door covered with highly ornate clay seals, with pictograms of a mountain top temple and the script "དགེ་འདུན་གྲུབ་པ།" (Gendün Druppa, the first Dalai Lama), the three Maelstrom commandos set about cutting down the rope that held the ceremonial cartouche, and then smashed through the door with a vicious desperation that clearly disgusted their hawk faced leader.

This time their helmet mounted red LED lights revealed a low-ceilinged tomb, sixteen feet square, filled with Tibetan religious relics, prayer wheels, cloth banners and some highly stylized black calligraphy portraying a monk meditating by a large underground lake, that had been painted on the white clay covered walls. In the centre of the floor were the remains of a small frail figure of a monk, wrapped in faded orange robes and seated in a classic crossed legged lotus posture. As the fresh air started the accelerated decomposition process that they had now become accustomed to when they opened any of these sealed rooms, Suzuki, Croc and Duke literally pulled the small figure of the monk apart. Casting the ritual beads to one side, they found a small worthless stone ring on the dead lama's left hand. As the treasure crazed men, pushed the remains to the ground, the three-sided blade of a stone ritual Tibetan phurba dagger fell from the skeletal fingers, just moments before the entire mummified figure crumbled to dust. With the final realization that there were no treasures to be found in the underground citadel, the six-foot five-inch Japanese operative finally lost his patience completely and turned on Issac bin Abdul Issuin.

"What is a non-special forces operative doing, telling us what to do? Do you even know how to kill someone, or do you just sit behind a desk and take credit?"

He looked directly at the hawk faced man, waiting for a response, and not getting one concluded,

"Ayah! You are as useless as all the things here,"

before kicking the pile of dust, that moments before had been the mummified monk.

"All weak and broken."

Abdul Issuin avoided looking directly at his accuser and appeared to be about to appease the massive Japanese commando, walking behind him in the tomb space and picking up the discarded ornate ritual dagger, decorated with a large lotus protruding from the hilt. Looking at the fine three-sided blade and feeling its weight, Abdul Issuin invisibly shifted his position away from his injured left side and, in a lightning fast thrust, buried the tip of the Tibetan phurba dagger just behind the Japanese operatives left ear into the external acoustic meatus, penetrating the brain and killing the massive man instantly. As the huge body slammed to the floor, with an incongruous lotus protruding from his skull, the hawk faced Abdul Issuin looked pointedly at the other two men.

"Well, some things still seem to work… do either of you doubt our mission?"

The two remaining men shook their heads, agreeing to end the treasure hunt and focus on completing their objective, without question.

With no further interruptions, the group of three men made much more rapid progress and soon reached the sheer cliff above the ocean, where they carefully gathered the COBRA drones back into their Sigma backpacks. With their night vision googles (NVG) they had no need to use a flare to get a view of the subterranean ocean, the NVG enabled them to see that the expanse of water was around six miles wide and at least thirty-one miles long, some parts reaching far beyond the range of their computer enhanced vision. The two Maelstrom operatives descended the stone stairway rapidly and, while they waited for their injured leader to complete his descent, they dispatched a small "Dragonfly" airborne reconnaissance drone over to the island. The UAV's complex sets of sensors covered all known spectrums and relayed a series of images back to the modified NVGs of the operatives.

To the consternation of the men, the infrared feeds from the island flyby showed not just the four members of Stewart's party, but also the startling discovery that the entire small one mile square space showed signs of life. As the three men hauled the pumice raft back from the island to the mainland jetty, the hawk faced Abdul Issuin assumed a worried look for the first time in this mission. Viewing the drone's detailed infrared images, he ordered his two men to prepare to engage with an unknown opponent.

Back on the island, Curren had decided to go and do some exploration on her own. O'Neill and Kwon had discovered some leather-bound documents, under the so called Holy Table, and had started translating them to Stewart. What had initially sounded interesting had quickly proved to be an exceptionally boring diary, covering months of overland travel from Constantinople to the Mongolian desert, that Curren thought should have been renamed "Dysentery, Donkeys and Dunes". With O'Neill and Kwon disagreeing about the exact meaning of pretty much every Latin phrase related to the emerald tablets, Curren had eventually excused herself and, taking her kerosene lamp, decided to walk among the statues and obelisks that littered the island around the central temple. She eventually found herself a stone seat in an area strewn with discarded sets of chain mail and a variety of sword designs from different periods and places. Sitting beside her kerosene lamp, Curren started eating some of the flat bread that had been provided by the Shamans for their excursion to the ancient citadel. Lost in thoughts of the people who must have left this strange assortment of armour and weapons, it took a few moments for her to recognize that, in the semi darkness, something was moving over her feet. Instinctively pulling her legs away, she looked down to where she had been resting her leather flat soled shoes and found the floor around her was alive with small white crabs, ranging in size from animals no larger than her small finger nail to ones the size of her thumb.

As she watched the tiny creatures fight with their claws over the crumbs of unleavened bread, Curren realized that, apart from their bleached white colour, the small creatures shared another unusual characteristic, they were devoid of the long eye stalks usually found on decapod crustaceans, and were therefore completely blind.

Feeling some pity for the tiny ten-legged creatures, Curren broke some of her bread into small pieces, and amused herself throwing bits on the ground and watching the sea of tiny white animals flow to the new food location and then engage in tugs of war, with their small claws waving in the air. As more crabs emerged, attracted by the commotion, what had once seemed cute, suddenly become an uncontrolled feeding frenzy. Larger crabs gradually arrived on the scene and, exhibiting a predatory intelligence, began to seek the source of the bread rather than fight for the small crumbs sought by their tiny offspring. Many of these larger animals, that were around the size of O'Neill's precious iPhone, had the bones of dead fish in their claws which they rapidly dropped and began to work in small groups, seizing the khaki linen material on the right side of Curren's long front button skirt with surprising force from their powerful front claws. With a growing sense of panic Curren rose and, abandoning her kerosene lamp, she pulled away towards the jetty, dragging a few of the more persistent crabs with her and tearing her thick linen skirt. Backing into a pair of strong arms, that she assumed must be Stewart's, she exclaimed,

"Thank God!"

only to feel the sting of a syringe penetrating the left side of her neck. As she crumpled to the floor she got a brief glance of a short haired blond man with blue eyes and a thick Australian accent, saying,

"Sweet dreams, cutie."

As Curren's world collapsed into delicious velvet blackness, "Croc" lifted the shapely forties something brunette over his right shoulder, and then fearlessly removed the three large white crabs that were hanging from her torn skirt, smashing their hard chitin exoskeletons under his Warrior combat boots, with a satisfactory cracking noise, on the wide stone pathway that led from the jetty. The smell of crushed crustacean on the ground caused the already excited crabs to swarm frantically towards the fresh meat, in a wave of menacing chelae that made the hardened SAS officer call for assistance.

The tobacco chewing Duke responded, confronting the oncoming wave of white eyeless crabs, some as large as house bricks, with his usual Ranger style, unleashing a series of suppressed 9mm rounds from his MP5, bursting the lead animals into fragments and sending the remaining crabs even wilder with excitement. In anger that Duke's excessive and thoughtless use of his weapon had lost them the element of surprise, Issac bin Abdul Issuin ordered his Maelstrom team to make a rapid advance into the centre of the island.

Inside the main temple, Kwon, O'Neill and Stewart had piled the sets of worn leather volumes, dating back for centuries and which had been discarded by the previous visitors to the temple, onto the top of the Holy Table. As the three men examined a set of maps and note books from a nineteenth century Roman Catholic cleric, Fr Benedict Lennson, who had transported the fourth emerald tablet, they heard six rapid loud cracks that Stewart immediately identified as suppressed 9mm automatic fire. Drawing his Ruger Super Redhawk revolver, Stewart moved to the narrow entrance and saw two men with red LED helmet lights hurrying towards him at double time, carrying a female figure. A familiar hawk faced man could be seen striding beside them, holding the barrel of his pistol to the unconscious woman's head.

Stewart walked calmly across the temple to a location behind the Holy Table, opposite the single entrance to the enclosed space. He then squatted with the sights of the massive revolver trained on the exact point where, moments later, three men entered, dressed in desert commando fatigues, wearing full body armour and carrying an array of deadly weaponry.

The shortest of the three, a blond-haired commando in his mid-thirties, carried the unconscious Helen Curren over his right shoulder. The other operative was taller by half a foot, his shaved head was covered with a sweat soaked bandanna, and he was clearly concerned about something behind them in the darkness, as his suppressed MP5 machine gun was pointing away, and not at Stewart and his colleagues positioned in front of them.

Issac bin Abdul Issuin held a sand coloured polymer Glock 17 pistol barrel precisely against the temple of the unconscious Curren. Looking at Stewart, he could see that the sights of a massive bore pistol were coldly aimed directly at his own hawk like face. Issuin had absolutely no doubt that, given the slightest opportunity, not only would the Scotsman take the shot, but he would not miss. Nodding at Stewart he said simply,

"So, we meet again…"

Stewart took in the Glock 17 held at his friend's head.

"Do not harm her, your dispute is with me…"

Abdul Issuin laughed.

"Ah yes, your old-fashioned sense of honour and compassion. Drop your weapon or she dies right now…" Knowing that Stewart would have no option but to comply.

Reluctantly, Stewart slowly put his hands above his head, walked around the table and surrendered his gun, grip first. With the Scotsman defenceless before him, Abdul Issuin delivered a blindingly fast Goju-ryu shutō-uchi open hand chop to the carotid artery on the side of Stewart's neck that sent the Scottish Knight unconscious to the floor, following up with a ruthless series of kicks aimed at Stewart's already broken ribs. Moments later, while being held at gun point by Duke, both Kwon and O'Neill received similar treatment from "Croc" and joined Stewart out cold on the flagstones.

Tavish Stewart woke slowly, struggling to decide if his neck or ribs hurt the most. After some reflection, he decided it was the ribs, as they made every breath an agonizing struggle. In the dim light from a single kerosene lamp, he could see that his wrists had been tightly bound with Ty-Rap Polyamide grey cable ties, attached to an ornate stone wall that he recognized as being located close to the jetty where they had originally landed on the island. Beside him were the unconscious forms of Curren, O'Neill and Kwon. Stewart noted his two male companions were tied, like himself, by their wrists to the stonework. Only Curren remained unrestrained, clearly their captors felt that the sedatives she had been administered would keep her unconscious for some hours. For the second time, Stewart was perplexed to see the Maelstrom commandos training their weapons away from their prisoners, as though there was some other threat in their environment.

Looking up at Abdul Issuin, who was clearly enjoying some private joke, the Scotsman noted with dismay that his hawk faced nemesis was now wearing the silver folio, with its three emerald tablets, and was also holding the obsidian dagger.

Sensing Stewart's thoughts, Abdul Issuin smiled,

"Yes, Stewart, I have something special planned for you, a goodbye gift from me. Once I have collected the final tablet, I will use this wonderful dagger of yours to slowly let your life blood, so I can think of you and your friends being consumed alive down in the deepest darkness of this city, when it is reburied in less than forty minutes time."

With that Issuin turned, as the unconscious figure of Helen Curren suddenly started to convulse and cough violently, bringing up copious amounts of water onto the stone pavement beside her. As she sat upright, gasping for air, the coughing began to sound more like a laugh.

Looking up at Issac bin Abdul Issuin, she smiled when she saw the silver folio round his neck and, in a trick of the dim light, the entire left side of Curren's face was cast into a dark shadow, that made Abdul Issuin take a step backwards in startled recognition.

In what was clearly Nissa Ad-Dajjal's velvet voice, Curren's mouth spoke,

"You have done well, Issac. Do not look so surprised. You know that this is one of my gifts."

To the evident confusion of the two Maelstrom operatives, their hawk faced leader bowed and handed the female prisoner the silver folio frame from around his neck. The figure of Curren stood and looked down at Stewart, with a depth of hatred that was almost physical.

"Sir Stewart, you should know that your Turkish friend is floating deep in the Aegean Sea."

"I doubt he went quietly." The Scotsman responded bitterly, and then added loudly,

"Helen! I know you are in there! Fight the bitch, it is your body not hers!"

Nissa Ad-Dajjal laughed.

"Do not waste your words. I had time to condition Ms Curren, when I had her on the Tiamat. She is mine now, just as much as Issac is..."

She reached forward and stroked the cheek of the ruthless hawk faced assassin beside her, making Abdul Issuin shudder with what was clearly pleasure and fear in equal measure. Instructing Croc and Duke to wait and watch the three bound men, the now clearly submissive Issac bin Abdul Issuin led the figure of Helen/Nissa towards the centre of the small island. Once inside the central temple complex, Nissa Ad-Dajjal totally ignored her hawk faced acolyte and approached the Holy Table with clear excitement. Scattering the ancient leather books and maps across the floor, she began to remove the emerald tablets carefully and systematically from the silver folio, placing them in the empty settings carved deep into the ancient stone table surface.

CHAPTER 49 – THE KEYS TO CREATION

"[illegible]" - The 17th Enochian Key "To Begin the End of the Endless Cycle" from Dr John Dee's "Claves Angelicae" 1583. Sloane MS. 3188.

Agharti, Citadel of the Djinn
South of the Gurvan Saikhan Mountains,
Southern Mongolia.
14:25HRS (GMT+8), 14th August, Present Day.

Back near the stone jetty on the small island, 2000 feet beneath the Gobi Desert, consciousness returned to the body of Father Chin Kwon, in spite of the blows he had received. Looking across at Stewart, he instantly noted the missing silver folio, the semi-conscious O'Neill beside him and then, finally, turned his gaze to the two heavily armed commandos standing on guard before him. Narrowing his eyes, as though he was assessing the weaknesses of the two SF operatives, he watched eagerly as the bald-headed US Ranger took a slow drink of water from a steel Summit water bottle, and then addressed him.

"Water? Please, sir. I am so thirsty. Can I buy a sip from you?"

Duke stopped drinking and regarded the priest, "Buy? What do you have of value?"

"Silver coins. Truly unique pieces…" Kwon struggled with his bound hands, and pulled free a small leather bag from his cassock pockets. O'Neill's eyes widened, as he recognized the leather coin bag from Rome. The young priest shook the purse so that it emitted a loud clinking sound of silver on silver, clearly tempting the American, who drew much closer. Seeing his offer was being accepted, the priest's face took on a look of wicked delight as his long fingers slowly pulled the leather draw strings loose and he reached inside the pouch. Bringing out a small coin, he placed it in his open left palm. It was clearly very old and, by the way the red light from the Maelstrom commando's head lamp caught its surface, it was pure silver. The front of the coin showed a man facing right, with a large, long nose and a laurel wreath around his head, with the Greek text "ΚΑΙΣΑΡΟΣ ΣΕΒΑΣΤΟV" embossed to the right side of the face. The reverse or "tails" side showed the Goddess Fortuna with her right arm extended so that her right hand, which held a large palm branch, was in the exact centre. As Kwon held the coin in the palm of his open hand, he slowly raised it so it was above his head and the full light of the red LED lamp shone onto its surface, adding,

"There is one thing about these coins…"

But the US Ranger was not listening, instead he grabbed the leather bag, roughly causing the thirty pieces of silver to cascade over the stone pavement. At that precise moment, the build-up of seismic pressures, created by the previous night's movement of millions of tons of sand and rock, triggered an earth tremor and an associated massive seismic electrical discharge, which arced in a thunderous lightning flash above the subterranean ocean and shook the small island violently. The two Maelstrom men were roughly thrown to the ground. The one called Croc fell to his knees in front of Stewart, while Duke landed on his back closer to Fr Kwon. Having being waiting for such an opportunity, Stewart unleashed a text book kneeling Mawashi-geri round house kick at the Australian's left hip, dislodging the Rockstead UN ZDP belt knife, and causing Croc to roll in an uncontrolled forward motion, straight into one of the nearby gaping holes. The sudden arrival of the SAS commando in the opening awakened something inside that made lots of scratching and scuttling noises, which were followed by the sound of thirty-two discharges from Croc's 9mm Glock 17, and ended with a piercing scream.

To his credit, Duke did not intend to abandon his partner. The big muscular American rose, pulled free a twenty-foot length of half inch nylon paracord from his backpack and, tying one length around one of the nearby Djinn stone statues, he wrapped the rest around his chest, and approached the six-foot-wide hole that had just consumed his mate, Croc. But the small thin silver coins scattered around him had made the wet stone pavement treacherous, and Duke's boots dramatically lost traction, taking him sliding down the short side of the slimy stone jetty, dislodging and unravelling the paracord around his chest so that it looped around his head and neck.

The American was pulled up short, hanging by his thick muscular neck over the twelve-foot high jetty edge, his legs dancing violently as he choked to death.

As Kwon watched the whole event unfold, with a terrifying lack of emotion, he completed his sentence about the coins.

"...they have a bad reputation."

Pulling the dislodged Rockstead dagger towards him with his feet, Stewart got hold of the knife and rapidly cut the Ty-Rap Polyamide grey cable ties, that had held the three men to the stone wall. While Kwon gathered up the silver coins and returned them to the leather purse, Stewart walked over to the jetty edge, fitted Duke's Silva Pro Line SL10 Red LED lamp on his own head and then cut the Ranger's body free. He remarked grimly, as he watched the floating corpse being suddenly jolted and then dragged, by an unknown predator, down into the black depths.

"Bon Voyage"

Back in the central Temple, Issac bin Abdul Issuin had watched as the consciousness of Nissa Ad-Dajjal strengthened its control over, and animation of the woman he had formerly known as Helen Curren. The transformation was remarkable. The mouth spoke with Ad-Dajjal's voice, the limbs moved in the same fluid and sensual manner and, as more time passed, even the facial features began to take on the stark beauty of his Domina.

As Abdul Issuin watched this wonder of transference, Nissa Ad-Dajjal was completely preoccupied making sure she had assembled the four emerald tablets correctly, pouring over the carved text that was revealed, now the four sections had been assembled together in the Holy Table.

The silence inside the temple was abruptly broken by piercing electronic beeps, as the falling barometric pressure alarms sounded simultaneously on Abdul Issuin's Suunto and Curren's Casio.

"What does this signify?" Demanded Ad-Dajjal, clearly irritated by the interruption.

"We must go now. The desert is reclaiming the city!" Exclaimed the hawk faced Abdul Issuin, becoming increasingly disconcerted by the complete indifference shown by his Domina towards being buried alive, and joining the countless skeletal remains.

"I do not care about such trivia. I have the ceremony to complete..." Shrugged Nissa Ad-Dajjal, as she pulled off the beeping watch from her wrist and cast it to the corner of the stone temple.

Thinking that his Domina did not understand the mortal danger, Abdul Issuin decided to take the situation into his own hands and, grabbing Ad-Dajjal firmly by the left arm, moved to extract the four emerald tablets and leave. Nissa Ad-Dajjal reacted in disbelief at the strong hand holding her arm and, reaching for the obsidian dagger on Abdul Issuin's belt, deliberately plunged the stone blade deep into his recently treated wound, leaving the dagger lodged deep in the abdomen, and causing the hawk faced Abdul Issuin to fall in agony to the floor. Realizing she should not leave this dangerous man armed, Ad-Dajjal then quickly removed the Glock and MP5 from Abdul Issuin's prone body, and directed the barrel of the H&K 9mm machine gun at her former lieutenant, stating coldly,

"How dare you think to control ME! If you are so keen to go, then leave right NOW!"

She let loose a three-round burst from the MP5, that expertly sprayed around Abdul Issuin's prone body, ricocheting wildly. Scrambling to his feet he rushed from the temple holding his bleeding side, the long obsidian dagger hilt still protruding from the wound, as he headed for the jetty and escape.

Once he was free, Tavish Stewart had searched his immediate vicinity for suitable weapons that he could use to equalize the odds when he faced Ad-Dajjal and her heavily armed jackal, Abdul Issuin. Picking through the numerous sets of armour, swords and shields discarded around the jetty area, he eventually settled for a half-length chain mail coat and a sixteenth century double edged German Beidhänder ("both-hander") sword, that had been banned from "civilized warfare" by the Swiss in the mid-1500s, but which closely resembled the Stewart clan ancestral claymore that he had practiced extensively with as a youth.

Leaving O'Neill to wait at the relative safety of the deserted jetty, where he could use his beloved iPhone as a torch, Stewart and Kwon walked together, each on a personal mission, one heading for the temple to confront Dr Nissa Ad-Dajjal, the other to deal with the ruthless assassin Issac bin Abdul Issuin. Stewart carried the five-foot long steel blade over his right shoulder, the mail coat clinking softly with each stride. Beside him, walking equally confidently to the temple, with an old-fashioned kerosene lamp to guide his way, was the entity animating Father Chin Kwon, his clerical dress now unbuttoned and flowing behind him, exposing the blood red silk on the inside of the robe and his still immaculate Sartoria Ripense grey pinstripe suit.

When the badly injured Abdul Issuin stumbled into the path of the two men, Kwon ignored the clearly wounded Egyptian and continued his steady pace to the temple, content to leave the two warriors to whatever might be their destiny. The sight of Sir Tavish Stewart in his chain mail coat and carrying a Claymore broad sword, might have struck Curren as amusing, but it sent an ice-cold chill down Issac bin Abdul Issuin's spine.

Stewart drew the double handed sword and pointed it expertly towards the hawk faced man before him, noting the blood flowing down his side, the obsidian dagger hilt still lodged deep in his body, and a complete lack of firearms.

Abdul Issuin looked expectantly behind Stewart.

"I knew I could not count on much from Croc, but what of Duke?"

"Got tired of hanging around." Replied the Scotsman humourlessly.

Abdul Issuin grimaced, and backed away from Stewart's blade, leaving as he did a trail of blood, the smell of which began to attract the attention of numerous small crabs that swarmed over the bottom of both men's trousers and boots. Fumbling with a clasp, Abdul Issuin drew the custom Bowie knife from behind his back into his right hand and, with an effort, pulled the obsidian dagger free from his own left side and held it in his left hand, dripping with his own blood.

Even though the man in front of him was clearly badly wounded, he was still extremely dangerous. Stewart responded to the threat of the two weapons with an expert double handed strike with the long sword, which smashed into the hilts of both knives, knocking both blades from his opponent's hands and causing massive cuts, that flowed copiously with blood over the stone paving. Suddenly, swarms of larger crabs emerged, attracted by the smell, and began grouping together to pull the injured man to the ground.

"Ibn El-Sharmoota!" Gasped Abdul Issuin, as he violently shook his legs in an attempt to get rid of the growing number of powerful claws pulling at his body. Stewart kept the advantage, by pushing the long sword blade into Abdul Issuin's adam's apple, forcing the hawk faced man back towards a set of massive Swiss cheese holes, which had numerous bucket sized crabs popping out of them, attracted by the noise and the increasing smell of blood.

Suddenly, two huge crustaceans the size of dogs emerged, each grabbing the terrified Abdul Issuin by the bottom of his blood-stained Dragon skin armour, battling to drag their prize down their respective holes. Stewart smiled, remembering how only minutes ago this man had coldly planned the Scotsman's own horrific death.

"Finally feeling the pinch, Issac?" Queried Tavish Stewart as he was just about to withdraw his sword, taking pity on the wounded man. Unexpectedly, a third even larger crab, emerged in a blur of speed from the dark waters, dragging the hawk faced man into the pitch-black depths, leaving nothing but the blood trail and the two discarded knives on the stone paving. Picking up the obsidian dagger and walking back towards the jetty, Stewart remarked,

"That was a bad case of the crabs..."

Some 2000 feet above Stewart, a storm was breaking, the sky had turned black, the winds were rising and sand was cascading down the sides of the ravine entrance way to the city of the Djinn.

O'Neill was pacing back and forth by the jetty when Stewart re-joined him. The Vatican Archaeologist looked expectantly,

"Abdul Issuin?"

"Something came up" Responded the Scotsman, while coolly gesturing for O'Neill to follow him.

Arriving at the central temple, they found the body of Curren, still animated by the consciousness of Dr Nissa Ad-Dajjal, and Fr Chin Kwon facing each other around the Holy Table, with all four emerald tablets set in their fixings.

Inside the small space, the air felt icy cold, making every breath appear as a thick mist, illuminated by the three kerosene lamps that were still burning around the Holy Table. The stone floor was covered in a mess of books and maps, that had clearly been thrown randomly from their place where O'Neill had left them, some hours earlier.

As O'Neill and Stewart approached the Holy Table, Curren smiled, but it was clear this was not the Curren they had travelled with over the past days. There was a strange light in her eyes, and her voice had taken on a darker and more seductive tone. Looking at the two men, she commented.

"Sir Tavish Stewart, Knight of the North."

Smiling at the irony as she noted the chain mail and the bloody claymore. Then her eyes moved on to O'Neill, who was holding his wooden crucifix and looking terrified.

"Dr Thomas O'Neill, Priest of Rome."

And finally, she turned to Kwon, who was standing with his clerical robes open, an ocean breeze causing the fabric to ripple slightly behind him.

"And a Devil. But not just a mere Prince of Hell … are you?" She smiled knowingly,

"And where is the dagger?"

Nissa Ad-Dajjal saw it held firmly in Stewart's hand, and nodded.

"So, everything is as foretold."

Stewart hesitated. Standing half way between Ad-Dajjal and Kwon in front of the four emerald tablets on the Holy Table, it was clear that he could only stop one person before the other could make the forty ninth invocation. Half closing his eyes, he could see the shimmering shape of the silver cords behind both Curren and Kwon's necks. Stewart knew from first-hand experience the evil that was Nissa Ad-Dajjal, and deliberately distanced himself emotionally from the fact that she currently looked like one of his oldest friends. Fr Chin Kwon on the other hand was an unknown. He had helped them but, by his own admission, this was an alliance of convenience, that would end abruptly once the threat of Ad-Dajjal was removed, and Stewart remembered only too well the carnage below the Hagia Sophia and the coins by the jetty.

Sensing Stewart's indecision, Nissa Ad-Dajjal became even more seductive.

"You know, Sir Stewart, once I make the call I can give you ANYTHING you desire…"

At that precise moment, Stewart's GShock countdown alarm sounded loudly, and Kwon smiled, looking at the obsidian dagger in the Scotsman's hand and sensing his indecision.

"Ah yes. Time's up. Who to strike?"

Ad-Dajjal looked greedily to the gleaming emerald tablets before her.

"Let me try, Stewart… You will have your every desire."

Tavish Stewart's indecision ended abruptly.

"Right now, I think my only desire is for you to go to Hell."

In a single smooth motion, Stewart's stone dagger cut the shimmering silver cords from the back of Helen Curren's head, making her body slump instantly to the floor, and prompting O'Neill to demand Stewart strike also at Kwon, to prevent him from making the forty ninth invocation, and creating god alone knows what.

Fr Chin Kwon and Stewart exchanged a slow knowing glance.

"Too late, Thomas. If I am right, he already made the forty ninth invocation eons ago, and this IS his creation. Anyone who has truly lived, knows there is no God of infinite forgiveness or love. Just an endless cycle of action and reaction."

Kwon nodded, and looked at the shocked O'Neill.

"Do not look so surprised, Thomas. And do not deny, you never suspected."

With that the body of the young priest collapsed, and the temple rumbled in a terrifying reflection of the growing storm above.

In the island's central temple, shrill barometric alarms sounded on Stewart's Altimeter Barometer Compass (ABC) watch and the identical model that was lying on the stone floor of the temple. Since both Curren and Kwon remained in a semi-conscious state, clearly unaware of who or where they were, Stewart gathered up the four emerald tablets from the Holy Table, returning them to the silver folio around his neck, before briefing O'Neill on how to carry Curren for maximum mechanical efficiency. Once Stewart was satisfied that the

Archaeologist would not slow them down too much, he removed his heavy chain mail and the two of them assisted the semi-conscious Curren and Kwon to the jetty, and on to the waiting pumice barge.

O'Neill's physical condition lacked the raw strength that Kwon had demonstrated on the previous crossing, so the transfer to the jetty was a struggle, requiring brief moments of rest before they completed the crossing. It was during one of these momentary respites, while the barge was approximately midway across the deep water separating the island from the high cliffs, that Stewart took off the silver folio and, after a moments reflection, threw it, along with the obsidian dagger and bag of silver coins, into the waves that now shook the barge, as the storm above them made the very bedrock of the Gobi shake.

The increasing ferocity of the vibrations that shook the subterranean tunnels inside the citadel, motivated O'Neill, giving him extra strength and, with Stewart leading the way, the two men stumbled along the trail of glowing blue ChemLight sticks left by the Maelstrom team, back to the ground level, only to discover the 100-foot-high entrance door almost completely filled with desert sand. While O'Neill gave up, falling to the floor sobbing, Stewart grabbed the pelvis from one of the nearby skeletons and, scrambling to the top of the ninety-foot-high pile of debris that had formed by the entrance, started frantically scooping away the sand and rock that barred their escape. Initially, his actions looked hopeless against the sheer volume of materials pouring in from the ravine outside but, gradually, Stewart cleared a human sized hole, through which they passed the two semiconscious forms of Curren and Kwon, before finally Stewart pulled the still sobbing O'Neill through the rapidly closing entrance way.

Outside, the winds had almost completed their work of reburying the ravine. Tons of sand and rocks poured over the high cliff tops on each side of the entrance way, turning the air into a choking cloud and quickly burying Stewart, O'Neill, Curren and Kwon up to their knees, close to the very spot that they had found the bones of Fr Benedict Lennson, the priest who had brought the final emerald tablet to Agharti. Just as it looked like they would join all the other bodies buried in the causeway, a thick hemp rope dropped down from the sheer rock face and the outlines of four thick set men, dressed in reindeer skins looked down on them.

After the unconscious forms of Curren and Kwon had been lifted to safety, Stewart tied O'Neill firmly to the thick hemp rope and gestured to Hujk for the four Shamans to begin pulling. The first sixteen feet of O'Neill's ascent went smoothly, but a sudden gust of wind buffeted the Archaeologist and smashed him violently against the cliff wall, causing his beloved iPhone, with its detailed record of their adventure, to cascade down into the sands and disappear into the exit hole Stewart had so recently cleared, prompting O'Neill to howl so loudly in despair, that for a moment his voice transcended the terrible roar of the wind.

With the four strong Shamans carrying Curren and Kwon, and with Stewart and O'Neill roped together, the group of eight figures made agonizingly slow progress in the increasing winds, blinding lightning and deafening thunder claps, up the shrinking two-mile slope of sand and rock, that was being lifted away from the mountain side to refill the desert floor, even as they attempted to walk up it. After over two hours of extreme exertion, all eight of them reached the safety of the small cave, and rolled shut the huge circular door.

That night almost everyone slept soundly. Stewart was so exhausted that he did not even bother to partake of the small flat bread meal the Shamans prepared, but instead just went into a deep sleep, bundled up in some furs on the stone floor of the cave. Curren and Kwon continued to lapse in and out of semi consciousness, and the four Shamans repeated their exploration of spirit with the Muscimol laced reindeer urine. Only O'Neill could not sleep, his mind tortured by having seen such sights, but not having any proof. He sat wondering at the injustice of life and, as the cave rocked and shook like a runaway railway carriage, he knew that in the morning the Gobi would have reclaimed its treasure for another 120 years.

Finally, in an utterly desperate attempt to escape his mental torture, O'Neill reached for one of the Yak bladders and, bracing himself for the disgusting taste of the reindeer urine, took a series of deep gulps, instantly regretting his rash action. After thirty minutes of shakes, sweats, violent nausea and increasing disorientation, O'Neill's exhausted body finally assumed the same mumbling, twitching unconsciousness shown by the four Shamans.

In O'Neill 's Muscimol fuelled dreams, the entity that had inhabited the young priest's body found himself on a vast dusty plain, with no trees or life as far as the eye could see. The ground was so dry that red dust particles blew in thick whirlwinds around him. The sweeping airborne soil played tricks on the eyes, transforming the timeless entity into a much taller figure that towered above the landscape. The shimmering air looked like flames covering him on all sides, dancing and casting hideous shadows onto the vast desolate plain around him. The thick swirling dust made his figure appear to be surrounded by six thick dark red wings, four of which covered his body and two of which spread wide into the sky around him, making it look like he was hovering menacingly, filling the entire heavens. Each of the wings were covered in large dark spots, that upon closer observation were serpentine eyes, blinking slowly, as they looked malevolently down on the sea of souls, who huddled together trying to cross a razor thin bridge between the physical and spiritual realms. In the towering entity's right hand was a long black sword engraved with glowing Enochian symbols, that moved to deny one specific figure their crossing over the Bridge of Souls, instead forcing that individual to remain in the physical realm, to reap the karmic consequences of her actions.

Shortly before dawn, the storm subsided and the Shamans rolled back the cave door, only to rush back in and make odd gestures. Not understanding what they meant, but hoping above all hope that some trace of the lost city remained, O'Neill rose, feeling disorientated, dehydrated, but also strangely at peace, as he walked unsteadily to the entrance. It was the sound of massive rotors that O'Neill noticed first, and then he saw an enormous 130-foot-long helicopter blocking the morning sun, as it rose over the sparkling surface of the Gobi Desert.

Fearing the crew might miss them, as they passed on further along the vast Gurvan Saikhan mountain range, O'Neill rushed back and woke Stewart who, stumbling into the light, fired the last of his three Pains Wessex Distress Signal flares. Twenty minutes later, the sand coloured eight blade Izdeliye 90 helicopter, with its large red star livery near the tail, hovered above them, lowering two men on winches down into the small clearing on the mountain top. Unclipping himself, and removing the sound muffler cap from his flight suit, Colonel Lev Averbuch Bachrach smiled, as he saw Stewart, two Catholic Priests and the London lawyer Helen Curren, being guided from a cave entrance by four Mongolian Shamans.

"Tavish! Your lady said I would find you here…"

Some minutes later, the Russian stood next to his friend, as three winch men lifted Curren, O'Neill and Kwon simultaneously up to the massive Izdeliye 90, that hovered above them. Then, after looking at the poor state of everyone, added,

"You all look like you have danced with the very Devil himself!"

"That is closer to the truth than you can imagine…"

Smiled Tavish Stewart, as he was winched up alongside Lev to the waiting helicopter, and began the long journey home.

At the bottom of the 17,000-foot-deep Hellenic Trench, the crushing water exerted over seven thousand pounds of pressure on every inch of her body, pulverizing every cell, rendering every ounce of flesh and bone into an agonizing pulp. Nissa Ad-Dajjal tried to open her eyes, but just felt the searing pain from the burst organs and her imploded skull. Slowly, she became aware that what remained of her body was entangled in a mess of thick twisted steel beams, that had once formed the skeleton of her magnificent ship, the Tiamat. These thick steel and titanium spikes had impaled her to a fig wood framed table that was carved with elaborate Sanskrit characters. With a silent scream, Ad-Dajjal recognized that she was bound to the "Sen No Yorokobi No Tēburu", and that her torment would know no end.

The End

EPILOGUE

EPILOGUE

"There is no real ending. It's just the place where you stop the story."
— Frank Herbert

Colonel Lev Averbuch Bachrach felt increasingly warm and uncomfortable, still dressed in his heavy wool Ground Forces uniform that had served him so well in the chill air of the Mongolian mountains. The summons to attend this urgent meeting had been delivered by two severe looking Presidential aides, who had been waiting for him at Sheremetyevo airport when his plane touched down this morning, giving him no opportunity to wash or change. He was sure he could detect a faint aroma of yak emanating from his clothing, as he sat nervously in a low backed chair in the Presidential Cabinet room located deep within the Kremlin's famous golden spired complex.

Seated at a single large felt covered desk in front of him, flanked by two elderly generals dressed in enormous peaked caps and a surplus of gold braid, was a short but powerfully built man in his sixties, dressed immaculately in a custom tailored Kiton suit, staring at him unnervingly. Two flags, one of The Russian Federation and the other of the Presidential Seal, stood on either side of the luxurious office chair while an impressive gold leaf fresco of the Presidential Seal was emblazoned on the wooden panelled walls.

Just as Lev's sweating started to become visible on his upper lip and forehead, the most powerful man in the Russian Federation, pulled a glass bottle from his desk drawer, with "Stolichnaya" written in gold cursive script on its label, above a drawing of a Moscow skyscraper. The President broke the seal and poured four large shot glasses, which were handed round, whilst the aides distributed copies of that morning's European newspapers, all with varying degrees of sensationalism, declaring the discovery by a Vatican Archaeologist of a lost civilisation.

"Do not keep us waiting, Lev. When we heard you had visited the fabulous lost city of the Djinn, even the Politburo wanted to hear what you had discovered!"

Lev, at last, started to relax and enjoy the sensation of the vodka as it warmed his throat,

"It was nothing. A small cave, with four locals camping there, Shamanic nomads. Inside the cave were eight yak bladders, filled with reindeer urine, that was heavily laced with the hallucinogenic fungi, amanita muscaria, and which had been almost completely consumed. I believe the Archaeologist himself had the last drop!"

Pouring another round, the President was clearly enjoying hearing a story highlighting the gullibility of these Westerners.

1554 miles West from the Kremlin, the warm afternoon sunshine poured into the living room of Helen Curren's three storey Clabon Mews home, highlighting the understated but stylish Laura Ashley furnishings and the sweeping long net curtains, exposing high sash windows that opened onto the cobbled street below. The increased ventilation was a concession to the stifling heat of the late September Indian Summer, the breeze also carrying in the sounds of busy London traffic passing through the nearby Cadogan Square, in the heart of Knightsbridge.

Tavish Stewart, dressed in one of his signature two-piece grey Ede and Ravenscroft suits, was sitting on a natural coloured Kingston Fabric Chaise End Sofa. Looking tanned and healthy, he had only recently returned from a short break at Cynthia Sinclair's family home in the Caribbean.

Opposite him, seated on a matching single seater, was a fragile looking Helen Curren, dressed in a Somerville college grey marl sweat top and pants, pouring F&M Jubilee blend coffee into two blue fish scale pattern china coffee cups, that perfectly matched the striking design of the F&M coffee tin.

In exchange for his cup, Stewart passed Curren a small gold envelope, which she opened with evident delight.

"The keys for a new Maserati!"

As Curren hugged Stewart in appreciation, he asked how she had been occupying herself during her recovery. Apparently, Jeffery Sonnet had been visiting frequently, eager to hear the details, such as Helen could remember, of their Mongolian adventure, although Stewart guessed that there were other more romantic reasons as well.

Curren had also discovered a new hobby, and began explaining about her recently acquired pet and how its survival against the odds had given her strength and confidence, so much so, that she would soon be returning to her Chambers.

While she explained about finding the animal by chance, when it fell from one of the folds of her dirty clothes, Curren led Stewart over to a large 650 litre Red Sea Max fish tank, artistically filled with small stones, that at first seemed completely empty.

"I asked at the pet shop, and they said to feed him chopped apples, grapes and bananas, but I have found that he really prefers meat..."

Curren threw in some strips of raw beef. Moments later, a tiny white crab came out and pulled the meat away, causing Stewart to look like he had seen a ghost, and comment.

"You are going to need a bigger tank."

1,100 miles East from Kensington, in one of the world's most exclusive conference rooms, Conrad De Ven, in his customary black Armani suit, walked down the long room alongside a new Papal assistant, a fresh faced Japanese priest dressed in a simple cassock, who carried a basket full of papers to be signed by the Pope.

Fr Chin Kwon took in his surroundings in evident wonder, the rich nineteenth century oak wood panelling, the long thin smoked Barovier & Toso glass conference table with Del Giudice dark leather chairs positioned around it, and the unique views from one of the top floors of the Apostolic Palace within the Vatican City. Reaching the end of the table, a nicotine stained hand wearing the Ring of the Fisherman (Annulus Piscatoris) took the papers, to begin the process of canonization for a nineteenth century Roman Catholic cleric, Fr Benedict Lennson, and paused to click an old Ronson and light a Turkish Royal cigarette.

Just over a mile away from the Vatican City, in the large C008 lecture theatre, within the Pontificia Università Gregoriana (PUG), Dr Thomas O'Neill was teaching the topic of "extraordinary influence", as part of this semester's offering of the post-doctoral seminar programme "Discarnate Intelligence: Theological and Historical Perspectives".

The afternoon's seminar was over and the lecture hall was slowly emptying, leaving O'Neill on stage with one of the patients, Mrs Susan Widee, the Dutch business woman from Leidsche Rijn in central Holland, who had participated in Verchencho's lectures the previous semester. O'Neill checked his faithful Nite watch, to see how long it would be before the attendants from the nearby Ospedale Pediatrico Bambino Gesù psychiatric clinic came to collect the patient. He started tidying up and, for the thousandth time, opened his battered MacBook and checked the "Find my iPhone" app which, as always, flashed "device not found".

Unnoticed by O'Neill, while he was occupied looking at the iCloud app, Mrs Susan Widee had risen from her seat and, in a series of slow strange steps, had come behind the desk. A shadow fell over O'Neill, as the woman's head tilted in a bird like fashion that was so familiar, and a distinctive male voice spoke in flawless British English,

"Still looking, Thomas?"

Less than a thousand miles away, at the Gülhane Eğitim ve Araştırma Hastanesi military hospital, Istanbul, in a clean private room within the internal medicine unit, normally reserved for senior officers, Zahra Sek was visiting her son Berat, who was thankfully recovering from the 400-foot ascent, when he had escaped from the sinking of the Tiamat.

Zahra put a pot of tall purple and pink autumn crocuses, taken from her own roof top garden, next to the bedside of her son, alongside several newspapers that proclaimed Berat Sek's heroism, risking his own safe decompression to save others from the Tiamat. Most of the front pages featured Berat's picture.

A deep voice from the bed alongside Berat, remarked.

"Handsome Devil..."

Zahra turned and responded, "Just like his father."

Mohammed Sek smiled, as his wife walked across and gently kissed him.

3709 miles to the East of Berat's hospital room, in a small oasis, twenty miles West of the Gurvan Saikhan Mountains, a group of six Mongolian men had brought their dozen camels to one of the numerous watering holes, that form the back bone of the ancient Silk Route. The group were all members of the same extended family, from the "Hecuiccheos" clan, grandfathers, fathers, uncles and sons, all working together as traders, just as their forefathers had done for generations. Their twelve distinctive heavily furred camels were laden with leather and canvas bags, filled with everything from T-shirts and cheap Chinese produced clothes to medicines. While the three younger men guided the Bactrian camels to the watering hole, the older members of the group made camp, preparing a small fire for their evening meal.

Some minutes later, as the men sat enjoying cups of a thick sweet black tea, poured from an old pewter jug, they noticed that something was spooking their precious camels, preventing them from drinking at the watering hole.

Leaving their steaming mugs, the entire family group approached the fifteen feet tall Burma reeds that covered the edges of the oasis, and began probing them with the long sticks that they used to guide the camels. As they explored the hidden recesses of the tall silk reed grasses, they discovered the form of a semi-conscious man lying face down. He was muscular, in his forties, around six feet tall and dressed in desert camouflage, that led the Hecuiccheos family to think he must be a lost military officer. The soldier must have been in some terrible battles, as he was covered in numerous wounds, stank of rotting fish and, judging by the state of his fingers, must have dug himself up through the sands, from one of the underground rivers, that legend says run deep beneath the Gobi.

Once at the campfire, the traders rolled the stranger on to his back and offered him some water. Seeing that the man was a foreigner, one of the younger men asked him in broken English, if there was anything he desired.

Taking a long sip from the water bottle, the hawk faced man smiled.

"Yes. Revenge!"

If you enjoyed reading this book please leave a review on social media so others can also enjoy the adventures of Tavish Stewart.

ABOUT THE AUTHOR

After leaving school, KRM Morgan would spend his free time practising the martial arts in his back garden, much to the amusement and sometimes consternation of his neighbours. Having attained black belt status, he went on to run clubs in some of the most socially deprived areas, before turning his sights to more academic endeavours. After completing many years of part time and self-funded studies, he took up a PhD scholarship in Psychology and Computer Science at Edinburgh University, which laid the foundations for a highly successful academic career, spanning a number of institutions in various locations across the globe. Having worked alongside the Police and Intelligence Services, both in the UK and abroad, helping to improve criminal intelligence analysis techniques, establishing educational programmes for women in the Middle East, and dealing with the challenges and opportunities of leading a higher education institution in one of the African Union's developing nations, he now lives quietly on the South Coast of England. When not working as a part time advisor for an educational think tank, he spends his free time writing action adventure novels, using his own experiences for realism, with a good measure of imagination thrown in.

Connect with K.R.M. Morgan

Twitter: @KRM_Morgan

www.ingramcontent.com/pod-product-compliance
Lightning Source LLC
Chambersburg PA
CBHW071144070526
44584CB00019B/2648
* 9 7 8 1 5 2 7 2 2 5 9 5 4 *